Beyond Integration

Beyond Integration

The Black Freedom Struggle in
Escambia County, Florida, 1960–1980

J. Michael Butler

The University of North Carolina Press CHAPEL HILL

Set in Espinosa Nova by Westchester Publishing Services
Manufactured in the United States of America

Portions of chapter 1 were previously published in somewhat different form in J. Michael Butler, "Economic Civil Rights Activism in Pensacola, Florida," in *The Economic Civil Rights Movement*, edited by Michael Ezra, 91–103 (New York: Routledge, 2013); reproduced by permission of Taylor and Francis Group, LLC, a division of Informa PLC. Portions of chapter 6 were previously published in somewhat different form in J. Michael Butler, " 'More Negotiation and Less Demonstrations': The NAACP, SCLC, and Racial Conflict in Pensacola, 1970–1978," *Florida Historical Quarterly* 86, no. 1 (Summer 2007): 70–92; reproduced with permission.

The paper in this book meets the guidelines for permanence and durability of the Committee on Production Guidelines for Book Longevity of the Council on Library Resources.

The University of North Carolina Press has been a member of the Green Press Initiative since 2003.

Cover illustration: Young marchers join hands for the 1.4-mile march, © Tampa Bay Times/ZUMA (photographer and specific paper unknown, labeled "Pensacola Demonstration 75," reference number ycl615)

Library of Congress Cataloging-in-Publication Data
Butler, J. Michael, author.
Beyond integration: the black freedom struggle in Escambia County, Florida, 1960–1980 / J. Michael Butler.
    pages cm
Includes bibliographical references and index.
ISBN 978-1-4696-2747-2 (pbk: alk. paper)—
ISBN 978-1-4696-2748-9 (ebook)
1. African Americans—Civil rights—Florida—Escambia County.
2. Racism—Florida—Escambia County—History. 3. Civil rights movements—Florida—Escambia County—History—20th century. 4. Escambia County (Fla.)—Race relations—History—20th century. I. Title.
E185.93.F5B88 2016   305.896'0730759990904—dc23
2015031949

To Tyler and Erinne

Contents

Illustrations

Acknowledgments

I have long imagined that preparing an acknowledgment of those who helped me in the preparation of this book, a project nearly fifteen years in the making, would either be similar to writing an obituary for the topic or preparing a lengthy acceptance speech for an award that does not exist. For those reasons, and a few more practical ones, I made it the last significant piece that I wrote prior to the work's publication. Yet because of the study's relevant nature and the number of people who contributed to the academic insights and conclusions that I ultimately reached, I found that expressing my gratitude was a fitting and—dare I say, enjoyable—way to cap a transformative intellectual and personal odyssey. The recognition of the numerous debts I have incurred during this manuscript's preparation is, therefore, done in a celebratory fashion with the realization that my study would not be as meaningful or thorough without the help of many people. I also apologize in advance to those who contributed to my research, writing, and thinking about the project that I fail to recognize in this public acknowledgment. Any errors of interpretation, fact, omission, or style within these pages are mine and mine alone.

I have been fortunate enough to work at an institution that has allowed me to complete this endeavor at a reasonable pace, particularly given our teaching load and institutional commitments. The administration and staff at Flagler College have supported me with this book well beyond my 2008 arrival. President William T. Abare twice took a chance on me and, for that, I will always be extremely thankful. Alan Woolfolk, our faculty dean, has been one of my greatest on-campus advocates. He sponsored many research excursions and provided a Fall 2013 sabbatical that allowed me to complete the initial draft. My department chair and fellow historian Wayne Riggs supported numerous funding requests which allowed me to finish the project in an efficient manner. Flagler has also connected me with a number of excellent colleagues in disciplines outside of history, particularly economist Allison Roberts. Allison not only took time away from her position as a new department chair to review my economic and educational figures; she challenged me to go beyond the basic facts I provided and locate statistics that revealed deeper truths about the nature of race relations in Northwest Florida. Without her guidance and tutelage, the final chapter would be much less powerful. Art Vanden Houten answered every political science question I shouted across the hall to his office with patience and clarity, and Hugh Marlowe, Jim Pickett, Doug McFarland, and Tracy Upchurch likewise demonstrated sincere interest in my project from their philosophy, communication, literature, and law perspectives. Terry Bennett satisfied my numerous printing requests in rapid fashion.

One of the benefits of teaching at Flagler College has been the chance to work with a tremendous library staff. Mike Gallen and Brian Nesselrode, the past and current Proctor Library directors, satisfied all of my book order requests and added numerous volumes to our expanding southern history collection. Blake Pridgen scoured the web, seemingly in good cheer, when I needed research aid and offered many interesting insights on the greater civil rights movement. If I ever had trouble with a citation—particularly in Chicago style—Katherine Owens took an almost incomprehensible amount of pleasure in helping me format properly. Finally, Peggy Dyess is the most efficient, friendly, and supportive interlibrary loan librarian I could ever want. I am also grateful to the many students, both past and present, who have expressed an interest in and asked thoughtful questions concerning my project. I remain convinced that they are some of the hardest working undergraduates I have ever encountered. Lyndsey Nauman, in particular, assisted with some mundane steps in the publication process and her husband, Andy Nauman, restructured and formatted the graphs that appear in my appendix.

Several other librarians and archivists also went above and beyond my research queries, such as Kenneth Dukes, Christy Manuel, and Marie LaCap with the Florida Department of Education, Guy Hall from the National Archives at Atlanta, James Mathis and Joe Scanlon from the National Archives in College Park, Carl Chatman and Barbara Rust at the Fort Worth National Archives, George Henderson at the Department of Justice's Civil Rights Division, David P. Sobonya with the FBI Records Management Division, and Peter Minarik, at the U.S. Commission on Civil Rights Southern Regional Office. Boyd Murphree and Deborah Mekeel assisted during my multiple visits to the State Library of Florida, Sara Logue and Randall Burkett made my experience at Emory University's Manuscript, Archives & Rare Book Library quite productive, and Jim Cusick and Michele Wilbanks did the same during my trip to the University of Florida's Special and Area Studies Collections. Allison Burke at ZUMA Press helped with a number of my image permission requests.

I am especially indebted to all of the people from Pensacola and Escambia County who satisfied my numerous questions and requests. It was not always easy to conduct primary source research from nearly 400 miles away, so I relied upon several people to obtain documents that were not at my immediate disposal. Wilma Davio provided invaluable data from the Escambia County Supervisor of Elections, while Ericka Burnett found similar materials as the Pensacola City Clerk. Jackie Dwelle and Teri Szafran supplied materials from the Escambia County School District, and Joel Hollon did a tremendous amount of research to supplement the data I possessed concerning county schools. Likewise, Dean DeBolt recommended I explore specific holdings in the University of West Florida Special Collections and granted permission to use images from the J. Earle Bowden Cartoon Archive in my book. Wendy Zirkin assisted with my Escambia High School yearbook inquiries, while Barbara Hoard and Calvin Avant gave me unprecedented and unlimited access to all of the Escambia-Pensacola Human Relations Commission's existing files. Finally, Ashley Joyner and Scott McDonald answered my records request through the Pensacola Police Department while Darci Cobb and Debbie Coburn provided documents through the Escambia County Sheriff's Office.

One of the benefits that scholars of the recent past have is the ability to interview those who lived the history we record. I cannot express enough the gratitude I have for those who gave me the privilege of interviewing them for this book, as not everyone that I approached wanted to speak about these often painful topics. Rev. H. K. Matthews turned what he initially said would be a thirty-minute interview into much, much more. Our subsequent discussions led to the publication of his memoir, during the writing of which he shared numerous photos, documents, news clippings, and, most important, hours of relevant recordings that he made during the late 1960s and 1970s. Matthews was the point person for almost everyone I contacted regarding the movement because those who lived through the tumultuous period still have a strong opinion—both positive and negative—regarding the minister. I am more indebted to Rev. Matthews in telling this story than any other single person and consider him a genuine friend, but I have consciously not allowed our relationship to cloud my historical interpretation and analysis of the events in which he was so intimately involved. I know he will understand my perspectives, even when he does not agree with them fully. Alain Hebert provided insight into the period from a perspective that I could not get elsewhere, and Ellison Bennett, LeRoy Boyd, Charles Carter, Horace Harrison, Raymon Harvey, Angela Huff, Mary Harrison Washington, Ora Wills, and Rev. James Young brought life to events that I discovered in secondary accounts. At the outset of my research I wanted desperately to understand attitudes and opinions that the white majority, particularly those in positions of authority, held concerning black activism during the 1970s. John Appleyard, Governor Reubin Askew, Jack Behr, Sheree Cagle, Kevin Flynn, Barbara Hoard, Lance Kelly, Roger Mott, Bob Ullrish, and Susan Watson, then, provided perspectives that many civil rights histories ignore. Many thanks to Katie Kelly Garrett for the interview leads, and to her family and friends for introducing me to Flounder's and sharing Escambia High School stories. Teníadé Broughton, Sarah Jonas, and Eurydice Stanley also provided me with potential interview candidates later in my research process who ultimately filled in some glaring research holes.

I would be remiss to not credit those who most impacted my intellectual growth as a graduate student at the University of Mississippi. Ted Ownby influenced me more than he will ever know and has remained a mentor and friend since I left Oxford. Charles Wilson is a close second to Ted in that regard and remains a model of humility and kindness in a profession that often lacks both. Sheila Skemp, Jeff Watt, Bob Haws, and Kees Gispen challenged and encouraged me at the appropriate times, Charles Eagles introduced me to the art of writing historically, and Winthrop Jordan ensured that I will never become a complacent academic. I regret never sharing those thoughts with him.

I have also had the good fortune of crossing paths with a number of scholars who have influenced this book in immeasurable ways. Paul Ortiz and Emilye Crosby provided valuable feedback on the original manuscript that contributed immensely to its current version, and they each have my eternal thanks. Jim Cobb, John Shelton Reed, Elijah Anderson, and Leonard Pitts Jr. shared thoughts and ideas that surface throughout my work, and Ambassador Andrew Young provided perspectives on movement coordination, limitations, successes, and challenges that influenced many of my ultimate conclusions regarding the topics. In addition, Chuck Grench, Iza Wojciechowska, Lucas Church, and Jad Adkins at the University of North Carolina Press have been accommodating, supportive, and extremely professional.

I am fortunate to have many personal friends who have expressed interest in my work and kept me grounded throughout the research, writing, and revision processes. Lindsay Moffett became an unlikely friend during our time together in graduate school and read nearly every word of this manuscript's earliest incarnations. He and his wife, Sarah Ann, gave me a place to stay during several of my trips to Escambia County and made me feel at home each time. Lenny Steverson has followed my work since our time at South Georgia College and remains one of my closest friends from within academia. Rob Skidmore uses a variety of colorful phrases when I get a little too full of myself, and Mark Valentin remains unconvinced that I have actually finished this book.

At the risk of sounding clichéd, I really have saved the best for last. My wife, Karen, has been with me since our first day of graduate school and has shared in my many professional and personal triumphs and failures. She has been a source of consistent perspective, and I am a better person because we have experienced everything together. I can barely find the appropriate words to describe what Tyler and Erinne have brought to my life. I know it seems "that book" was sometimes more important that anything to me, but such was never the case. I dedicate the work to them both and hope that it returns a small fraction of the pride and happiness that they provide me every day.

Abbreviations and Acronyms

AME	African Methodist Episcopal Church
CPSA	Escambia County Concerned Parents and Students Association
ECCL	Escambia County Community League
EHS	Escambia High School
FAC	Florida Advisory Committee to the U.S. Commission on Civil Rights
FBI	Federal Bureau of Investigation
FDOE	Florida Department of Education
FDOT	Florida Department of Transportation
HRC	Human Relations Commission
KKK	Ku Klux Klan
MFC	Movement for Change
NAACP	National Association for the Advancement of Colored People
NAS	Naval Air Station
NFRC	North Florida Reception Center
NOW	Neighborhoods Organizing Workers
PAL	Pupil Assignment Law
PCM	Pensacola Council of Ministers
PHS	Pensacola High School
PPD	Pensacola Police Department
SCLC	Southern Christian Leadership Conference

UKA	United Klans of America
UMC	United Methodist Church
WEAR	television station
WCOA	radio station
WSBR	radio station

Beyond Integration

Introduction

Conflict, Power, and the Long Civil Rights Movement in Northwest Florida

> A good many observers have remarked that if equality could come at once the Negro would not be ready for it. I submit that the white American is even more unprepared . . . The reality of substantial investment to assist Negroes into the twentieth century, adjusting to Negro neighbors and genuine school integration, is still a nightmare for all too many white Americans.
>
> —MARTIN LUTHER KING JR., *Where Do We Go From Here: Chaos or Community?*

On February 24, 1975, approximately five hundred African Americans gathered at the Escambia County, Florida, sheriff's department in Pensacola to demonstrate against what they considered a grave injustice. Two months earlier, Deputy Douglas Raines shot and killed a young black named Wendel Blackwell from a three-foot distance. Despite the existence of significant evidence that suggested foul play, a local grand jury quickly declared the incident to be "justifiable homicide" and the local sheriff, Royal Untreiner, refused to take disciplinary action against Raines.[1] The incident represented the latest in a series of conflicts between the local white power structure and black residents, who had grown increasingly frustrated with their social, cultural, and economic marginalization in Northwest Florida. Rev. H. K. Matthews, president of the county Southern Christian Leadership Conference (SCLC) and the person that area blacks recognized as their primary leader and spokesperson, organized a series of nonviolent demonstrations that reminded many of the previous decade's civil rights campaigns. Blacks routinely gathered at the county sheriff's department headquarters, carried protest signs, sang familiar spirituals, chanted popular slogans, and prayed. The demonstrations that Matthews coordinated had occurred nearly every evening for the previous two months, and the February 24 protest did not deviate from earlier patterns. Matthews knew that the sheriff's department's patience with the demonstrations had grown thin, but he did not anticipate the severity of their retribution.

The crowd that formed on the twenty-fourth was in jovial spirits. They conversed with deputies, joked with each other, and sang uplifting religious choruses. As he had done numerous times on previous evenings, Matthews addressed the crowd through a bullhorn. He repeated black grievances through the amplifier—they demanded the termination of Raines, for starters—and led the assembly in prayer. Another minister then took the horn from Matthews and led the crowd in the same mantra that he had conducted at earlier demonstrations: "Two, four, six, eight, who shall we incarcerate? Untreiner, Raines, the whole damn bunch!" Soon after the chant ended, seventy nightstick-wielding deputies moved into the crowd. They arrested forty-seven blacks on misdemeanor charges, including Matthews, but after three days added felony extortion counts to the charges against him and a fellow minister. The case went to trial four months later and an all-white jury found the two men guilty of the felony counts. Deputies testified that Matthews threatened to "assassinate," not "incarcerate," the county sheriff and deputy, which explained the extortion charges. While his accomplice received probation, a judge sentenced Matthews to five years of hard labor in the Florida State Penitentiary.[2] The controversial sentence crippled the once-vigorous civil rights movement in Northwest Florida, and served as the starting point of a fifteen-year-long research project that has culminated in the completion of *Beyond Integration*.

I found a brief description of the Matthews ordeal in a U.S. Commission on Civil Rights report titled *The Administration of Justice in Pensacola and Escambia County* while researching my dissertation as a graduate student at the University of Mississippi. I conducted a preliminary investigation into the arrest, the events that led to it, and the subsequent impact it had on the local civil rights movement. My dissertation began as a community analysis of the Biloxi, Mississippi, civil rights movement and turned into a comparative study of the two similar areas after I discovered the federal report. The materials that I discovered pertaining to Pensacola and Escambia County fascinated me most during the research and writing process, and I continued to examine the topic after I received my doctoral degree. Rev. H. K. Matthews read my brief account of the Pensacola movement and asked me to edit his memoir, which I agreed to do. The experience added to my understanding of the civil rights movement in Escambia County, made me aware of the struggle's importance

in a thorough understanding of the post-1960s black freedom movement, and fueled my desire to produce a more comprehensive study of
the topic. My work with Matthews raised several questions on both the
micro and macro levels that I wanted to address in a larger project.
When did the local movement begin, what issues most concerned local
African Americans, and which people and organizations mobilized the
black masses in Northwest Florida? How did those answers change after
passage of the Civil Rights and Voting Rights Acts in the mid-1960s, and
how did the movement progress into the 1970s? What impact, if any, did
the post-1960s movement have upon the political, social, and economic
conditions that existed for African Americans as the twentieth century
ended? I considered the same questions that numerous other movement
historians, particularly those that followed the influential works of John
Dittmer and Charles Payne, posed in their local studies, but I wanted to
tell the story of how a community handled the *aftermath* of a relatively
peaceful process of school and public facility desegregation. How did a
city like Pensacola, which implemented integration plans with little overt
white resistance, experience such tremendous racial unrest a decade later?
What issues did de jure integration not address in Northwest Florida,
and how did whites and blacks settle their grievances in the era beyond
integration? Finally, how did the movements of the 1960s and 1970s impact the lives of whites and blacks in Escambia County for the remainder of the twentieth century? In the process of addressing these and
numerous other issues, *Beyond Integration* examines both the development
and consequences of desegregation in the state's Panhandle region and
reaches conclusions that heighten our understanding of the accomplishments, shortcomings, and nuances of the post-1960s U.S. black freedom
struggle.

Escambia County experienced challenges to codified racism that characterized numerous other southern communities during the transformative 1960s African American civil rights movement. In 1960, for
instance, black parents filed a lawsuit to integrate public schools in Escambia County. Two years later, a sit-in movement desegregated public
facilities in downtown Pensacola. Elected city officials formed biracial
committees that addressed discriminatory policies and laws, and an indigenous group of black ministers provided indispensable leadership for
the dispossessed in Northwest Florida. Voter registration campaigns,
labor strikes, and youth mobilization efforts consequently surfaced in
Pensacola during the decade. Unlike many other locales throughout the

region during this era, area whites and their civic leaders met each successful challenge to their perceived racial supremacy with relative calm. They opened their businesses to blacks and grudgingly implemented new laws without the massive resistance that characterized similar developments in communities that received national attention, such as Little Rock, Birmingham, Selma, and St. Augustine. Yet something changed during the 1970s, and racial conflict engulfed Pensacola. The majority of my work examines the contentious encounters that occurred during the post-1960s era and presents them as a continuation of the greater struggle for racial equality in the American South. In so doing, *Beyond Integration* contributes to the growing body of scholarship that emphasizes what historian Jacqueline D. Hall termed a "long civil rights movement."[3]

"The dominant narrative of the civil rights movement," according to Hall, conforms to a timeline that begins with the 1954 *Brown v. Topeka Board of Education* decision and ends with the assassination of Rev. Dr. Martin Luther King Jr. Hall challenged scholars to expand their focus beyond the reductive conceptualization "which distorts and suppresses as much as it reveals" and "prevents one of the remarkable mass movements in U.S. history from speaking effectively to the challenges of our time." Such a narrative typically characterizes the movement as a grand moral struggle of good versus evil, as simple as, both literally and figuratively, black and white. In addition to Jacqueline Hall, Charles Eagles implored historians over a decade ago "to muster even greater historical imagination" and "write new histories of the twentieth century movement and its era in a more detached, well-rounded, balanced manner." In particular, Eagles maintained, "more attention needs to be paid to the period after 1968 and the legacies or ramifications of the movement."[4] While not all historians agree with the "long civil rights movement" framework, many have validated and expanded the challenges that Hall and Eagles made for movement reevaluation.[5] In her examination of Claiborne County, Mississippi, for instance, Emilye Crosby repudiated the "outdated narrative of progress" with an "accompanying assumption that our nation has actually confronted and solved the problems generated by segregation and white supremacy." Similarly, J. Todd Moye demonstrated that African Americans in Sunflower County, Mississippi, engaged "in a forty-year struggle for civil rights," while Cynthia G. Fleming concluded "the struggle to realize the promises made by the civil rights movement over a generation ago continues" in Wilcox County, Alabama. *Beyond Integration*, like these monumental studies and others that Hasan Kwame Jeffries, Laurie Green, Francoise Hamlin, and Tomiko Brown-Nagin produced, challenges the "dominant narrative" in ways both chronological and topical, which provides a more complex and realistic assessments of the gains, progression, and continued significance of the U.S. civil rights movement.[6] The chronology alone of the Pensacola struggle supports the "long movement" conceptualization, but my study also contributes many unique features to the existing scholarship.

While historians have extended their community studies into the post-1960s period, *Beyond Integration* focuses primarily upon the 1970s as crucial in appraising the realization and limitations of the previous decade's legal gains. In Escambia County, 1960s civil rights activism shaped economic and political decisions that impacted African Americans for the remainder of the twentieth century and revealed areas where white power remained entrenched. Timothy Minchin emphasized the shift in movement goals from political and legal rights to improved economic opportunities and status into the 1970s, but his work focused on black mobilization in the textile and paper mills in several southern locales. I extend his conclusion regarding the economic limits of legal victories for African Americans beyond those industries alone and focus on a single county. In addition, most scholarship that traces movement developments into the 1980s emphasizes political realignment and highlights locations where black voters were a substantial part or even majority of the electorate, or both. Yet my work examines a southern community where black voters were a distinct minority, as they were in much of the region. The crucial differentiation means that African Americans in Northwest Florida shared more commonalities with blacks who resided outside of areas that are disproportionately represented in movement studies, such as Atlanta, Birmingham, and the Mississippi Delta. *Beyond Integration*, therefore, presents the post-1960s black freedom struggle in Escambia County as one whose particular features—including but not limited to African Americans as a voting minority with limited electoral power—contribute to a more complete understanding of the movement's nuanced, complex, and often contradictory consequences. More significantly, my study demonstrates that the Escambia County freedom struggle evolved in the 1970s as one that highlighted the previously unquestioned power that local whites retained and utilized to protect their remaining social, economic, and political privileges as the racial majority, and the resistance African Americans encountered when they challenged entrenched white entitlement. In Northwest Florida, the movement did little to alter the white-dominated systems of control that shaped local race relations into the twenty-first century. The conclusion is an extension of an argument that Michelle Alexander proposed in *The New Jim Crow*.

In her provocative study, Alexander argued that the U.S. criminal justice system, the "War on Drugs," and its resultant mass incarceration of African Americans has created "a new racial caste system" that she compared to the series of legal codes and racial mores that separated the races in southern states between 1876 and 1964. The widespread imprisonment of black males that began in the 1980s and continues, Alexander maintained, produced "a stigmatized racial group locked into an inferior position by law and custom" removed from "the mainstream society and economy." Some scholars have criticized Alexander's methodology, generalizations, conclusions, and popular appeal, but her book provides civil rights historians with a model from which to gauge the limitations and shortcomings of the 1960s movement. Alexander's emphasis on "systems of control" is especially interesting. She defined such systems broadly and categorized mass incarceration, slavery, and Jim Crow as the three social structures that created and maintained racial hierarchy in the United States. Systems of control, however, are much more multitudinous and specific to local conditions and circumstances in the post–Jim Crow South than Alexander proposed. In Escambia County, for instance, the sheriff's department, board of education, county commission, and Pensacola City Council operated as the primary institutions that maintained racial hierarchy in the area. They were the bodies that provided "the tangible and intangible benefits," Alexander claims, "to those who are responsible for the system's maintenance and administration."[7] My work demonstrates that the white-dominated systems of control in Northwest Florida planted the seeds of this "new Jim Crow" during the 1970s in seemingly unrelated areas, such as the county's educational system, law enforcement policies, social service offerings, and employment practices. *Beyond Integration*, then, does more than expand the existing chronological conception of the black freedom struggle in an isolated community among ordinary people. It synthesizes scholarly thought on social change, theories of racial inequality and its contemporary consequences, and recent African American history to make several arguments that contribute to a greater understanding of the civil rights movement's legacy for blacks and whites alike.

First, the study demonstrates that although the 1960s movement destroyed the visible and most dramatic signs of racial discrimination that permeated Northwest Florida, it did not address the many forms of institutionalized racism that survived the 1960s. The victories that civil rights leaders won in both Congress and the courtroom proved vital, but such progress had its limitations. "Legislation," according to Charles Payne, "serves our need to render history understandable by giving us convenient benchmarks, and we may be tempted therefore to exaggerate its influence."[8] Judicial decisions and legislative mandates did not, in short, challenge the white maintenance of their institutionalized racial superiority. White leaders in Pensacola claimed that due to the legal rights that blacks obtained during the 1960s, African Americans could not claim justifiably that systematic racism still existed. The barriers that limited black social, political, and economic advancement, many whites insisted, ended when public facilities and schools integrated. White notions of black inferiority became stronger with each deliberate legal step toward racial equality that occurred in Northwest Florida. When African Americans in Pensacola attacked the vestiges of racism that remained beyond complete implementation or were altogether outside the reach of legal and legislative jurisprudence, white restraint ended. The challenges that black activists posed to the white-dominated systems of control in Escambia County materialized in the 1970s over two issues—the use of Confederate images at a local school and allegations of police brutality against black citizens. In 1973, African Americans organized a boycott of all county schools to protest the Confederate imagery that existed at Pensacola's Escambia High School (EHS), the area's largest and one of its least integrated institutions. Consequently, a federal judge declared that the "Rebels" nickname, the "Johnny Reb" mascot, and use of the Confederate battle flag at EHS violated the court-ordered peaceful maintenance of an integrated county school system, and he ordered the icons removed. Students of both races participated in sporadic rioting, led boycotts, and organized mascot votes and countervotes at the school until 1978. During the same period, several violent incidents perpetrated by white law enforcement officers against African Americans also fueled racial confrontations that peaked with the 1975 arrest and trial of H. K. Matthews, the charismatic personification of black unrest in Pensacola. Matthews spent sixty-three days in prison before Governor Reubin

Askew commuted his sentence. Askew's successor, Governor Robert Graham, later issued the minister a full pardon. Matthews left Florida soon thereafter, leaving a void in leadership for local African Americans and providing an example of what could happen to anyone who challenged white systems of control in Pensacola. The beliefs and values of whites and blacks collided publicly and sometimes violently over the contrasting meanings Confederate symbols and police brutality possessed for each group in Northwest Florida during the 1970s. Most important, *Beyond Integration* contends that conflicts over the two issues related directly to the power whites possessed over the making of pertinent policies, procedures, and practices, and the difficulty blacks had in influencing those systems of power. The most significant racial encounters that surfaced publicly, then, transpired over issues that possessed conflicting meanings for those involved and related directly to the failure of civil rights campaigns to alter the power imbalance that characterized Escambia County race relations into the 1970s and beyond.

Second, this study demonstrates that the discord that surfaced in Pensacola regarding the possession, use, and exercise of power increased divisions both within and between civil rights organizations and local black groups. This fragmentation first surfaced within the African American community during the 1960s along professional and class lines and progressed with time. Evangelical black ministers organized public direct action campaigns, which worked effectively against de jure forms of discrimination in the previous decade and against the de facto forms of racism that persisted in Escambia County into the 1970s. Upper class black professionals condemned the protests as relics of a bygone era and publicly criticized those who organized and participated in the public demonstrations. Black elites believed that only the political process could deliver substantive improvements for African Americans, and they responded to the challenges which emanated from the masses by filing legal suits against discriminatory political practices. The federal judiciary eventually restructured the electoral process for local offices in Pensacola and Escambia County, but political realignment resulted in little substantive social and economic advancement for most African Americans in Northwest Florida as the twentieth century ended. The finding highlights the internal complexities that civil rights groups encountered when they challenged white political hegemony in Pensacola and Escambia County, and it demonstrates that class-based tensions between blacks increased, as a minority within the African American minority capitalized upon the limited economic, political, and educational opportunities that the movement produced.

In addition, Escambia County's long civil rights movement illuminates the conflict that existed between the SCLC and National Association for the Advancement of Colored People (NAACP) and the complex relationships each organization had with its national and state chapters as the 1970s progressed. Both groups faced a multitude of problems on the national level after the 1960s ended, and each had an active branch in Florida's Panhandle region. The NAACP and SCLC in Escambia County worked together on many successful campaigns, and leaders encouraged members to possess membership in both organizations. Yet tensions between those who advocated legal and direct action campaign tactics eventually turned the groups against each other, particularly as the two organizations struggled for membership, contributions, and national relevance. One of the tragic consequences of the 1970s Escambia County freedom struggle is that the struggles of the NAACP and SCLC at the national levels impacted—even undermined—their local chapters when they most desperately needed assistance. The struggles of each organization at the national level weakened local campaigns in myriad ways and contributed to a growing irrelevance of each organization in Northwest Florida as the 1980s began.

A fourth contribution of *Beyond Integration* to existing scholarship is that it accentuates the white response to the local black freedom struggle. Understanding those who opposed African American activities, how they did so, and why they felt it necessary enriches the area's historical importance and sharpens analysis of the movement's accomplishments and shortcomings. Historians Joseph Crespino, Kevin M. Kruse, and Matthew D. Lassiter have examined the movement of white southerners to the Republican Party and expanded understanding of "moderation" and "conservatism" in the post-1960s era. Crespino, in particular, maintained that white elites in Mississippi used "strategic accommodation" tactics to preserve "practical segregation" in their state.[9] My work extends this focus on the white response to movement-initiated changes, reveals that effective white resistance to the Escambia County freedom struggle did not surface until the 1970s, and maintains that it differed substantially from the massive resistance campaigns that characterized many prior southern movements. The United Klans of America (UKA) attempted to resurrect its moribund organization in response to the African American protests that gripped Northwest Florida between

1973 and 1978. Pensacola Klavern 109, in fact, sponsored many local activities and became the largest UKA unit in the country. Its influence faltered as rapidly as it rose, though, which indicated that white Pensacolians rejected the extremism that the UKA represented. The repudiation of Klan activities and the begrudging tolerance of integration, though, did not equal white acceptance of African Americans as their social, political, or economic equals. In Northwest Florida, white leaders accommodated to federally mandated desegregation measures while retaining their racial and class-based privileges through the implementation of at-large election systems, "freedom of choice" school programs, and political compromises that they reached quietly with county and state leaders. At the popular level, most Escambia County whites interpreted continued black demands for a loosely defined freedom with a loss of white liberties. Their frustration surfaced in defense of Confederate imagery at Escambia High, the call for increased "law and order" measures against perceived criminals, the condemnation of an intrusive federal judiciary, and an assertion of "majority rights." The white power structure denounced UKA belligerence, inflammatory rhetoric, and mobilization effort. Yet the repudiation of extremism and token concessions to judicial mandates were tactics that white officials used to counter civil rights mobilization, satisfy federal authorities, and retain virtual segregation in most practical applications. An examination of the long civil rights movement in Escambia County, then, reveals the depth and complexity of post-1960s white resistance, adds to an understanding of popular white conservatism, and demonstrates how systems of power stonewalled and delayed the promise of meaningful racial change in the region.

The geographical area that this book examines also contributes to existing civil rights studies and demonstrates that Florida experienced its own vibrant, rich, and complex black freedom struggle. The popular perception of "Florida's regional exceptionalism"—that it was different, more progressive, and less racist than other Deep South states—first characterized the works of southern apologists such as Ulrich B. Phillips. In 1949, political scientist V. O. Key perpetuated the characterization in *Southern Politics in State and Nation*, where he labeled Florida "a world of its own." Key considered the state "scarcely part of the South" and claimed Florida only "occasionally gives a faintly tropical 'rebel yell.'" His depiction ignored the fact that Florida led the nation in per capita lynchings between 1882 and 1930, but it influenced many subsequent scholars.[10] Yet as early as 1946, journalist and folklorist Stetson Kennedy published accounts of racial segregation and violence that contradicted the widespread narrative and placed Florida firmly within the contemporary southern social order. Historians such as Steven F. Lawson, David Colburn, Joe M. Richardson, and Jerrell H. Shofner first challenged the issue of Florida's regional exceptionalism and, since the 1990s, numerous others affirmed that segregation, exploitation, violence, and white supremacy characterized race relations in twentieth-century Florida. *Beyond Integration* extends this emphasis into the post-1965 era and broadens Irvin Winsboro's argument that "the reality of Florida's past is more complex and racially ciphered than much of the historiography and journalism recognizes."[11]

Simultaneously, however, Pensacola and Escambia County possessed many features that also distinguished the region from others during its 1970s civil rights conflicts. The Pensacola Naval Air Station provided a substantial federal presence in the area, employed thousands of white and black civilian residents, and relocated families from around the nation to the area, which provided a degree of population diversity absent in many southern locales. It was also a region that developed no consistent patterns for handling conflicts between black and white citizens. Neither tradition, violence, nor progressive civic leadership, the methods that Numan Bartley highlighted in his influential study of white resistance, characterized the area's approach to racial unrest.[12] Because the white power structure in Northwest Florida developed no systematic methods for dealing with challenges that civil rights activists posed to the local status quo in the 1960s, civic leaders contrasted later unrest with erroneous memories of a racially harmonious past in Northwest Florida. Civic authorities responded with genuine surprise, then, when African Americans questioned the existing systems of control during the 1970s and considered black leaders to be outside malcontents who inflamed mass passions for their own selfish reasons. Vengeance and retribution, rather than understanding and compromise, characterized the response white authorities exhibited to the racially charged events of the post-1960s. From the 1970s through the 1990s, therefore, Pensacola and Escambia County possessed many elements that situated it culturally within the South, but the Panhandle also resembled many locations across the nation that had to deal with the aftermath of integrated schools, economic disparities between whites and blacks, working class resentment of continued civil rights protests, and divisions between the African American middle-class beneficiaries of the previous decade's freedom movement and those who experienced no change in their living standards. The Florida Panhandle is an important location for examining the post-1960s freedom struggle because the region possesses characteristics that make it both uniquely southern and like other communities throughout the nation that still confront similar issues.

Furthermore, this work suggests that the typical academic characterization of local movements as primarily top-down or bottom-up in structure or operation is reductive and simplistic. Historical understanding of the movement has evolved from its conceptualization by scholars such as Aldon Morris and Harvard Sitkoff as a hierarchical, church-centered struggle that charismatic leaders and national organizations drove to an emphasis on grassroots activism and campaigns "local people" initiated to transform their communities. My study demonstrates that both approaches formed an approach to organizing for African Americans in Northwest Florida that stretched from the early twentieth into the twenty-first century.[13] The NAACP and Pensacola Council of Ministers provided the local movement with its first two major objectives, the integration of county schools and downtown lunch counters, and both utilized mass public campaigns to obtain each goal. The success established a pattern of top-down activism that area ministers, renowned national organizations, and young blacks continued into the 1970s. The Pensacola NAACP and, later, Escambia County SCLC filed legal suits, organized selective buying campaigns, and held marches through downtown streets. Local ministers coordinated mass meetings, denounced racism from their pulpits, and met with white civil leaders as representatives of the greater black community. The limitations of such traditional methods became clear during the 1970s as African Americans turned their attention to issues that defied legal regulation, such as police brutality and the use of Confederate images at the county's largest public high school. Sit-ins, economic boycotts, mass meetings, and nonviolent demonstrations did little, however, to alter practices that reinforced the racial status quo and, in fact, inspired whites to preserve the power they possessed over such matters under the guise of majority rights. The local black organizing approach succeeded when it confronted segregated schools and public accommodations and, to a lesser extent, employment discrimination, but it ultimately failed to reform the white power systems during the post-1960s era. The Escambia County freedom struggle, then, demonstrates the compatibility of top-down and bottom-up organizing traditions at the local level and reveals the failure of such measures to bring meaningful political, economic, or cultural change to African Americans in the twentieth century's final decades.

Finally, *Beyond Integration* concludes that the political and educational changes which transpired as a result of lawsuits that black elites filed brought limited political change to the region and did little to shift the balance of white-dominated power to the marginalized in Northwest Florida. Tremendous economic and cultural division, therefore, still permeates Escambia County race relations because the systems of control that whites utilized to preserve their authority, supremacy, and social prestige as the twentieth century ended remain firmly in the hands of a privileged majority. The depth of white supremacy's entrenchment in Northwest Florida rendered all subsequent challenges futile, which resulted in dire consequences for local African Americans. Existing socioeconomic and demographic data suggests white and black residents remained as separated in the 1990s as they were when the Voting Rights Act passed in 1965. The election process for county and city positions changed in the 1980s, but the procedural and jurisdictional transformation brought little substantive change for the majority of Panhandle residents. Black voting power, it turns out, was not the key to reducing the economic disparities between the races or improving the living, educational, and employment conditions for African Americans. The legal suits did result in the election of few black officials on a token basis, but they did not deliver the equality of opportunity that upper-class black leaders anticipated because a distrust of elected officials and an unwillingness to accept that the political process, even when revised, could bring racial improvements is a legacy of the 1970s Escambia County black freedom struggle. Consequently, suspicion and cynicism still characterize contemporary local race relations.

The mistrust became abundantly evident in the oral histories that I conducted for this project and, more tellingly, with the potential interviews that I could not obtain. Numerous individuals, both white and black, declined my interview requests because of the topic's sensitive nature. It is only through the few contacts I made in Pensacola that other opportunities to obtain oral histories opened. Yet even with a reference from a trusted source or two, I still encountered a general reluctance to share personal thoughts, recollections, and opinions related to the subjects of race, power, and legacy of the local freedom struggle. The wife of a former activist, for instance, initially consented to sharing her story with me but withdrew hours before the appointed interview time because the memories of her experiences "are still too painful." I received numerous responses similar to the one that a white alumnus of Escambia High School provided to my interview inquiry when she asked, "What is your agenda?" The realization that events that occurred over thirty years ago still arouse such visceral responses indicates how important it is to finally address them in a public medium. Escambia County is not alone in that regard. Such a conclusion balances the optimistic narrative of progress that characterizes many local movement studies and stimulates a long-overdue dialogue concerning issues that possess very real consequences for whites and blacks in the contemporary United States.

Beyond Integration is organized both chronologically and topically. Chapter 1 surveys the development of race relations in the area through the 1950s and examines two separate campaigns against white supremacy that different segments of the black community in Northwest Florida launched. A group of black parents, most of them middle and upper class professionals, filed the monumental *Augustus* school desegregation suit and turned to the national NAACP for assistance. Local ministers initiated a second and more direct confrontation with discriminatory practices in their hometown. The men and their supporters formed the Pensacola Council of Ministers and chose downtown streets and lunch counters, instead of the courtroom, to wage their protests. Each battle operated independently of each other, but their successful outcomes transformed the city in a number of ways. Chapter 2 highlights the transformation of the local movement after area blacks lost their most dynamic leader in 1964. The transfer of W. C. Dobbins to a church outside of Florida changed the nature and the focus of the continuing black freedom struggle. Rev. H. K. Matthews asserted himself as the leading spokesman for area blacks and confronted the persistence of de facto forms of racism in an increasingly hostile racial climate. The local movement evolved after the legislative victories of the Civil Rights Act (1964) and the Voting Rights Act (1965) to address minority employment, poverty, and the institutionalized forms of cultural discrimination that permeated county schools. The remainder of *Beyond Integration* examines the nature and consequences of the continuing black freedom struggle in Northwest Florida during the 1970s.

Chapter 3 documents the struggles of the Escambia County SCLC against two cultural manifestations of institutionalized discrimination that surfaced during the late 1960s—the use of Confederate images at

Escambia High School and repeated acts of police brutality. Blacks believed that whites who attended EHS used its Confederate nickname and imagery in racist and intimidating ways. Interracial fighting on campus and subsequent SCLC school boycotts led to a showdown over the use of Confederate symbols in county schools, and one black family took legal action to remove the iconography. Confederate symbols, their attorneys argued, violated the still-open county school integration suit because it undermined the maintenance of a unitary educational system. A federal judge ruled on behalf of the African American plaintiffs, called the symbols "racial irritants," and ordered the school board to remove all related imagery. The controversial decision, though, represented something more than a simple mascot dispute to each race. The symbols issue embodied the black struggle against cultural forms of racism that existed in Northwest Florida, while whites viewed it as an unacceptable assault on their perceived rights as a racial majority. While inter- and intraracial tensions increased in the verdict's wake, the deaths of seven African Americans broadened the already voluminous racial divide that existed in Escambia County.

Chapters 4 through 7 examine how the deaths of five fishermen collectively known as "the Atlanta Five" and the shooting death of two unarmed black men by white deputies brought local blacks and law enforcement officers into direct conflict with each other, and the consequences each confrontation had upon the black freedom struggle in Northwest Florida. In response to the 1975 Wendel Blackwell shooting, Rev. H. K. Matthews and Rev. B. J. Brooks, the Pensacola NAACP chairman, organized mass meetings, economic boycotts, and nightly picket lines on county property to protest the suspected murder. The UKA capitalized upon the growing white impatience with the Panhandle's long civil rights movement and formed one of the organization's largest and most active chapters in Pensacola. Klavern 109 organized rallies in downtown Pensacola, which sparked counterdemonstrations from the national SCLC. The organization's president, Ralph Abernathy, pledged to use the Pensacola events to stage a national SCLC resurgence, which angered NAACP leaders and sparked a battle between the two civil rights groups in Northwest Florida that had disastrous results for the area movement. The arrests, trial, and convictions of H. K. Matthews and B. J. Brooks, a subsequent federal investigation concluded, "'broke the back' of the civil rights movement in Pensacola."[14] The sentences created a leadership void within the African American community, exacerbated tensions between professional and working class blacks, and demonstrated the limits the local organizing tradition faced when it confronted de facto forms of racism.

The final three chapters of *Beyond Integration* examine the ramifications each conviction had on the area's black freedom struggle from the mid-1970s through the twentieth century's end. Violence resumed at Escambia High over the presence of Confederate images and magnified how the arrests and trials of Brooks and Matthews weakened local civil rights groups. Student rioting captured national attention and ensured that city and county officials could no longer deny that the symbols caused the racial unrest on campus. White authorities determined that "clouds of interracial revolution" threatened to consume Pensacola, a warning that African American leaders had issued for nearly a decade. Considerations besides their racially offensive nature, though, determined the selection of a new nickname, mascot, and accompanying imagery at Escambia High in 1977. In the aftermath of the symbols controversy, several area black elites filed suit to change the electoral process in the city and county. The plaintiffs, all middle- to upper-class professionals, condemned the previous decade's direct action campaigns, mass meetings, and public protests. The men insisted that only political changes, specifically the district-based rather than at-large election of county commissioners, school board members, and city councilmen, could improve social and economic conditions for black residents. A federal judge agreed and ordered a modification of the local electoral process in *McMillan v. Escambia County*. In 1984, Pensacola and Escambia County implemented new election procedures for public office. Existing demographic data, however, indicates that political alterations did little to change the social and economic disparities between African Americans and whites in Northwest Florida during the 1980s and 1990s. The area continues to endure repeated incidents of police brutality against black citizens, and attempts to organize in either traditional or new ways provide little relief for Panhandle residents. The failed campaigns of the 1970s, therefore, created a deep mistrust of traditional institutions, such as the political process and formal civil rights organizations among African Americans, and did little to alter the economic and educational inequities that divided the races in Escambia County into the twenty-first century.

Beyond Integration, therefore, raises several issues that deepen historical understanding of the long civil rights movement and leads to a reconsideration of its accomplishments and legacies in one southern community. The post-1960s black freedom struggle in Pensacola and Escambia County reveals elements that apply to racial conflicts in many other locations across the nation, explores the themes of change and continuity in movement scholarship, and contributes to a greater understanding of inequality's frustrating persistence in American society. Legislative decisions desegregated public facilities in 1964 and guaranteed black suffrage in 1965 but, as Charles Payne noted, those mandates did little to alter the white belief in and exercise of their racial superiority. African Americans thus continued their campaigns against racism into the years beyond integration with an expanded definition of what constituted freedom and equality.[15] Martin Luther King Jr. noted such in 1967 and wrote that blacks "have proceeded from a premise that equality means what it says and they have taken white Americans at their word when they talked of it as an objective." Whites, though, "proceed from a premise that equality is a loose expression for improvement. White America is not even psychologically organized to close the gap—essentially it seeks only to make it less painful and less obvious but in most respects to retain it."[16] The Pensacola story illuminates these conflicting interpretations and demonstrates that the death of de jure segregation fueled black campaigns against de facto forms of racism. African Americans defined, though, what constituted the most visible forms of persistent discriminatory treatment at the local level. In Northwest Florida, undoubtedly as in many other areas both north and south, black activists did not regard political participation, unemployment rates, housing issues, public transportation, recreational spaces, segregated residential zones, or the availability of equitable social services as their primary obstacles to full citizenship. The movement shifted focus from obtaining legal rights to having the power to influence decisions that local blacks believed represented only the interests of whites in positions of authority. The celebration of Confederate iconography in an official public setting and brutalization of African Americans by white law enforcement officials represented to area blacks the two most important manifestations of their powerlessness to influence the white-dominated systems of control in Escambia County.

Local whites, though, viewed the conflicts much differently. White civic officials and their most vocal constituents considered African American protests against the maintenance of law and order and images that honored the past sacrifices of those who embodied regional freedom from outside oppression as another attack on their rights as the racial majority. The integration of schools and public facilities was one thing, and local whites responded to the social transformations with relative restraint. Yet as King observed in his final book, whites treated the passage of laws as the final "reality of the reform" and "felt that the Negroes had gained so much it was virtually impudent and greedy to ask for more so soon." As a result of federal legislation, most notably the Civil and Voting Rights Acts, many white southerners maintained that racial discrimination became obsolete and even interpreted theirs as a color-blind society. In the early 1970s, for instance, Alabama journalist H. Brandt Ayers proclaimed the era of a "post-racial" South "in which the nation can find hope and an example," while author and Mississippi native Willie Morris declared his region could disperse "more than a few crucial lessons to other Americans" regarding race relations. One influential white civic leader in Northwest Florida similarly noted that continued local black protests in the early 1970s "was beginning to grate on the nerves of the vast majority of Americans who believe in flag and country, in church, and in living a peaceful life devoid of constant harassment and disruption."[17] Any willingness to accommodate social change in Pensacola and Escambia County ended when African Americans attacked the images that represented the very identity of many white Panhandle residents and demanded the power to abolish the symbols from public view. White resistance solidified when black protests spread into the realm of law enforcement practices, policies, and procedures, which provided white authorities the opportunity to cripple the area's once vibrant public movement. What remained of the local freedom struggle continued in a legal suit to increase black political power. The plaintiffs won their case, but the electoral changes brought few economic and social changes for area African Americans due to reasons that represent the legacy of the 1970s black freedom struggle. Black powerlessness to access or directly influence white-dominated systems of social control, therefore, embodied the changing nature of the post-1960s civil rights movement, maintained divisions between whites and blacks in Northwest Florida, and impacted local race relations into a new century. Further examination of the success, or lack thereof, that African Americans experienced in obtaining access to or impacting decisions made by the systems of control in communities across the nation will increase our understanding of the continuously evolving and always complex nature of U.S. race relations.

CHAPTER ONE

Patterns of Protest in Escambia County

The colonial history and location of Florida had a tremendous impact on the development of race relations in the Panhandle, as it possessed a degree of religious pluralism, economic prosperity, and ethnic diversity absent in much of the South. Bountiful employment opportunities, in particular, attracted large numbers of freedmen to the area during the postbellum era and contributed to the rise of a confident black middle class in Pensacola. African American economic and political assertion continued into the twentieth century, and a chapter of the NAACP came to the city in 1919. Yet the activism did not occur without resistance, and white hostility to black advancement increased in the years following World War II. The uneasy coexistence that characterized race relations in Florida's Panhandle threatened to unravel as the 1960s progressed.

The area that became Escambia County experienced one of the earliest European attempts to colonize North America when Spanish explorer Tristan de Luna established a settlement at Pensacola Bay in 1550. The colony collapsed within two years because of many factors, but Andres de Pez claimed the area again for Spain in 1686 and named it "Panzacola" after the long hair common to native men and women. Twelve years later, Don de Arriola established Pensacola as the Gulf of Mexico's first permanent European settlement. Competing European kingdoms exchanged Pensacola thirteen times before the twentieth century due to its desirable location, including a one month period when the colony's possession changed four times between warring nations. Spain ceded Pensacola to the United States on July 17, 1821, and Andrew Jackson served as West Florida's governor until 1828. Except for its brief Confederate period, Pensacola remained a U.S. possession from 1821. As Jane Landers and other scholars have demonstrated, African American resistance to racial oppression became a primary theme of Florida history during its colonial era.[1] The quest for black freedom continued into and beyond the U.S. Civil War.

The Civil War devastated Pensacola industries but, as it did throughout Florida, the Reconstruction years initiated unprecedented growth in the Panhandle. The historian Paul Ortiz argued that the postwar "economic expansion of Florida depended on the subjugation of black labor," and Pensacola was no exception. The lumber trade, naval stores, railroad construction, and fishing industry created employment opportunities, but they were "the most dangerous jobs that paid the lowest wages."[2] Yet the prospect of employment attracted white migrants to an area that remained attached to southern cultural traditions. In 1870, only 40 percent of white Escambia County residents claimed Florida as their birth state, while another 47 percent were born in another southern state. The trend continued into the twentieth century, as 60 percent of the area's white parents and 83 percent of black parents migrated to Pensacola from elsewhere in the region between 1900 and 1910. By the beginning of the twentieth century, Pensacola was the state's largest port, the primary commercial center for northwestern Florida and southwestern Alabama, and the region's only connection to national markets.[3] It was also an area where African Americans initiated an open struggle to secure greater freedoms in Northwest Florida.

Historians have recently highlighted Florida's role as a bastion of white supremacy in the Reconstruction and Jim Crow South. Irvin D. S. Winsboro and Abel Bartley maintained, for instance, that "a racial climate of separate-but-unequal was the norm in Florida long before the *Plessy v. Ferguson* decision provided the legal basis for this in 1896," while Michael Newton labeled the state "one of the Klan's strongest and most violent realms." Tallahassee legislators made Florida the first southern state to adopt the convict lease system and poll tax, and revoked the Pensacola city charter in 1885 due to the impact blacks had in electing their civil leaders. In *Emancipation Betrayed*, Paul Ortiz argued that while segregation and white supremacy in the proverbial Sunshine State was "as brutal as anywhere in the cotton south," African Americans in Florida initiated "the first statewide social movement against Jim Crow." Panhandle blacks joined separate militia units, organized public Emancipation Day celebrations, initiated a successful boycott against segregated city streetcars, and formed their own trade unions and fraternal organizations, groups that Ortiz deemed "the backbone of the Florida movement."[4] Yet in 1909, city officials prohibited miscegenation and interracial cohabitation and segregated multiple public accommodations.[5] Unsurprisingly, the county experienced its first recorded lynching during the transitional era. On July 29, 1908, a mob of 1,000 whites dragged Leander Shaw, a black male accused of raping and attempting to murder a white woman who lived six miles north of Pensacola, through the city's downtown streets to his public execution. The mob hung Shaw at Plaza

Ferdinand, riddled his body with bullets, and mutilated the corpse. Photographers took pictures of the scene and sold them as souvenirs throughout the city. Local African Americans avoided the plaza for over a year to protest the death.[6] In 1914, federal intervention stabilized Northwest Florida's struggling economy, became the most important element in Escambia County's financial rejuvenation, and escalated area racial tensions.

On January 20, 1914, thirty-two men, seven aircraft, and two surveillance balloons established the Pensacola Naval Air Station (NAS). Due to the outbreak of World War I, the promise of employment opportunities sparked another wave of rural migration to Pensacola. White newcomers outnumbered African Americans and accepted jobs considered undesirable a few years earlier. Only menial labor or domestic positions remained open to blacks, and 60 percent of Escambia County African Americans had no job at the decade's end. Many simply left the area during the Great Migration in search of employment in the North, and white supremacy continued to permeate Northwest Florida.[7] Throughout the decade, the *Pensacola News Journal* glorified the Confederacy, justified white supremacy, published cartoons and editorials that negatively stereotyped blacks, supported the Ku Klux Klan, and sensationalized crimes that blacks allegedly committed.[8] Some African Americans responded to the increased anxiety by joining the Pensacola chapter of the NAACP, which formed on June 15, 1919. It was Florida's second local branch and it enrolled seventy-three members in its first year of existence. The organization identified the white primary, a crucial element in the preservation of white supremacy locally and regionally, as its immediate concern, and it sponsored voter registration and membership drives into the 1940s.[9] Escambia County whites, though, provided little overt brutality to black mobilization efforts from the 1920s through the Second World War due in part to the economic stability that the federal government provided.

The Naval Air Station brought large federal appropriations to the area during the depression through World War II, provided jobs for many workers, and saved several local businesses from financial ruin. In 1923, the federal government dispersed $2.3 million to military and civic personnel in the county. By 1930, the government distributed $4 million to the area as 25 percent of Pensacola residents derived their salaries directly from the federal government. The situation continued through the New Deal, as federal work relief and national defense funds provided

Pensacola with government allotments unmatched in most southern locales. From 1933 through 1936, Escambia County received $23 million in "New Deal appropriations for navy-related projects alone. Federal support created jobs and Pensacola's population increased from 31,000 in 1920 to 60,000 by 1940.[10] The Second World War created more work in Escambia County due to increased activity at the NAS. By war's end, the federal government employed 30 percent of Pensacola's labor force, contributed over $180 million to the local economy, and created a labor shortage that again drew thousands of migrants to the area. Federal intervention also sparked growth in other local industries such as shipbuilding, construction, retail, and naval supplies. As a result, Pensacola's population grew by 61 percent between 1940 and 1950, while the county experienced a 51 percent increase during the same period.[11] Yet the conclusion of World War II ended many employment opportunities the conflict had created four years earlier. The Pensacola Shipyard and Engineering Company, for example, employed 7,000 workers in 1942 but closed when the war ended. "The Navy," Pensacola city manager George Roark complained, "had drawn a red ring around the city of Pensacola which prohibited not only the building of ships but anything else due to the fact that it might interfere with the NAS activities." In short, the conclusion of war meant the liquidation of thousands of jobs in the Pensacola area. The local economy depended heavily upon federal spending, and it decreased when World War II ended.[12] Racial animosity in Escambia County intensified during the postwar period as black and white workers competed for the remaining employment opportunities and white politicians at the local and states levels tightened their control of the ballot box.

The chances of black victory in a general election remained slim in 1945, but the end of the poll tax and white primary weakened majority control of the voting process. In fact, the *Pensacola Journal* speculated that blacks could claim up to nine elected positions in Escambia County if the NAACP mobilized the full postwar voting potential of African Americans. To head off black electoral success, in 1945 the Florida legislature changed the election process for all state county offices from single-member districts to at-large positions. Over thirty years later, a federal judge concluded that "racial motivations were a main force" behind a transition to at-large elections because the single-member district system gave African American candidates their only chance of winning a local election in Florida. The at-large elections, a $1,000 filing fee for public office candidates, and the geographical and population size of Escambia County essentially barred African Americans from winning spots on its commission and school board, the two most important and influential political bodies at the county level.[13] The city council, however, retained its district-based election process, a fact that captured widespread local attention in the months following one of the twentieth century's most important Supreme Court rulings.

On May 17, 1954, the Supreme Court ruled segregated schools "inherently unequal" in its *Brown v. Board of Education* decision. Political scientist Michael Klarman's "backlash thesis" contends the verdict made race the focus of regional politics and catapulted into public office the white politicians willing to use any necessary means to preserve Jim Crow. The ruling, Klarman maintained, "produced a southern political atmosphere in which racial extremism flourished." Florida state senator and Escambia County resident John Rawls, for instance, decried the decision because it encouraged "the reprehensible, unnatural, abominable, abhorrent, execrable, and revolting practice of miscegenation which is recognized, both in conscience and the law of the state of Florida, as a criminal offense." On May 31, 1955, the *Brown II* decision required local school systems to make only a "prompt and reasonable start toward full compliance" with their original verdict and that integration proceed "with all deliberate speed." The two rulings did not unleash a torrent of hatred upon blacks, as politicians at the local and state level believed it to be easy to circumvent both orders. The historian Richard Kluger declared that Florida legislators, in fact, submitted the "most extensive and spirited brief" the Supreme Court received to "slow the desegregation process" in their state. Still, Pensacola city councilmen openly discussed whether the case would increase federal intervention in their affairs or embolden blacks to disrupt the local political structure.[14] The 1955 city council election justified their anxieties.

Although the *Brown* decisions did not directly encourage Charlie Taite to run for the city council's Ward Two position, the sensitive racial atmosphere that existed in the verdict's aftermath exacerbated the white response to his candidacy and near victory. Since 1931, a council-manager structure governed Pensacola. The system divided the city into five wards that each placed two citizens on the city council. Ward residents determined one representative, while a citywide vote selected its other. Council members appointed a mayor from their ranks, but the title possessed no executive authority. The council seats, then, represented the most important positions of political authority in Pensacola, and no African American ran for a council spot in its first twenty-four years. Charlie Taite, a minister and member of the Pensacola NAACP, decided to buck local tradition and campaign for a seat in his residency district, Ward Two, after a white employee at the Kress department store in downtown Pensacola refused to serve a hamburger to him and his daughter at the establishment's lunch counter. The only way to change the discriminatory practice, Taite believed, was as a city councilman. The close ratio of white to black residents in his ward gave the forty-one-year-old hope that he could win the election. In the spring of 1955, Charlie Taite became the first African American to run for a spot on the Pensacola City Council.[15]

Taite's candidacy and subsequent campaign alarmed city politicians. A representative for Congressman Robert Sikes, the district's state house member, offered Taite a job at the Naval Air Station and $10,000 to withdraw from the race. He refused the proposal. On election day, Pensacola radio stations broadcast multiple announcements that asked listeners to contact anyone they knew who lived in Ward Two and urge them to vote before the polls closed "or we will wake up the next morning with a black city councilman." After the voting ended, Taite and a small group of supporters went to observe the ballot count at City Hall. Much to their surprise, they learned that the votes had already been counted and Admiral C. P. Mason had won the election. The city registrar submitted an official result of 929 to 765 votes in Mason's favor. Taite filed a complaint concerning the vote count with the State Attorney's office, but was told that his grievance was a private matter for which he needed to hire an attorney. Taite decided not to waste any of his additional time, energy, and limited funds on the election and conceded the seat to Admiral Mason. The city council ultimately appointed Mason the mayor of Pensacola and took steps to prevent similar future black campaigns.[16]

Events occurred outside of Pensacola weeks later which further exacerbated racial concerns in the city and throughout the region. On December 1, 1955, police in Montgomery, Alabama, arrested Rosa Parks for not surrendering her city bus seat to a white passenger. Four days later, local blacks refused to use city buses as part of a greater protest against discrimination. The Montgomery bus boycott lasted 381 days and ended with the court-ordered integration of city buses. The historian Samuel Hyde argues that while Montgomery lies one hundred and twenty miles northwest of Escambia County, the city is an integral part of the Gulf South because of its shared cultural and social characteristics.[17] In May 1956, another bus boycott began in Florida's capital city. The Tallahassee protest lasted until the city commission rescinded their segregated seating ordinance on public transportation in 1957. Events that occurred on the regional and state levels had local consequences, as each Gulf South boycott captured white attention in Northwest Florida. Both protests occurred in state capitals less than two hundred miles from Pensacola and potentially threatened white supremacy in Florida's Panhandle, particularly in the aftermath of the Taite-Mason election.[18] In the midst of such growing African American assertiveness, the Pensacola City Council took steps to dilute local black voting power.

On July 24, 1956, the council changed the boundaries of Ward Two, the district where Charlie Taite lived, to incorporate more white voters. The board gerrymandered the district to render blacks a nonthreatening voting minority in all of Pensacola's single-member districts for future city elections. Councilmen unanimously endorsed the change, according to one member, to specifically prevent "a recurrence of what had happened in 1955." Approximately two years later, the Pensacola City Council changed the selection process of its members from the single-member ward to the at-large election system. City voters, regardless of the district where they lived, elected all ten council members as a result of the procedural change, much as county voters selected school board and county commission members. The city council held no public meetings or public forums, passed no resolutions, nor voted to recommend the significant change to the state legislature for its approval. Instead, councilmen discussed the idea at informal gatherings and dinners that they attended with influential local citizens, legislators, and newspaper editors to keep the plan out of the official record.[19]

The at-large election process, Councilman Julian Banfell explained, would save future members the trouble "of reapportioning to keep so many blacks in this ward and so many whites in that ward," while fellow representative Red McCullough warned of "a salt and pepper council" if the election process remained unaltered. A popular vote, though, had to approve the measure before it became policy. In the weeks leading to the October 6, 1959, referendum election, the News Journal repeatedly endorsed the proposal because it "would create extensive changes in the operation of the city government." Editor Paul Jasper declared the at-large method "advantageous" because under the current system "small groups which might dominate one ward could not choose a councilman. Thus one ward might conceivably elect a Negro councilman although the city as a whole would not. This," Jasper wrote, "is the prime reason behind the proposed change." One thousand seven hundred and twenty-two voters approved the measure while only 307 cast ballots to retain the ward-based system. The *Journal* praised the result and Jasper found "no interest on the part of Negro voters who might have felt discriminated against" due to the procedural change, which indicates that he, at least, recognized its true intent.[20]

Elsewhere in the state during the 1950s, the murder of Harry T. Moore and the Groveland Four case indicate that white Floridians used violent measures to maintain the social, economic, and political privileges that came increasingly into question during the 1950s. The Pensacola City Council, though, demonstrated that white systems of control also retained power in less dramatic yet more pervasive—and equally insidious—ways during the same era. City leaders preserved the existing political power imbalance by wrapping their measures in the guise of civil reform and electoral progress. Such seemingly color-blind actions maintained racial hierarchy by weakening potential political resistance from black voters. The legal scholar Reva Siegel labeled the evolution of white tactics to retain power "preservation-through-transformation," and civic officials in Northwest Florida shifted their obstructionist methods in the aftermath of the 1955 city council elections. The tactics reflected an overall pattern that characterized the state in the wake of *Brown* and continued into the 1960s, which was to delay integration for as long as possible while both demonstrating to the courts that Florida was developing an implementation policy and projecting a public façade of cooperation and moderation concerning racial change.[21] The position that the *Pensacola News Journal* assumed during the council referendum election, in particular, illustrated both the influence its editors possessed regarding civic issues and its primary purpose of sustaining the social status quo. The combination made the newspaper a bastion of white power and a powerful ally to the systems of control in Escambia County over the next twenty years. Its emphasis on community stability, particularly economic progress, made the *News Journal* editor an influential local figure and what the historian James McGovern called "a person who is in on the major decisions to shape the fate of this community."[22] Like many other newsmen throughout the South, then, *News Journal* editors often used their forum to frame the preservation of white supremacy as in the interest of communal stability.

The *News Journal* printed several letters that demonstrated that white racial attitudes in Escambia County became more belligerent between the *Brown* decision and the 1959 city government referendum. Several readers blamed Communist intervention for racial activism and stated that the NAACP sought to weaken the nation internally. "I fully believe," one writer opined, "that this whole" civil rights "mess is engineered by a bunch of communist sympathizers who wish to show the mass murderers from Moscow that they are acceding to his demands." Others ridiculed the religious arguments that some integrationists used and disputed "this baloney about us all being Children of God." Some writers used little reasoning to justify their race-obsessed ramblings, such as one who proposed the federal purchase of Ethiopian land and a forced black relocation to avoid a racial war from engulfing the nation. Other letters called integration "the worst injustice ever perpetuated against any civilized people," claimed the Supreme Court did not consider "the rape cases being done by Negroes to our white women in Florida," stated "I would not want my children to marry a Negro," and declared that "forced racial integration solves nothing." Contemporary patriots "would be better off if we were in Cuba," a particularly cantankerous letter declared, because "you could at least shoot back" against oppressive government forces. The region's current racial crisis, the letter concluded crudely, indicated that "you are either a man or a monkey and just because you don't wish to be a monkey you are beaten and clubbed into submission."[23] The letters that *News Journal* editors published regarding racial issues, then, revealed a growing white intolerance with regional challenges to the existing racial status quo. The unease escalated when area blacks initiated their own indigenous protests.

As the 1960s began, African Americans in Escambia County launched two separate assaults upon white supremacy in the Panhandle. Each campaign came from different segments of the community and reflected a division in the methods that local blacks used in their pursuit of racial equality. A group of black parents, most of them upper- or middle-class professionals, turned to the national NAACP in their efforts to integrate Panhandle schools. Local ministers initiated a second and more public confrontation over racial injustices and chose downtown streets and lunch counters, instead of the courtroom, to wage their protest campaigns. Although each battle operated independently of each other, their outcomes transformed the city. Few blacks, though, understood the impact school desegregation and sit-ins would have on the long civil rights struggle in Northwest Florida.

On May 13, 1959, the African American physician Dr. Charles A. Augustus filed an application with the Escambia County School Board for the admission of his daughter, first grader Karen, into Pensacola's all-white Oliver J. Semmes Elementary School. It marked the first formal attempt to integrate a secondary school in the county. Augustus, an Oklahoma native and Howard University College of Medicine graduate, had recently established a practice in Pensacola and applied for Karen's transfer, he told friends, because Semmes Elementary lay within walking distance of his home. Lillie Mae Robinson followed Augustus and submitted the required paperwork to have her daughter, Coemaxile, admitted to the fourth grade at Semmes Elementary with Karen Augustus. The school board ignored each petition and assigned both children to segregated Brown-Barge Elementary. The *Pensacola Journal* published a report of the action and white callers besieged each family with threats. City police officers had to guard each residence until the warnings subsided.[24] The resistance and hostility that local whites exhibited provided only one barrier to the integration of Escambia County's public school. A far more imposing obstacle faced Augustus and Robinson at the state level.

Almost three years earlier, the Florida State Senate unanimously accepted a bill a Pensacola judge authored entitled "An Act Relating to the Management of the Public Schools at the Local Level." Governor LeRoy Collins signed into immediate effect what became known as the Florida Pupil Assignment Law (PAL) and the Escambia County School Board accepted it on August 22, 1956. The PAL represented Florida's most transparent attempt to circumvent the *Brown* ruling and foreshadowed the state's tendency to delay and stonewall inevitable racial changes. The law gave county school boards the power to deny integration requests, established an almost impenetrable way for local authorities to maintain their dual educational systems, and never mentioned race. First, the PAL instructed county boards to assign pupils in way that maintained "the orderly and efficient administration" of public schools. The Senate charged county school boards with maintaining "the health, safety, education and general welfare" of its pupils by "taking into account such sociological, psychological and like intangible social scientific factors" when they determined student assignments. Second, state legislators approved the utilization of standardized tests as a way for counties to measure a student's academic aptitude, "social attitudes, adjustment, and maturity" levels. They also advised the use of a "summary statement from teachers regarding the social acceptance of (the) students being reassigned," as well as consideration of the "economic welfare" of the applicants and their families. County school boards, therefore, could deny transfers based solely upon their interpretation of the best interest of those who desired school reassignments. Finally, the PAL established numerous procedures that complicated the transfer application process. For instance, parents had to apply for their child's transfer in writing either ten days before schools opened, ten days after they opened, or any "such other date as the [county] board may specify." In addition, the parent had to personally deliver their request to the principal of either their child's current or prospective school or the county school superintendent, all of whom had to approve the application. The school board then had to accept each request with a unanimous vote. Despite its reputation as a "moderate" southern state in regard to race relations, passage of the PAL demonstrated that Florida whites "did not reject the spirit of massive resistance" but employed a method to delay school integration that differed from the belligerent public confrontations that later surfaced in other Deep South locales such as Little Rock, New Orleans, Oxford, and Tuscaloosa. Escambia County's systems of control—in this case, the board of education—developed ways to retain power that circumvented or delayed the application of federal mandates, which connected it to communities throughout the former Confederacy.[25] Not surprisingly, the school board rejected the Robinson and Augustus transfer requests on November 12. Each family appealed the decision to the state board of education, which upheld the county ruling. Frustrated at both the local and state levels, Augustus and Robinson decided to use legal action to integrate local schools.[26]

On February 1, 1960, the same day that the Greensboro, North Carolina student sit-ins began, Charles Augustus, Lillie Mae Robinson, Calvin Harris, Abraham Tolbert Sr., and David L. White Sr. filed a class action lawsuit on the behalf of all black parents in the area against the Escambia County School Board and superintendent to desegregate every public school in their district. Although two other school integration suits existed in Florida at the time, the *Augustus* case, as it came to be known, differed because it demanded integration of the county's entire school system and not a specific school or grade. The suit also demanded the desegregation of county school faculties and staff, which made it even more distinct because it offered a broader interpretation of the *Brown* decision than any previous school suit. Charles F. Wilson, the plaintiff's attorney and only practicing black lawyer in Pensacola, crafted the unique legal strategy and asked the national NAACP to finance the ensuing court battle. The organization consented, and Thurgood Marshall and Constance Baker Motley joined Wilson as the parents' counsel.[27]

Media outlets throughout the state and nation, including the *New York Times*, noted the significance of *Augustus*. The *Southern School News* called the suit "Florida's most sweeping court challenge" to segregated schools and called the action "somewhat more than token integration" because "it was filed in Pensacola, at the tip of the state's Northwest Panhandle, where segregation sentiment is strongest." The *Pensacola News*, on the other hand, hoped the suit "may take months, perhaps years, to settle" and urged the board to "spend several thousand dollars" to combat integration. Ten days after parents filed their suit, the county school board unanimously declared "an all-out defense" against the case and hired two Pensacola law firms with county funds to represent it. On February 19, board attorneys filed a motion to dismiss the case on the basis that the parents did not follow proper PAL procedures and that no legal basis existed for the integration of school personnel. Threats and acts of intimidation accompanied the legal resistance whites used to delay school integration. Abraham T. Tolbert Sr., a navy civil service employee and plaintiff in the *Augustus* suit, had an eight-foot cross burned in his front yard. Minutes after he extinguished the flames, an enraged Tolbert telephoned the county sheriff's department, reported the incident, and told them he needed no help because he owned several firearms. Deputies rushed to the home and found Abraham Tolbert sitting on his front porch holding a shotgun. He told the officers that he would kill anyone who attempted to burn another cross on his property.[28] As racial tensions surrounding *Augustus* increased in Pensacola, Judge G. Harrold Carswell made his first ruling in the school suit.

In his June 23 written opinion, Carswell relieved school staff and faculty from the *Augustus* case. *Brown*, he determined, made "no ruling that [the] assignment of teachers, principals, and other school personnel on the basis of race or color is a 'violation of the equal protection clause adhering to students.'" The judge called black requests to integrate school faculties "an absurdity" and "mere nonsense." For the remainder of 1960, Carswell made no effort to resolve the suit. His ruling and deliberation surprised few, as one attorney called Carswell "the most openly and blatant segregationist of federal district judges." Indeed, Carswell once told an audience, "Segregation of the races is the only practical and correct way of life in our states," and wrote in a Georgia newspaper, "I yield to no man in the firm, vigorous belief of white supremacy, and I shall always be so governed." Carswell's involvement in *Augustus* and his initial decision to exempt staff from the case predicted a lengthy, fierce struggle for classroom integration in Escambia County.[29]

On January 16, 1961, attorneys presented their cases in the *Augustus* suit. Three African Americans testified before Judge Carswell at the session and each sought reassignment for their children. All who spoke insisted they filed the suit because they lived closer to the forbidden schools, not because they challenged the existing racial structure in Pensacola. The defense countered with two arguments—the school board rejected the black requests because of overcrowding at the chosen school and not racial factors, and that they followed the Florida Pupil Assignment Law in making their decision. Yet the plaintiffs' lead attorney, Constance Baker Motley, produced evidence that the county school board accepted the transfer requests of two white students to Semmes Elementary after it denied black applications for assignment to the same school, which proved the overcrowding argument a baseless excuse. One administrator also admitted the county separated all reassignment requests by race to simplify transfer decisions. In her closing argument, Motley targeted the PAL as her primary grievance. The Escambia County School Board used the obstructionist legislation "to perpetuate the racial and segregated situation" of area schools and maintain their dual educational system, which made the law unconstitutional. Judge Carswell promised his decision before the May court term began.[30]

Carswell made his first major decision in the *Augustus* case on March 16. To the surprise of many, the judge ruled that the Escambia County School Board violated *Brown* by excluding black students from attending previously all-white schools. In an April 12 meeting between the county school board and their lawyers that they closed to the public, board attorney William Fisher said the officials had no alternative but to comply with Carswell's ruling. Board member L. D. McArthur asked about the consequences of resistance, to which Fisher replied, "You'll probably go to jail." After a heated discussion, the board instructed its attorneys and school superintendent W. J. Woodham to prepare a new policy regarding "the integration problem." The county school board submitted its plan to Judge Carswell on June 14, which he accepted on September 8, 1961. Because the new student transfer procedure contained many stipulations meant to discourage black applicants, limited school integration, and kept all power in the assignment process under the school board's control, NAACP attorneys appealed the Carswell plan to the Fifth Circuit Court of Appeals on the day he endorsed it.[31]

After resisting integration for as long as possible, the Escambia County School Board reluctantly assigned thirteen black students to eight previously all-white area schools on May 23, 1962. The body rejected forty-four other transfer requests. The following day, the Fifth Circuit Court of Appeals heard arguments concerning Escambia County's dual educational system. NAACP attorneys called board efforts unsatisfactory and asked for complete system desegregation in compliance with *Brown*, including the integration of school personnel. The hearing represented the first time that requests to integrate school faculties and staffs appeared before a federal court. School board representatives, on the other hand, cited their previous evening's announcement as a measure of compliance and asked the court to dismiss the entire suit.[32] The court denied the request, ruled against the Escambia County School Board, and issued a key verdict concerning the coming school year.

On July 24, 1962, the Fifth Circuit Court of Appeals unanimously agreed that the county school board violated *Brown* and used the Florida Pupil Assignment Law to maintain classroom segregation. The court also reversed Judge Carswell's decision concerning faculty integration and stated, "The district court erred in striking all references to non-student personnel from the complaint, because this phase of the case involves disputed questions of fact and law which should be decided." The reversal represented one of Carswell's fourteen civil rights decisions that higher courts reversed. The ruling conceded that the board "has now gone a considerable part of the way toward compliance with desegregation of the public schools," but concluded it "has not gone far enough." The court ordered the county to integrate its first two grades in the fall of 1963 and at least one grade per year thereafter. Although the decision crippled Escambia County's dual educational system, it did so slowly. The decision did not order immediate and total integration because it feared "undue confusion" in the area, and postponed staff reassignments until pupil desegregation "has either been accomplished or has made recommended substantial progress." Like the original *Brown* verdict, the Escambia County ruling gave no deadline for compliance to all of its provisions. Yet despite the order's vague time frame, the county school board desegregated ten area schools in the weeks following the verdict's announcement and appealed the Fifth Circuit's ruling. Nine of Florida's sixty-seven counties possessed desegregated schools during the 1962–63 school year, but Escambia represented the only system that operated under a federal court order.[33]

Media outlets from across the nation converged on Pensacola as a number of its schools opened to both black and white students for the first time. The *News Journal* advocated a peaceful integration process and stated that Pensacola "has the opportunity of demonstrating to the nation that it is an orderly, law-abiding community, not one in which hoodlumism [sic] is permitted or in which force is substituted for reason." Editors speculated the first school days would progress normally "unless there is untoward interference from outsiders."[34] On August 27, 1962, twenty-one blacks aged six to sixteen broke the racial barrier at ten county schools. With the exception of a white man who shouted at a photographer outside of Pensacola High School (PHS) from his automobile, reporters noted that the day began, progressed, and ended peacefully. Local whites cited the uneventful proceedings as evidence of their tolerance and lawful communal character. A county deputy called the opening "a feather in Pensacola's cap," while city police chief Dexter Caldwell reported no untoward incidents. Superintendent Woodham stated the day "more than met our expectations" and said local whites "are certainly to be commended" for their nonviolent response to school desegregation. In addition, the *News Journal* praised county leaders, school officials, principals, teachers, and parents for the uneventful opening and declared African Americans must "now prove themselves able to keep abreast of their fellow white students." Newspapers across the state also used the uneventful day to conclude, "Florida is an example to the South in upholding law and order in a situation which can always explode in ugly fashion when local authority refuses to take control or citizens ignore their responsibilities to the court."[35] Some evidence, however, suggests that a less harmonious atmosphere surrounded school integration.

Karen Augustus, who walked three blocks from her home to Semmes Elementary, said that students and faculty treated her so contemptuously during her first day that she did not want to return. Augustus earned all As in her academic courses during the school year, but her teacher gave her a C in citizenship each quarter to prevent her from making the school's Honor Roll. "If it had to be done over," Augustus later remarked,

Carolyn Roberson, white dress, center, walks past white students at Pensacola High School on August 27, 1962. Roberson was one of twenty-one black children to integrate ten previously all-white Escambia County schools in the Pensacola area. AP Photo/Jim Bourdier.

"I wouldn't want to be the one thrown in the kettle." Horace Harrison, one of four blacks who integrated PHS, summarized his year at the school as a "great personal sacrifice." In addition to the daily ostracism and insults he received, Harrison attended no extracurricular functions such as school dances or sporting events "because it was too dangerous." He feared white attack and remembered that "you could never relax. I always had to be aware of where I was and who was around me" to avoid potential violence. Whites pelted his home with rocks and rotten fruit, made several threatening telephone calls to family members, and burned a cross in his yard during his senior year. Another student who integrated PHS described her first year as "hostile" and recalled that whites punched her, assaulted her in the hallways, and made her sit alone in classes. White Pensacola High students went for days without uttering a word to any of the four black students. "If I had to do it again, I wouldn't," one recalled, because "it was not an environment that makes you feel good about yourself." In addition, a white caller informed PHS administration that he planted a bomb on campus to kill the four blacks who integrated the institution. Officials cleared the building, discovered no explosives, and reported that their "first day was just like any other." Pensacola High evidently experienced its share of bombing threats.[36]

On November 29, 1962, the Fifth Circuit Court of Appeals accepted Judge Carswell's "Order to Modify" his original school integration request. The new order demanded the complete integration of all county first- and second-grade classes, instructed the county school board to integrate at least one grade per year in successive years, and ordered local officials to eliminate geographical segregation by redrawing school districts. Finally, the modified plan left the *Augustus* case open indefinitely. Although approximately fifty blacks entered previously white schools at the beginning of the 1963–64 academic year, the county's dual educational system persisted. In 1964, 40,072 whites and 7,914 blacks attended public schools in the county. Only 112 blacks attended schools with whites, and no whites attended black-majority schools.[37] The Escambia County School Board resisted further integration in numerous other ways. It rejected over one-third of African American student transfer requests to majority white schools in 1964–65 due to overcrowded schools, low standardized test scores, emotional immaturity, and incomplete transfer applications. The board also granted transfers for white students who had lower standardized test scores than black applicants, turned in their applications after the submission deadline passed, lived farther away from the schools they transferred to, and gave no reason for requesting the transfer on their applications. NAACP attorneys charged, then, that the school board possessed "no uniform transfer criteria" and used their powers "in an arbitrary, inconsistent, and conflicting manner" against African Americans. As of March 1965, thirty-three of Escambia County's fifty-one public schools had no black students, no white attended a predominantly black school, no African American teacher had a white student in their class, and the school board admitted that it still denied black transfer requests solely due to the "socioeconomic welfare of the [black] students and their families."[38] Because of the continued inequities and efforts of white officials to delay greater desegregation measures, NAACP attorneys continued their efforts to accelerate classroom integration in Northwest Florida through the judicial process as the decade passed.

The progression of the long civil rights movement in Escambia County, then, exhibited features that both mirrored patterns that developed elsewhere in Florida and other Deep South states and established characteristics of a unique local freedom struggle. The Reconstruction and Jim Crow–era experiences of Panhandle African Americans replicated those of blacks in neighboring states, which shatter the myth of Florida exceptionalism that often characterizes popular perception of state race relations. The postwar movement also reveals that events which attracted national attention, such as the *Brown* decision and Montgomery bus boycott, had local repercussions. Finally, and most importantly, the 1955 Pensacola City Council election and use of the Pupil Assignment Law to delay school integration demonstrated that while the local power structure rejected the flamboyant and violent massive resistance tactics that occurred in some other southern cities during the same era, white-dominated systems of control in Escambia County used less dramatic yet more effective methods to protect their interests and preserve the existing racial status quo for as long as possible. The effort of white power systems to retain their privilege and control while not directly referencing notions of racial superiority or inferiority, a preservation of power through a tactical evolution, would characterize the Northwest Florida movement for the century's remainder.

While *Augustus* meandered through the court system, another black protest movement developed and transformed Escambia County in unprecedented fashion. The second wave of local challenges to Jim Crow, however, differed substantially from school desegregation efforts. The former utilized an approach that depended upon the endeavors and support of a few middle- to upper-class black professionals, while the lower and working class black majority generated the latter. The social, economic, and political conditions that typified the Panhandle in the late 1950s provided the atmosphere necessary to generate an indigenous movement, but the African American community lacked a local leader who could—and would—mobilize the masses. That situation changed when Rev. W. C. Dobbins arrived in Pensacola. Just as in numerous other locations across the region, the most formidable threat to Jim Crow in Florida's Panhandle emanated from the black church. Dobbins organized mass protests against stores in downtown Pensacola that depended upon black patronage, yet segregated their dining facilities and refused to hire blacks. The ensuing downtown campaign utilized direct action protests and depended upon mass action to achieve their goal, tactics that the national NAACP discouraged and often refused to endorse. The result was a movement that both complemented and challenged the methodical, single-issue, top-down approach that the NAACP used in its pursuit of racial equality in Northwest Florida.

William Curtis Dobbins was born in Athens, Alabama, on April 30, 1934. He entered the ministry as a teenager and earned degrees from Alabama A&M, Scarritt College, and Gammon Theological Seminary. He also began correspondence graduate studies through Yale Divinity School before he left a church in Montgomery, Alabama, to become the minister of Pensacola's St. Paul United Methodist Church (UMC) in 1959. Soon after his arrival, Reverend Dobbins became an active member of the local NAACP. Like Rev. Martin Luther King Jr., who influenced the young minister greatly, Dobbins made social justice the focus of his ministry and used biblical teachings to justify civil rights activism. According to Dobbins, Christ cared for the whole person in addition to addressing their spiritual needs. He healed the sick and fed the poor, thus caring for the physical well-being of people while He comforted their souls. Dobbins related his theological interpretation to the state of contemporary southern blacks. As Christians, he argued, African Americans had an obligation to work for social justice. Dobbins published many of his beliefs in a regular column he wrote for the Pensacola *Colored Citizen* titled "From Where I Stand." Several of his congregation members and, more important, fellow ministers agreed with Dobbins's insights and scriptural interpretations. The significant support he received led to the formation of the Pensacola Council of Ministers (PCM) in 1960. The group, whose motto was "Equality of Treatment for All People," initially consisted of forty-eight black clergymen from various denominations and dedicated itself to achieving racial equality in the county. The involvement of area ministers and their congregations marked a turning point in the local movement. For the remainder of its duration, the church and its more charismatic ministers played a central role in leading and organizing the black community's fight for justice in Escambia County.[39]

The vital role the African American church would occupy in the Pensacola movement first became clear during the city's 1961 sit-in campaigns. Dobbins targeted two groups as essential in the emerging local civil rights struggle. He organized the first group, consisting of black ministers, by forming the PCM. In addition, Dobbins believed that young people had to become active participants in the movement if it was to succeed. Before his arrival, the local NAACP Youth Council existed in name alone; its adviser, an unmarried twenty-seven-year-old named Raymon Harvey who worked at a black-owned pharmacy, referred to the group as "dormant." It had at most five teenaged members and had never applied for formal recognition from the national office. Sensing the opportunity to awaken the moribund organization, Harvey voluntarily relinquished his leadership role to Dobbins, primarily because Dobbins possessed more status in the black community as a minister. Harvey also recognized that Dobbins possessed the leadership abilities that local blacks so desperately needed. Dobbins named Harvey the group's coadviser and relied heavily upon the Pensacola native during his work with the youth council. Harvey, in turn, considered Dobbins to be his mentor and the primary reason he became actively involved in the area freedom struggle. In 1959, Dobbins sent the Pensacola NAACP Youth Council's application to the national headquarters, where it was almost immediately accepted. Twenty-one blacks ranging from twelve to twenty-five years old joined the youth council at its initial meeting.[40]

Dobbins had a dramatic impact upon those who joined the group. Youth Council member Mary Harrison Washington remembered the "impressive" minister as "a young, enthusiastic person who was very articulate and had a brilliant mind." Her younger brother, Horace Harrison, became a member of the youth council because of the "charisma" and "leadership qualities" that Dobbins possessed. According to Washington, "When Rev. Dobbins would speak, everyone would listen because he always had something important to say. He did not waste words." Other youth council members called Dobbins "one of my heroes," "intelligent, personable, well-mannered," "powerful and strong," and recalled that his group "loved him. We really loved him." The minister, then, personified and perpetuated the top-down model of activism that formed a central component of the local approach to organizing. The youth council met with Dobbins and Harvey every week to discuss local and national issues that pertained to African Americans. By the first weeks of 1960, therefore, W. C. Dobbins had the primary pieces in place to wage a successful campaign against Jim Crow in the Florida Panhandle. The stimulus for such a program came on February 1 when four North Carolina A&T students occupied a segregated Woolworth's lunch counter. With his attention fixed on Greensboro and the subsequent sit-ins that spread across the region, Dobbins repeatedly asked youth council members, "What is Pensacola doing to end segregation?"[41]

The students and their advisers decided to first request that local merchants voluntarily desegregate their dining facilities. Dobbins and council leaders wrote letters dated March 30 to the managers of S. H. Kress, Woolworth, and W. T. Grant stores in downtown Pensacola asking them to end their discriminatory practices and thus avoid "the necessity of such 'sit-down' or picketing demonstrations." Dobbins also wrote a letter to the *Pensacola News Journal* that explained and endorsed the youth council's demands. While none of the correspondences threatened direct action if proprietors ignored their requests, each expressed hope that stores "will seek to end all discriminatory practices without the loss of any Negro business and of their own volition." Each establishment ignored the youth council's request, so Dobbins and nine others entered the white-only dining area at the Pensacola Woolworth's at noon on April 5. The group stood quietly behind lunch counter stools that white customers occupied and left approximately five minutes after their entrance. As they departed the store, group spokesman Raymon Harvey left a note that explained, "This is a phase of our protest demonstration against unfair, unethical, and unchristian [sic] practices of many nationwide variety stores." The letter promised future demonstrations and announced a black selective buying boycott of downtown merchants during the upcoming Easter season. Despite what the *Pensacola Journal* called "a brief, almost unnoticed demonstration," five robed Klansmen marched into the store the next day and offered their services to the manager in the case of future protests.[42]

During the remainder of 1960, as the *Augustus* case consumed the attention of the NAACP's local adult branch, W. C. Dobbins engineered a massive crusade to integrate downtown lunch counters and based his plan on the Greensboro model. The Pensacola direct action protests reflected a great deal of planning and required unprecedented local support to succeed. Dobbins coordinated the operations under the auspices of the PCM, the NAACP Youth Council and, to a lesser degree, the adult branch of the Pensacola NAACP. Dobbins believed that the PCM would provide leadership by spreading news of the protests from their many pulpits. PCM members prepared their congregations for direct action by often preaching against racial inequalities. The NAACP Youth Council met weekly and became increasingly enthusiastic about participating in downtown campaigns. Dobbins planned to use the students in lunch counter sit-ins, believing that whites would be less likely to attack youngsters. Black ministers justified the coming demonstrations both spiritually and politically, while youth council members provided the zeal and volunteers for the lunch counter sit-ins. Dobbins also utilized the NAACP to recruit adult volunteers and engineered a fund raising drive in October 1960 that lasted through the following spring to cover the bail and fines that students would likely incur during the protests. Support from the church Dobbins pastored, St. Paul UMC, was vital to any protest's success. Many NAACP members and local black professionals, including several physicians, dentists, teachers, and attorneys, attended St. Paul. Their advocacy and financial support of the demonstrations carried weight both in the black community and among white merchants who would lose their substantial business.[43]

Dobbins began the campaign in January 1961, when he and other PCM and NAACP representatives individually approached downtown business managers and asked them to both integrate their lunch counters and hire at least one black employee. None complied. The minister also petitioned a coalition of local white businessmen called the Pensacola Retail Merchants' Association for assistance, but received no assurances. In response, the PCM placed a full page advertisement in the *Pensacola News Journal* that listed group demands. It named downtown businesses that possessed segregated lunch counters and refused to hire black employees, and urged the black community not to patronize those stores until their owners addressed African American grievances. As weeks passed without progress, the PCM initiated the second stage of Dobbins's plan to integrate downtown lunch counters.[44]

While negotiations with business leaders stalled, Dobbins and Harvey chose five young blacks to participate in Pensacola's first sit-in. The fact that the adult leaders selected those who participated in the city's first sit-ins and did not solicit or include volunteers is a significant departure from most other such demonstrations that characterized the region after the Greensboro protests. It also indicates that the Pensacola sit-ins were carefully planned and well-reasoned affairs, not spontaneous or emotional reactions against the racial status quo. The two men met privately with the five chosen youth in the office of the local civil rights attorney Charles Wilson. The students did not know the purpose of the meeting until the minister spoke. Dobbins explained why he chose them; he wanted the protestors to be at least fifteen years old, active NAACP Youth Council members, and good students. The men knew that whites would accuse students of "rabble-rousing" and "trouble-making," so they placed an emphasis on character when they chose the demonstration participants. Each student had a good reputation with no past disciplinary problems, and was brave enough to face hostility but disciplined enough not to respond to it. Dobbins also chose them based on their parents' employment situations. He did not want anyone to lose a job because of their children's activities, so parents had to own their own businesses or work for a black employer. Most importantly, Dobbins and Harvey had to trust each student completely, as they wanted the sit-ins to surprise local whites. Dobbins told the assembled youth that any leaked information would give downtown merchants the upper hand. They could lock out all blacks, call the police, or assemble a mob of hostile onlookers. If the white community found out, violence could transpire. In fact, they told no other youth council or NAACP adult member about the coming sit-ins besides their parents, who had to give their permission for each child to participate. All five of the students decided to take part in the initial protest.[45]

On the June morning of the first Pensacola sit-in, the teenagers met with Dobbins and Harvey at Central Life Insurance for final instructions. The students had to have a book or magazine to read while sitting. They could not, under any circumstances, respond to the taunts and jeers of onlookers or make eye contact with those who harassed them. They had to surrender any nail files, penknives, or anything else that whites could label a weapon. They could not touch any merchandise in the stores for fear of shoplifting accusations, and they had to possess a small amount of cash in the unlikely case that restaurant workers served them. Dobbins gave each individual a dime in case they needed to use a telephone for any reason. The two adults then drove the volunteers to Woolworth's in separate vehicles at approximately 11:30 A.M. Dobbins chose the protest time to coincide with the café's lunchtime rush. To avoid arousing suspicion, each student entered the store separately and pretended to shop in the department store. Once all five arrived, they walked together into the dining area and took seats in different sections of the café. According to Washington, the white employees "were in total shock" and "did not know what to do." The manager told them to leave, but the students ignored his command. The few whites who dined in the area left almost immediately, and no other patrons entered. While the students quietly occupied their counters and tables, Harvey and Dobbins watched their activities through the front window from outside of the department store. After approximately two hours, the students left Woolworth's and returned to Central Life Insurance Company to review the day's protest and coordinate activities for the following day. Within days of the initial demonstration, the number of young people who volunteered to participate in the sit-ins tripled. Dobbins and other members of the PCM carefully screened their backgrounds and motives before authorizing their participation.[46]

The scheduled demonstrations continued throughout June on every day of the week except Sunday. Approximately fifty black youth participated in the 1961 sit-ins, which spread to lunch counters at other department store lunch counters such as Kress, J. J. Newberry's, and Walgreens. The protests followed a similar pattern: students entered the stores simultaneously, sat individually at their counters, and asked to place an order. When café workers refused to serve them, they remained seated and read in silence. Dobbins and Harvey always monitored events from a distance and allowed no adults to join the demonstrations. Although the sit-ins followed the same structure, they occurred on varying days and times so that whites could not predict their occurrence. Dobbins organized the demonstrations in such a manner to serve two purposes. First, the sit-ins revealed local black frustration with segregation. The fact that the protests occurred at all reinforced Mary Harrison Washington's conviction that the young blacks—and their mentors—rejected the racial status quo that existed in downtown facilities. The second purpose of the methodical organization of the sit-ins related to their economic objectives. The demonstrations occurred when they did and as often as they did to prevent the restaurants from earning a profit. As the sit-ins progressed, the number of whites who shopped at the targeted businesses declined and those who did frequent the stores would not enter a dining area if any black occupied a seat. Merchants also encouraged protestors, albeit unwittingly, when they closed their counters or locked their doors to prevent a demonstration. Either way, the establishment lost money as a result of the choices their proprietors made, which accomplished the economic objectives of the sit-in organizers and participants. For these and numerous others reasons, then, the historian William Chafe has maintained that the sit-ins "represented a new stage of black insurgency" throughout the region.[47]

Although the number of customers dwindled as the protests continued, the crowds of curious spectators grew. So, too, did white impatience with the demonstrators' determination. Many harassed the young blacks who sat in the forbidden dining areas. White teens even held a " 'reserved seat' sit-in" at Woolworth's, where they took café seats and relinquished them to white customers alone, to trump youth council activities. These counterdemonstrators were emboldened by a police force that had no intention of protecting blacks engaged in civil disobedience. Verbal harangues escalated into violence and officers often refused to protect the black demonstrators from physical assaults. During the June 15th sit-ins, assailants burned one protester with a lit cigarette and sprayed insecticide in the eyes of another. The next day, a white teenager slashed a black teenager with a knife. On June 17, a white onlooker threw battery acid in the face of a demonstrator. One black witness watched a cook sprinkle crushed glass over food before he served it to a NAACP Youth Council member. Police arrested no whites and laughed at or ignored their actions. Conversely, officers arrested blacks for a wide range of offenses including trespassing, illegal boycott, public cursing, loitering, vagrancy, jaywalking, unlawful assembly, resisting arrest, and "feeding a parking meter," among others. On some occasions, officers retrieved items from the store, placed them in demonstrators' pockets, and then arrested them for shoplifting. The experiences deepened the already present mistrust of law enforcement that later dominated the Pensacola movement. Authorities also incarcerated Dobbins for interfering with an officer in the discharge of his duties, disorderly conduct, and contributing to the delinquency of a minor "by inducing Juveniles to carry picket signs." The *Pensacola Journal* reported that a city judge found Dobbins guilty of both charges and fined him three hundred dollars, but police records noted that the court found the minister not guilty of any crime. Regardless of the verdict, passersby fired shotgun blasts into his house and the Dobbins family slept in the homes of his congregation members during the earliest weeks of the sit-ins. Other adult NAACP members found signs posted on their property that read, among other things, "Don't let the sun set on your head in this town," "War," and "Stay away from lunch counters, Niggers." The Ku Klux Klan (KKK) signed each warning, yet City Manager Churchill Mellon blamed the disturbances on "nominal leaders" who were "unable to control the CORE-oriented youth," even though the Congress of Racial Equality did not exist in Escambia County. The *Pensacola News Journal* scarcely mentioned the sit-ins but reported all downtown arrests.[48] White resistance, though, combined with the adolescent exuberance that the sits-ins embodied, inspired Pensacola's black community in their first mass protest against the existing white power structure.

The PCM and Pensacola NAACP Youth Council both played indispensable roles throughout the local sit-in campaign, which provided a pattern for later black mobilization efforts. The PCM organized weekly mass meetings at different churches throughout the city during the protests to discuss their progress and inform the community of youth council activities. Many of the mass meetings proved so popular that people stood along the walls and in the aisles of sanctuaries. The final segment of each meeting, which Dobbins called "the pep talk," proved especially popular with those gathered. Dobbins contacted Dr. Martin Luther King Jr. and asked him to speak at one of the PCM mass meetings. He could not attend, but SCLC officers and King confidants Ralph Abernathy, Fred Shuttlesworth, and C. K. Steele did on separate occasions. Adult members of the PCM and NAACP also took shifts in the waiting area at the city jail to ensure that police did not physically abuse those arrested during the sit-ins. Adult volunteers packed the county courthouse when young activists had to face a judge, where they sat in the section reserved for whites. Both organizations collected money at the mass meetings and used the funds to bail protesters from jail and pay their fines. The NAACP Youth Council also participated in the mass meetings, distributing a newsletter "to truthfully inform the community of the activity of the youth council, relative to sit-in demonstrations," in hopes that adult blacks "will conscientiously support our efforts to achieve a just goal." The one-sheet documents summarized each day's activities and listed all arrests. The first such report, for instance, noted that police incarcerated fourteen blacks during six days of protests.[49] The newsletters and mass meetings were effective because they kept black activists and adults connected at critical stages of the downtown movement. The unprecedented resolve and cooperation that connected the PCM and the youth council forced civic leaders to intervene in the local protests.

The PCM's downtown campaigns came to a temporary halt when white officials agreed on July 12 to negotiate compromise terms with PCM and NAACP leaders, including Dobbins, to end the protests. The Pensacola Chamber of Commerce's board of directors voted 8–6 to initiate the settlement because "numerous downtown merchants" reported significant financial losses due to the sit-ins and asked the chamber to intervene on their behalf. Weeks later, the Pensacola City Council became involved in the talks when it formed a "Special Committee" to "look into the problem of the Negro sit-in demonstrators." Three whites and three blacks joined the six-member body. Interestingly, two of the first three whites the Special Committee asked to serve in the group declined, including *Pensacola News Journal* editor Marion Gaines. The whites who accepted the invitation included committee chair Judge Theodore Bruno, Ralph Barrett, and Jack Sison. The community council nominated African Americans Dr. E. S. Cobb, Rev. George Harper, and C. J. DeBolt to serve on the Special Committee, and they all accepted the appointment. It is unclear from surviving records why the council invited the people it did to serve on its committee or what their qualifications, backgrounds, or employment histories were. The fact that elected white representatives selected them, though, indicates that Special Committee members would do as little as possible to alter the existing status quo. The newly constituted committee met for the first time on November 29, 1961, "to determine policies and approach" the group would take concerning the sit-ins. Members decided to meet separately before year's end with black leaders, the chamber of commerce, and the Pensacola Retail Merchants' Association to resolve the demonstrations.[50]

Rev. W. C. Dobbins reaffirmed the PCM and NAACP Youth Council objectives when he met with the Special Committee. Most importantly, Dobbins reiterated, downtown lunch counters must desegregate. The committee shared the demands with the Merchants' Association and city and county authorities. Business leaders agreed to finally integrate their dining areas, provided that "it was a countywide endeavor," and city officials endorsed the plan. Pensacola's city manager and city attorney and the Escambia County community council, sheriff's department, and county attorney agreed to any integration procedure that the Special Committee and Merchants' Association approved. With all of the necessary agencies in agreement, the Special Committee proposed a blueprint for desegregation that its members believed satisfied every group involved. The sit-ins would commence the next year "on a controlled basis" alone. Black leaders would inform the Special Committee of the exact place, time, and day of their planned demonstration and committee representatives would, in turn, contact the targeted establishments and officials at both the city and county levels. After an unspecified number of protests occurred, the establishments would integrate their dining facilities. The plan allowed the sit-ins to continue and businesses to symbolically resist without the accompanying unrest of the previous year's operations, but they would conclude with African Americans ultimately obtaining the right to dine at downtown lunch counters. The Special Committee's plan would, therefore, satisfy blacks by allowing their demonstrations to resume, progress peacefully, and obtain their most important goal. The committee's proposal obtained white acceptance because it gave them the opportunity to offer quixotic resistance and seemingly capitulate to desegregation demands under persistent, unrelenting pressure.[51] The concession of inevitable changes on terms that placated white elites and kept black power over the integration process at a minimum became a feature that characterized the local movement for its duration.

The Special Committee meticulously planned the controlled sit-ins, which commenced on February 21 at 2 P.M. Committee members even met with members of the local media to inform them of the sit-ins and "request their cooperation insofar as publicity was concerned." The committee, in other words, asked the primary media outlets in Escambia County to ignore the coming activities. The sit-ins lasted for one hour and occurred on consecutive days during their first week as "test runs" to determine the practicality of later demonstrations. According to Dobbins, "all tests ran smoothly" and black protesters encountered "no incidents of any kind." Three stores, though, declined to participate in the staged protests. The refusal of Plee-Zing Market, Pfeiffer's Drugs, and Easley Drugs to cooperate with the Special Committee's program indicated that their integration plan did not receive unanimous support. Still, the success of the first two sit-ins convinced the committee to continue them into March. Consensus concerning the organized plan deteriorated rapidly, though, as the new month began. Some businesses informed the Special Committee that it lost enormous revenues and received several telephone calls from agitated white patrons because of the sit-ins. Blacks also complained of the restrictions that white merchants imposed on their protests and threatened to break their agreement with the Special Committee. In response to the increasingly fragile state of its project, the committee suggested that downtown establishments either integrate their lunch counters immediately or allow blacks to conduct sit-ins on unannounced days and times in the coming weeks. Although some businessmen threatened to close their stores rather than desegregate, the city's Retail Merchants' Association announced that its members would integrate all of their dining facilities on March 12, 1962.[52] The date marked the official integration of downtown lunch counters in Pensacola. With their objective accomplished, the city council's "Special Committee" dissolved. Civic leaders at both the city and county levels praised the committee's work and later used it as the model for a biracial city committee.

Inspired by the NAACP Youth Council, who wanted to channel their energies into a new project almost immediately, the PCM turned its attention again toward downtown businesses, this time for their refusal to hire African Americans. Dobbins suggested that the PCM and Pensacola NAACP establish picket lines in front of establishments that refused to employ blacks. Selective buying had always accompanied the sit-in campaign, but the boycott now took center stage. Unlike the sit-ins, though, Dobbins asked adults to participate in the store protests. The minister modified his previously successful tactic because schools had reopened in Escambia County and he wanted the demonstrations to take place from the time stores opened until they closed. The PCM and some NAACP members recruited volunteers who marched in shifts throughout the day. The youth council made placards for picketers and walked in the lines when they were not in class. The signs had a variety of slogans on them such as "Justice Is Not Served," "Don't Shop Here," and "Your Dollar Is As Good As The Next," among others. When the young protestors participated in the boycotts, their numbers swelled lines down both sides of Palafox Street, the main thoroughfare in downtown Pensacola. Adults and youth alike distributed fliers that discouraged shoppers from entering stores that refused to hire African Americans. Youth Council member and sit-in participant Horace Harrison recalled that demonstrators particularly discouraged black consumers from crossing the picket lines and "would try to talk them out" of entering the businesses by explaining the purpose of the protests. Several other youth council members used a more direct tactic to achieve their goal and pretended to photograph all black shoppers. Their cameras had no film, but the threat served its purpose. Harrison estimates that 90 percent of the local black community avoided downtown during the campaign and shopped in other places, such as the suburban Town and Country Plaza. The boycott had a great impact on other area establishments. Nolan's, a downtown grocery store where white owner Ernest Nolan refused to hire black cashiers, lost $10,000 and 90 percent of its business during the first month of protests. Only after Nolan hired a number of black cashiers and a department associate did the boycott there cease. The direct action protests became so effective that some Pensacola businessmen agreed to address black grievances only days after the demonstrations began.[53]

By the end of 1962, over thirty downtown stores had either hired black employees, integrated their dining facilities, or both. The *Montgomery Advertiser* called the Pensacola movement "extremely successful," and Dobbins estimated that the campaigns satisfied 80 percent of NAACP and PCM goals. Florida NAACP field secretary Robert W. Saunders noted in his annual report of state activities that the Pensacola Youth Council "in cooperation with local ministers . . . successfully desegregated all lunch counter facilities in downtown stores." Saunders declared the operation one of the most "outstanding activities" a Florida NAACP branch sponsored in 1962, despite the fact that the state office offered no assistance to its Panhandle chapter and the adult branch remained preoccupied with the *Augustus* suit.[54] That the NAACP, an organization that preferred to work methodically through the judicial process to secure racial changes, recognized and praised a local campaign that utilized nonviolent resistance and student protesters indicated the downtown Pensacola campaign's potency. It also demonstrates the adaptability of the state NAACP to accept and even praise direct action campaigns when they resulted in positive outcomes. The organization's desire to balance legal actions while acknowledging the efficacy of grassroots activities reveals the complexities that characterized the relationships between the NAACP national, state, and local offices.

The downtown campaign was a watershed moment for race relations in Northwest Florida, but it also reveals a great deal concerning the motivations, planning, and implementation of the sit-ins and subsequent boycotts. While the *Augustus* case worked methodically through the judicial system under direction of the national NAACP and threatened to dismantle segregation in the sole area of education, the sit-ins and boycotts utilized different techniques. The downtown crusades required an unprecedented degree of calculation and cooperation among Panhandle blacks. The PCM, NAACP Youth Council, and some NAACP adult branch members each played specific roles during the demonstrations and accomplished together what would have been too much for any single group to obtain. The endeavors also involved African Americans, both students and adults, in direct action protests for the first time since World War II ended and increased the role that area black churches played in the developing Northwest Florida freedom struggle. City churches provided African Americans with a dynamic group of indigenous leaders that the Pensacola movement desperately needed. Rev. W. C. Dobbins, in particular, was crucial to the success of the downtown sit-ins and boycotts. He organized and inspired area ministers, students, and NAACP members with no help from outside organizations in the first significant mass crusade against Jim Crow in Escambia County. Neither Dobbins nor any other member of the Pensacola NAACP petitioned the national branch for assistance during the campaign. The PCM invited Martin Luther King Jr. to Pensacola, but only to provide support and motivation. No group wanted King, the SCLC, or any other civil rights leader or organization to take control of the movement in Northwest Florida. The success of Pensacola's downtown campaigns thus established the black church as the center of civil rights activity in the area. The importance of black pastors and their congregations in challenging racial discrimination from the grassroots level remained a feature of county race relations for the next twenty years. Dobbins, then, combined and coordinated the efforts of an indigenous ministers' organization, members of the local NAACP chapter, carefully selected student demonstrators, a prominent black church, and economic reasoning to commence the integration of city lunch counters and employment rolls. The triumphant downtown campaign provided local blacks with a common experience in community mobilization and their success bred confidence in the righteousness of their cause and effectiveness of their method—a top-down organizational approach that depended upon mass participation. It also illustrated that black economic power was a collective force that a diverse range of community members—youths and adults, sacred and secular, men and women, rank-and-file and elite—could utilize to bring significant racial change. Perhaps most important, though, is that the downtown undertakings combined with the *Augustus* suit to provide a two-front assault on white supremacy in the Panhandle. The tactics and their subsequent success provided a pattern of protest that African American leaders would reprise during later campaigns against white supremacy in Northwest Florida.

CHAPTER TWO

The Movement Evolves

After downtown department stores desegregated their lunch counters, Dobbins petitioned civic leaders to establish a biracial committee in Pensacola. Civic leaders initially ignored Dobbins's suggestion, but Pensacola mayor Charles Mason urged the city council and county commission to form a biracial committee "to keep channels of communication open between the two races" in the city. The city council's Special Committee, which worked diligently with white and black leaders to obtain peaceful integration during the sit-ins, provided the organizational and functional blueprint for the new group. On June 13, 1963, the city council created the Pensacola Biracial Committee to serve in an advisory capacity to councilmen and county commissioners. The motion passed unanimously and the council appointed the first members to the Pensacola Biracial Committee. W. C. Dobbins was not selected to serve on the committee whose creation he so passionately advocated because civic leaders considered his public activism "extreme and demanding."[1]

Like the Special Committee, three blacks and three whites served as the initial members of the Biracial Committee. The city council chose educated, middle- to upper-class professionals to serve on the committee. Dr. E. S. Cobb, Howard King, and Robert Walker represented the African American community, while Dr. E. V. Anderson, Rev. Paul Duffey, and Frank Fricker served as its white members. Only one member, Cobb, served on the original community council. At its first meeting, the group unanimously elected Fricker, the vice president of the Weis-Fricker Mahogany Company, its chairman and chose King, a Naval Air Station employee, as secretary. At its second meeting the committee added two whites and two blacks, both from the middle and upper professional classes, to the group. The established civic and professional constituency of the Biracial Committee exhibited a disconnection between the group and the majority of Panhandle residents. The exclusion of W. C. Dobbins from membership—despite his repeated requests to serve—meant that the committee did not represent the interests of the local black majority, but that was neither the committee's intent nor purpose. Its primary duty, the committee chair declared, "is to check into the background of Negro-white relations in the Pensacola area in an attempt to provide a basis for future work." City leaders intended the group to serve as a conduit between elected officials, businessmen, and black organizations to minimize racial unrest in Northwest Florida while preserving the power of white elites over the integration process.[2] The Biracial Committee, in short, was an extension of the city's white power structure and represented its desire to control black mass activism at the local level.

In addition to local circumstances, events that transpired approximately 250 miles north of Pensacola influenced the development of the city's Biracial Committee. The SCLC chose to stage its first national campaign against Jim Crow in Birmingham for multiple reasons, and "Project 'C' for Confrontation" proved crucial to the U.S. civil rights struggle. SCLC used nonviolent direct action tactics during Project C, such as selective buying campaigns, sit-ins, marches, and mass meetings to generate "creative tensions" with local authorities. Birmingham's police commissioner, an avowed segregationist and temperamental racist named Theophilus Eugene "Bull" Connor, proved an ideal opponent for the campaign that Dr. Martin Luther King Jr. led. On April 18, 1963, six days after local police arrested him for violating a court-ordered injunction against marching, King released his "Letter from the Birmingham Jail." The letter responded to the published disparagement of King and SCLC activities that eight local white ministers signed, and it represented the most eloquent defense of nonviolent direct action that the movement produced. Approximately two weeks later, the "Children's Campaign" unleashed the unbridled wrath of Connor, who authorized the use of high pressure city fire hoses and trained police dogs against the defenseless young protestors. Media coverage of the city's brutality drew international condemnation and inspired President John F. Kennedy to announce his support of a federal civil rights bill. The historian Glenn T. Eskew argues that "the climax of the civil rights struggle occurred in Birmingham" because it forced a reluctant Kennedy administration to become an active agent of political change regarding black rights.[3] The Birmingham campaign, therefore, had a tremendous short term and long term impact on race relations in the nation, region, and Escambia County.

The Pensacola Biracial Committee defined its purpose in the context of Birmingham and most "wanted to avoid the turmoil and disruptions" that engulfed the Alabama city. In one of its first resolutions, the committee blamed the Birmingham conflict "on undue outside pressures, both individual and governmental." Pensacola needed the Biracial Committee, its members argued, to address disagreements between white and black residents without "unnecessary interference from outside our community." The organization pledged "to avoid such tensions, demonstrations and racial strife in our beloved city" and "handle all our problems on a local basis under local leadership." Committee members even privately agreed to make formal recommendations or public announcements only after a unanimous vote, and pledged to serve the community "without fanfare and without disruption." The group reached out to the local media, particularly the *Pensacola News Journal*, to further validate its actions. In the first recorded comment that a Biracial Committee member made, Dr. E. V. Anderson praised the newspaper for providing a "public service" to the community during the downtown demonstrations and integration of public schools. In essence, the white physician applauded editors for ignoring or minimizing the contentious nature of each event.[4] The response of the local media and civic leaders from the city and county indicates, though, that they viewed the Biracial Committee as an organization whose primary role was not to improve relations between blacks and whites, but to prevent future demonstrations from occurring in the county and city.

The *News Journal* endorsed the committee's formation because it offered the area "a means of communication between races" that would address black concerns before they became "possible causes of friction and disorder." Marion Gaines, the paper's editor, published many editorials and letters that revealed a blatant hostility toward black activism. Gaines opined, for instance, that protestors "are going to extremes" with their demands for equality in Birmingham. Their use of "mob demonstrations contrary to local ordinances or in violation of court injunctions," he concluded, "injures rather than aids solution of interracial problems." The Biracial Committee's "highest priority," Gaines wrote, should be the "peaceful handling of complaints" from local African Americans, or else "street demonstrations" like those in Birmingham would occur in the Panhandle. The *News Journal* also published correspondence from white readers that labeled direct action a "savage" tactic that "immature minds" utilized. "The Negro," the author maintained, "is being used as the tool of Communism." Another praised Alabama governor George Wallace as the "one man in this country with the nerve and guts" to resist integration. The newspaper printed a letter from an African American reader who urged the activists to "stop crying and marching all over the country creating excitement," and reminded them that "Jesus never forced himself on anyone." The *News Journal* even gave history lessons to shed light on contemporary racial affairs. Relations "are close and cordial" between whites and blacks in the South, it claimed, because "the Negro guarded faithfully the defenseless women and children whose husbands and fathers were fighting" during the Civil War. In addition, the paper characterized "the Southern Negro" as "religious," "true and plain," and "opposed to the means now being employed to right the wrongs which must be righted." The formation of the Biracial Committee, the paper maintained, meant that "Pensacola has wisely chosen to keep the fire out of our community." *News Journal* editors, then, perpetuated the view that the Biracial Committee's primary purpose was to keep the demonstrations and activities that engulfed Birmingham from occurring in Pensacola. The committee encountered its first challenge when African American leaders issued a series of new demands.[5]

On August 16, 1963, the city NAACP requested the immediate integration of all area theaters, drive-ins, golf courses, bowling alleys, public pools, medical facilities, beaches, YMCA and YWCA facilities, and popular area tourist attractions. The organization also wanted all locally owned businesses, not just downtown establishments, to serve black customers by 1964. In addition, NAACP leaders requested that local soft drink companies, grocery chains, lunch counters, fast food restaurants, and bus companies hire black applicants, and that the city hire blacks in its parks and maintenance departments, city hall, and all of its utility companies. Finally, the group urged the Pensacola Police Department (PPD) to allow its few black officers to patrol all city neighborhoods and arrest anyone who broke the law, regardless of the offender's color. At the time of the petition, black officers could only arrest those of the same race, while white policemen could arrest anyone. If city officials and business leaders ignored their concerns, the Pensacola NAACP promised to "use its might and resources to bring whatever action deemed necessary to achieve our ultimate goal, which is *complete and total civil liberties* [emphasis in original]."[6] The city council responded by having the Biracial Committee delay African Americans from initiating any direct action campaigns in the city.

The Biracial Committee privately implored both the NAACP and the PCM to allow it to obtain concessions through negotiations with white authorities before the two groups organized public protests. Committee chair Wallace King, a white NAS employee, urged the groups to "not push faster than lasting progress can be made" and warned that "demonstrations or ultimatums at this point" would only " 'solidify resistance' to integration." Public activism, committee member Howard King maintained, "was not the way to get things done" in Northwest Florida. Yet the Biracial Committee possessed no real power beyond an advisory capacity to the white-dominated systems of control at the city and county levels and functioned, as Wallace King observed, "to keep an ear to the ground for organized authority." Committee members, working on behalf on the white power structure, considered segregation "a moral issue that should and could be solved by our own initiative" not "legal compulsion," and proposed a May 1, 1964, deadline for the voluntary integration of all theaters, restaurants, motels, and hotels in Pensacola. After weeks of often tense negotiations between the NAACP, PCM, and the Biracial Committee, the organizations agreed to support the voluntary integration plan and organize no direct action campaigns "as long as time is used constructively" and "negotiations are continued in good faith" between local businessmen and committee members to desegregate their establishments. Committee members privately urged numerous local civic leaders "with a proven track record of community service" to implement changes or else "pressure will be brought into the situation either by local Negroes or by the Federal Government," yet the city council and the county commission refused to publicly endorse or support its committee's voluntary integration plan. Consequently, only one area institution, the city's annual Fiesta of Five Flags, publicly pledged to integrate.[7]

In its seven-page "May 1 Report," the Biracial Committee admitted that its voluntary desegregation plan failed, yet proclaimed "we find no reason for pessimism." The report concluded that "Pensacola can be justly proud of its fine record in the field of race relations" because, in comparison to much of the region, the city's "Negro and white leaders have quietly gone about the task of making adjustments in community life with a minimum of difficulty and very little publicity." From its perspective, the Biracial Committee considered the voluntary desegregation plan an unmitigated success. The proposal eliminated public protests in the immediate future, delayed integration, and maintained the white power structure's power and influence in Northwest Florida. Pensacola NAACP president Calvin Harris called the voluntary program "disappointing" and worked with the PCM to revitalize nonviolent demonstrations in downtown Pensacola. Those threatened protests, however, never materialized due to the progress and eventual passage of what the *Pensacola Journal* labeled "that controversial measure."[8]

While the Pensacola Biracial Committee championed a program of voluntary integration, the Civil Rights Act made its way through Congress. Among its eight provisions, the legislation ended segregation in public schools, the workplace, and in public and private accommodations, provided equal employment opportunities, and prohibited the unequal application of voter registration requirements. It passed the House of Representatives on February 10, 1964, and came to the Senate for debate on March 30. Nineteen southern senators initiated a filibuster that did not end until June 10. Despite the determined resistance, the Senate passed the bill on June 19, and President Johnson signed the Civil Rights Act into law on July 2.[9] The Pensacola Biracial Committee, then, urged the community to integrate its public facilities voluntarily while Congress passionately fought over the future of the twentieth century's most important piece of federal civil rights legislation. White business owners, employers, and managers in Escambia County rejected the committee's proposal due to what they viewed as possible federal coercion as much as they did because of local circumstances. The intense debate that existed over involuntary integration at the national level, then, meant that the voluntary desegregation of local accommodations in Northwest Florida had little chance to succeed. Rejection of the Biracial Committee's program represented the last gasp of local whites to resist integration, regardless of the plan's origin. With the passage of the Civil Rights Act, local establishments had to desegregate or face federal chastisement. The Pensacola Biracial Committee, NAACP, and Pensacola Council of Ministers, therefore, shifted their collective emphases after July 2, 1964, from obtaining access to public accommodations to monitoring the pace and process of desegregation. As the movement adjusted to the monumental change at both the local and national levels, African Americans in Escambia suddenly and unexpectedly lost their most important advocate.

Less than a month after the Pensacola Biracial Committee released its "May 1 Report," the United Methodist Church transferred Rev. W. C. Dobbins to a pastorate in Sylacauga, Alabama. His new assignment officially began on July 1, 1964, the day before President Johnson signed the Civil Rights Act into law. The relocation and promotion followed UMC procedure and no surviving records indicate that his civil rights activities prompted the reassignment. Still, Dobbins's departure left a tremendous leadership void for African Americans in Northwest Florida. According to one minister, local blacks had "nothing but respect" for Dobbins because "he was the one that really opened our eyes to the social injustices" they endured. Several ministers remained active NAACP members, but most were advanced in age and none filled Dobbins's role as spokesman for the county movement. Local NAACP president Calvin Harris seemed a possible successor to Dobbins, but he was not a minister. Harris did not have access to the congregations that pastors led and lacked the instant credibility and social status that African American clergy possessed. Consequently, the Pensacola Council of Ministers dissolved as a grassroots civil rights organization within six months after Dobbins left the Panhandle and the adult branch of the Pensacola NAACP grew complacent in the wake of his transfer.[10] Yet one of the followers Dobbins left behind, a fellow minister named H. K. Matthews, soon became the most vocal advocate for racial justice in Pensacola and filled the need for a charismatic leader upon which the local organizing tradition depended.

The civil rights movement in Escambia County experienced a dramatic transformation in the period that followed the monumental downtown campaigns, but the transfer of W. C. Dobbins to another state came at a transitional time in the local movement, for the passage of the Civil Rights Act changed the nature and the focus of the continuing black freedom struggle. The early 1960s, though, established several protest patterns that county blacks replicated when they encountered racial injustices over the next fifteen years. Nonviolent demonstrations, mass meetings, public assemblies, economic boycotts and selective buying campaigns, and voter registration drives became staple tactics when local people protested the persistence of segregation and discriminatory treatment. Yet the white power structure—in this case, the Pensacola City Council—also maintained its influence over the desegregation process and minimized the degree of area racial changes. The city's Biracial Committee developed in response to both local and regional direct action campaigns, and it publicly pledged to open communication between blacks and white systems of economic, political, and social control. The Biracial Committee, however, represented the interests of white elites and worked to minimize racial unrest through the implementation of measures that kept power in their hands. The committee addressed black demands with token concessions, voluntary programs, and other ways that minimized or stonewalled challenges to their ultimate authority. Escambia County's civil rights movement, therefore, encountered tremendous resistance as the decade progressed. Rev. H. K. Matthews continued the protest patterns that his mentor utilized in an increasingly hostile racial climate.

Hawthorne Konrad Matthews was born on February 7, 1928, in Snow Hill, Alabama. His mother died six weeks after giving birth to H. K. and his father returned to his home in nearby Camden soon thereafter. Lucy Purifoyd Johnson, the widowed maternal grandmother of H. K., raised the abandoned child as her own son in the predominantly black community of Snow Hill. After he graduated from high school in 1947, Matthews attended classes at both Alabama State College and Alabama A&M. He joined the army in 1951, served in an integrated unit during the Korean War, and was wounded in combat. He received an honorable discharge in June 1955 and returned to Snow Hill for a brief period. Matthews moved to Pensacola later in the year and worked a variety of odd jobs while living with friends and relatives. He also started drinking heavily and became a self-professed "slave to the bottle." In 1957 Matthews married and began a new family, but his habit persisted. Two years later, his life changed dramatically. He quit drinking, lost his grandmother to an extended illness, and entered the ministry. In October 1960, Matthews delivered his first sermon at Allen Chapel African Methodist Episcopal (AME) Zion Church. His preaching duties soon brought Matthews in contact with another enthusiastic young minister named W. C. Dobbins.[11]

The two men formed a bond shortly after meeting. As Matthews put it, "Rev. Dobbins took me under his wing and taught me a lot about the ministry and the conditions blacks in our time faced." He referred to his mentor as "the master teacher" because he spoke constantly to both his congregation and fellow ministers about the social injustices that permeated Pensacola. Matthews eventually served as the substitute pastor for Dobbins at St. Paul UMC, became an early member of the Dobbins-led Pensacola Council of Ministers, and represented the PCM in meetings with the county's Special Committee during the downtown demonstrations. Dobbins also appointed Matthews as adviser to the NAACP Youth Council after the downtown campaigns ended. Matthews's rise drew the attention of blacks and whites alike, and each group responded to his personality in contrasting ways. Matthews's fiery speaking style, confrontational nature, and admitted habit of using inflammatory rhetoric and tones when addressing racial injustice earned the admiration of many local blacks. His combative temperament, by Matthews's own admission, differed tremendously from his mentor's deliberate style. Not surprisingly, many Panhandle whites despised the more outspoken minister.[12] The position gave Matthews leadership experience and exposed him to socially conscious young blacks, a group that he connected with immediately and who became his most ardent supporters. His dynamic personality, close relationship with Dobbins, boundless energy, popularity among the youth, and religious fervor did not go unnoticed by his fellow ministers.

Matthews made such a positive impression on the area's veteran activists that a group of them asked the energetic minister to expand his leadership role within the black community after Dobbins left Florida. Matthews accepted their challenge. In the following weeks, what remained of the PCM publicly declared their support for Rev. H. K. Matthews as the new leader and spokesperson for the local civil rights movement. Over the next fifteen years, Matthews remained the central figure in Escambia County's black freedom struggle. He initially approached his appointment with great trepidation, though, struggling internally with a sense of his own inadequacies and lack of experience in the movement, particularly when compared to Dobbins. Matthews believed that he had to do more in the regional struggle for racial justice to both prepare him to lead his community and to validate his selection as the movement's primary figure.[13] In 1965, then, the thirty-seven-year-old preacher acted upon his convictions and traveled to Selma, Alabama.

On March 3, 1965, Dr. Martin Luther King Jr. announced that a march from Selma to the Montgomery state capital in support of black voting rights would take place the following Sunday. H. K. Matthews believed that because he now occupied a very public role in the Pensacola civil rights struggle, he should join King in the demonstration. The situation provided Matthews with what he believed an invaluable opportunity to learn more about nonviolent techniques and practices from a first-hand perspective. Matthews left Pensacola on the Friday afternoon of March 5 and attended a mass meeting at Brown Chapel AME Church when he arrived in Selma later that evening. The next day, which became known as "Bloody Sunday," permanently altered the life of H. K. Matthews. He choked on tear gas that the police shot into the crowd and an officer hit him repeatedly with a club, even after the minister fell to the ground and covered his head to escape the blows. Matthews received numerous bruises, lacerations, and a severely damaged knee that plagued him for the remainder of his life. The experience inspired him to work even harder for racial justice in Pensacola when Matthews returned to the city three days later.[14]

March 7, 1965, therefore, had an immeasurable impact on the black freedom struggle in Escambia County, as well as the United States as a whole. Bloody Sunday led to the passage of the 1965 Voting Rights Act, which represented the last major legislative victory of the national civil rights movement, but it also represented a turning point in the black freedom struggle. African Americans now turned their attention from de jure forms of segregation to more de facto expressions of white supremacy. Campaigns like the one in Selma eliminated the existence of codified racism, but other obstacles to full black citizenship persisted in the Panhandle, as they did throughout the region. Furthermore, whites believed the toppling of legal pillars that maintained their racial superiority should eliminate automatically all complaints blacks had with the existing social system. As the *Pensacola News Journal* argued in the days following President Lyndon B. Johnson's announcement of his support for federal voting rights legislation, blacks "have attained all of the really important legal objectives they have battled for during the past decade." The editorial continued that blacks could now achieve the jobs, economic advancement, and other social gains "the more restless members of the race" desired. "But," the piece continued paternalistically, "these things cannot be acquired by making demands, conducting demonstrations and marches, staging sit-downs, or by violating the laws of peace and order." Black efforts "to force a reluctant public to recognize and grant equality" must "be diverted to personal improvement" and to cultivating the "responsibility to properly use the freedoms which have been made available."[15] The black freedom struggle that continued beyond 1965, then, faced a new kind of white resentment and resistance because many readjusted their understanding of the struggle after the Voting Rights Act. Whites now equated the collapse of de jure segregation via federal intervention with the full arrival of racial equality. In the wake of the legislative victories, some whites believed that blacks no longer had anything to protest. In addition to the influence that Selma exerted on the national black freedom struggle, it also had an important impact in Pensacola. His experience on Bloody Sunday bestowed an increased degree of legitimacy upon the outspoken minister, and area blacks thereafter looked upon Matthews as someone who transcended local importance; he had participated in an event of national significance. As one Pensacola NAACP member recalled, Matthews "was the person that we all kind of looked to for a sense of direction" because "he had marched with other civil rights leaders," traveled "in and out of Pensacola to go to important national meetings," and "had the pulse of what was really happening on a national level." His work both in and outside of the Panhandle placed him in a nearly unassailable position of prestige with many local blacks.[16] Perhaps most important, though, the Selma experience reinforced Matthews's growing belief that he received a divine calling to lead the Pensacola movement.

Religion played an indispensable role in Escambia County's civil rights movement from the time W. C. Dobbins formed the Pensacola Council of Ministers in 1961 and constituted a key component of the local organizing approach. Clergy members organized each direct action campaign and their churches served as centers of the grassroots mobilization efforts. After Dobbins left Pensacola in 1963, religion maintained its primary position in the local movement. Area ministers implored Matthews to take a leadership role due in large part to his status as an AME Zion preacher and his commitment to carrying out what many blacks viewed as God's work. Matthews maintained that he accepted the position due to his religious convictions and believed leadership of the local black community was an ordained appointment that he could not refuse. Bloody Sunday only strengthened Matthews's belief that God chose him for a special task in Escambia County, as heavenly intervention prevented him from "being hurt worse or even killed" that day. Matthews, therefore, left Selma with the unshakeable belief that "God can be called on and be relied upon in times of social turmoil." He viewed his strength, determination, and spiritual awareness as gifts that God expected him to use on behalf of the socially, economically, and politically powerless in Northwest Florida. Matthews, therefore, characterized his civil rights activism as "working for God" and utilized the concepts of justice and deliverance supported through Christian principles to demand immediate racial equality.[17]

For H. K. Matthews and his growing number of followers, religion justified their demands for social, political, and economic equality. Their devotion to God demanded action that would deliver tangible results for the powerless and destitute in this world. Although the Pensacola movement became an exercise in religious faith for most of its leaders and participants, its intended outcomes never assumed secondary importance to its spiritual expression. The ends were secular—the extension of citizenship rights for all—but its means—the language, motivations, and understanding of the struggle—were spiritual. Matthews presented the plight of African Americans in Escambia County and, indeed, throughout the nation, as a result of the white failure to recognize the common humanity and natural equality that they shared with blacks. It became the Christian obligation of God's children, regardless of their color, to protest all forms of racism and prejudice that endured in Northwest Florida. The spiritual realm provided a way through which Matthews understood and explained the economic and cultural challenges that his followers faced in the years following the passage of the Civil and Voting Rights Acts. Matthews, however, rejected the concept of prophetic Christianity, which is the belief that redemptive suffering would force an unwilling power structure to make substantive, tangible changes that it opposed. The state of the bigot's soul mattered little to Matthews; he did not emphasize the Gospel's transformative nature for the oppressor when addressing white racism. "It was never my intention," he maintained, "to change anybody. I did not think our actions would change anyone and, quite frankly, did not care" if they did. What Matthews demanded was the treatment that blacks deserved as people created in God's image. After the sit-ins, for instance, Matthews proclaimed that any white who served him at the newly integrated lunch counter could "hate my guts, but I could care less. As long as he served me my food, took my money, and called me 'sir,' that was all I wanted." The fact that Matthews did not care for the redemption of Panhandle racists is a departure from the popular belief—particularly in the African American church—that the movement intended to save the black man's body and the white man's soul.[18] Unlike prominent religious leaders at the national level such as Martin Luther King Jr., John Lewis, and Andrew Young, Matthews did not obtain an advanced theological education or rigorous intellectual training. He was a philosopher of the folk who advocated nonviolence because it proved thoroughly compatible with his religious beliefs. The ideology and its application reinforced the spiritual nature of the local movement for its participants and they were not concerned with how it might affect their enemies. Religion, then, supplied a way for Matthews to illustrate and comprehend the existence of de facto forms of inequality in the evolving black freedom struggle, but it did not offer blacks their means of deliverance. Only mobilization and non-violent activism could bring social change.

Upon his return from Selma in 1965, Matthews made revitalization of the NAACP Youth Council his top priority. He organized meetings with interested young blacks and challenged them to become involved in the ongoing freedom struggle by joining the youth council, whose membership grew to over 150 people within eighteen months. The group elected Matthews as their sole adviser in 1967. The rejuvenated council became a crucial part of the rapidly evolving local freedom movement, for Matthews and his organization were thoroughly compatible with each other. His direct, down-to-earth personality and willingness to confront discrimination in an intolerant, often combative manner made him extremely popular with those he mentored. Youth council members considered Matthews an "honest" and fearless leader, a "highly respected citizen of our community," and "a giant" who "did not back down from anybody or anything" in his demands for justice. The organization provided Matthews with an enthusiastic group of volunteers who demanded equal treatment and who had their adviser's vigor and passion. Some council members had participated in the downtown sit-ins and demonstrations, but most were high school students who joined the group between 1965 and 1968. Matthews initially concentrated youth council activities against local establishments that remained closed to black customers after passage of the Civil Rights Act, and direct action protests or the threat of such campaigns integrated local skating rinks, bowling alleys, movie theaters, and the Pensacola YMCA during the late 1960s.[19] One particular campaign, though, became the stuff of local legend and enhanced the reputation of H. K. Matthews among young activists in Northwest Florida.

In April 1969, four nursing students from Florida A&M University entered Stuckey's Laundromat in Ensley, a town which lay approximately ten miles north of Pensacola. The ladies wanted to wash their clothes, but a white employee pointed out signs that designated the establishment as segregated and refused to let them use the machines. The frustrated students contacted the NAACP Youth Council and recounted their experience. Matthews rode past the laundry and noticed a large "White Only" sign posted outside of the entrance. He discovered that the Meredith Lumber Company owned the establishment and sold materials to blacks next door, but refused them access to the laundry. The reverend decided to protest the business in a unique way; the youth council would obey the sign. In less than a month after they learned of the Stuckey's placard, Matthews and several young blacks entered the building, occupied every vacant washing machine, and placed one article of white clothing in each appliance. Curious whites milled around the laundromat and one of them called the police. An officer told Matthews that his group had to leave the premises because the establishment "is for whites only." Matthews responded that the youth abided by the sign's command and broke no law because they washed white clothes alone. The officer made no arrests and asked them to leave when their task ended, but the group dried the clothes in the same manner. The business closed permanently rather than integrate in the aftermath of what the youth council dubbed their "wash-in."[20]

H. K. Matthews became a hero to many in the black community because of his unique tactics and outspoken nature. He did not alter his rhetoric to make his words more palatable to either race or any social class and confronted the local white power structure with little concern for his personal safety. He was a very public spokesman for African American concerns, as he appeared frequently on a weekly community affairs program that the white-owned Pensacola television station WEAR—an ABC affiliate—broadcast, and wrote regular columns for the *Pensacola News Journal* and the *Pensacola Call and Post*, the city's only black newspaper. In some ways, then, H. K. Matthews became "a sincere revolutionary" to many Escambia County blacks. He did not just want access to previously segregated facilities, but he demanded equal treatment in the most literal sense. Blacks deserved dignified treatment as full citizens, an increased share in the nation's economic promise, and equal access to the educational opportunities that whites claimed as theirs alone. Matthews so inspired local African Americans that an area magazine declared his name "a synonym for civil rights in the Northwest Florida Panhandle" in 1971. The self-righteousness he projected about racial affairs made ambivalence regarding his message practically impossible. Unsurprisingly, his assertiveness and often confrontational manner struck Panhandle whites as insolent, insulting, and self-serving. Whites who found themselves on the receiving end of Matthews's ire perceived him as "something of a scoundrel": a "dishonest," "extremely inflammatory," and "very angry man" who manufactured nonexistent racial conflict for his own egomaniacal benefit and insatiable need for publicity. Many considered Matthews "a showman" who "was trying to be another Martin

Luther King" at the expense of tranquil race relations in Escambia County.[21] White civic leaders were not alone in their rising revulsion toward Matthews. The multiracial Pensacola Biracial Committee also refused to work with Matthews or any organization affiliated with him in addressing mutually acknowledged racial problems in their city, particularly employment inequities.

The Pensacola Biracial Committee officially changed its name to the Pensacola Human Relations Commission (HRC) on August 15, 1966. Despite the new title, the five white, five black member body continued to act in an advisory capacity to the Pensacola City Council and the Escambia County Commission and operated as an extension of the local power structure. *Pensacola News Journal* editor Marion Gaines, for instance, chaired the HRC from 1966 to 1971, and the two bodies selected African American members from the ranks of the educated and professional elite, particularly those who worked at NAS.[22] The HRC publicly acknowledged black underemployment as a significant issue as the 1960s progressed and launched several programs to increase minority hiring on a voluntary basis. The efforts addressed black grievances while providing white business owners the power to control the amount and pace of integration that occurred in their establishments. The commission, for instance, planned several "job training programs" in 1968 to teach "disadvantaged" blacks skills such as the "proper behavior, etiquette and personal grooming required to obtain jobs." The group also planned a "Human Relations Day," organized occasional interracial worship services throughout the city, investigated the conditions of public recreation facilities in the county, and hosted a seminar for interested civic groups that addressed "Unemployment and Under-Employment of the Disadvantaged."[23] The HRC, in other words, responded to black concerns regarding local economic disparities in ways that did not challenge the racial status quo and perpetuated segregation in practice. The group also criticized nearly every NAACP activity that it addressed in committee meetings, such as protests against the *Pensacola News Journal*, a month-long selective buying campaign against downtown businesses that employed no blacks, and the group's involvement in labor strikes at Baptist and Sacred Heart hospitals. The HRC also rejected the NAACP's recommendation that it fill a membership vacancy with H. K. Matthews due to his public activism. Those who supported Matthews and the NAACP viewed black HRC members as "Uncle Toms" who "are bought and paid for by the white power structure" and undermined African American social and economic progress. HRC members understood the perceptions that blacks had concerning its members, but they defended their conservative actions. Rev. H. C. Calloway, for instance, claimed that "Uncle Tom was a Christian gentleman and that's all I want to be."[24]

The enmity that characterized the relationship between the Human Relations Commission and the NAACP reveals that class-based tensions permeated the civil rights movement in Escambia County as the 1960s ended. On one hand, the HRC represented the interests of upper-class professional, business, and civic authorities. The preservation of social order represented the HRC's main objective. The group wanted to minimize public protest and used more reactive, voluntary measures to address the economic divisions between the races in Northwest Florida. The NAACP, on the other hand, publicly demanded the immediate end of de facto discrimination, particularly in the area of black employment. Matthews and his followers considered African Americans who served on the HRC as accommodationists who either shared in the interests of their fellow white committee members or hoped to profit in some way from their complicity. The HRC, according to the working and lower-middle-class blacks whom Matthews championed, represented "the classes, not the masses" in Pensacola. Indeed, commission chair Marion Gaines defended the interests of the area's business and professional leaders, refused to work with groups who actively protested local racial inequalities, and thus embodied the authority that white systems of power still possessed after the token integration of schools and public accommodations in Northwest Florida.[25] Between 1966 and 1969, then, the racial chasm in Escambia County grew due to the white ability to control the pace, nature, and amount of social change and the inability of African Americans to influence such decisions. At the same time, H. K. Matthews grew increasingly frustrated with what he interpreted as a plethora of unnecessary rules, regulations, and restraints the NAACP imposed upon local chapters.

The minister experienced the restrictions directly when he became president of the Pensacola chapter of the NAACP in 1968. Matthews resigned from the position months later because "I did not want to check with the headquarters every time I wanted to arrange a demonstration or organize a campaign." NAACP tactics, he believed, absorbed valuable time and resources that local members could better spend organizing their communities. Indeed, the historian Timothy Minchin has examined NAACP activism after 1965 and concluded the organization "continued to be defined by its belief in litigation as the best means to combat racial injustice" across the South. The frustration that Matthews had with the group, though, went both ways. National NAACP officials grew increasingly displeased with his provocative public pronouncements and the demonstrations Matthews organized. The national office consequently threatened to dismiss him as leader of the Pensacola Youth Council before his resignation as president of the adult chapter.[26] Yet his struggles with the national NAACP had an impact upon Matthews and caused him to question the practicality of depending solely upon one group to mobilize local blacks. As a new decade began, he introduced another civil rights organization to Pensacola.

H. K. Matthews formed the Escambia County chapter of the Southern Christian Leadership Conference in February 1971 and became the branch's first president. Matthews started the Northwest Florida office because he believed the area needed an organization to complement the NAACP and compensate for its shortcomings. "It was not the tactics," Matthews explained, "but rather the non-tactics of the NAACP that most concerned me." Respect for Dr. King first attracted Matthews to the SCLC and he sought to follow in his hero's footsteps. Matthews also admired SCLC protest methods and the almost unrestricted autonomy the national office provided its local chapters. Despite the SCLC's decline as an influential civil rights organization following King's 1968 death, Matthews supported the group because he believed it presented the best opportunity for black social and economic advancement in Northwest Florida.[27]

The Escambia SCLC grew from forty-five to over three hundred members in its first year of operation. Many also belonged to the Pensacola NAACP, which had over six hundred registered supporters. African Americans possessed dual membership because Rev. B. J. Brooks, president of the local NAACP chapter, and Matthews emphasized the importance of activists joining each organization. The two groups, according to Matthews, acted "as one, basically, because the leadership and membership was so united. When we had mass meetings, we did not have a NAACP mass meeting or a SCLC mass meeting. We had a community mass meeting," which Matthews and Brooks led together. The two men, in fact, met "almost daily" to plan and discuss protest plans and strategies, and always met with local officials together to appear united in their aims and objectives. The strategy had a practical outcome, as white leaders preferred to negotiate with the more quiet and less demonstrative

Brooks. The NAACP and SCLC leaders noticed the trend early in their working relationship and used the personality difference to their advantage when they met with civic leaders to discuss racial issues. White authorities negotiated more willingly with Brooks than they did the more loquacious, blunt, and sometimes confrontational Matthews, although the two leaders had the same outcome in mind during such sessions.[28] Yet unlike the local NAACP, the Escambia SCLC president possessed almost total control of his group. Matthews divided the chapter into three committees. The Field Staff Committee was led by Rev. Nathaniel Woods, who organized membership drives and solicited support for the new group. F. L. Henderson chaired the Labor and Industry Committee, which monitored Pensacola businesses to ensure they followed fair hiring policies. Finally, Rev. Otha Leverette oversaw the Educational Committee. Leverette became especially important to the organization because he presided over a small group known as the Escambia County Community League (ECCL) before the SCLC formed. He brought ECCL members into the group along with fragments of the local Black Baptist Ministers Alliance. Leverette's main duty as committee chair was to investigate the unequal treatment of faculty and staff in county schools. Each committee chair reported solely to Matthews, which ensured that he influenced every aspect of the county SCLC. According to one area publication, SCLC members considered Matthews "a saint left here to fill in the holes of justice and defend the rights of black people to live, work, learn, and play in the mainstream of a wealthy America." White residents in the Florida Panhandle, however, despised Matthews more with each of his public campaigns.[29] The organization continued to emphasize black underemployment, but another issue soon drew its attention.

In his 1941 work on race, violence, and regional culture, *The Mind of the South*, W. J. Cash described the post-Reconstruction Era southern "policeman" as a "simple soul primarily interested in keeping his job" who used his authority to enforce white supremacy and, thus, satisfy the social and economic elite. Gunnar Mydral developed the theme more deeply three years later in the monumental study *An American Dilemma*, where he noted that police brutality occupied a central purpose in the preservation of white supremacy throughout the South. More recently, scholars have highlighted police actions and inactions during past civil rights campaigns. Gail O'Brien, for instance, argued that "the police operated as the frontline guardians of an arbitrary criminal justice system and a social order that controlled black Americans in their relations with whites but that offered blacks little protection from whites or from one another." Hasan Jeffries linked the rise in southern police violence to the decrease in postwar lynchings as a method of white racial control, while Laurie Green argued that law enforcement officers "*were* the face of racial violence during the civil rights era, whether their assaults were conducted as part or outside of official police business [emphasis in original]." Violence exerted by law enforcement also plays a significant role in the narrative of late 1960s urban race riots, when the concept of "police brutality" became a national concern and provided a catalyst, if not the central reason, for African American mobilization in the years beyond integration. Those incidents did not occur in a vacuum, but represented the primary role that the police played in the maintenance of white supremacy, particularly during times of ongoing social upheaval. "White police officers," the historian Leonard Moore demonstrated, "emerged as the protectors of white privilege and the opponents of black progress." This became particularly true in the South before, during, and after the 1960s movement.[30] The courts, official government agencies, and white opinion endorsed and implicitly encouraged discriminatory practices by local police, whose oppressive actions took numerous forms. Claims of police brutality ranged from harassment, the use of abusive, demeaning, and racist language, beating those in police custody, and acts of sexual exploitation to wrongful arrests and the lethal shooting of blacks for relatively minor offenses. Law enforcement in many southern cities, then, exacerbated racial tensions and fueled black mistrust of white authorities. This was apparent in Pensacola where, according to H. K. Matthews, "there has never been a complete trust of law enforcement by African Americans." The mistrust of local police first became a major concern during the 1961 sit-in campaigns after officers placed batteries in the pockets of young demonstrators and arrested them for shoplifting.[31] Although blacks protested the practices of the PPD, the Escambia County Sheriff's Department earned a particularly notorious reputation among local blacks for their racially motivated acts of brutality.

The sheriff's department employed dozens more officers, had fewer employment requirements, and paid lower salaries than the PPD, all of which contributed to the ECSD's image as an unprofessional bastion of white supremacy. Sheriff's department cruisers patrolled black neighborhoods, many believed, to "harass and harm, not help" its residents. Lee Humphrey, the editor of Pensacola's only black-owned newspaper, maintained deputies "retained uncomplimentary stereotypes of black people" into the 1970s. The county SCLC documented several instances in which white deputies pulled over black motorists when they broke no laws, issued tickets for nonexistent offenses, and even brutalized some who questioned an officer's actions. Racial profiling, therefore, intensified the relationship between blacks and area officers long before the phrase entered the nation's vocabulary, and SCLC leaders maintained that African Americans believed "they were looking at the enemy" any time they saw a sheriff's deputy. The treatment of black prisoners within the county jail supported such declarations. The Escambia County Sheriff's Department refused to provide black prisoners with medicine, meals, showers, clothing, and attorney visits, and segregated their cells into the 1970s. The department also maintained six "special confinement cells" called "bullets" due to their stainless steel walls and round, symmetrical design. Each bullet measured six feet wide by eight feet high with no solid covering. A metal grid allowed air, light, and rain to enter each cell, which contained no toilet, sink, bunk, or mattress. A hole in the polished steel floor allowed waste to exit the enclosure. Prisoners housed in the bullets were typically stripped naked, denied regular meals and showers, and not allowed to communicate with anyone outside of the jail. The sheriff's department acknowledged that it used the bullets for "mentally disturbed persons" and " 'disciplinary' purposes," but one inquiry revealed that the department regularly placed African Americans into the cells "for no reason whatsoever" other than their race. Deputies locked as many as twelve blacks in a single bullet at one time for "making too much noise," and some prisoners spent up to twenty-seven consecutive days in the cells.[32] The tensions that grew between black Pensacolians and county officers in the years following the federally mandated desegregation of public accommodations, therefore, often brought the groups into direct conflict with each other. In 1969, the NAACP Youth Council listed "police brutality" as one of their two primary concerns for the coming decade, and several altercations between officers and young blacks during the late 1960s confirmed the youth council's apprehensions.[33] One incident, in particular, indicated that the precarious relationship between the Escambia County Sheriff's Department and the local black community would lead to racial conflicts in the area.

On a July afternoon in 1970, two nineteen-year-old African Americans named Beulah May Glover and Willie James Huff III spent the day at a county beach that blacks primarily patronized. When the two did not return home that night, their families searched the area where the teens said they intended to swim. One family member found Huff's automobile at the site but no sign of the two, and called the Escambia County Sheriff's Department to report the teens missing and request help in locating them. The deputy who answered the call refused to travel "way over there" to the beach "to look for somebody in the dark." The officer advised the search party to "walk up and down the beach and they might find them," noting that the two "were probably alright." The next morning, the lifeless bodies of Glover and Huff were found. The county coroner discovered no signs of a physical struggle on either body, located water in the lungs of both victims, and confirmed that the two had drowned. Family members, though, suspected that Glover and Huff died under more dubious circumstances, and rumors spread throughout the black community that the white deputies who patrolled the beaches killed the two and hid their crime with the drowning allegations.[34] Because African Americans distrusted white authorities, the coroner's report strengthened black suspicions that county officials conspired to hide the true nature of Glover's and Huff's deaths. Instead of satisfying questions surrounding the teens' deaths, the coroner's findings sparked four nights of racial unrest in Pensacola.

African Americans responded to the deaths of Glover and Huff by rioting in downtown Pensacola from July 31 through August 3. Groups of angry youths threw Molotov cocktails into white-owned businesses, threw bricks at passing automobiles, overturned one vehicle, intentionally set fires at specific locations across the city, and shot at fire engines that fought the flames. Young blacks also converged on the *Pensacola News Journal* office and told reporters who spoke with them that deputies killed Glover and Huff "because of their race." City officials, however, publicly proclaimed that "no indication of racial overtures" characterized the unrest, and Police Chief D. P. Caldwell ordered his officers not to speak to reporters about the nightly violence. City police and county deputies finally ended the rioting after its fourth evening. Officers arrested approximately fifty blacks on charges that included loitering, assault and battery, inciting to riot, and attempted arson. City leaders praised them for doing "a magnificent job of restraining themselves" for, as one supervisor noted, "no guns were drawn and not one person was clubbed" by deputies. Editors at the *News Journal* equated black rioters to the Ku Klux Klan "of many years ago" and opined that the "South had finally suppressed one crop of bigots of one race only to find we're raising another crop in another race." The HRC called an emergency meeting in response to the riot and formed a six-man subcommittee to investigate both the deaths of Glover and Huff and the causes of subsequent black unrest. Although the panel eventually ruled that the two teenagers died due to an "accidental drowning," it cited black "distrust for the majority of the law enforcement personnel who are charged with the protection of all it's [sic] citizens regardless of color" as the systemic cause of the subsequent riots. "Rumors about the deaths of these two young people were not 'THE' [emphasis in original] cause of the disturbances," the committee declared, but that they "were brought on by a multitude of things including the harassment by some white policemen, and the steady patrolling of the black areas by policemen, and the refusal of so many white employers to hire blacks in meaningful employment."[35] The fact that civic authorities did not publicly release the HRC findings confirmed that African American frustration with the county sheriff's department posed a significant obstacle to interracial peace in Northwest Florida. The appointment of a new sheriff mollified black suspicion of area law enforcement officers only temporarily.

In 1970 Florida governor Claude Kirk removed Sheriff Bill Davis from office following a grand jury indictment on multiple ethical and criminal charges. Royal Untreiner, a Pensacola native and former University of Florida athlete who became a Federal Bureau of Investigation (FBI) agent in 1934, replaced Davis. Untreiner rose through the organization's ranks and captured the attention of bureau director J. Edgar Hoover, who became a mentor and close friend to the young agent. Untreiner served as a "Special Agent In-Charge" of fifteen different FBI field offices and molded many of his leadership qualities after those that his role model possessed, including an unwavering loyalty to those he commanded. Untreiner returned to Pensacola after his 1956 retirement from the FBI and won elections to the state legislature and county commission. His professional background and "law and order" political platform evoked hope from black leaders that the strained relationship between the sheriff's department and African Americans would improve.[36] Their optimism was unfounded, as the issue of police brutality and the suspected killing of unarmed blacks resurfaced less than a decade later with more dire consequences for Escambia County race relations.

While the Northwest Florida SCLC increasingly focused its attention on the alleged mistreatment of African American residents, Escambia

County public schools integrated on token levels at best. During the 1965–66 school year, only 902 of the 13,211 blacks who attended county schools attended previously all-white institutions. The number of blacks who attended formerly all-white institutions increased the following year, but they constituted only 2.8 percent of the county's total students. NAACP attorneys filed a motion to accelerate school integration in Northwest Florida, and Judge Carswell implemented a "freedom of choice" plan for the Escambia County School District on April 14, 1967. The decree kept the onus for school desegregation on black parents who had to formally request the relocation of their children to predominantly white schools.[37] "Freedom of choice" programs, much as they did throughout the South, preserved the dual system of education in Northwest Florida. A 1967 federal report claimed the plans "produced little integration. White pupils seldom, if ever, chose to attend majority black schools, and black children, perhaps apprehensive of hostility by the overwhelmingly white majority, rarely chose to attend white schools." As the 1967–68 term began, twenty county schools had no white pupils, fifteen had no black students, and African Americans constituted less than 5 percent of the student population at thirty-one formerly white schools.[38] A May 1968 Supreme Court decision, though, accelerated the pace of school desegregation across the South.

In its *Green v. New Kent County (VA) School Board* ruling, the court declared freedom of choice an ineffective and unacceptable method of school integration. The historian James T. Patterson called the decision "a major milestone in the history of judicial steps toward" public school desegregation because "it gave specificity to the vague and ineffective phrase, 'all deliberate speed.'"[39] Before he could issue a ruling on the NAACP motion, though, President Richard Nixon appointed Carswell to the Fifth Circuit Court of Appeals.[40] Local whites lost an important ally in their struggle to maintain segregated schools because Carswell's replacement proved much less sympathetic to their cause. Winston E. "Bo" Arnow, a Florida native and World War II veteran, served as a municipal judge in Gainesville before his 1967 nomination to the U.S. District of Northern Florida. Arnow excelled in legal research and civil procedure and possessed a reputation as a strict constructionist who, while politically conservative, followed higher federal court orders "to the letter, even if he may have personally disagreed with the decision."[41] His initial decision regarding school integration, therefore, marked a conspicuous start to his influential tenure in Escambia County. Judge

Arnow ruled the school board's freedom of choice plan violated *Green* on January 23, 1969, and ordered members to issue new integration procedures based on reorganized school attendance zones. The judge instructed obstructionist board officials and resistant local whites to "face up to reality" because "the time is now" to comply with previous rulings and end Escambia County's dual educational system. The school board submitted a new plan to Arnow on April 18, and he used it as the basis of an order he released three days later.[42]

The April 21 mandate represented the most thorough attempt to integrate the county's public school system, due in no small part to Arnow's conviction that he possessed a "mandatory obligation to provide a unitary school system effective now" for Escambia County. The most important component of the revised proposal stipulated that no Escambia County school would house only blacks during the 1969–70 term. The significant order also integrated twenty-one schools where little or none had occurred, ended dual busing routes, paired four primarily segregated elementary schools, closed three others, restructured two to serve grades six through eight, reassigned faculty members based on racial considerations to achieve a 75 percent white to 25 percent black balance in each school, and required that each institution submit annual reports concerning the racial distribution of their student bodies to the court. Judge Arnow anticipated great public resistance to the order and warned against such actions. If white parents initiated a "mass exodus" from county schools, Arnow declared, the court would implement a busing plan for every institution. Finally, the April decree kept *Augustus* open because Arnow believed that board integration efforts "may need further examination and rearrangement from time to time." The court, therefore, retained jurisdiction in the suit and promised to intervene when necessary. The county school board accepted the changes with no open resistance at its next meeting. Escambia County's dual educational system, at least in theory, was finally dead. *Augustus* lay dormant for the first time since its 1960 filing as the new decade began.[43]

Judge Winston Arnow's revised school desegregation edict was a unique event in the continuously evolving black struggle for racial equality in Northwest Florida because it again made local classrooms a primary focus for both races. For blacks, the court-ordered end of the dual education system represented a necessary and long overdue step toward a more thoroughly integrated society. Educational equality became both practically and symbolically important, as blacks pursued educational opportunities with the same passion that they sought economic advancement. The two issues, in fact, were inseparable. African Americans realized that the county's predominantly and exclusively all-white schools provided greater educational opportunities than others in the area, particularly those with substantial black majorities. The facilities, textbooks, athletic equipment, libraries, and other amenities were more advanced and newer than those at predominantly black institutions. African Americans believed that attendance at such schools prepared them more thoroughly for their postgraduate lives and careers. Through access to more advanced schools that had previously integrated on a token basis, if at all, young blacks could increase their economic, employment, and social prospects as adults. Yet schools represented a symbolic victory for blacks as well, for they represented the last bastion of white resistance to de jure segregation in Escambia County. Long after public accommodations integrated their facilities, schools in Pensacola and elsewhere across the South refused to integrate completely. Arnow's order, therefore, was important to local blacks because it ended the maintenance of racial separation in the last significant public domain where it survived. The realization of racial equality in a post–Jim Crow region, then, began with black access to the best public schools.

The end of segregated schools in Escambia County was just as crucial to whites, albeit for completely different reasons. The federal rulings integrated public schools, but acquiescence to the court orders did not translate into the acceptance of black students on an equal basis or end white belief in their own racial, intellectual, and cultural superiority. On the contrary, federal intervention increased white defensiveness regarding racial issues and strengthened the resolve to apply court-ordered integration plans on white terms alone. To many, Arnow's measure symbolized the most glaring instance to date of unwanted federal intrusion into the Panhandle's racial affairs. Desegregation, whites believed, had already transpired. Schools that either race predominantly attended reflected their neighborhood compositions, not a nefarious scheme by school board members or white parents to subjugate black students. Recalcitrant whites blamed a small group of malcontents that H. K. Matthews and the NAACP led for inflaming racial animosities and making unreasonable demands of reasonable people. Intervention from the federal courts represented an unwarranted intrusion into local affairs and only increased white hostility toward changes in the city's racial status quo. The issue for many became how to best protect and display white supremacy within a unified educational system. In the wake of the judicial edicts, therefore, a surge of unprecedented massive resistance rose in Escambia County, and schools became the primary battleground in the evolving struggle for racial equality in Northwest Florida as the 1970s began. Pensacola High School became the first such institution where blacks questioned the meaning of complete integration in a unitary system of public education.

In the fall of 1969, the Escambia County School Board chose PHS to host a football exhibition featuring the Pensacola Naval Air Station squad. The school band planned to play "Dixie" as a part of its "Fiesta of Five Flags" halftime show, but several blacks who belonged to the ensemble objected to the song. The band director gave them an ultimatum— play the tune or fail their music course. The students took their dilemma to Matthews, who also despised "Dixie" because he believed it romanticized antebellum plantation culture. School officials refused to compromise with the dissenters or meet with Matthews, so he decided that the black students who participated in the halftime festivities should make their sentiments clear. When the band began to play "Dixie" near the end of their halftime routine, most of the group's black students lowered their instruments and walked off the football field. Many white band members kept playing, unaware that the students had abandoned their marching formation, while some stopped in astonishment as their classmates left the group. Blacks in the crowd cheered the protest, except for a few parents who shouted at Matthews angrily. Stunned silence characterized the response of white crowd members. In the days that followed the episode, PHS officials reversed their policy on "Dixie," removed it from the band's song list, and did not fail any blacks as punishment for their actions.[44] The confrontation over "Dixie" represented much more than a mere disagreement concerning a song to both whites and blacks. The cultural triad of music, football, and historical memory played central roles in the evolution of race relations during a pivotal time in the area's history.

In an essay that the *Pensacola News Journal* published in the aftermath of the PHS incident, editor J. Earle Bowden, a self-professed "Civil War buff," termed the local white population a "sleeping tiger" that blacks constantly "prodded with a stick" because they "want his dinner." Quite tellingly, the paper portrayed black activists as disruptive thieves. The agitators did not demand what belonged to them, the illustration indicated, but wanted to take things from the white citizenry that African

Americans had no right to claim. "The silent majority of Americans," Bowden warned, "are growing angry" with continued black demands. The protest concerning "Dixie," from the white perspective, became the latest in a developing pattern of social disruptions. H. K. Matthews responded to the *News Journal* editorial in a manner that characterized his demonstrative personality. In a letter to editors that the paper published, Matthews provided his own analogy regarding the sleeping tiger. Blacks, according to Matthews, did not want the writer's dinner, but they did demand the portion that rightfully "belongs to us." He agreed that "people are growing angry," but stated that African Americans, not whites, "have become so angry until they don't intend to sit still and take your repression any longer. For you see," Matthews continued, America is "supposed to be just as much the black man's country as anyone else's, though it doesn't work out that way." The polarizing minister pledged to "fight to the bitter end to gain the freedom that is rightfully mine."[45]

The latest in a series of public exchanges between Matthews and the *News Journal* revealed much about the state of Northwest Florida race relations as the 1960s concluded. The editorial highlighted the difficulties blacks encountered in their fight against white systems of control in the years beyond integration. African Americans protested no specific law but a practice which, to many, fostered an atmosphere of continual indignity and disrespect. While the playing of "Dixie" violated no statute, it perpetuated the black belief that they remained second-class citizens in Northwest Florida. The campaign against the possession and use of power to exercise unmitigated authority over the public commemoration of a divisive past, and not a legal code, ensured that many whites grew exhausted with black demands for racial equality more rapidly in the decade's final years. The *News Journal* editorial reflected such frustration. Finally, the PHS incident and subsequent public pronouncements demonstrated the divisive nature of Confederate iconography in the desegregated South. The debate over "Dixie" foreshadowed the tensions that consumed Pensacola during the 1970s. The use of Confederate imagery at PHS had ended, but a countywide struggle over the controversial cultural symbols had only started.

Race relations in Escambia County, therefore, reached a crucial juncture as the 1960s concluded. Blacks and whites in the Panhandle had begun to address how federal civil rights legislation and judicial decisions would affect the area's entrenched racial hierarchy. The integration of public facilities and token desegregation of county schools represented surface alterations, but white supremacy remained relatively intact through the 1960s. The civil rights movement in Northwest Florida likewise transformed between 1965 and 1970. A new stage in the struggle for racial equality began in which blacks and whites struggled intensely over what would constitute a redistribution of power, the meaning of equal citizenship, and the nature of change and continuity that would characterize race relations in the wake of the 1960s civil rights movement. Many whites became increasingly frustrated with black demands as the 1960s ended and perceived claims of continued inequality as unwarranted because desegregation had occurred. Racial animosities built as white systems of control increasingly refused to yield additional concessions to blacks, particularly in the economic and cultural realms. The civil rights movement in Northwest Florida, then, had not ended, but continued to evolve as a new decade began. Over the next ten years, county schools became the primary battleground in a conflict over the display, use, and defense of cultural symbols. The struggles would demonstrate the limits and shortcomings African Americans encountered when they applied the promises of the civil rights movement to the acquisition of meaningful power in Northwest Florida.

CHAPTER THREE

Cultural Imagery, School Integration, and the Lost Cause

The integration of the Escambia County public school system accelerated as the new decade began. Judge Winston Arnow refused to issue a comprehensive busing program for the district because such a plan would literally bankrupt the county system. He did, though, order schools where "little or no integration occurred" to implement student busing in 1970. The county bused 2,711 blacks and 18,689 whites to schools during the subsequent term. The number of students bused to school increased to 20,400 white and 8,130 black students during the 1972–73 academic year.[1] Blacks and whites reflected frustrations with the demographic and cultural upheaval at their schools in myriad ways. White teachers, administrators, and students treated the few blacks who entered schools that previously excluded them as pariahs. Teachers separated them from their white classmates and forced blacks to occupy desks at the back or in solitary rows inside of the room. Instructors also ignored African Americans during class periods, held them to different academic standards than those they had for white students, and punished blacks who committed the most minor offenses while not holding whites accountable for similar infractions. According to Assistant School Superintendent Roger Mott, most teachers only "tolerated" black students, at best, and "did not treat them as equals" with their white pupils. Mott believed that whites "treated [African Americans] as if they were doing them a favor" by serving as their teachers. White parents also resisted accelerated school integration in a variety of ways both subtle and blatant. As the number of black teachers in previously all-white schools increased, for instance, white parents petitioned the school board to forbid them from paddling white pupils. They made no objection to white authorities who administered the same punishment to black students. Parents did not want their kids to attend classes or socialize with members of other races, and their children often reflected these prejudices. They sat at separate lunch tables, stayed away from each other at recess, and avoided contact during physical education classes. Few blacks participated in student clubs, athletic teams, or extracurricular activities. At schools where blacks expressed an interest in such pursuits, whites held meetings at off-campus sites after school hours ended, or in their parents' homes to discourage black participation.[2] Public schools in Escambia County, much as they existed in many other systems throughout the South at the same time, were integrated in name but segregated in practice.

The attitudes of black students had also transformed by the 1970s. Unlike their predecessors a decade earlier, the African Americans who attended integrated schools in 1970 had been sensitized to the existence of white racism by a decade of civil rights activism. The younger generation had been exposed to the concept of Black Power, the assassination of Martin Luther King Jr., and the images of cities that burned as a consequence of interracial confrontations. The African American students who entered integrated schools in the 1970s, therefore, wanted more than just the court-ordered desegregation of facilities; they demanded complete integration and total inclusion in an area of society that previously excluded them. Racially motivated fighting, then, occurred regularly in county schools during the early 1970s. Incidents ranged from students throwing bricks and bottles at each other at bus stops to melees involving over one hundred students that required police intervention to quell. Interracial brawls let to the cancellation of several school days at Pensacola High School and the installation of armed deputies at Woodham High School for approximately four months.[3] White officials aggravated the developing racial crisis in county schools by simultaneously minimizing its existence and placing responsibility for any unrest on black students.

The county school board acknowledged that principals had reported "a small number" of fights between white and black pupils to board headquarters, but officials blamed the conflicts on "outside forces" that influenced the students involved. School board members also attributed the clashes to "normal adolescent differences which can lead to clashes between black and white, as well as black against black or white against white." Interracial skirmishes, the board maintained, were an expected aspect of public school culture and not a symptom of greater interracial turbulence between students. Kids, after all, will be kids. Woodham High's principal attributed unrest on his campus to "the large influx of blacks" that enrolled in the school. The new students refused to join student clubs, athletic teams, and leadership programs, participation in any of which, the principal reasoned, "would have provided greater identification of black students with their new school" and resulted in "better communication" between African Americans and administrators. School officials at many levels, then, believed scuffles between white and black pupils were exaggerated, expected, and brought on by the actions and attitudes of the African American minority.[4] As the integration of county schools continued and racial tensions deepened in the aftermath of the *Augustus* rulings, white displeasure with classroom desegregation surfaced in circuitous ways. One of those involved Confederate images, which became an emotional, divisive, and ultimately destructive issue.

Escambia High School was the first scene of the tremendous racial unrest that inundated Pensacola during the 1970s. EHS represented one of the largest and least integrated learning institutions in the area at decade's onset. During the 1970–71 academic year, for instance, 33,140 students out of 46,987 enrolled in county public schools—roughly 70 percent—were white. Whites constituted 93 percent of the student body, though, at Escambia High. Furthermore, class-based divisions fueled tensions between white and black students at EHS. The school lay in an area of Pensacola that possessed a heavy concentration of working-class residents. The county bused black students to EHS from some of the poorest housing projects in Pensacola. As a result, one county school official opined that a "core group of rednecks" and "hot blacks," each of whose "raison d'etre was fights, conflicts, and battles," attended Escambia High. Yet its iconography most distinguished EHS from other Panhandle schools. Escambia High opened in 1958, a year after the integration of Little Rock's Central High School captured international attention. During the school's inaugural term, students elected "Rebels" as the school mascot, adopted "Dixie" as its official song, and chose the Confederate battle flag as its symbol. Each year a different student earned the opportunity to dress in Confederate gear as the EHS mascot, "Johnny Reb," at official functions and sporting events, many of which took place at the school's "Rebel Bowl" stadium. Those who did not serve as the EHS mascot displayed their school spirit at events such as the "Confederate Ball," an annual affair where males dressed in Confederate uniforms escorted females dressed in antebellum hoop skirts. Homecoming week at EHS mirrored a Sons of Confederate Veterans function, complete with appearances by Civil War reenactors. The male and female school chorus clubs called themselves "Southern Gents" and "Rebelaires," and students read "The Rebelog" campus newspaper. When Sidney Nelson became principal of EHS in 1964, the faculty welcomed him with a new Confederate battle flag to display in his office. He later recalled the presentation as "moment of great pride." Confederate imagery also adorned two cement monuments near the school's main entrance that commemorated EHS students killed in combat during the Vietnam War, while two banners adorned another statue that stood beside the school's "Rebel Cannon." Even Snoopy waved the Confederate flag on school bulletin boards.[5]

Implicit and sometimes blatant racism underlay white pride in such symbols. When Linda Wingate entered Escambia High in 1966 as its first black student, whites conspicuously used the flag as a symbol of their resistance to her presence. Each classroom in the school contained Confederate battle flags, as did each administrator's office. EHS yearbooks from the early 1970s stereotyped blacks as comical, ignorant, or isolated individuals. In the 1972 *Escambian*, for example, the most prominent photograph of a black student portrayed a barefoot young male dressed in ragged overalls, a sleeveless flannel shirt, and straw hat fishing off a pier while sporting an enormous grin. In the same annual, a window-washing custodian represented one of the few black staff pictures in the book.[6] The area's largest high school remained its most segregated, and black students felt increasingly ostracized and unwanted by EHS students, teachers, and administrators. African Americans who attended EHS believed themselves targets of the school's Johnny Reb mascot, whom they claimed sought them out at school functions and mocked them to the delight of other whites. Black leaders claimed that school officials encouraged the intimidating use of Confederate images in the presence of black students and masqueraded their racist intents under the guise of school spirit. Indeed, EHS principal Sidney Nelson dismissed black objections to the school's imagery as a "desperate" attempt to "get attention." The school's battle flag became particularly provocative, as white students carried miniature flags in their pockets, waved them in the faces of black students, flew them outside of school bus windows, and even sewed the banner onto their clothes. During the early 1970s, Escambia High's Confederate imagery proliferated as the symbol of white resistance against further classroom integration in the area, and the most important of the symbols was the Confederate battle flag.[7]

The historian John Coski labels the flag "the most familiar, potent, and embattled of all Confederate emblems" in his examination of the standard. Instead of possessing a fixed or absolute meaning, he contends, the symbol's use determined its meaning and affected how people perceived it in the post–World War II era. The flag first became associated with white supremacy and racial separation during the States' Rights

Party convention in 1948, which gave the banner "a more specific connotation to the civil rights movement and to racial integration." The connection intensified after the 1954 *Brown* decision. The Confederate flag became a familiar emblem in cities such as Little Rock, Oxford, Birmingham, St. Augustine, and anywhere else blacks challenged the region's racial order. African Americans, then, "came to view the Confederate battle flag as a symbol of racism because they encountered it in situations in which white people *intended* it as a symbol of racism [emphasis in original]." Coski maintains that "the meaning of the flag changed forever" after the Supreme Court ordered the immediate and total integration of public schools in 1969. Many whites used it as a symbol of resistance to greater integration, as they had since 1948, but others also defended it more vigorously when blacks demanded its removal from public spaces. The more that African Americans protested the flag's presence and the more successful their claims became with the support of federal courts, the more vehemently whites defended the flag as representative of a selective "heritage" which oppressed minorities within and, sometimes, outside of the immediate community attacked. The assault on the flag was seen as insensitive or hostile and sparked backlash from whites who defended their right to fly the embattled banner at any cost. As a 1971 Southern Regional Council report explained, "In what used to be ordinary times, when student bodies were more—or—less homogeneous, agitation over such matters as school songs and colors no doubt could be regarded as 'inconsequential' and 'trivial.' The point," the Atlanta-based organization concluded, "is that these are not ordinary times and student bodies are not homogeneous." The council's study was particularly applicable to Escambia High.[8] Although school integration occurred without incident at EHS in 1966, circumstances transpired six years later which demonstrated that the school did not escape racial turbulence, but experienced delayed discord.

During the 1972 football season, the EHS squad wore the rebel flag on their golden helmets for the first and only year, which made quite a fashion statement when paired with their blue and orange uniforms. Black students displayed an unprecedented degree of anger toward the symbols during the term. At the football team's pep rallies, for instance, blacks refused to stand and sing "Dixie" along with other students as the band played the tune. Such protests only escalated use of Confederate icons to intimidate African American students, and scuffles between black and white students increased in size and severity as the year progressed. On November 17, 1972, EHS principal Sidney Nelson canceled classes for two days after interracial fighting again disrupted school operations. Nelson blamed the disturbance on overcrowded conditions and summoned sheriff's deputies to patrol the campus and deter further violence. White parents, though, made numerous telephone calls to the school in which they threatened to lynch black students. Racial tensions consumed EHS over the following weeks as whites increased the use of the Confederate flag as a symbol of their supposed racial supremacy. Groups of white students marched in unison up and down school halls singing "Dixie" and waving the battle flag in the face of every unwanted person they encountered. They targeted lone blacks, surrounded them in hallways, and chanted slogans such as "Rebels all the way," and "Niggers go home." The situation became so dangerous that some blacks refused to board their buses. A white mob occupied one such vehicle and their leader dared onlookers to "get on, Nigger, if you want to die." Cars packed with whites, not all Escambia High students, drove around the campus blowing horns and shouting racial epithets at African Americans while flying the Confederate colors. Some whites brought a Ku Klux Klan hood to EHS and sprayed the group's letters on school property. Not surprisingly, fights broke out between white and black students on almost a daily basis. B. J. Brooks and other black adults visited Principal Nelson collectively and as individuals to discuss the volatile situation, but the administrator refused to meet with them. The racial animosity that characterized Escambia High reached its peak on December 13, 1972, and ultimately consumed the region.[9]

On that pivotal day in Pensacola's racial history, a group of black and white students again exchanged insults and punches in the EHS cafeteria. The December 13 incident, though, escalated into a full-fledged race riot that engulfed the entire school. Between 150 and 200 students joined the fray and used serving trays, chairs, garbage cans, and tables as weapons in what one witness described as "a western-style brawl." The few sheriff's deputies at the scene did little to quell the fighting, and one white officer even sprayed mace into the eyes of a black deputy who attempted to stop the fracas. The tumult spread to the front lawn and parking area, where over 400 students assaulted each other with rocks, bricks, bottles, and other projectiles. The barrage of debris also struck police and school officials who tried to intervene in the melee. Sergeant Jim Edson later told reporters, "I had enough stones, bricks, and mortar thrown at me to pave a driveway." Deputies restored some order to the campus nearly thirty minutes after the riot began, and Principal Nelson canceled classes for the remainder of the day. It marked the second time in less than a month that the school closed due to interracial violence. Deputies confiscated a plethora of weapons from the thirty-eight whites and nine blacks they arrested during the altercation. Nelson suspended twenty-four students, including one who required hospitalization for injuries he sustained during the encounter. State representative and Pensacola native R. W. "Smokey" Peaden arrived on campus shortly after the school closed and described what he witnessed as "a hell of a mess."[10]

In the hours following the fight, county schools Superintendent J. E. Hall organized an impromptu meeting between his school board, EHS staff members, Escambia County sheriff Royal Untreiner, and concerned parents to discuss the situation. For most of the six-hour session, the predominantly white audience demanded swift and harsh action against future agitators and offered their services to county authorities, but did not address possible reasons for the disturbance. Sheriff Untreiner promised more arrests in the event of future incidents, while Sidney Nelson pledged to extend student suspensions and "deal severely" with riot instigators. Nelson closed the assembly, which accomplished very little, by announcing that his school would open the following morning.[11]

Classes at EHS resumed with no major disturbances on December 14. Attendance figures at the school plummeted, though, because many parents feared additional violence and withheld their children from classes. Forty-seven police officers patrolled school hallways during the day and arrested ten juveniles for trespassing and possessing weapons. Pensacola NAACP president B. J. Brooks and white school board member Richard Leeper spoke to classes throughout the day in hopes of defusing the situation. Brooks visited the campus on his own volition because he wanted "to make sure there was no violence on the part of our children," but the staggering number of Confederate flags that white students exhibited, particularly on tee shirts and baseball caps, reinforced his belief that "blacks were being intimidated" by white use of the symbols.[12] While law enforcement officials worked to secure the campus, area whites offered several theories that explained the EHS disturbance. The *Pensacola Journal*, for example, blamed overcrowded facilities. State legislator Smokey Peaden, a former Pensacola police officer who obtained most of his support from working-class whites and had a reputation as a "tough, almost brutal guy," blamed the trouble on "a small minority of hoodlums" and "young thugs." He also criticized local law enforcement officials and school administrators for allowing "troublemakers" to control the school and requested a grand jury investigation of the disturbances. The use of words like "minority," "hoodlums," and "thugs" represented thinly veiled references to the black students who attended Escambia High. Peaden admitted that he "was looking for a fight" over the symbols issue and declared, "We need teachers with the backbone to stand up and do what is right, a principal and superintendent that will back them up, and law enforcement officers who will back them up." Escambia County School Superintendent J. E. Hall echoed Peaden's belief that isolated malcontents instigated the riot. Hall, who served as the first principal of EHS, declared that when "we can get those students out who do not want to go to school, the problem will be resolved." Deputy School Superintendent R. C. Lipscomb offered yet another theory to explain the discord. "Over-supervision," Lipscomb explained, led to the "open rebellion" of black students. EHS, he believed, "was a permissive school and when the rules and policies were enforced to bring about order, this created more problems because the kids resented the structure being imposed."[13] While several white officials vehemently denied that racial problems caused the EHS conflict and used terminology that placed responsibility for the disorder on African American students, no public figure approached the belligerence of Wyon Dale Childers.

W. D. Childers, a former Escambia County teacher and door-to-door hula hoop salesman, was elected to the state senate in 1970. Childers represented the district that included EHS and drew his support primarily from working and lower-class whites who lived in rural areas. Childers's constituents were the region's most adamant supporters of Confederate imagery, and they considered Childers their political champion. One journalist called him "the George Wallace of Escambia County" due to the racist demagoguery that Childers used, while another attributed his popularity to the fact that he "talked like a redneck" in both accent and content. Childers visited EHS a day after the violence occurred and interviewed those present during the unrest. The senator acknowledged that a majority of black students he spoke with blamed the incident on their animosity concerning the school's imagery, but Childers deemed the problem more "deep-seated" than a symbols disagreement. He virtually ignored black concerns and pledged to unearth the "real problems" at Escambia High, although he did not explain what they could be. Childers also defended the Confederate imagery as part of the school's "heritage and tradition" and ridiculed blacks who criticized the symbols. "You haven't seen any white groups trying to get the name of Booker T. Washington High School changed after integration," Childers proclaimed. Due to such comments, a state NAACP official declared Childers "a throw-back to the days of Senator Bilbo," the infamous legislator who personified white supremacy in Mississippi from the 1920s through the 1940s.[14] White officials, therefore, blamed the EHS violence on overcrowded classrooms, isolated vagrants, cowardly staff members, and lenient disciplinary standards, while black students, parents, and civil rights groups considered Escambia High's Confederate icons as the primary reason for the trouble. Childers's comments demonstrated that white officials dismissed black objections to the imagery, defended the symbols as school tradition, and criticized those who disputed their meaning. Area civil rights leaders realized that the African American community had to unite and act in dramatic fashion to capture white attention concerning their objections.

One week after the EHS riot occurred, H. K. Matthews, B. J. Brooks, and Otha Leverette met with the county school board and presented a list of items on behalf of the local SCLC and NAACP that they believed would alleviate area racial tensions. The petition first demanded the abolition of Confederate images at Escambia High, including the Rebel nickname, the band's playing of "Dixie," and the display of Confederate flags at school functions. Its placement as the first demand reflected that local blacks viewed the icons as their primary concern and the reason for racial violence at EHS. NAACP leader B. J. Brooks called the Confederate images "a revulsion" because they represented "a whole set of white attitudes toward blacks" that "must go." The petition also requested the promotion of black school system employees, appointment of an African American assistant principal at EHS, and dismissal of all charges against students and staff members arrested during the disturbances. Furthermore, the group proposed mandatory suspensions for students who wore Ku Klux Klan hoods to school, posted signs supporting the group, or distributed racist leaflets, all of which occurred prior to the December 13 fight. If the school board did not satisfy each request, Matthews threatened, the 14,400 blacks who attended public schools in Escambia County would boycott classes in the new year. Local black leaders appeared united in their effort to end white resistance to integration at Escambia High, and their resolve captured the attention of the Florida NAACP. Two days after the school board received the petition, State Field Director R. N. Gooden traveled to Pensacola in support of the demands and pledged to remain in the area until white leaders satisfied each of the requests. Gooden and State Coordinator Otis Williams also disseminated news of the Escambia County struggle to NAACP branches throughout Florida to obtain organizational solidarity against the use of Confederate images.[15] The reaction of local white officials, though, ensured that a heated struggle concerning the demands loomed.

Hours after Matthews promised the black student boycott, county school board members, Superintendent J. E. Hall, EHS administrators, and other concerned whites met at board headquarters to discuss the matter. The threatened boycott concerned school officials considerably because the county's annual funding derived from January attendance figures. Board members estimated that county schools would lose $40,000 per day in state funding if a majority of black students participated in the boycott. More problematic, the board believed, were the significant numbers of white parents who would withhold their children from schools in fear of racial violence during the coming weeks. Despite black protests to the contrary, school officials denied that EHS symbols played any role in the intensification of local racial tensions. Only school board member Richard Leeper, the sole school board member who visited the school after the riot ended to personally gauge the situation, acknowledged that the symbols played any part in the EHS upheaval. Leeper told board members that the abolition of Confederate symbols "has now become a rallying cry for the blacks," but recognized that only Principal Nelson or EHS students possessed the authority to ban school symbols. The school board, Leeper conceded, could do nothing concerning the imagery. The board took no formal action regarding the demands but promised to solve the conflict before students returned from their holiday break on January 2.[16]

While the SCLC and NAACP petition concerned school board members, it infuriated whites and aroused suspicions that outsiders manipulated local blacks for their own nefarious purposes. State Representative Smokey Peaden deemed the boycott threat part of a greater African American conspiracy to close Escambia High permanently due to its Confederate iconography. School board chairman Peter Gindl cited an imaginary past of interracial harmony in Pensacola and questioned whether "our blacks would even resort to such tactics" as petition writing. Richard Leeper summarized school board sentiment by saying that blacks possessed "no justification whatsoever for a walkout" because community leaders would address "every problem" the petition mentioned "in good faith." The threatened boycott, Leeper told *Pensa-cola Journal* reporters, represented "a cruel exploitation of school children."[17] The newspaper needed little encouragement to denigrate black leaders, as several articles blamed them for the racial unrest that engulfed Escambia High.

The *Journal* published an editorial on December 29 that blamed the school's racial problems on overcrowded classes and stated that a boycott "would be tragic, for the only hope of blacks to attain the economic level of whites is to upgrade their general education level." It also cautioned black leaders that their actions could "get out of hand and lead to violence, which for the most part this community has avoided during nearly twenty years of full-scale, court-ordered integration." In another editorial, *Journal* editors questioned whether area black leaders "can muster complete solidarity for a school walkout."[18] In addition to the editorials that dismissed all black concerns regarding the iconography at EHS, the *Journal* published letters that castigated African Americans. One reader blamed them for "pushing people to the point where they are beginning to demand the semblance of a right-wing dictatorship to restore some order" in the county, and said that Brooks and Matthews "are only hurting the chances of accomplishing goals which" they established with their boycott threats. Another resident criticized objections to Confederate imagery and lamented the fact that "the last vestiges of the Old South are gradually disappearing" in Northwest Florida. The author professed with unconcealed bitterness that "'Dixie' and the Confederate flag means as much to the school-spirited Escambian" as "'We Shall Overcome' and the clinched fist do to every proud soul brother." G. H. Lanius called those whom "Dixie" offended "merely trouble makers who would use any flimsy excuse to foment discord." His note concluded that if blacks "think that this wonderful country is such a terrible place to live, why don't they go to Africa or the Soviet Union?" Pensacola resident Harry Harris similarly deemed black demands "preposterous," while Rob Parrish reminded whites that Confederate deity Robert E. Lee "started the proud heritage of Escambia High's 'Dixie' and the Stars and Bars." B. D. Springer criticized the NAACP for advocating school absences because uneducated blacks "are a detriment to all of society." White Pensacolian Jim Willis wrote perhaps the most combative letter that the paper published. "We will continue," Willis pledged, "to play the non-racial, regional song called 'Dixie' which was written by a man from the north and yes we will continue to call ourselves the rebels as we did before we were integrated." Willis echoed sentiments present in other letters by concluding that "some outside force is directing and controlling the agitation" area blacks displayed.[19]

Local newspapers played a significant role in the way residents reacted to racial disturbances that occurred in their communities, and the *News Journal* both mirrored and sharpened area white resistance. The 1968 Kerner Commission, which concluded the "nation is moving toward two societies, one black, one white—separate and unequal," revealed that whites made up more than 95 percent of national newspaper writers and over 99 percent of editors. Most African Americans, the commission concluded, therefore considered "the newspapers as the mouthpieces of the 'power structure.'" *News Journal* editors "reflected the culture and the attitude of the community in general," placed responsibility for interracial peace upon African American leaders, and reflected the growing white intolerance with black demands and protest tactics in the early 1970s.[20] Their biased coverage and frequent commentaries also inflamed white passions concerning the attack on Confederate images at Escambia High. The paper's rabid advocacy of the controversial symbols indicated that the issue resonated with whites throughout the area and was not simply a matter that only concerned EHS students, parents, or alumni. The unrest over "Rebels," "Dixie," and other Confederate images represented more than a debate concerning mascots, musical tastes, or a piece of cloth. The conflict symbolized a greater struggle concerning the realization and limits of school integration, white resistance, and the power of African Americans to influence the racial status quo. The situation became even more combustible because it involved Lost Cause imagery.

The Lost Cause emerged in the South after the Civil War ended and transformed the region's military defeat into a moral and cultural triumph. Lost Cause ideology, according to Emory M. Thomas, "held that the southern cause was not only undefiled by defeat but that the bloodbath of war actually sanctified the values and mores of the Old South." The Lost Cause commemorated southern suffering, sacrifice, and defeat to ensure that it would not lose meaning, and ultimately preserved the region's sense of moral and cultural superiority over the depraved Yankee. The historian Charles Reagan Wilson argues that evangelical Christianity infused the Lost Cause with spiritual meaning, making the concept a "civil religion" throughout the South. The region did not lose the war, its promoters maintained, due to divine punishment. God permitted the South to perish on the battlefield because He had a greater plan for the region. The South suffered because its people were God's favored, not because He had forsaken them. Defeat was a purification ritual, a "baptism in blood," from which the South would emerge as even more pure and spiritually superior to its materialistic and sinful counterparts to the north. The Lost Cause, whether defined primarily as "myth," "civil religion," or "tradition," transformed defeat into victory, shame into honor, traitors into holy warriors, and provided the primary rationale in the development of a distinct and supposedly superior southern cultural identity in the postwar region. Dreams of a separate political nation gave way to belief in the South's cultural supremacy, and the Lost Cause provided the foundation of this incredibly popular—and enduring—regional identity. In addition to various myths, rituals, organizations, and theological beliefs, symbols associated with the Lost Cause became central in the perpetuation of a separate southern cultural identity into the twentieth century. The Confederate soldier, the nickname "Dixie," and, especially, the Confederate battle flag, had numerous consequences for southern race relations during times of cultural unrest. To question the presence or meaning of Lost Cause symbols was to challenge a core element of white southern identity.[21] In times of tremendous social, cultural, and racial changes, such as during the busing of students to integrate public schools more fully, the presence and meaning of the symbols assumed even greater importance to both whites and blacks.

Southern whites perceived themselves as under siege by the federal government, its judicial system, and an unsympathetic national media as the 1960s ended and the 1970s began, and increased school integration measures were one symptom of their greater victimization. In his study of political conservatism in post–civil rights Mississippi, Joseph Crespino argued that "the innovation of modern conservatives was in taking the explicit racism out of southern massive resistance while maintaining its essence." Indeed, white parents and students in the Panhandle grudgingly accepted the changes and tolerated black students, teachers, and administrators, but still viewed the institutions as "our schools" and for "our community." Whites in Escambia County, and in areas throughout the South during the early 1970s, simply did not accept that public schools also belonged to African Americans. Furthermore, local whites used their status as the racial majority to justify resistance to additional changes. They could not be forced to accommodate the voices of a few, whites maintained, when the majority opposed. To the white majority in Northwest Florida, then, public schools may have integrated, but they still belonged under white control. The objection to Escambia High's Confederate icons represented the issue where county whites asserted their majority privilege, repudiated black objections, and defended the images in vehement defiance to greater social change. The fact that the symbols in question represented the Lost Cause made them even more combustible. White southerners, Charles Wilson demonstrated, combined beliefs in their racial supremacy and cultural "tradition" in Lost Cause commemorations and observances, including celebration of its symbols. The existence of segregation, Wilson maintained, provided "visible evidence that the Lost Cause lived." The successes of the civil rights movement and accompanying attack on the images of the Lost Cause, conversely, represented an attack on the entire "southern way of life" in the 1970s.[22] The Lost Cause provided a simplified, romanticized view of the past and regional identity in times of cultural anxieties, and its defense peaked when southerners faced a regional identity crisis. Still, the Lost Cause did more than just bolster regional self-esteem or provide the foundation of a separate, superior cultural identity from the rest of the nation. It also provided a vehicle through which county whites defended their perceived supremacy in the years following desegregation without directly addressing racial issues.

The *Pensacola News Journal* published numerous articles, editorials, and letters that addressed the symbols issue and reflected white beliefs and attitudes. *Journal* editors proposed that a student vote should determine the fate of EHS's symbols, and published a biting editorial that further criticized black objections to the Confederate icons and condemned African American leaders. "The hopes and chances of the black youth of the community are worsening," editor J. Earle Bowden declared, because "militant blacks strut and fret" to advance their own personal agendas. The paper's editors refused to name specific black leaders because, according to Bowden, it "would only create the martyrs upon which boycotts and demonstrations of this sort grow and feed." Furthermore, the piece declared, Confederate symbols represented "a long-standing tradition" in Escambia County. The paper expressed particular concern that black leaders targeted "Dixie" as a "cause for complaint in this situation, for it is the one area in which we think they are entirely wrong." To support his claim, Bowden maintained that a northerner wrote "Dixie" which made the tune "part of the nation's heritage." Besides, he argued,

"Even Abe Lincoln enjoyed it." The article acknowledged that while some southern whites used the Confederate flag to proclaim their racial superiority, "It is part of the proud tradition of many whites whose ancestors fought a war not for the continuance of slavery but in defense of what they believed was their constitutional right to govern themselves."[23]

Bowden and other community leaders acknowledged that black objections to the EHS symbols represented much more than just a debate concerning a school mascot or nickname. The editor noted that people "from generations of segregation" most ardently defended the Confederate images and that prominent white chamber of commerce members considered any mascot change "a problem." Assistant School Superintendent Roger Mott observed similarly that the symbols "brought two cultures into a clash with each other," with the Escambia County School Board representing "the old culture" of segregationist rule and H. K. Matthews becoming "the black point man" in the local clash. Board members viewed Matthews as the primary reason for the problems they faced concerning the Confederate symbols, so they defended them vigorously both for their meaning and because the greatest critic of white supremacy in Pensacola opposed them. John Appleyard, an influential civic booster in Escambia County, claimed most whites blamed blacks who were "trying to stir up trouble and make this a site where something will happen that will draw publicity to them," and that this was the source of all icon-related tumult. The mascot dispute, Appleyard believed, "was just a shame and it shouldn't have happened." From his view, the fact that civil rights leaders attacked Lost Cause images "gained them no friends," did the continuing movement for racial equality "a great disservice," and "simply made people angry," for the symbols represented the very foundation of a regional identity that had experienced numerous challenges over the past decade. Objection to Lost Cause imagery, according to one local civic leader, "was certainly counter to the culture of that particular generation" of white southerners.[24] The fact that whites used seemingly color-blind reasons such as heritage, history, and tradition to defend Confederate images complicated the situation for African Americans, for they could not cite the explicitly racist language to prove that racism still persisted at EHS. The evolving system of racialized social control in Northwest Florida, therefore, maintained hierarchy and white privilege much as it did in years past. The white response to the EHS symbols controversy, which the *Pensacola News Journal* most publicly advocated, demonstrated that Lost Cause ideology and iconography both remained central to southern white identity, particularly in times of cultural turmoil, and served as the vocabulary that whites used to defend their perceived racial superiority.

While the local defense of Lost Cause imagery coalesced, Escambia County school superintendent J. E. Hall announced a compromise that satisfied blacks, angered whites, and increased white intransigence concerning Confederate icons. On the morning of January 1, 1973, representatives from the Pensacola NAACP and Escambia County SCLC met with Hall to temporarily resolve the symbols issue at EHS and avoid the looming black student boycott. Superintendent Hall "grudgingly" promised to drop all charges against each EHS student and faculty member arrested during the disturbances, removed every deputy from school grounds, and appointed a black staff member to counsel the school's three hundred African American students. Most important, the superintendent placed a moratorium on playing of "Dixie" at school functions "until inter-racial councils can decide on official schools songs and symbols" at Escambia High. H. K. Matthews and B. J. Brooks canceled their planned boycott but promised its resumption if the Biracial Committee did not determine the symbols' fate within thirty days. The compromise proved short-lived. The Escambia County School Board opposed Hall's proclamation vehemently and several members appeared on live television within hours of his announcement to nullify the decision. Board members maintained that Hall did not possess the power to make such an agreement without their consent and that they had the support of the area's most powerful politicians in Smokey Peaden and W. D. Childers. "I don't have the authority to call a moratorium on 'Dixie,'" Childers echoed, "and neither does Mr. Hall." With the support of each representative, therefore, the Escambia County School Board refused to honor Hall's proposal. According to the superintendent, the board viewed him as "too accommodating" to blacks, so the body "pulled the rug out from under me" and undermined his decision to avoid the boycott. Because he believed the school board negated his compromise "for political reasons," Hall "washed his hands of the issue" and allowed the board to handle the situation as they saw fit. At an NAACP meeting later that evening which the organization initially called to discuss Hall's compromise, B. J. Brooks announced that the boycott would begin because of the school board's position. "Everything that we have tried to work out in a peaceable way through negotiation," he told his audience, "has been aborted" by the county school board.[25] The black student boycott of

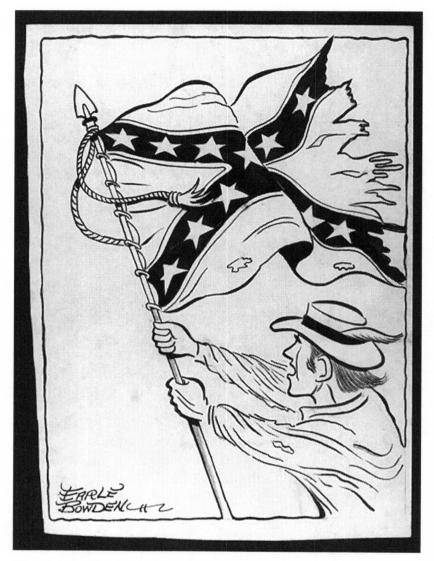

"The Banner of Brave Men," an April 26, 1967, illustration by *News Journal* editor J. Earle Bowden, demonstrates the local white attachment to Confederate imagery. J. Earle Bowden Cartoon Archive, University of West Florida Libraries.

Escambia County public schools began, as originally planned, the next morning.

Superintendent Hall did not release school attendance figures on January 2, but the *Pensacola News* estimated that over 44 percent of area students missed classes due to the protest. While classes resumed at Escambia High, the school board met and proposed a compromise to the black community. The group pledged "to discourage provocative activities, such as songs, signs, and symbols, in order to provide a peaceful and productive educational environment" at EHS. The board also requested state intervention to establish racial harmony at the school. Peter Gindl stated that mediators from Governor Reubin Askew's office should meet with parents "of those who want an education" but not speak to representatives from "dissident groups." B. J. Brooks noted the irony of board officials requesting assistance from impartial moderators and stated, "When the white community calls in outsiders, they say they are merely trying to preserve the peace. When the blacks call in people, we are accused of bringing in troublemakers, lawbreakers, and agitators." Senator Childers, however, went even further than the county school board in his repudiation of black leaders. He lashed out at the NAACP's "unlawful" boycott and promised that county schools would lose no funding because of the protest. Despite its alleged illegality, Childers sarcastically deemed the protest successful because the absence of black students made the day "real nice and peaceful" in county schools. Teachers, he claimed, surely "have forgotten what it was to work under such peaceful conditions" since integration occurred. The boycott, he concluded, created "a real good educational atmosphere for white students."[26] Yet Childers did much more than ridicule the collapse of public education for which he held desegregation responsible. He threatened the livelihood of a key civil rights leader in Pensacola.

In one of his many commentaries concerning the EHS situation, Childers feigned surprise that B. J. Brooks organized "this insurrection against the school board" because "his salary is paid by state dollars." The senator claimed that Brooks, who worked for the Florida Department of Transportation, should "use his energies to build the roads that we so badly need in Northwest Florida" instead of fomenting racial discord. Childers's reference to Brooks's occupational status incensed SCLC official H. K. Matthews, who called the thinly veiled threat "economic genocide."[27] To many, Matthews's statement undoubtedly represented another in the long list of hyperboles that the minister often used to illustrate social realities. Yet as often was the case, his claim had merit. The realization that B. J. Brooks earned a paycheck from the state of Florida attracted interest from Tallahassee. The investigation of Brooks's occupational background, in fact, represents the first issue related to the EHS situation that appears in the papers of Governor Reubin Askew. Memoranda to the governor reveal that the state police commissioner and Florida Department of Transportation (FDOT) kept Askew informed of the tumult in his hometown, conducted a background check of B. J. Brooks, and viewed the NAACP official's job as a way to intimidate and potentially silence him.

State authorities found that Brooks had attended Baptist Theological Seminary in Beatrice, Alabama, and served as ordained minister at Mt. Lily Baptist Church in Pensacola. He obtained his job with the FDOT in 1970. A representative from Askew's office contacted two of Brooks's immediate supervisors and asked them to "keep us informed of any new developments" related to the reverend's civil rights activities. A memorandum addressed to Governor Askew revealed that the FDOT investigated ways to use possible violations of state employee regulations against the NAACP president, but they found none. The department, for instance, checked into whether Brooks had "acted inappropriately or violated any state law or personnel ruling or policy applicable to his employment" due to his civil rights activities. Possible offenses included organizing NAACP initiatives "on state time," "using state equipment" to do so, or not clearing leave time with his supervisors before taking it. Yet "action by the DOT" against Brooks, the correspondence read, "would be shakey [sic]."[28] The importance of the correspondence regarding Brooks's position with the FDOT is twofold. First, it shows that state authorities in the early 1970s searched for any available means, including economic coercion, to silence those who continued to lead the struggles for racial equality in their communities. Second, and more importantly, the memoranda regarding Brooks indicates that the governor's office closely monitored the racial climate in Pensacola after the initial Escambia High riot in 1972. Askew, then, chose a course of deliberate noninvolvement in the racial politics of his hometown from an early date. The stance he took concerning the Panhandle unrest is notable because Askew, according to one scholar, "chose to embrace integration, including busing, as an opportunity for the South to lead the nation by example in overcoming America's racial dilemma."[29]

Reubin O'Donovan Askew entered politics as assistant solicitor for Escambia County in 1956. Voters sent him to the state House of Representatives in 1958 and the Florida Senate in 1962, where he served until 1970. According to the historian David Colburn, Askew's working-class background and "almost evangelical espousal of traditional American religious and moral values enabled him to assemble a constituency that cut across a range of Florida voters." Askew's 1970 gubernatorial victory over Claude Kirk, the governor who tried to block implementation of a desegregation order in Manatee County during his term in "the most direct and spectacular challenge to federal authority since the heydays, of Orval Faubus, Ross Barnett, and [George] Wallace," strengthened Askew's image as a political "neopopulist." The young governor appointed blacks to a number of state positions during his tenure, including the first black cabinet member in one hundred years and Florida's first African American Supreme Court justice. More controversially, Askew took a pro-busing stance during a heated state referendum on the issue. Despite Askew's opposition to the 1972 referendum, 74 percent of voters approved the constitutional amendment against forced busing and it passed in every county. The governor's popularity initially suffered due to his position on the straw vote, and his political opponents capitalized on his controversial stance during the year's elections. Despite the temporary backlash in his home state, Askew's "political courage" was extremely popular within the Democratic Party. He delivered the keynote address at the 1972 Democratic National Convention and declined the opportunity to serve as George McGovern's vice-presidential candidate during the subsequent campaign. Askew's political star rose so rapidly that many considered him a leading candidate for the Democratic Party's 1976 presidential nomination.[30] His deliberate evasion of intervening in his home county's racial conflicts, then, was politically expedient. Involvement in such a controversial and potentially violent situation— in his home city, no less—threatened to abort his long-term political ambitions in their infancy, as his first significant political misstep had come when he opposed popular sentiment concerning an emotionally charged, racially based issue. He would not make a similar mistake by becoming mired in the controversy surrounding Confederate images in Escambia County, a local issue that possessed potentially national ramifications.

Additional evidence exists that demonstrates the governor deliberately circumvented involvement in the Escambia High symbols issue. Dr. Claud

Anderson, the state education coordinator during Reubin Askew's time in office, kept the governor apprised of the EHS icons dispute, racial violence, and student protests. In a memorandum that suggested the course of action Askew should take regarding the issues, Anderson advocated a path of willful ignorance. Anderson advised that they both "minimize . . . our involvement in this situation" and suggested the governor's office maintain "a low profile" concerning the circumstances at Escambia High. The education official promised to issue "safe or neutral statements" regarding the inflammatory topic. Anderson also informed Askew that black leaders in the Panhandle, including state and county NAACP representatives, desired a "brief meeting" with the governor to obtain assurance that he understood their objections to the Confederate symbols. Anderson advised the governor to "not meet" with black leaders because intervention from Tallahassee would undermine any "mediating group's efforts" to settle the crisis. No such effort, however, existed. Still, Askew followed Anderson's recommendations and refused to intervene in Escambia County's racial affairs for the duration of his time as governor. When he responded to the situation, it occurred in a personal reply to a direct query and never appeared in a public declaration. In two such cases, for example, Askew declared that all decision-making responsibility in the EHS crisis rested with the Escambia County School Board, its district superintendent, the state department of education, or all three. Askew's determination to avoid taking any public position on Pensacola's racial tumult extended to official visits he made to the Panhandle. During his time as governor, Askew brought additional state law enforcement personnel with him when he traveled to Pensacola in the event demonstrations or protests erupted at any of his public appearances.[31] Askew's failure to exercise strong leadership in the area of race relations in his hometown represented one of his major shortcomings as Florida's executive.

While the governor's office charted a course of benign neglect concerning racial disquiet in Northwest Florida, the state NAACP expanded its efforts in Escambia County. On January 3, a day after the black student boycott began at EHS, state NAACP coordinator Otis Williams and state field director R. N. Gooden returned to Pensacola and promised to support the local branch until whites satisfied all of their demands. The following day, the national NAACP declared Escambia County's struggle the "top priority" of its eleven-state southern region. R. N. Gooden also announced a selective buying campaign directed at white-owned

Rev. H. K. Matthews (left) and Rev. R. N. Gooden prepare to lead a demonstration, 1975. © Tampa Bay Times/ZUMAPRESS.com.

downtown stores during the coming weekend and declared, "The purpose of this economic 'walkout' would be to demonstrate the power of the movement to the business community." B. J. Brooks and H. K. Matthews held daily meetings at local churches to organize their coming protests. The fiery Matthews told the congregation at one such meeting that his goal "is to send a message to the nation that Pensacola is not an All-American city. It's nothing but a racist, red-neck community." He also called blacks who did not support the demonstrations and boycotts "a bunch of dumb Niggers" and promised to "deal with those folks." Brooks debated Senator Childers on local television and explained his group's position during the contentious program. African American leaders, therefore, prepared their community for a long battle with white officials concerning EHS's provocative images in a manner consistent with the area's organizing tradition against discriminatory practices. The *Pensacola News Journal* monitored area developments closely and informed its less observant readers, "A vintage civil rights-type controversy appears to be in the making for Escambia County."[32] Black insistence on achieving each of their goals and the white refusal to comply made the subsequent proclamation a shock to all.

Florida NAACP field secretary R. N. Gooden announced a compromise concerning the Escambia High situation on January 5. After two days of secret meetings between Gooden, Superintendent Hall, the county school board, and unidentified white businessmen, the black student boycott ended. Interestingly, neither state officials nor leaders of Pensacola's African American community participated in the negotiations. As a result of the sessions, the school board ordered a biracial student group at Escambia High to write new words for the "Dixie" tune, allowed blacks to make up assignments they missed during the boycott, and pledged to hire more black staff members at the school. The board also declared the Confederate images "racial irritants very real to one race and not yet recognized by the other." In exchange, Gooden ended the boycott and canceled the weekend's selective buying campaign. Those who negotiated the settlement hailed it as a victory for racial peace that "other communities could use and learn from." The compromise also pleased Senator W. D. Childers, who called it "a triumph of democracy."[33]

Matthews and Brooks said nothing about Gooden's resolution because they considered it an incomplete and temporary solution. Most importantly, the compromise ignored EHS symbols, the issue that mattered most to local blacks. The decision to retain "Dixie" as Escambia High's official theme song represented a particularly bitter defeat to local civil rights leaders. Gooden had reached an agreement with white leaders that did not satisfy indigenous demands at a time when Pensacola blacks demanded crucial concessions from white authorities. The NAACP's compromise demonstrated that the state office did not always represent the interests of its local chapter and even, in this instance, undermined the activities of its county branches. As a result, the tension between NAACP officials at the local, state, and national levels increased as the decade progressed, which weakened the Northwest Florida movement at a crucial juncture. In addition, the agreement solidified white resistance to additional African American demands. The *Pensacola News Journal* published letters from angry readers who called black objections to the Confederate symbols "childish, immature, and of no consequence to serious minded young people and adults." The protests only occurred, it continued, because "this is all that the NAACP has to complain about." Another asked, "The Negro insists that 'Dixie' and Rebel remind him of bad things" but "what of the white missionaries that were eaten and beheaded not too long ago" by Africans? Pensacola resident Thomas Flower demonstrated the racial polarization and resentment that permeated Escambia County after the boycott's end by stating, "They demand their own culture; likewise, it is the right of the white man to demand his own culture."[34]

A day after the boycott officially ended, the *Atlanta Daily World* outlined the symbols controversy and called the Escambia County school protest "the first recorded case of a successful, or at least partially successful, action against the racist practices which are defended by some on the grounds that they represent a link with 'tradition.'"[35] In reality, area black leaders considered the school boycott a partial success at best. Matthews, Brooks, and Leverette voiced black objections to the Confederate symbols during the campaign, explained why the icons offended so many, and demanded their removal at EHS. Yet the protests and their outcome only exacerbated mistrust between local blacks and both the white community in Northwest Florida and outside civil rights organizations. Instead of allowing area leaders to solve racial disputes on their own terms and obtain compromises that satisfied those involved as much as possible, individuals from outside of Escambia County intervened for their own reasons and reached settlements that satisfied few. R. N. Gooden and W. D. Childers departed Pensacola after the symbols announcement, which left local people to deal with the consequences of an agreement that they did not want and did not negotiate. The token concessions undermined the authority of local black leaders and further deepened the racial animosities that so divided Escambia County concerning the possession and exercise of civic power. The heightened uneasiness between blacks and whites and persistence of the Confederate images issue, which symbolized the greater racial struggle over the power that systems of control still possessed, became apparent after African Americans resumed classes at Escambia High.

CHAPTER FOUR

Racial Irritants

On January 10, the day after black students returned to Escambia High School, whites initiated a protest of their own when someone noticed the Confederate flag that adorned a trophy case in the school lobby was missing. Rumors circulated that African Americans had stolen the banner, which further aggravated an already sensitive white student body. Hundreds of angry students gathered on the school's front lawn and decided to converge on the downtown school board office and air their grievances directly with Superintendent J. E. Hall. No one in the crowd or at board headquarters knew that a white staff member had removed the flag from the case and hidden it for safe keeping before classes began that morning. The banner returned to its original location before the day ended, but only well after the latest protest began.[1]

Over three hundred whites arrived to board headquarters and demanded that Superintendent Hall address their concerns regarding the symbols compromise. Hall spoke nearly one hour with approximately fifty students who told him that blacks, not whites, had initiated all racial problems at school. A "small group," they claimed, attacked whites in school bathrooms, stole their money, called them "honkey, whitey, and white trash," and gave each other "black power salutes" after their actions. To make matters worse, the students claimed, Escambia High administrators punished victims instead of the victimizers. Only a student vote, the group claimed, would protect their rights as a majority group and alleviate campus unrest. Hall agreed and assured everyone present that despite the board's earlier decision, EHS students alone would resolve the issue. He called an emergency meeting of the county school board for the following day to discuss the vote.[2]

When the contentious January 11 session ended, a white sheriff's deputy named Otis Davis announced the formation of the Escambia County Concerned Parents and Students Association (CPSA) and invited all who were interested to attend the group's inaugural meeting the following night at Pensacola's municipal auditorium where state legislators W. D. Childers, Tom Tobiassen, and R. W. Peaden would address the developing crisis. Nearly four thousand whites attended the assembly. Davis addressed the crowd first, urged an indefinite boycott at EHS, and claimed he formed the group because a black minority stifled majority opinion. One person who attended the gathering said "resistance to integration, whether in schools, church, or socially" served as the group's main philosophy and compared the group to the White Citizens' Councils of earlier generations. The forum, which began with audience members waving Confederate battle flags and repeatedly singing "Dixie," soon became a shouting match between those who urged restraint and those who wanted to take more drastic measures. Enraged whites grabbed the main podium microphone and made impassioned and, at times, incomprehensible pleas. Childers, Tobiassen, and Peaden arrived late to the auditorium, but each addressed the crowd and promised to support popular opinion. Childers made the surprising yet crowd-pleasing announcement that due to his intervention, EHS principal Sidney Nelson promised to hold a student vote to decide the symbols' fate in four days. A majority vote, Childers claimed, would decide if Escambia High would remain the Rebels with all accompanying images preserved. A multitude of triumphant rebel yells followed the declaration. Some whites carried the celebration into the evening and rode through Pensacola with their Confederate flags flying as they harassed and assaulted unfortunate black bystanders.[3]

In response to the possible EHS student vote, local blacks resumed the public schools boycott on January 15 because "that song and that flag," according to B. J. Brooks, represented "slavery and servitude" to most African Americans. In spite of the protests, in the following days, Escambia High students were to vote to either retain or abolish their "Rebel" nickname and mascot, the "Dixie" fight song, and the display of Confederate flags at school functions. Principal Sidney Nelson refused to cancel, postpone, or modify the election because it was "what the white youngsters right now are pushing for." The county school board tacitly endorsed the student election and refused to intervene because the vote "does not interfere with the educational process" at EHS. In what one district judge later called "a foregone conclusion," each symbol's measure passed by a substantial margin; 2,354 students voted to retain the "Rebel" name and mascot while only 179 opposed, 2,257 elected to retain the flag against 259, and 2,239 voted to keep "Dixie" while 290 rejected the song. Five hundred seventy-five students did not cast ballots, including the vast majority of the school's 238 black students who attended school on January 16. The vote transpired without incident, as ten deputies patrolled campus during the voting period.[4]

In response to the overwhelming decision, Pensacola NAACP President B. J. Brooks announced an indefinite continuation of the student boycott while SCLC established three "Freedom Schools" at black churches throughout the county. State NAACP president Otis Williams addressed the EHS situation at the association's January 20 annual conference in Orlando, and promised a boycott of every public school in Florida if local officials could not settle the Escambia High dispute by January 23. The decision had little to do with the organization's concern for African Americans in Northwest Florida. R. N. Gooden told Williams that the symbols ordeal provided a way "to revive the NAACP in this state." The Pensacola struggle even captured the attention of the NAACP's national office for similar self-interests. In a special report concerning the Escambia County situation, an NAACP official declared that "the mobilization of ministers and the black community is fantastic" in Northwest Florida. The situation captured the organization's interest, though, for financial reasons. According to the NAACP, the symbols dispute provided the national office with an opportunity to conduct a local fund-raising event where "many memberships can be obtained."[5] While civil rights groups and leaders on the local, state, and national levels addressed the EHS situation in different ways for a variety of often self-serving reasons, one family tried to resolve the controversy through the judicial process.

Escambia High student Belinda Jackson and her mother, Merenda Kyle, filed an injunction for an immediate ban of the "Rebel" nickname, the playing of "Dixie," and the display of Confederate flags at EHS on January 19. Ed Duffee, an African American NAACP attorney from Tallahassee, represented the plaintiffs and tied their injunction to the still open *Augustus* school integration case. Duffee maintained that the symbols "disrupted the educational process and denied the black students the opportunity to acquire a public education on terms equal to those enjoyed by other students" at Escambia High. The school board's failure to remove the offensive icons represented "symbolic resistance" to a unitary public school system, which violated prior *Augustus* orders. Crucially, Duffee cited a previous case in his petition that provided a legal precedent for the situation in Escambia County.[6] He based his "Motion to Intervene" on *Smith v. St. Tammany Parish (LA) School Board*, which concerned the display of Confederate battle flags on public school property. Judges in the District Court for the Eastern District of Louisiana ruled that since *Brown*, the banner "has become a symbol of resistance to school integration and, to some, a symbol of white racism in general." The court called the flag "an affront to every Negro student in the school, just as the display of the Black Panther flag would be an affront to every white student in a school whose principal was a Negro," and ruled that the banner "is not constitutionally permissible in a unitary school system where both white and black students attend school together." Plaintiffs in the *Smith* case successfully argued that "meaningful integration" prohibited the official display of "all Confederate flags, banners, signs expressing the school board's or its employees' desire to maintain segregated schools, and all other symbols or indicia of racism." The retention of Confederate imagery in an integrated, unitary public school district, the court maintained, "is no way to eliminate racial discrimination 'root and branch' from the system." The Fifth Circuit Court of Appeals upheld the District Court ruling on June 1, 1971, and provided Jackson and Kyle with a powerful legal precedent.[7]

The "Motion to Intervene as Plaintiff" in the *Augustus* suit captured attention from elsewhere in Florida. State education commissioner Floyd Christian informed Escambia County school officials that *Smith* all but guaranteed victory for the black plaintiffs, while the *Miami Herald* published a feature story on the situation. On January 19, the same day Kyle filed her injunction, legislators W. D. Childers, Smokey Peaden, Grover Robinson, and Tom Tobiassen spoke at an EHS assembly that celebrated the symbols vote. Approximately seven hundred white parents gave the politicians a standing ovation for their defiant defense of school images. Peaden took credit for each black student arrested and claimed "majority rights" justified the controversial election. Childers responded to the situation with even more hostility, as he implored "proud and responsible" whites to "stand up and speak out for our rights and our personal freedoms" and "not be intimidated by blacks." African Americans, Childers declared ominously, "do not understand the seriousness of the white backlash" concerning their protests. Local officials shared the sentiments that Childers and Peaden so vociferously expressed. School board chairman Peter Gindl, for example, told the *Miami Herald* that Escambia County "is George Wallace country" where white "people believe in fighting for what they believe in." Panhandle whites, he claimed, "have been pushed far enough" and "want to stop everything that's been taken away by courts in the past." Gindl concluded that, "there's no more room for negotiations" on the Confederate symbols issue. Deputy county school superintendent Roger Mott likewise lauded Childers because he

"Super Childers," an editorial cartoon published in the News Journal,
November 23, 1980, reflects a local perspective of the influential state legislator.
J. Earle Bowden Cartoon Archive, University of West Florida Libraries.

"correctly read the mind of the general public" and summarized white
attitudes toward the crisis by stating, "When you come to a conflict that
is irresolvable, the biggest wolf eats first."[8] White systems of power, including the *Pensacola News Journal*, defended their interests as a racial majority in the aftermath of the icons vote.

Paper editorials blamed black outsiders for instigating trouble and
deemed the symbols controversy "much ado about nothing." The paper
also called the school boycotts "a dismal failure" and said only "a hard
core of black students" refrained from attending classes, despite school
board reports to the contrary. *Journal* editor Paul Jasper claimed he did
not understand the furor concerning Confederate images and concluded

flippantly, "You have to be black to understand blacks."[9] The publication of letters that criticized black actions simultaneously reflected and fueled white bitterness concerning the Escambia High's symbols debate. On January 13, Mrs. Winfield Brady wrote that area black leaders "want to make a lot of noise" because white people "don't want them here." Eight days later, a writer characterized black protestors as "a bunch of fools" and claimed their protests revealed "a monkey-see, monkey-do attitude." Another person could not "fathom what is so offensive about 'Dixie,'" while Bob Martin proclaimed, "Were I a Negro, I would enjoy hearing a song of Dixie, because I would know I was part of Dixie and Dixie was part of me." The letter continued that as a black, "I would not be bitter toward the south for enslavement of my ancestors, because they were already slaves and nowhere in the world could they have been sold to a more benevolent people or given heritage in so great a land." The racially charged correspondence rambled even further with proud references to the southern accent, a negative portrayal of Africa, and references to black mammies. In another letter that mirrored Martin's in content and tone the author wrote, "If black students in the Escambia schools would obtain possession of a Confederate flag and march down Palafox Street to the tune of 'Dixie,' it would be about the most civilized thing that could happen in this country." On February 4, J. A. Turner blamed black leaders for "this boycott mess" while Starr Brown concluded, "God help us now that our country has come to the point of fighting and bickering over something as small as the symbols of a local high school." Eddie White criticized black claims that the symbols reminded them of slavery and asked, "How can they be reminded of something they have never been?" He further called R. N. Gooden "a big mouth out-of-towner" who "owes this county an apology," and thanked Childers and Peaden "for standing up for the rights of the majority to preserve our past." On the same day, Mrs. E. N. Tinkham best revealed local attitudes toward blacks when she penned, "My grandfather owned slaves, and they loved him dearly. When slavery was abolished, they cried and did not want to leave."[10] She did not relate it to contemporary matters and did not need to, for its implications were clear. A ruling that Judge Winston Arnow made concerning the symbols further exacerbated white rancor.

Arnow heard the request to temporarily ban Confederate imagery at Escambia High on January 24. The plaintiffs' attorney reiterated two arguments throughout the proceeding. First, he argued that the symbols alone incited racial violence between students at Escambia High. Second, and most important, Ed Duffee maintained that the county school board's failure to remove the offensive icons represented "symbolic resistance" to a unitary public school system, which violated prior *Augustus* orders. The federal court's verdict in *Smith v. St. Tammany Parish School Board* seemingly validated Duffee's argument. The school board's lead attorney, Edward T. Barfield, denied that his clients violated any of the *Augustus* terms and blamed the unrest on a small group of problem students at EHS who wanted "to rebel against authority and not go to school and not attend class." He also maintained that any decision against the mascot, Confederate flag, or "Dixie" would violate the first amendment rights of EHS students because they chose the symbols through a majority vote, and that race had no influence whatsoever upon the choice of school images. The "athletic teams of the University of Mississippi," he claimed, inspired the decision.[11] He failed to explain how sporting events at Ole Miss influenced a high school student symbols vote in Northwest Florida.

Judge Arnow opened the hearing by granting Jackson's "Motion to Intervene as Plaintiff" in the *Augustus* suit. The decision marked an important point in local race relations because it linked the Confederate symbols debate and Escambia County school integration in a legal setting. Arnow's second ruling, though, tempered black enthusiasm. The judge dismissed the plaintiff's request to ban the playing of "Dixie" at Escambia High functions because state law prevented county school boards from prohibiting the playing of the song in any of its institutions. The requests concerning the "Rebel" nickname, mascot, and Confederate flag usage, though, violated no existing statutes. After the judge issued his two rulings, four individuals testified in the EHS symbols hearing. Ed Duffee called two black Escambia High students, Belinda Jackson and Linda Packer, and Pensacola NAACP president B. J. Brooks to the stand. Only R. C. Lipscomb, the deputy school superintendent, testified for the defense.[12]

Each of the black witnesses testified that Confederate images intensified racial animosity at EHS and led to the December riot. Fighting between white and black students began, Jackson summarized, because "the whites want to keep the Confederate flags and song 'Dixie' and name 'Rebels,' and the blacks do not." Brooks echoed her sentiments by stating, "All of the tension is situated around the Confederacy symbols," which he deemed "racial irritants." The problem with the images, according to each of the black witnesses, was that whites used them as a symbol of their perceived racial supremacy. The images made "blacks feel as though they are not included in the student body," Jackson argued. She also noted that whites pinned Confederate emblems to their clothing and said that "the only purpose for wearing those flags was to irritate us." Each black witness testified that whites maliciously used the iconography as a constant reminder of their belief in African American inferiority. Only the removal of Confederate images at EHS, Brooks argued, would satisfy Escambia County blacks.[13] An exchange that occurred between Winston Arnow and Belinda Jackson revealed the symbols' importance and meaning to black students.

The heated conversation began when Jackson said that her school's images reminded blacks of a war whose primary cause was the preservation of slavery. Arnow interrupted the testimony to interject his own opinions concerning the Civil War. "Slavery," he proclaimed, "was on its way out" when the conflict began and "was not the real reason" the South seceded. Arnow asked why "Dixie," which "originated down south and is a pretty song," offended black students. "Because," Jackson responded, "being black, we were the slaves." Arnow admitted that, "I am puzzled a bit by" the connection blacks made between the Confederacy and slavery because he could surely trace his ancestry and "find where some of my people were slaves." Jackson countered that white students used their symbols to threaten and intimidate blacks. She felt so unsafe that she had withdrawn from EHS and attended no public school in the area. Arnow responded to Jackson's declaration with a torrent of questions that reflected his incredulity and failure to comprehend the basis of African American protests. "Young lady," he asked, "are you sure you are putting first things first in this thing? Is all this really important to you? Isn't getting an education in which you come forward in the world and face the world and have all the education we can provide you, isn't that the thing that should be first and paramount with you and all the children in that school, and their parents? You are willing to let your education suffer because of the display of symbols and those kinds of things?" Arnow ended his questioning of Jackson by asking, "You don't think you have a chip on your shoulder?" She denied the allegation and remained firm in her decision to remain out of school until the Confederate symbols at EHS were removed.[14] The dialogue that occurred between the judge and student was crucial, for it characterized the opposing positions clearly. Black students knew the images were used to reinforce their positions as an unwanted, unwelcomed, and inferior minority, while whites in positions of power and authority—the local systems of racial control—considered the objectors petty, insolent, and, quite frankly, ungrateful for the benefits that integrated schools provided. After Lipscomb's testimony that a few black rabble rousers alone caused the EHS tumult, Winston Arnow issued a monumental court order that he based on the *Smith v. St. Tammany Parish* precedent.

The Escambia County Public School System, Arnow declared, had a judicial mandate "to eliminate root, stock, and barrel anything that prevented us from having a unified, desegregated" education system. Its failure to resolve the EHS dispute violated prior *Augustus* rulings, so Arnow issued a temporary injunction against the Confederate icons because they "have become and are symbols of white racism in general and offensive to a substantial number of black students in attendance at this school." The First Amendment, Arnow stated, did not protect the images because whites at EHS used them maliciously for the sole purpose of "taunting and offending black students," which led to "a breakdown" of campus order. The injunction went into effect the following Monday, January 29. Arnow ruled that a flag could remain in the school's trophy case, on two school monuments, and on yearbooks and class rings for the 1972–73 school year. No student, though, "can display or wear the Confederate Battle Flag on his person." Arnow ordered large images covered, such as the rebel flag that adorned the football stadium's press box, and placed deputies on the campus to prevent further rioting. He gave each side twenty days to submit a mutually agreeable implementation plan to the court, after which he would determine the injunction's status as permanent or temporary. Unsurprisingly, whites and blacks responded to the judgment in contrasting ways. Politicians promised to fight the ruling, the county school board pledged to appeal the decision, and African American leaders ended their countywide school boycott.[15]

On January 29, black students resumed classes at Escambia High. Two days later racial violence again engulfed EHS as over three hundred students clashed in one wing of the school. Principal Sidney Nelson dismissed classes after officers gained control of the situation and stationed deputies on each school bus to prevent even more fighting. Only twenty blacks returned to class the following morning. In Tallahassee, state representative Smokey Peaden heard about the latest round of tumult at Escambia High the day after it occurred. He told Representative John Ryals and Tampa newsman John Hayes, "Those niggers make me so mad.

If I had anything to do with it, I would get a shotgun—no, a submachine gun—and mow them down." As if the threat of use of automatic weapons did not suffice, Peaden urged Escambia County deputies to pick up any black "that shoves a white student around" and throw the "trouble maker . . . through the wall." The Tampa television station aired the comments during its evening newscast, and African Americans throughout Florida demanded Peaden immediately resign from the legislature. R. N. Gooden called the politician "an instigator of violence" and demanded his impeachment. Peaden initially claimed, "I never said anything like that in my life" but admitted making the comments "in a joking manner" when presented with the recorded evidence. He therefore refused to abdicate his position in the House, apologized to anyone "who took offense" to his humorous statement, and pled guilty to only trying "to create unity" in Pensacola. Florida House speaker Terrell Sessums accepted the explanation, refused to discipline the official, and even commended Peaden because "it takes a tall man to stand up and admit he said something he should not have said." Sheriff Royal Untreiner also supported Peaden publicly and said the "elected representatives of this county . . . have a right to say what they feel."[16] The representative's unique sense of humor, though, was subsequently overshadowed as racial disturbances spread to other Escambia County schools.

Interracial fighting at PHS and Booker T. Washington High School prompted black student walkouts at each institution on February 1. R. N. Gooden summarized the racial atmosphere by stating, "You can feel the wave of hate in the streets of Pensacola like a powder keg" waiting to explode. He appealed once more for state intervention and declared, "I hope Governor Askew is real proud when his home city explodes in a riot." No longer able to ignore the volatile situation, the governor sent Florida education commissioner Floyd Christian to Pensacola on February 4. Christian brought twenty riot control officers from the state highway patrol with him to help the county sheriff's department maintain order on campus and made permanent and temporary leadership changes at EHS. He promoted black teacher Willie J. Brown to the position of assistant principal, placed Principal Sidney Nelson on administrative leave, and appointed Deputy School Superintendent Roger Mott as temporary EHS principal. In Mott's estimation, Nelson had "mismanaged" the symbols crisis, riots, and student vote in many ways and "needed time away" from the school because the growing racial tumult was "not something he could handle." The number of missed classes due to the

Sheriff's deputies and riot squad officers guard one of the entrances to Escambia High, 1976. Pensacola Historical Society Collection, UWF Historic Trust.

cancellations and suspensions that Nelson levied threatened the school's accreditation, as the number of minimum contact hours between students and teachers approached dangerously low levels. More crucially, though, Mott perceived that Nelson sided with white students in the symbols conflict and sympathized with "white rednecks" who clung to Confederate symbols as part of their segregationist identity. In fact, the last thing Nelson told Mott before he started his state-enforced sabbatical from EHS was "don't let the blacks win."[17]

On February 14, the Escambia County school board asked Judge Arnow to repeal his injunction against Escambia High's Confederate iconography or else the issue "is going to be settled in the streets." A group of EHS students and parents assembled a list of twenty-four "White Irritations" that they distributed throughout the county. The document reveals the primacy of race in the EHS maelstrom, as every point vilified African Americans in some manner. The first item, for instance, claimed that "Blacks should have respect for the American flag and the

National Anthem, which the majority of them don't." Other points accused African Americans of "just trying to make trouble by taking away our symbols," "trying to change history," and refusing to "let the majority of the school be happy." Perhaps the most inflammatory irritant claimed, "Blacks expect things because they are black, yet they cry when they don't receive things because they are black."[18]

African American students and teachers at Escambia High, unsurprisingly, encountered consistent harassment after Arnow's decision. B. J. Brooks explained the deteriorating situation in a letter to NAACP general counsel Nathaniel Jones. "We do not want to take the children out of school again," Brooks confessed, "but this seems to be the only way to get results." If blacks continued to endure abuses, Brooks believed, "someone could get hurt or killed, according to the threats that I am getting from white citizens." Although Brooks expressed hope that the national office could devise "a better way for black citizens to obtain justice" than local leaders had utilized, he suspected that violence would soon engulf the school once more.[19] His correspondence became prophetic when racial unrest resurfaced at Escambia High on March 22. Over 150 black students, frustrated because teachers would not let them make up work they missed during previous boycotts, gathered in the school gymnasium, refused to attend class, and demanded that Principal Sidney Nelson address their issues. Nelson telephoned H. K. Matthews and requested that he visit the campus and mollify the students. The principal also contacted the sheriff's department and requested deputies disperse the assembly. Nelson finally appeared before the frustrated group and demanded they return to class, leave the campus, or face arrest. The frustrated students complied and slowly exited the gym. Fights began between exiting blacks and white students who had gathered to taunt the group as the building emptied. Twelve police officers already stationed on campus arrested thirty-five black and fifteen white pupils. Nelson met Matthews, who arrived at the conflict's apex, and told him that students would not go to jail if they dispersed peacefully. Matthews subsequently stood on the steps of a school bus parked in front of the main entrance at EHS and addressed the crowd through a deputy's bullhorn. He begged students to cease fighting, repeatedly asked them to obey officers, and promised that "nobody is going to jail." Deputies immediately arrested Matthews after he made his announcement, transported him and the thirty-five other blacks to the county jail, and placed them in the prison courtyard without informing them of their crime. Two hours later, deputies pressed felony charges against Matthews for inciting a riot.[20] The arrests and charges foreshadowed patterns that later epitomized the local struggle, and also deepened divisions between black leaders in Northwest Florida.

After the latest incident at Escambia High, black elementary school principal Henry McMillan formed the Escambia County Coalition and proposed an alternative to the traditional pattern of local black protest that the NAACP and SCLC perpetuated. McMillan, a forty-year school system employee, criticized Matthews and Brooks for their confrontational direct action campaigns and challenged their positions as local black spokesmen. He disparaged the two for using their pulpits to organize demonstrations and said that as a Catholic, "We just don't get up and promote political campaigns in church." The educator expressed particular distaste for H. K. Matthews, whom McMillan said misrepresented NAACP and SCLC objectives for personal gain. The minister's visibility and public activities, McMillan declared, did not "necessarily make him a black leader" and due to whose activities, "the black community doesn't know about the thousands of white people who are perfectly fair and honest in their objectives." McMillan wanted the Escambia County Coalition, which he declared "is not and doesn't pretend to be a civil rights group," to focus their energies on the political process. Only through running for political offices and becoming more involved in the electoral system, McMillan maintained, would elected officials respond to black needs. The accessibility of commissioners at the city and county levels would bring meaningful racial change to Escambia County as, McMillan observed, "the demonstrations and confrontations of the 60s that drew attention to the black's [sic] problem and destroyed unfair laws have now become counterproductive." Direct action protests, he claimed, "were valid during those times" but "racial and discriminatory" statutes "have been stricken and therefore those tactics are no longer necessary." The actions of Brooks and Matthews, McMillan claimed, "create an atmosphere of mass hysteria that make any real progress impossible." Only "the calm, thoughtful consideration of facts by all persons that are truly concerned with the community," particularly members of the city council and county commission, could bring peace and racial uplift. H. K. Matthews vehemently rejected McMillan's claims, while B. J. Brooks stated that the NAACP's philosophy "is poles apart from that of the Coalition." The *Pensacola News Journal* acknowledged that "a power struggle for leadership in the black community" became more apparent after

Matthews's arrest and stated, "we associate ourselves completely with the goals" McMillan espoused. The deteriorating situation at Escambia High School, then, deepened the divide between both whites and blacks in Escambia County. The mass arrests and public criticism that Henry McMillan levied against them radicalized Matthews and Brooks and strengthened their demands that white leaders acknowledge their concerns.[21]

White resistance to civil rights activities likewise stiffened as a result of Matthews's arrest and alleged crime. The state subpoenaed twenty-seven witnesses to testify against the reverend, but an all-white jury declared him not guilty of the felony riot charges. Matthews claimed the prosecution failed because their witnesses "could not get their lies straight" concerning the words and actions he used on March 22.[22] Although their first attempt failed, local white leaders would again use police action and the judicial system to stifle the county freedom struggle. For the duration of Pensacola's civil rights movement, white politicians, police officials, and judges blatantly used their power and influence against local black leaders, particularly H. K. Matthews. Judge Winston Arnow proved the only white official who used his power on the behalf of racial justice in Northwest Florida.

On July 11, Judge Arnow heard arguments from both sides in the *Augustus* case concerning the permanent status of Confederate symbols at Escambia High. Unlike prior hearings on the topic, defense testimonies dominated the July proceedings. Eight whites, including six EHS students, Principal Sidney Nelson, and school board member Richard Leeper testified for the defense while two black students from the school testified for the plaintiffs. It is unclear why Ed Duffee, the NAACP attorney, called only two witnesses, but it foreshadowed future questions regarding his ability to effectively challenge the Panhandle's white power structure. Defense witnesses repeated a familiar theme—none of the violence at EHS "had anything to do with this flag." The blacks who testified, though, provided numerous instances in which whites used Confederate images, particularly the flag, to humiliate and intimidate them. Anixibia Strong said that whites stood across the street from school grounds and waved the flag while they chanted, "Niggers go home." As Strong explained, "You can't expect a black student really to want to be a Johnny Reb and march up and down the field and carry a Rebel flag" because Confederate imagery "symbolized inequality among students at the school." The testimonies of white witnesses unwittingly supported black claims. EHS student David Howell, for instance, admitted the inseparable connection between his school's battle flag and the word "nigger." Nicky Scapin, another white EHS student, admitted that many defended the flag because it represented a hatred of blacks "and everything they stand for." Similarly, Richard Leeper acknowledged that waving a Confederate flag in a black face "was done for the purpose of belittling or degrading" black students. Principal Sidney Nelson also conceded that blacks possessed "a real strong feeling about 'Dixie'" and observed they refused to stand when it was played at school functions. Furthermore, he confessed that the fights which occurred on his campus in 1973 transpired because "the temper of the white youngsters" increased when they realized that blacks "were doing away with their symbols." The testimonies of white witnesses, therefore, undermined their own arguments that no connection existed between white racism and the Confederate iconography at Escambia High. The contradiction appeared so obvious that after defense rested, Arnow collectively asked its witnesses, "Why was it important to the rest of you to keep the symbols" if they "were offensive to a few of the students?" The hearing transcript recorded no response to the judge's query. Although school board attorneys intended to use more witnesses at the hearing, the judge canceled testimonies after the first day because he feared they would further arouse emotions and increase racial unrest in the community. Instead, he instructed attorneys from each side to submit written arguments that summarized their positions.[23] On July 24, Arnow banned Confederate images from Escambia High School on a permanent basis.

In his fourteen-page opinion, Arnow called the symbols "racially irritating," declared they "generated a feeling of inequality and inferiority among black students," and deemed them "a source of racial violence" at the school. Furthermore, Arnow called the Confederate battle flag "a symbol of white racism" that white students and parents defended "deliberately for the purpose of offending black students." His opinion acknowledged that "removal of the symbols may not eliminate racist beliefs," but their continued presence would "continue to be a source of racial tension and a cause of disruption."[24] Six white EHS parents appealed the decision on their children's behalf, while the school board allocated $15,000 of county money to fund their legal struggle to preserve the symbols. In a bitter editorial, a "disappointed" *Pensacola News Journal* called "Afro hair-dos" and "the clinched fist of black power" offensive to whites and asked, "What's going to be a 'racial irritant' tomorrow?" It also noted that "courts never banned the Swastika," chastised "this willy nilly censorship," and compared Arnow's verdict to destroying the Alamo "because some Spanish-Americans now believe the acquisition of Texas was a land grab by the imperialist war monger, the United States." Paper editors emphatically declared, then, "We reject Judge Arnow's decision." While the case awaited an appeals hearing, EHS sports teams were called the "Escambians" but the school had no official mascot. A student vote during the first quarter of the 1973–74 year adopted the "Raiders" nickname and mascot, but Principal Nelson resigned his position before the election because of the "mental and physical exhaustion" the symbols controversy caused.[25]

As the 1970s progressed, then, the civil rights movements in the Florida Panhandle shifted from the Escambia High School campus and county school headquarters to the federal district court. Judge Winston Arnow based his injunction against Confederate images at EHS on past legal precedent and because they disrupted the peaceful maintenance of a unified school system, not because he believed them to be racially offensive. The ruling addressed black grievances without acknowledging the reasoning behind their complaints, which demonstrates that Arnow's order did not alter the power imbalance that characterized race relations in Northwest Florida. The decision also reinforced the local movement's organizing tradition, as individual leaders used their affiliations with civil rights groups at the state and regional levels to obtain favorable outcomes in which local residents played supporting roles. Arnow's mandate widened the divide that existed between activists and the black upper-class elite, temporarily defusing mobilization against the iconography, and did nothing to ensure the more equal treatment of African American students in district schools. While the injunction failed to alleviate the racial status quo, it solidified white resistance to greater changes and mobilized the local systems of control to protect their remaining social, economic, and political advantages as the racial minority. The symbols controversy, therefore, represented more than a quarrel over mascots and nicknames. The issue revolved around the white possession and implementation of power and the limitations blacks faced when they challenged it in the years beyond integration.

Tensions at Escambia High subsided for the remainder of the 1973–74 school term after the school's latest mascot change, but Pensacola remained a community bitterly divided along racial lines. The acrimony grew substantially when a fatal police shooting of an African American "sent a wave of unrest through the black community in Pensacola." On April 22, 1974, twelve armed Escambia County sheriff's deputies surrounded a downtown grocery store where an escaped black prisoner named Bobbie Lee Smith had been spotted. Three officers entered the store after a prolonged standoff to apprehend the accused fugitive. Deputy Lucien Mitchell, a man who had been involved in three previous fatal shootings and had a reputation among blacks as "Pensacola's Wyatt Earp," gunned down Smith once inside. The twenty-one-year-old died instantly. Officers at the scene initially declared Smith unarmed at the time of his death. The state attorney's office, which the *Pensacola Journal* admitted "is an arm of the law enforcement establishment and works hand in hand with the police on a daily basis," conducted the only formal investigation into the incident. White investigators interviewed all of the deputies involved, each of whom were also white, and released a two-page report that declared the shooting an act of self-defense. The attorney's office declared that Smith had actually charged Mitchell while holding an ice pick, and the deputy fired his pistol to protect himself. The report ignored many key issues, such as why initial statements proclaimed Smith unarmed. Still, the Escambia County Sheriff's Department exonerated Mitchell of any wrongdoing. Black leaders responded to the investigation and state attorney's report with outrage. SCLC president H. K. Matthews called Mitchell "a trigger-happy" killer and feigned surprise that Smith "became armed two or three days after he was killed." Pensacola NAACP president B. J. Brooks questioned why a group of sheriff's deputies could not apprehend an individual armed with an ice pick without killing him. The NAACP and SCLC demanded Mitchell's immediate suspension and sent numerous telegrams to Governor Reubin Askew that requested a state grand jury investigation of the incident and suspected cover-up. Neither Askew nor the sheriff's department acknowledged African American complaints, which, according to the *Pensacola Voice*, left the black community "in an angry mood over the incident."[26] Although the sheriff's department, state attorney, and governor's office ignored the situation, the Escambia-Pensacola Human Relations Commission validated black concerns.

The HRC, formerly the Pensacola Biracial Committee, met monthly during the EHS unrest but made no public pronouncements or recommendations concerning Confederate images. The organization stuck to its policy of nonintervention in area affairs unless a group requested their assistance, and none asked. While the situation at Escambia High escalated, the HRC experienced a number of substantive changes. First, the Escambia County Commission joined the Pensacola City Council to fund the HRC in 1972. The organization officially changed its name to the Escambia-Pensacola Human Relations Commission and renewed its pledge to "promote fair and equal treatment for citizens" in the Panhandle, but now fell under the control of the white power structures at both the city and county levels. Second, the HRC shifted its focus from employment and economic issues to the tenuous relationship between blacks and local law enforcement as the issue that most threatened the delicate racial peace in Northwest Florida. Finally, the HRC used funding it obtained from a 1973 federal grant to open its own office and hire a full-time executive director and staff, elements that gave the commission a newfound purpose and false sense of autonomy. On May 17, 1974, HRC members chose a twenty-six-year-old white journalism graduate student at the University of West Florida named Alain C. Hebert from a pool of twenty-two applicants as the commission's first executive director. Hebert, a Ft. Lauderdale native and self-described "unknown outsider" in Northwest Florida, believed the HRC should serve "as a safety valve of some sort" and act as "a neutral third party advisor" when interracial conflicts surfaced. Yet Hebert had little idea that the local white systems of control intended to continue using the commission to maintain its ultimate authority. Although he emphasized fair housing and equal employment opportunities as priorities upon entering the position, the conflict between local blacks and the county sheriff's department consumed the HRC during Hebert's tenure.[27]

Mistrust between area residents and local law enforcement had influenced race relations in Pensacola for well over a decade and increased precipitously during Royal Untreiner's time as sheriff. Many white officials and their constituents adored Untreiner because, according to white civic booster John Appleyard, the sheriff "had a pretty good understanding of what the culture was" in the area and championed the white majority's opinion on issues involving race. County whites considered the former FBI agent a "super cop" who "didn't take crap off of anybody." Untreiner's department was also "an extremely powerful force" in Northwest Florida historically, and possessed "much more power than the county commission it served." The sheriff, HRC director Alain Hebert observed, possessed "an aloofness" because of the power and autonomy he possessed and "looked down upon" those who criticized his department, particularly African Americans. Consequently,

Sheriff Royal Untreiner, 1978. Pensacola Historical Society Collection, UWF Historic Trust.

Panhandle blacks possessed "a firm belief" that "the Escambia County Sheriff's Department was racist" in its policies and practices. H. K. Matthews publicly declared Untreiner "a bona fide racist" and "complete bigot," while many African Americans referred to him sarcastically as "the Lord High Sheriff." The HRC organized meetings between local black leaders and department officials, but the sheriff viewed the committee "as more of an annoyance than a help" and rarely attended the sessions. The failed meetings reinforced the power that the sheriff's department retained in preserving the area's racial status quo and the impotence of African Americans and the HRC to alter it.[28]

In the wake of Bobbie Lee Smith's death, the Pensacola City Council asked the HRC to investigate the shooting and prepare a report concerning the divisions between police officers and blacks in Northwest Florida. The HRC study concluded grimly that "a state of increased community tension does exist and the issue centers around the fear of police brutality," which represented "a threat to the city's very existence." To alleviate tensions, the organization recommended a number of new officer firearms policies. First, the HRC suggested the city or county remove an officer who killed a citizen in the line of duty from active service, with pay, until the department investigated the episode. Second, the HRC urged reassignment for exonerated officers if the situation under review inflamed area racial tensions. Third, the report requested law enforcement agencies to develop, publicize, and distribute a coherent policy for filing a citizen's complaint against abusive officers. Finally, the HRC recommended that all law enforcement personnel undergo psychological testing and "participate in accredited courses concerning the fields of human and personal relationships." The Pensacola city manager rejected all HRC recommendations, which demonstrated that the white power structure expected the HRC to preserve—not critique or threaten—the racial status quo.[29] The HRC's critical report in the aftermath of the Smith shooting and conclusion that a culture of institutionalized police brutality (a relatively new phrase in the racial discourse of the 1970s) threatened to tear Pensacola apart proved prophetic in less than eight months after the organization made its claim.

On November 29, 1974, five black men left their Atlanta homes for a weekend fishing excursion in Pensacola. The Panhandle trips had become a common ritual for the friends and they made numerous such escapes to Escambia County. This visit, though, ended in tragedy, as their boat disappeared during an early morning storm and was found at daybreak floating empty in the city's Santa Rosa Sound. Rescue units from Pensacola, New Orleans, and Mobile searched for the missing men but speculated that they drowned in the turbulent overnight waters. A coast guard spokesman, however, called the circumstances surrounding the disappearances "weird" because workers found a full ice chest, two fishing tackle boxes, two half empty gasoline containers, and five life jackets on the boat. The men, he told reporters, "could not have been out fishing" because most of their equipment remained in a camper on shore. Officials further wondered how each man succumbed to the inclement conditions while their belongings remained intact on board, and noted that the boat's anchor rope had been cut. The coast guard reported their findings to local reporters and initiated a search for survivors. After two days of exploring the sound and Pensacola Bay, search efforts temporarily ceased. Rescue director M. K. Renfroe reported no unusual findings and concluded that Robert Walker, Leroy Holloway, Lonnie Merritt, John Sterling, and Marvin Walker, a group journalists dubbed "the Atlanta Five," perished in a boat accident. Officials shifted the search and rescue efforts to a recovery operation and patrolled local waters eight days after the men vanished to find their surfaced bodies. While authorities conducted their search, relatives of the men grew increasingly suspicious concerning the disappearances.[30]

Escambia County law enforcement officials contacted the men's families and told them that their relatives likely drowned in a boating mishap, but all questioned the assumption and the evidence provided to justify that an accident occurred. All of the men, for instance, were frequent boaters and could swim well. They had traveled to Pensacola together since 1952 and were familiar with area waters. In the days following the disappearances, furthermore, one family member received a call from an anonymous individual who claimed he spoke to one of the missing men hours earlier. The caller claimed that the five men "had been captured by whites and were being held in what seemed to be a castle" somewhere in the county. Before the person could elaborate, the telephone connection ended abruptly. The helpless yet hopeful family members contacted the Atlanta-based SCLC, informed the group of the strange circumstances surrounding their loved ones' disappearance, and requested assistance from organization president Ralph Abernathy.[31] The Atlanta Five case provided the SCLC with a tremendous opportunity to recapture some of its lost prestige, but the organization's intervention would have detrimental consequences on the long civil rights movement in Escambia County.

Ralph David Abernathy became SCLC president soon after Martin Luther King Jr., the organization's founder, was murdered in 1968. Abernathy remained dedicated to King's philosophies but faced many problems during his nine-year presidency, many of which existed beyond his control. Succeeding King as SCLC leader, in fact, was Abernathy's primary obstacle. King's tragic assassination elevated him to martyr status and guaranteed his eternal role as the personification and symbolic figure of the civil rights movement, a status that no one could live up to. With the death of King, the SCLC lost its founder, leader, and public identity. To make matters worse, Abernathy was admittedly unprepared to lead the organization and plagued by self-doubt. He simply did not possess the charisma, intellect, celebrity, or ability to relate to people of all races and economic backgrounds that the SCLC president needed. Abernathy, according to long-time SCLC official Andrew Young, never developed his own leadership skills and was ultimately "frustrated by his inability to be Martin Luther King." In addition, a mass exodus of many top SCLC officials deprived the organization of both funding and legitimacy during Abernathy's time as president. Coretta Scott King, Andrew Young, Jesse Jackson, James Bevel, and Hosea Williams, among others, left the group in the years following Dr. King's death. The membership decline and rise of numerous rival organizations left SCLC financially devastated. By 1973 the organization that once claimed 150 paid employees and a $1 million annual payroll had become a "broke and disorganized" group with seventeen staff members and a $75,000 debt. Personal conflicts between Abernathy and other civil rights leaders developed that further deteriorated SCLC's reputation. Abernathy later conceded that as the 1970s progressed, SCLC lost its "fighting edge and the single-minded allegiance of our people, who were beginning to look in other directions for leadership."[32] In addition to the personal and financial struggles SCLC faced, Abernathy and his organization had to deal with the changing nature of the civil rights movement.

Growing black disillusionment with the direct action campaigns of the 1960s and the rise of more confrontational organizations rendered Abernathy's dedication to King's nonviolent strategies increasingly obsolete. Demonstrations and campaigns against de jure forms of segregation proved more effective because they often achieved a tangible goal, such as the integration of dining counters. De facto segregation, though, proved much more difficult to combat, as most did not understand the connection between poverty and the denial of civil rights. King understood the challenges de facto racism posed to civil rights for all citizens later in his life and anticipated "the inevitable counterrevolution that succeeds every period of success" in his final book. Young observed that by 1970, the movement "had achieved surface change: the abolition of segregation, a spectacular increase in voter registration, and so forth . . . [yet] the various devices of direct action had taken us about as far as they could" because white "opposition was far too hardened." SCLC historian Thomas Peake observed that whites and blacks alike held "less confidence by the end of the decade (the 1960s) that the nation was economically and spiritually capable of solving its racial problems." By 1970, therefore, most people observed that "the civil rights era was over for all practical purposes." Peake described the period as one of "white backlash reinforced by the view that blacks had gained all that the American system could appropriately guarantee." The slow pace of racial change since 1965, the movement's northern and urban shift, a growing distrust of activist organizations, and white liberal indifference all represented changes that national movement leaders faced. Most important, white resentment concerning continued civil rights activism transcended the popular realm and became a crucial component of the Republican party's "southern strategy" during the Nixon administration. The SCLC responded to the changes by remaining, according to one observer, "in a dazed fixation on the past" which allowed "King's memory to stagnate." The SCLC's 17th annual conference legitimized such concerns and demonstrated that SCLC, according to Young, faced "difficult times" which "called for new ideas. And we weren't coming up with any."[33]

Abernathy launched a national SCLC membership and fund-raising drive to resurrect the dormant organization at its 17th annual conference in Philadelphia, Pennsylvania, on August 17, 1974. Abernathy placed great importance upon the meeting because of the "trying times in the life of this organization." He sent a letter to all SCLC board members and chapter presidents that urged them to attend the convention because "all is not well in SCLC's household." He also asked each SCLC official to contribute "at least $500" at the convention. In addition, Abernathy proclaimed August 11 as "National SCLC Sunday" and implored ministers "to please take a special offering and urge your congregations to give liberally so that I can report your gift in Philadelphia." He requested that each pastor give "no less than $100" and wanted them to contribute between $300 and $500 to the national office. Abernathy appealed to the memory of Dr. Martin Luther King Jr., "our fallen and sainted leader," in his solicitation and reminded SCLC members, "it has been lonely trying to carry on the mantle of leadership which was thrust on my shoulders." He anticipated thousands of people from across the country to attend the organization's vital meeting, but fewer than three hundred people attended. The SCLC, according to Thomas Peake, "was hoping to see some solid evidence of renewal in 1974, only to find that the organization had not yet reached the bottom of its decline."[34] The Atlanta Five case hastened the organization's spiral into national irrelevancy at the expense of the continuing struggle for civil rights in Northwest Florida.

In December 1974, therefore, SCLC desperately needed an opportunity to regain its lost prominence, rehabilitate its tarnished image, and fill its dwindling coffers. The Pensacola situation provided Abernathy with his best chance to date of fulfilling the goal. The incident involved missing blacks from the home state of a nationally recognized governor and presidential candidate, occurred in one of the South's most racially tense areas, involved law enforcement officials, and captured the attention of local civil rights leaders. The situation possessed the familiar characteristics of early 1960s campaigns and contained the elements needed for a potential SCLC revival, particularly in Florida. The Panhandle, Rev. C. K. Steele observed, provided SCLC its "greatest" opportunity "in the attempt to begin reorganizing the state." Pensacola, he reported, "is pretty much 'open turf' with the NAACP gaining strength" and therefore "definitely worth the effort" for SCLC.[35] With the possibility of national exposure and his organization's resurgence at stake, Abernathy committed himself completely but briefly to the case. He met with a group of the boaters' relatives, listened to the circumstances concerning the alleged drownings, and dispatched an SCLC investigator named Doris Mason to Pensacola to collect more information concerning the case. Although Mason found no direct evidence suggesting foul play, Abernathy suspected otherwise and held a press conference where he publicly announced that white racists in Escambia County had murdered the Atlanta Five. Abernathy asked volunteers "to go with me to Pensacola and search for the bodies" the following day, and he and two other SCLC officials arrived in the Panhandle on December 12.[36]

The Atlanta contingent first met with local SCLC leaders H. K. Matthews and Otha Leverette to discuss the disappearances. All suspected that area whites murdered the Atlanta Five, so Abernathy received an enthusiastic response to his rapidly developing conspiracy theories surrounding the deaths. Matthews and Leverette accompanied SCLC officials to their visit with Sheriff Royal Untreiner, who told the group his office would not investigate the mishap. Abernathy considered Untreiner's abrupt response "highly insulting" and it stoked SCLC concerns that the sheriff's department had knowledge of, and possibly conspired in, the abduction of the black boaters. The frustrated group next visited Pensacola's University Hospital to view the bodies of Robert Walker and John Sterling, the latter of which surfaced earlier that day. Abernathy saw no signs of foul play and noted "the two bodies appeared in normal condition," which led him to conclude that hospital authorities showed them "two fake bodies." As Abernathy reasoned, "if a body stayed in the water that long the salt and animal life would almost destroy it." The "normalcy of the bodies," then, indicated that "county hospital personnels [sic] are involved in the deaths or possibly involved in the cover up." Abernathy's entourage next visited the area where authorities located the two bodies. Although they supposedly capsized at the same time, rescue workers found Walker and Sterling over two miles from each other. The distance, to Abernathy, made little sense. He believed they should have surfaced closer to each other, regardless of tide patterns, weather conditions, or other mitigating factors. The vast area between the two, Abernathy maintained, proved their assailants dumped the bodies in different locations. Rescue workers also predicted that water temperatures and other scientific factors indicated that another body would surface within twenty-four hours. Officials recovered two more bodies before daybreak the following morning. "How in the world," Abernathy asked, "could they promise us that they were going to find a body the next day?" The sudden discovery of the bodies, which coincided with his visit to Pensacola, convinced the SCLC president that the conspiracy surrounding the men's disappearance surpassed his initial suspicions. The speciousness of his arguments indicates that little could have convinced Abernathy that the Atlanta Five died accidentally.[37]

With local leaders Otha Leverette and H. K. Matthews at his side during an afternoon press conference, the SCLC president concluded that the Atlanta Five were murdered and "law enforcement agencies in Pensacola may have been involved." At a mass meeting later that evening, Abernathy promulgated the SCLC conspiracy theories concerning the Atlanta Five case. Matthews and Leverette each spoke at the assembly, which secured their connection to SCLC accusations in the public eye, and Abernathy reported that the Atlanta Five "were taken and beaten and killed by racist, segregationist forces in Pensacola." He also appointed H. K. Matthews over all SCLC activities in Northwest Florida because the region "needs to be organized," and promised the reverend would "expose how backward this section of Florida is." Furthermore, Abernathy demanded that the local, state, and federal governments launch separate investigations into the incident. "We don't intend," Abernathy insisted, "for this to be another case where black men are destroyed and nothing is done about it at all." *Pensacola Journal* reporters attended the meeting and published the inflammatory rhetoric in its next issue. Abernathy departed the following morning for Boston, Massachusetts, but he reported his findings and suspicions concerning the case to the *Atlanta Constitution*. "Due to the facts of this tragedy and to rumors in the Pensacola black community," the SCLC concluded that the five Atlanta fishermen "died by the hands of persons unknown." The organization's use of a phrase that historically characterized lynchings and Abernathy's repeated accusations of "foul play" on behalf of the Escambia County

Sheriff's Department insured that the story of the Atlanta Five reached a regional and, ultimately, a national audience.[38] Official reports concerning the deaths only exacerbated acrimony between the SCLC and white officials in Northwest Florida.

The Escambia County Sheriff's Department released its autopsy reports of the five Atlanta residents on December 14. The findings collectively ruled that each man perished accidentally and concluded, "There are absolutely no signs of foul play involved" in the deaths. National and local black leaders remained suspicious in spite of the autopsy results. Abernathy argued that drowning did not exclude the likelihood of murder, while Matthews stated that local blacks "have to believe that foul play was involved" in the episode. SCLC representative Tyrone Brooks even accused local law enforcement officials of "suppressing crucial evidence" in "one of the biggest mass murders this state has ever seen." Despite SCLC misgivings, police officials closed their investigations of the drowning case on December 16.[39] The decision encouraged Abernathy to bring national attention to the Atlanta Five ordeal.

In the weeks following his Pensacola visit, Abernathy wrote letters to Florida governor Reubin Askew, Georgia governor Jimmy Carter, Representative Andrew Young, the Florida State Attorney's office, the FBI, and the United States Justice Department imploring them to support the SCLC's investigation into the Atlanta Five case. As a result of Abernathy's persistence, Askew, Carter, and the Justice Department launched independent investigations into the Atlanta Five case. None of the inquiries discovered suspicious evidence in the case and each declared the men "victims of an unfortunate and tragic accident." Abernathy expressed "no surprise" in the investigation results because they concerned black victims, while Tyrone Brooks told *Jet* magazine that SCLC had "to do what the U.S. government and the state of Florida would normally be doing if these men were white, and that is searching for the killers." Although the national publication reported that the organization's "findings indicate that the fishermen died of horrible foul play," no one produced evidence that substantiated SCLC allegations.[40] Local whites, particularly *Pensacola News Journal* editors, responded angrily to the charges and blamed black leaders of inciting racial unrest in Escambia County.

On the same evening that the sheriff's department released its autopsy results, the *Journal* published an editorial that deemed Abernathy a race-baiting "demagogue" comparable to ex-Mississippi governor and virulent racist Theodore Bilbo. "Every word (Abernathy) said," the essay continued, "was based on the same kind of rumor promulgated by some paranoid mind in this community every time there is the slightest mystery concerning the death of a black." The piece blamed "outside agitators" for their city's racial tumult, claimed that racism existed "on the part of blacks as well as some whites" in the area, and concluded, "only time will tell what harm [Abernathy] has done to the quest for racial harmony in West Florida."[41] Sheriff Untreiner expressed similar sentiments in a letter to Governor Askew. In contrast to what he told SCLC officials, Untreiner claimed he devoted "thousands of hours of volunteer work" and "thousands of dollars" to the case. He asked the local FBI office for assistance, the sheriff maintained, but they "refused to investigate the matter" due to a lack of evidence that suggested foul play. Untreiner concluded his letter to Askew by stating bitterly, "It seems to me very ungrateful that these people (Abernathy and Matthews) should be acting as they are." The *Pensacola Journal* published another editorial less than two weeks later that called SCLC allegations "a compendium of misquotes, suppositions, and rumors presented as facts" and blamed the organization of causing "these racial hatreds which have plagued the nation since its birth." The article concluded, "The tragedy is not yet over" because no one realized "how many whites will be pushed into the racist mold due to Abernathy and the SCLC's false accusations."[42] The reactions of Untreiner and *News Journal* editors indicated that they, and undoubtedly many of the Panhandle whites they represented, placed the burden of racial accord squarely upon the shoulders of black leaders. The Pensacola-Escambia Human Relations Commission, though, found an impartial investigation of the Atlanta Five case nearly impossible because of the intransigence that had already developed between white authorities and their African American critics.

The HRC's inquiry into the Atlanta Five situation found that the sheriff's department's lack of communication and refusal to cooperate with outside organizations aggravated an already difficult situation. Untreiner rebuffed all HRC inquiries regarding the case and the agency received information "as it was being released directly to the public." The lack of official cooperation allowed "rumor mongering and finger pointing" to dictate public discourse concerning the Atlanta Five, which allowed their deaths to "become another flash point" in an already polarized community. In the most objective, honest, and likely assessment of the Atlanta Five situation, the HRC "could not find enough evidence that there was a cover up" and concluded that the men died in "a horrible accident." Abernathy added the HRC to his list of groups that conspired to conceal the murders, but some local activists consequently tempered their support of the SCLC in wake of the HRC report.[43] Approximately two weeks after the men perished, Pensacola NAACP president B. J. Brooks called Abernathy's charges "untimely" because he made them before examining all facts in the case. "The charges of foul play," Brooks reflected, "should not have been made." New Escambia County SCLC president Otha Leverette likewise admitted, "I don't believe now there was foul play" and "I don't feel anything is being covered up" by local whites concerning the Atlanta Five. To Abernathy, such comments reinforced his belief that local African Americans feared white repression and lived in a racist county. Matthews never wavered in his public support of SCLC activities, but his stance on the issue softened as no new evidence surfaced. He also complained privately that Abernathy "did not help matters by coming in, making all of these loud proclamations, and leaving me to clean up the mess." Yet the minister never wavered from his claim that "Pensacola is one of the most racist towns I've ever been in."[44] His bold rhetoric and affiliation with the national SCLC reinforced Matthews's status as the most influential black leader in Escambia County during the mid-1970s and, consequently, made him the primary target of incensed whites throughout the area at the same time.

The Atlanta Five case, then, acted as a racial Rorschach test for a variety of groups and individuals in Escambia County—it exposed what each collectively believed about the state of contemporary race relations in Northwest Florida. Local whites viewed the case as the latest in a growing number of unjustified claims that racist activities, practices, and beliefs still permeated Escambia County. Abernathy and the Atlanta-based SCLC recognized the incident as an opportunity to reestablish the group as a leading civil rights organization, a status it lost rapidly after Martin Luther King Jr.'s 1968 death, and to rebound from the disastrous Philadelphia conference. The divergent responses of the county NAACP to SCLC claims concerning the Atlanta Five also indicated an increasingly fragile bond united the two local organizations. Although the Pensacola NAACP initially supported SCLC actions pertaining to the missing men, the former distanced itself from the latter's charges and ultimately repudiated SCLC claims within a month of the disappearances. The organization, Pensacola NAACP president B. J. Brooks claimed, used "suppositions and suspicions instead of solid facts" to conclude whites murdered the men.[45] The disagreement was the first in a series of events that would ultimately sever the once inseparable bond between the NAACP and SCLC in Northwest Florida. The Atlanta Five case, much like the controversy surrounding Escambia High School's Confederate imagery, also represented a power struggle against the perseverance of institutionalized racism in Northwest Florida that surfaced in ways which possessed different cultural meaning for those involved. Panhandle blacks, particularly H. K. Matthews and his supporters, viewed the Atlanta Five controversy as yet another instance in which racism characterized all interaction between African Americans and the local white power structure. Black citizens, they believed, had legitimate reasons to suspect foul play in the disappearances, but nothing they did prompted a direct response from the county sheriff's department. The failure of Sheriff Untreiner to address local black suspicions—much less modify his decisions or departmental policies—reveal the limitations African Americans faced when they tried to extend the civil rights triumphs of the previous decade into meaningful change regarding policies and practices that had contrasting cultural meaning for the races. The Atlanta Five incident, like the struggle over EHS symbols before it, heightened white resentment over the continuous assaults against cultural mores and rendered later black protests, no matter their merit, simply intolerable to their adversaries. The anger that each side held against each other carried over when another incident further immersed Escambia County in racial unrest. Black and white responses to the death of Wendel Blackwell, then, indicated that each group's patience with each other had finally expired.

CHAPTER FIVE

Who Shall We Incarcerate?

At 10:30 P.M. on December 20, 1974, an Escambia County Sheriff's Department dispatcher contacted officer Douglas Raines about an armed disturbance in downtown Pensacola. The operator told Raines a vehicle that contained two armed black male robbery suspects traveled in his direction. As Raines approached the crime scene, a car going in the opposite direction sped past his cruiser. Raines noticed that a black man, later identified as Wendel Sylvester Blackwell, drove the green Plymouth Fury. The deputy suspected that the speeding motorist was involved in the robbery, so he turned his vehicle around to stop and question the man. Raines's cruiser caught up with the Plymouth and signaled it to pull over, but the suspect refused and made several turns down one-way streets in an attempt to lose his pursuant. Blackwell nearly ran over another deputy, Roger Tyner, who stood outside of his cruiser when the Fury passed. Tyner joined the chase, which approached speeds of ninety-five miles per hour. Raines finally ended the fifteen-minute pursuit when he rammed the Fury on its rear bumper in an attempt to force it into Highway 29's wide grass median. The tactic did not work as planned, and both vehicles came to sudden stops in the middle of the highway.[1] What next occurred became the focus of intense debate.

Deputy Raines departed his cruiser as soon as it came to a full stop with his .357 magnum revolver raised at Blackwell, whom he repeatedly commanded to exit the vehicle. According to Raines, who talked to department investigators about the incident soon after it happened, Blackwell "reluctantly" exited his car while shielding the right side of his body. Raines ordered Blackwell to turn and place his hands on the Fury's roof, but he instead cupped them behind his head and continued to face the officer. Raines claimed that Blackwell made a sudden movement toward him with his right hand, which he dropped from behind his head. The deputy then shot the suspect in the forehead from a distance of approximately three feet. Deputies Tyner and Leonard Rogers, who joined the chase in its later stages, arrived on the scene as Blackwell collapsed to the ground. Contrary to Raines's testimony, Rogers reported that Blackwell exited his car "real quickly" as the deputy approached with his weapon drawn. Rogers heard the gunshot and "saw blood spurt from the man's head," but he never witnessed Blackwell move his hands in a threatening manner. Deputy Tyner also arrived at the scene in time to see the shooting but did not witness anything unusual about Blackwell's behavior. Tyner and a civilian passenger who rode with him saw Blackwell place his hands behind his head just before Raines fired and got out of the car to check on the deputy. He said that after Raines shot Blackwell the officer crouched over his fallen victim, walked to his car's rear bumper, and bent over shaking his head from side to side. As Rogers and Tyner tried to comfort Raines, Rogers noticed that Darryl Mumford, a civilian who accompanied Raines on patrol that evening, stood next to Blackwell's body holding a .22 pistol. Rogers assumed it belonged to Blackwell and instructed Mumford to drop the gun. With the exception of Doug Raines, every man present at the shooting first saw Blackwell's pistol when Mumford held it.[2]

An ambulance and numerous police officers arrived minutes after the shooting occurred. Sergeant Don Powell and state investigator Bill Lynch escorted witnesses to the sheriff's department, recorded their testimonies, and concluded that Raines shot Blackwell in self-defense. The department took no disciplinary action against the deputy and gave him two paid days off because of his "emotionally upset" state. Sheriff Royal Untreiner ordered no internal investigation of the incident and summarized Raines's action by stating that Blackwell "pulled the gun on him, his life was in danger, and he shot him." Untreiner remained unwavering in his support of Raines, despite the fact that a supervisor described the deputy in an annual evaluation as "uncooperative, fault finding, resents supervision, and a chronic complainer." Many local blacks, though, questioned the circumstances surrounding, and the individuals involved in, Wendel Blackwell's death.[3]

The victim's family expressed misgivings toward the sheriff's department's assessment of the incident for several reasons. They argued that Wendel had never before been in trouble with law enforcement and cited the absence of a criminal record to prove their point. Elaine Blackwell, like many other African Americans before her, described the county sheriff's department as uncooperative and even hostile to questions regarding her husband's death. Pensacola NAACP and Escambia County SCLC representatives tried to discuss the incident with Sheriff Untreiner, who angrily questioned "why every time some black was killed that he had to be bothered" by the two groups. The organizations launched a joint investigation into Blackwell's death, which raised additional questions. "We simply did not believe that Blackwell had a gun in his hand or that it was lying under his head when he fell," H. K. Matthews concluded. "Either Raines or his civilian rider," the reverend maintained, "put it there." The NAACP and SCLC demanded that Deputy Raines take a polygraph concerning his lethal actions, urged Untreiner to suspend him from duty until all investigations were concluded, and asked State Attorney Curtis Golden to launch a grand jury inquest of the killing. None occurred, which deepened black suspicions that a white conspiracy existed within and extended beyond the Escambia County Sheriff's Department.[4]

Blackwell's death, much like the Atlanta Five disappearances, had important ramifications for local blacks and meant more to them than an isolated fatality. It represented the pinnacle of local black apprehensions concerning county law enforcement officials and brought African Americans into direct conflict with the local white systems of control. Suspicions that the sheriff's department conspired to conceal the true fates of the Atlanta boaters inflamed the already blazing black resentment of police officers in the Panhandle, and those tensions reached a dangerously high level in the aftermath of Wendel Blackwell's death. As 1975 began, the *Pensacola News Journal* observed that the Blackwell shooting "is arousing more racial feeling in this community than did the drownings" because black leaders, particularly Matthews, used the incident to inflame the "hatred many blacks feel toward law enforcement officers" in Northwest Florida. "That hatred," editors maintained, "is fed each time a black is killed in a confrontation with the law because no matter what the circumstances, Matthews will term the death 'a racist murder.'" The animosity between black and white officials over both cases grew so vitriolic that Curtis Golden asked the Escambia-Pensacola Human Relations Commission to investigate and prepare a public report on the Blackwell shooting.[5] The state attorney's office hoped that the HRC's findings would mollify racial tensions, but the opposite occurred.

The HRC's activity increased in the months after Alain Hebert became executive director, but the conflict between the sheriff's department and black residents remained the organization's greatest challenge.[6] Although the white power structure in Northwest Florida established the HRC to minimize discord while preserving the racial status quo, Hebert believed his committee serviced the entire community and not a specific group of political or economic elites. When given a mandate to research the Blackwell shooting, Hebert used his office to conduct an objective investigation and offer conclusions that would improve county race relations. In the course of their inquest, commission members interviewed several people who were with Blackwell on the night he died, examined the witness statements and interview notes taken after the shooting, and reviewed many of the sheriff's department's relevant policies. The subsequent HRC report reached several important conclusions, the most important of which pertained to what happened in the immediate moments before and after Raines shot Blackwell. No one supported Raines's contention that Blackwell made a sudden movement and dropped his hands before he was shot. Three witnesses said that Blackwell had both hands above his head when Raines fired, and none of them saw a weapon in the victim's hand. Daryl Mumford, the civilian who rode with Raines, said the deputy approached Blackwell after he shot him and turned the body. Mumford approached the fallen body, saw a .22 "lying under the suspect's head," thought Blackwell survived the shot, and moved the pistol because he did not want the suspect to use it against anyone on the scene. Vickery and Rogers first saw the pistol when Mumford held it and both told him to drop the gun. Furthermore, the deputies moved their vehicles from the spot on the highway where they first stopped before investigators arrived. Mumford, according to the HRC, "contaminated valuable evidence" and the deputies compromised "all evidence present at the scene" when they moved their cruisers. The HRC also noted several inconsistencies between Raines's version of events and the statements that others made, and claimed "several questions" the state attorney's investigative staff used were "leading" and "affected the conclusions reached in their investigations." HRC executive director Alain Hebert maintained the Blackwell shooting did not happen in a vacuum, but that Raines "was very much a reflection of his environment" at the sheriff's department. As long as deputies "stayed within semi-legal confines," Hebert believed, they had "passive permission" to treat African Americans as they wished and "nothing was going to happen about it." The HRC's report, therefore, recommended a grand jury investigation of Blackwell's death and that Sheriff Untreiner transfer Raines to a position within the department that did not require use of a firearm until the review ended. State attorney Golden requested HRC assistance only to ignore its recommendations.[7]

In response to Blackwell's death, H. K. Matthews, B. J. Brooks, and Otha Leverette organized a series of mass meetings to coordinate local African American protests against the Escambia County Sheriff's Department. The meetings revealed several features that characterized the mid-1970s Pensacola movement. Most importantly, the assemblies demonstrated that the local African American church played an indispensable role in the local freedom struggle beyond the 1960s. Reverends Gooden, Brooks, Matthews, and Leverette provided both structure and direction for local blacks in their fight for racial justice. County churches also remained the headquarters of movement activities. The ministers held their meetings at the two largest African American churches in the city, Allen Chapel AME Church and Greater Mount Lilly Baptist Church, and they served as before and after demonstration assembly points. The importance of the church as a vital leadership and logistical institution in the black community is not surprising, as historians have long noted the importance of area churches in their movement studies. What scholars often neglect, however, is what the historian Michael Eric Dyson calls the "radical remnant of the black church" and the role it played in inspiring, motivating, and providing the foundation for community movements in the civil rights South.[8]

The "radical remnant," Dyson contends, is "driven by the belief that the universe belongs to God, that truth is not trapped in church sanctuaries, and that God transmutes hostile powers to achieve the divine will." This unique component of African American Christianity inspired visions of civil virtue and social justice among its adherents. Those who embraced the concept, Dyson maintains, "take on a more liberal theological outlet to combat black suffering, and eventually, class oppression." The radical remnant, in short, "tirelessly works to make politics reflect the justice that prevails in God's kingdom."[9] In 1959, Rev. W. C. Dobbins became the first black leader in Northwest Florida to use the theological argument to support his demand for social change. His teachings greatly inspired Matthews, who stressed the importance of faith during his tenure as Pensacola's most influential black spokesman. As his leadership abilities matured and white resistance in the Panhandle stiffened, Matthews depended even more upon the radical theology that had earlier characterized the ministries of Bishop Henry McNeal Turner, Bishop Alexander Walters, Rev. Reverdy C. Ransom, and, Matthews's hero, Martin Luther King Jr. Several surviving audio tapes document the importance of the radical remnant at key junctures in the Pensacola movement's organizing tradition.

Matthews used a tape recorder to document many of the mass meetings he organized and attended after the Blackwell shooting occurred.

He began the practice because the *Pensacola News Journal* repeatedly misquoted blacks, including himself, during the 1960s struggles and resumed the tactic during the EHS controversy. Matthews eventually taped SCLC press conferences, radio programs, and other materials that pertained to the Pensacola black freedom struggle. Approximately twenty hours of the recorded materials survive and they provide an account of grassroots activities that historians can rarely access. Most importantly, the tapes reveal that elements of continuity and change characterized the long civil rights movement in Escambia County. The centrality of radical black Christianity linked the struggles of the 1960s and 1970s, but the emphasis ministers placed on accessing, influencing, and altering the power that local systems of control exercised over the persistence of white supremacy beyond the legal or legislative realms represented a new feature in the movement's evolution.

The first mass meeting local ministers held after Blackwell's death occurred on January 2, 1975, at Greater Mount Lilly Baptist, the church where Reverend B. J. Brooks pastored. Brooks, Matthews, and Leverette organized the meeting to address both the Blackwell shooting and the intense racism that characterized the Escambia County Sheriff's Department. Each minister's primary goal, Brooks proclaimed, was to force Sheriff Royal Untreiner "to the conference table where we could discuss" Blackwell's death and "prevent this type of thing from happening again." Untreiner, though, refused to meet with the leaders, so Brooks announced that state NAACP field secretary R. N. Gooden had returned to Pensacola to help organize indigenous demonstrations and alter the department's discriminatory practices. Gooden, who had not been in Pensacola since the Escambia High School symbols dispute, attended the meeting and pledged to remain in the city until the Blackwell investigation ended. Each minister announced that the mass meetings, marches, and downtown demonstrations—tactics that preceded racial changes in the previous decade—would continue until the Justice Department and a local grand jury investigated the Blackwell shooting. The men also insisted that Sheriff Untreiner suspend Douglas Raines until the inquiries ended, force the deputy to take a polygraph test concerning his actions, and hire more black deputies.[10] The meetings represented much more than just a forum where black leaders aired grievances concerning and demanded concessions from the white establishment. They became the practical and emotional center of the revitalized Escambia County movement.

The tone and content of the 1975 mass meetings resembled a religious revival more than a political or civic assembly. The gatherings usually lasted over two hours and each of the ministers addressed the audience at different times during the evening. Congregation size frequently exceeded five hundred people and participants stood against sanctuary walls to hear the nightly messages. A minister always led the congregation in a number of conventional opening hymns such as "Leaning on the Everlasting Arms," "Pass Me Not, O Gentle Savior," and "Precious Lord." Traditional spirituals and "freedom songs" such as "Nobody Knows the Trouble I've Seen," "Ain't Gonna Let Nobody Turn Me Around," and "We Shall Overcome" were also popular selections. When the singing concluded, Brooks customarily recited a Bible passage concerning the night's theme and led the group in prayer. At one meeting, Brooks summarized the ministers' primary goal by stating, "Doug Raines has to leave the sheriff's department" or "we're going to close this county down." Yet Brooks warned that "if we drop the ball and forget about" Blackwell's shooting, "white folks are going to have a field day beating niggers' heads" in Pensacola. Matthews next addressed the congregations on a nightly basis and made announcements that pertained to recent developments or applied to future gatherings. Gooden most often delivered the evening's sermon, but Matthews and Brooks shouldered the responsibility at different times. Regardless of who delivered the nightly message, the theme remained the same: theirs was "a Holy struggle" against white supremacy in Pensacola.[11]

Matthews typically offered an introduction that reinforced the Christian nature of their actions before Gooden spoke to the congregation. Matthews called their meetings "spiritual meetings" and pledged "to tell God's truth" for "as long as there's breath in my body." He always reminded those in attendance that Christ Himself proclaimed the equality of all people and urged listeners, "Do not be afraid of doing right because God is on our side." The habits and practices of local white leaders, then, violated Christian principles. Religious reasoning superseded constitutional and legalistic arguments in part because laws did not regulate the changes African Americans desired. "If the church is not the place for peaceful protest" against racism, Matthews therefore asked, "then where is the place?" A reliance upon God, he ensured, guaranteed that "right will prevail." Gooden echoed the sentiment and proclaimed, "I feel good about the struggle because I know God is able." The popular hymn "God Will Take Care of You" also reflected the confidence blacks had in the righteousness of their campaign.[12] The theme of divine justification appeared most clearly in Rev. R. N. Gooden's sermons.

One of the first points Gooden stressed at the mass meetings was the need to transform their encounter with the county sheriff's department "into a revival." He declared that local African Americans "are in the throes of a confrontation with the white power structure" and that "justice and freedom in Pensacola are long overdue." The Christian faith offered the only hope for racial reconciliation in Northwest Florida for, as Gooden proclaimed, "The only way that the white man and the black man will be able to walk together is through Jesus." For the ideal to occur, blacks had to utilize what Gooden called "righteous pressure." He characterized the Pensacola movement as a struggle between "evil" and "righteousness," explaining that "We are living in a city and dealing with men who know nothing about God." Yet Gooden urged the crowd to treat whites as their brothers because all races "have the same Heavenly Father." He urged listeners to follow the examples of Martin Luther King Jr. and "another great fighter for freedom and justice," the Apostle Paul. Gooden also reminded the congregation that "love is the most dangerous weapon in the world," prayed publicly for the whites who oppressed them because "God changes people," and proclaimed that "God is in this movement." The Pensacola movement possessed an optimistic tone in its early stages because of the religious nature that characterized it.[13] The religious foundation of the mid-1970s struggle provides a significant degree of continuity between the decade's black activism and the local civil rights campaigns of the 1960s, yet references to the uneven power relationship between white authority and the racial minority represented a change—albeit subtle—in the movement's emphasis.

The *Pensacola News Journal* responded to the mass meetings with bitter criticism. The *Journal* published a January 8 editorial which decried Matthews, Brooks, and Ralph Abernathy, "their mentor," for fomenting racial discord in the county. Their latest commentary, though, singled out Matthews as the man the white power structure considered most responsible for Panhandle unrest. "Each time a black is killed in confrontation with the law," the paper claimed, Matthews "will term the death a 'racist murder.'" Editors also accused the outspoken minister of "trying to produce something out of nothing," "making unfounded accusations against law enforcement officers," and rendering racial cooperation "continuously more difficult." Editors admitted Untreiner could alleviate racial tensions by hiring more black deputies, but doubted any would apply because Matthews had demonized law enforcement officials for local African Americans. A later edition stated that the meetings, marches, and boycotts "serve no good purpose," "foment trouble among students at local schools," and "further divide the races" in Escambia County. To validate its insights, the *Journal* published a letter from Sheriff Untreiner that commended its "fine editorials" and efforts "to enlighten the people of this county about the whole matter." In spite of the inevitable criticism, the Pensacola NAACP began a selective buying campaign against downtown stores on January 11. Brooks asked area blacks to not buy from downtown merchants, to refrain from buying milk or bread at county groceries, and to instruct their children to not use the lunchroom facilities at county schools in protest of Blackwell's death. "We have to resort to whatever means are at our disposal to bring justice to the forefront," Brooks declared, because white authorities continued to ignore African Americans. As Matthews put it less delicately at one mass meeting, "If you want to hear the white man holler, squeeze the dollar!" The day after the boycott began, state attorney Curtis Golden empaneled a grand jury to investigate the Blackwell shooting.[14]

Jurors listened to nearly five days of testimony from forty witnesses involved in the incident. Outside the courthouse where the jury convened during what Gooden dubbed "showdown week" over the young man's death, African Americans carried signs that read, "Justice is Color Blind" and "Justice Now." Gooden reiterated that "nothing short of the removal of Deputy Doug Raines will satisfy us" and warned, "If this local Grand Jury does nothing we will camp on the capital grounds" in protest. Its decision tested the threat, for six days after it convened the Escambia County Grand Jury formally declared Blackwell's death an act of "justifiable homicide." Raines, the eleven-page report concluded, "acted in a reasonable and prudent manner" because he "believed himself to be in imminent danger of death or great bodily harm" by an armed Blackwell. Raines did nothing to inflame the conditions before the shooting and, therefore, could not legally be suspended for his action. The grand jury also stated that Sheriff Untreiner "acted lawfully in his handling of the investigation and could not be removed from his office" for any reason. The body recommended that the sheriff's department recruit, train, and hire more blacks and remove deputies from active duty with pay when involved in a citizen's death. Yet it also encouraged blacks to "make a concerted effort to ride with regular deputies under the Sheriff's Office present policy" so that they would better appreciate law enforcement duties and the dangers officers faced. Brooks called the report a "mockery of justice" and promised "a long struggle" for racial equality in the area, while Matthews warned ominously, "This is the last time a black man will be killed in Pensacola and nothing is done about it." R. N. Gooden called the sole black who served on the grand jury a "hand-picked establishment nigger" who "accepts what the white man says," and promised the decision would lead to local blacks "raising some hell in the streets." Over four hundred blacks gathered in downtown Pensacola to protest the grand jury's conclusion, and ministers petitioned Governor Reubin Askew for assistance at the evening's mass meeting. White spokesmen, on the other hand, praised the decision. Sheriff Untreiner said the findings "vindicated" his position, while the *Pensacola News Journal* stated that anyone "guided by the evidence and sound reason and judgment used in everyday life" would "have reached a similar conclusion." Paper editors fired yet another shot at black leaders by declaring, "We find it regrettable that some elements of the community, using emotion instead of reason, are not in agreement with the finding." Area residents, the essay concluded, "will just have to live with whatever these persons choose to do" until their "sense of reason returns."[15] While local attention remained focused on the grand jury's controversial conclusions, federal judges made a crucial decision regarding the dormant Escambia High School symbols controversy.

On January 24, the Fifth Circuit Court of Appeals lifted Judge Winston Arnow's injunction against Confederate images at EHS and ruled that he went "further than necessary" to ease racial tensions at Escambia High. Judge Paul Rooney wrote the majority decision and maintained that the court reached its verdict not because of racial concerns, but to protect school board sovereignty. The court also called its ruling inconsequential because Escambia High had adopted a new mascot and nickname eighteen months earlier. Rooney suggested the school board "might be better served by letting well enough alone" and not allow EHS to abandon its new "Raider" mascot and nickname, and he compared the battle flag to the Nazi swastika. The sole judge who voted against the verdict wanted the Confederate imagery at EHS immediately reinstated because a "threatening minority" of blacks intimidated board officials. The objecting opinion sarcastically noted that blacks would next "favor local ordinances making it a misdemeanor for a spectator to give a spontaneous rebel yell after Escambia scores a touchdown" or request that federal agents serve as school cheerleaders. In response to the ruling, Arnow gave the Escambia County School Board until May 1 to develop a policy governing symbols and nicknames at all schools.[16] The appeals court judgment, however, did not end the symbols controversy and it later resurfaced as a crucial tool of white resistance to black cries for equality. Yet few community leaders noticed the ruling because of the controversy that surrounded Blackwell's death. Their attention instead focused on the state capital.

Matthews, Brooks, and Gooden led approximately one hundred SCLC and NAACP members from Pensacola to the governor's mansion in Tallahassee on January 31 and held a candlelight vigil in memory of Wendel Blackwell. Thirty minutes after the silent demonstration began, Governor Askew agreed to meet with Gooden, Matthews, Brooks, Leverette, and Elaine Blackwell. They informed the governor during their hour-long meeting that violence would engulf Pensacola unless he suspended Raines and removed Untreiner from his position as Escambia County sheriff, a new demand. Leverette reported that many area blacks armed themselves for protection because they feared white police officers. "If another black is shot" by a white deputy in Pensacola, Leverette warned, "we are going to be walking in blood." Askew ended the meeting with no promises but the group returned to Pensacola convinced that the governor would intercede on their behalf.[17] Askew did contact Escambia County's Sheriff Untreiner in the days following the Tallahassee meeting and urged him to meet with area black leaders and open communications between the sheriff's department and the black community. Untreiner agreed to meet black representatives and scheduled a conference for February 21.[18] Black leaders celebrated the chance to finally air their grievances with a key component of the white power structure, but the most important consequence of the Tallahassee trip was the development of a new impediment to Pensacola activists—the state and national NAACP.

In the days leading to the Tallahassee demonstration, Governor Askew received word of the coming caravan and called Florida NAACP president Charles Cherry. Askew had worked with Cherry on previous issues and asked that he prevent the protestors from carrying through with their plans. Cherry asked Reverends Gooden and Brooks, both NAACP officeholders, to postpone their trip, but they ignored the request. Cherry reported the perceived insubordination to the national office and the "March on Tallahassee," as the NAACP called it, created a rift between the local and state offices that never mended fully. Although Gooden deemed the march a success because it captured the governor's attention and brought Royal Untreiner "to the conference table," Gloster B. Current, the national NAACP director of branches and field administration, reprimanded the field secretary for his endeavors. In a letter to Gooden, Current admitted, "I was a little disturbed that a local branch would undertake such a venture without the knowledge and authorization of the state and national offices." Current promised to monitor the Pensacola situation but warned "it will be most important that the state, regional and national offices be kept advised of prospective actions before they are engaged in."[19] Mistrust and suspicion thereafter characterized the relationship between the Pensacola NAACP chapter and its state and national supervisors for the duration of local protests. While the NAACP imposed its chain of command upon local leaders, black protests continued in Northwest Florida. Unbeknownst to them, the Escambia County Sheriff's Department had begun surveillance of African American activities.

From February 6 through 28, Sergeant Jim Edson filed daily field reports that documented black movement in downtown Pensacola. The reports recorded the nature of each gathering and noted their locations, the number of participants involved, and how long each demonstration lasted. Edson submitted his reports to Sheriff Untreiner, which indicated that the sheriff ordered his sergeant to monitor and document black actions. The surveillance reports, therefore, reflected the department's determination to terminate black activism and a concerted effort to quiet specific leaders. They also revealed that protests occurred at the county jail and courthouse complex on a nightly basis and grew more intense as white leaders ignored black demands. Edson noted, for example, that twelve blacks carried signs in front of the county jail for approximately thirty minutes on February 6. The next day, twenty-five blacks circled the prison and remained on the premises for nearly three hours. Edson wrote that thirty to forty vehicles circled roads that surrounded the courthouse blowing their automobile horns at 11 P.M. on February 11. The procession only stopped when several blacks gathered in front of the building and demanded to speak with Sheriff Untreiner immediately. Four days later, eighty to ninety blacks surrounded the county courthouse perimeter and on February 18, approximately seventy vehicles brought black demonstrators to the facility.[20] Edson's notes also revealed a change in the mood and tone of the continuing protests.

Edson called the earliest demonstrations "orderly," but his descriptions changed as the days passed. Whether the papers accurately recorded events at the prison, reflected Edson's imagined fears, or contained several blatant fabrications later became a matter of grave importance. The earliest field notes indicate only that black protestors carried signs and dispersed quietly after short periods. The reports grew more descriptive, though, as the demonstrations persisted. Edson identified Matthews and Brooks specifically as group leaders and wrote that they delivered speeches to the assemblies, led the protestors in songs, and conducted chants that demanded Raines's termination. He also wrote that African Americans hurled profanities and insults at officers as the protests continued. Deputies gathered inside the courthouse and sheriff's department building out of black sight on several occasions "in the event there would be any trouble." On February 19, Edson wrote that Matthews and Brooks led a chant which stated, "Two, four, six, eight, who we gona [sic] assassinate? Doug Raines, Sheriff Untreiner and all these deputies." The sergeant noted that the group leaders "pointed to the five members of the crowd control squad that were standing in front of the door." The following evening, Edson estimated that sixty-five automobiles brought 141 blacks to the premises who conducted "the most vocal demonstration that we have had at this time." Edson even lamented in his report, "Now they have gone to the practice of referring to us as pigs." Officers followed protestors home in unmarked vehicles after the ninety-minute rally to further monitor their activities.[21] The growing protests, therefore, revealed that blacks believed persistent demonstrations represented their only outlet to express disenchantment regarding the uneven balance of local power. The gatherings grew as white officials refused to acknowledge black concerns with Blackwell's death. Despite the escalating dissension, Governor Askew told his advisers that racial tensions in his hometown "are easing" and "are not as bad as some people say."[22] The February 21 scheduled meeting between Untreiner and black leaders supported Askew's contention, but the proposed forum never occurred.

A lack of communication between black spokesmen and white officials again stymied efforts to resolve their differences. The conference failed, in short, because Brooks, Matthews, and Gooden never agreed with Untreiner's proposed meeting time or location. The sheriff wanted to meet with black leaders in the early afternoon, but most of their supporters worked during those times. Untreiner also scheduled the assembly at the Escambia County Health Department auditorium in a

African American protestors, with H. K. Matthews front and center,
confront Escambia County sheriff's deputies, 1975. © Tampa Bay Times/
ZUMAPRESS.com.

debatelike setting before an audience. Matthews feared that Untreiner
would avoid the primary issues and force them to answer questions from
hostile whites at the assembly. He suggested a closed evening meeting
between leaders at a local church. Untreiner never responded to Matthew's request, and appeared at the auditorium as planned at 3 P.M. State
attorney Curtis Golden, two representatives from the governor's office
in Tallahassee, and *News Journal* reporters accompanied Untreiner to the
meeting. When no African Americans appeared, Untreiner used the forum to criticize their leaders, motivations, and tactics. He told those present that he and Golden had responses to black concerns "but they are
not the answers these people want to hear." Gooden, Matthews, and Leverette informed approximately two hundred people of the day's events
at a mass meeting later in the evening. Matthews, as usual, most clearly
articulated black anger. He attacked the *News Journal* for fomenting racial hatred and said its editors "pounce upon every opportunity they get
to bring attention to the fact there are people in the black community
who disagree with Matthews, Gooden, and Leverette," despite the fact
"we speak for more black people than anyone else in the community."
Matthews's speech became more impassioned with each injustice recited.
He ended the meeting by leading those present in another protest to the
Escambia County Sheriff's Department.[23]

According to reports that two deputies at the scene prepared, Matthews promised them that his group "would meet force by force" from white officers, "would take care of anyone that tried to stop them," and concluded another assassination chant by pointing at the squad leader and shouting, "And you too Jim Edson!" Although Matthews did not know it, officers at the scene captured the evening's activities on a tape recorder. Edson's reports cited Brooks, Matthews, and Leverette as crowd leaders, despite the fact that Brooks did not attend the particular demonstrations due to illness. Edson did not mention Gooden's presence at the rallies, which indicated a concerted effort by law enforcement officials to specifically quiet local activists. Edson's description further claimed that the protestors obstructed all access to the department, would not let deputies through the barricades, spat on and made obscene gestures toward deputies, and damaged police vehicles.[24] The officer's notes conjured images of a situation that verged on anarchy, even though deputies arrested none of the supposedly dangerous, potentially violent protestors. The sheriff's department, instead, decided to silence Matthews and his constant companion, Rev. B. J. Brooks, with force.

The night that forever changed the black freedom struggle in Escambia County, February 24, 1975, began as many previous evenings had. Local leaders held a mass meeting at Mount Lilly Baptist Church and led the congregation to their nightly demonstrations at the Escambia County Sheriff's Department, courthouse, and jail. Before departing the church, Brooks repeated his routine command for those "who thought they might become violent to stay home," for this group of almost five hundred African Americans represented the largest assembly on county property since the boycotts began nearly two months earlier. Once together, the crowd resumed their usual routine of songs, prayers, and chants. Black "marshals" that Brooks and Matthews appointed scanned the crowd as they did at previous demonstrations to ensure that no one possessed weapons or threatened officers. Some participants carried signs that proclaimed, "Raines is a murderer" and "Do away with Douglas Raines." One eleven-year-old possessed a sign that stated, "Blackwell: Gone but not forgotten." Sergeant Edson saw the placard and told the child, "Boy, you've got the wrong sign. Hell, I forgot the nigger the next day." Matthews prayed, led some songs, and directed group cheers through a bullhorn. The crowd chanted in unison, as they did during previous demonstrations, "One, two, three, four, five, we ain't going to take no jive," and "We're gonna stop, stop, the racist cops." Reverend Jimmie Lee

Savage later took the bullhorn from Matthews and led the crowd in a familiar chant which declared, "Two, four, six, eight, who shall we incarcerate? Untreiner, Raines, the whole damn bunch!" The night's demonstration grew so boisterous that prisoners housed in the county jail responded to the activity for the first time by singing, chanting, and pounding their prison bars in unison with those gathered outside of their cell walls. Although the crowd laughed, joked, and reflected a generally festive mood, white observers possessed different perceptions of the evening's demonstration.[25]

Deputies claimed that the crowd's mood darkened as the 11:00 P.M. shift change began. One officer claimed the "good-humored" rally turned "more hostile," "very threatening," and "frightening" as additional deputies arrived. Officers who tried to leave department headquarters when their afternoon shift ended claimed that the crowd congested each doorway so that no one could enter or exit the building. Protestors, deputies reported, even blocked driveways and would not allow sheriff's vehicles to enter or leave the premises. Those who made their way through the masses stated that blacks threatened, jostled, spit on them, and "took swings" at them with "billy clubs." Edson noted that several blacks possessed weapons, exhibited them "in a rude, careless, angry, and threatening manner," and displayed knives to intimidate officers. Deputy James Cardwell claimed that Matthews told him through a bullhorn, "Boy, we'll eliminate you too, if you don't straighten up," while others said that Matthews pointed their way after he repeatedly promised to "assassinate" them. Unlike previous demonstrations, Sheriff Untreiner personally observed the one on February 24 and claimed that Matthews told him, "If you try to stop us" from assembling, "there will be trouble." The crowd grew so unruly that Untreiner ordered Sergeant Edson to end the demonstration. Edson commanded all present to leave the premises and said everyone risked arrest if they refused. Because he claimed that that numerous people threatened him and his officers, Untreiner ordered seventy nightstick wielding deputies to dissipate the group ninety seconds after telling them to leave the premises.[26]

County deputies waded into the crowd swinging nightclubs and arresting anyone who offered the slightest resistance. "The entire incident," Edson wrote, "was over after twelve minutes." Many protestors received minor injuries during the melee and required treatment at local hospitals, despite Edson's contention that "there were no injuries reported to any of the crowd or the officers involved." One juvenile, for instance, needed stitches after an officer hit him in the head with a club, while two officers beat a seventeen-year-old unconscious as he tried to cross an adjacent street. Riot squad members also wrestled a young girl from her grandfather's arms to arrest the elderly demonstrator. Untreiner defended his officers' actions and explained that black militants led a radical mob to the station intent on storming the jail and hurting his deputies. Blacks who suffered injury, the sheriff explained, received them while running from the police, falling over each other, or resisting arrest. To support his claims, Untreiner said his officers confiscated six clubs, six shotgun shells, three knives, and a bayonet from the group, despite the fact that no one else saw the alleged evidence and deputies arrested only four blacks for possessing small clubs.[27] Sheriff Untreiner even commanded *Pensacola News Journal* reporters to help deputies apprehend and arrest demonstrators. Curtis Golden watched the events unfold and informed the newsmen that if they refused the order, police would arrest each of them. Untreiner also demanded that the journalists not report his order or describe the tumultuous scenes in their articles. Each complied and ignored the deputy-initiated violence. The next morning's paper declared, "No confrontation between officers and blacks" occurred and that protestors and officers outside of the jail "mingled" and "swapped light, playful banter" as the night progressed. Officers arrested thirty-four adults and thirteen juveniles on misdemeanor unlawful assembly and malicious trespassing charges during their sweep of the prison grounds. The *Journal* published the names, addresses, and charges of each African American arrested. In addition, Golden added felony extortion counts to the Matthews and Brooks charges the day after their misdemeanor arrests. Police witnesses accused the men of leading chants that threatened to kill Untreiner, Raines, and Governor Askew. The extortion allegations stemmed from the claim that Brooks and Matthews used a violent crowd to intimidate Untreiner into removing Raines from active duty against his will. The sheriff claimed to possess a taped recording of the chants that justified the felony charges. A commentator for the *St. Petersburg Times* called the additional allegations against Brooks and Matthews "a clever application of the law, and perhaps the only time that a felony extortion statute has ever been used to crush a civil rights demonstration." A local judge set bonds for Matthews and Brooks at $22,000 each because of the felony charges.[28]

Matthews viewed the extortion counts as another desperate attempt by the sheriff's department to intimidate and silence him, much like the

Escambia County deputies arrest African American demonstrators, 1975.
© Tampa Bay Times/ZUMAPRESS.com.

baseless charge of inciting a riot that he faced a year earlier. He anticipated some sort of retribution for the role he played in the nightly demonstrations, but neither he nor Brooks expected the mass arrests, the
"sadistic" and "blatant brutality" that deputies used against the crowd,
or the felony charges levied against them. Both men vehemently denied
using the crowd to force Sheriff Untreiner to do anything against his will.
Matthews also learned that after he posted his own bail, a local judge lowered Brooks's bail amount to $7,000. The NAACP produced the funds
needed to free Brooks and Otha Leverette, but not Matthews. After he
posted bail, Matthews promised, "There will be more protests and more
people coming to join us in our struggle for racial equality" because
"black people are getting sick and tired of being misused and mistreated"
in Escambia County. Untreiner, on the other hand, portrayed the black
leaders as revolutionary felons who threatened Raines, Askew, and himself with death.[29] The arrests, though, concerned more than a conflict
between the sheriff's department and leaders of two civil rights organizations. A popular local radio talk show demonstrated that the prison incident also evoked passionate reactions from many Pensacola residents.

On February 25, local radio station WCOA held a regular call-in program titled "Pensacola Speaks." The arrests dominated the hour-long forum, which revealed the monumental divide that separated the races in

Escambia County. White callers revealed three primary themes during the program's duration. First, they expressed unanimous contempt of the recent civil rights protests in their city and portrayed area blacks as violent insurrectionists. One caller claimed, "They are intent on making trouble" while another called black residents "terrible" citizens who "belittle our law." Second, whites praised local law enforcement for arresting blacks at the county prison the previous evening. A listener lauded the sheriff's department for "doing an excellent job," despite the fact African American leaders "are attempting to coerce law enforcement" leaders into acting against their will. One of the show's first participants set the tone for discussion by stating, "I personally believe that law enforcement agents last night acted in a proper way and they did a thing that was long overdue." County deputies, he concluded, "have tolerated these people long enough." Another male deemed the arrests "a good judgment" and surmised that if they had not occurred, blacks "would have put a bomb in the county jail." Many white callers specifically commended Untreiner for arresting "black troublemakers." One woman voiced her approval "that Sheriff Untreiner is at last trying to put an end to all this violence that has been going on" and called the arrests "a necessity" because, "We don't need any trouble in this community." One participant even defended the Ku Klux Klan and suggested the group become more active in the county, while another similarly warned blacks that "violence begets violence."[30] Finally, whites divulged venomous contempt for Matthews during the radio show. One reminded her audience that Matthews "was trying to start up a riot" at Escambia High the previous year and "was intimidating" white students who attended the school. Another declared Matthews a shameless self-promoter who appeared on local television station WEAR so often, "I thought he might be the owner of it." The most hostile call of the evening came from a white man who stated that Matthews "resorts to violence" only to "fill his collection plate on Sunday mornings." The caller further demanded "vital proof he is minister . . . because I don't think he is" one. The irate white continued that Matthews "cannot be a disciple of God but must be a disciple of Satan, otherwise he wouldn't be leading his people down the road of destruction." The man concluded his diatribe by calling Matthews "despicable."[31]

The same installment of "Pensacola Speaks" received a number of calls that came from local blacks. In fact, the show accepted only a few more calls from whites than it took from African American listeners. The black callers also revealed three elements concerning the nature of their struggle. First, they expressed their dedication to peaceful Christian principles while on the air. Their comments were much less hostile than those that came from their white counterparts. The first African American who spoke during the show assured whites that "peace is what we want," while he urged fellow blacks, "Let us march in prayer." Another believed "blacks and whites should get together and associate more" because "we've got to live in the world together." One woman expressed sadness with the state of race relations in Escambia County and said, "God doesn't want all of this to be going on." Others cited the Bible to conclude "People are people," while another declared, "I am calling for love" and "I pray to God we will have peace in Pensacola." The second theme that characterized black calls was that practical reasons explained their discontent. One individual, for instance, stated that the protests occurred because "there should be more black policemen" and "more black officials because we pay taxes and are American citizens," while another simply concluded, "Get the Sheriff out of there and all of this wouldn't be going on." Finally, African Americans expressed support for their embattled leader during the radio broadcast. One caller lauded Matthews for "doing a wonderful job" and "holding the black people together" in the face of such massive resistance. The caller also questioned white vilification of the reverend when "he's not putting hoods on his head" or "burning crosses in people's yards, which is really against the law."[32] Regardless of their subject matter, then, black callers remained calm and often reaffirmed their adherence to Christian principles in the local freedom struggle, which separated them from the virulent statements that most white callers made. One African American, though, did convey the anger and frustration that characterized white calls during the February 25 program. The call came from Matthews, who identified himself on the air before he addressed listeners.

Matthews telephoned WCOA after he heard the white caller question his ministerial credentials and speculate upon his motivations for organizing the black community. The same listener regularly called the radio program to criticize and ridicule civil rights workers, particularly Matthews. On this evening, the reverend had enough. He told the show's host that the person's constant attack of black demonstrators on station airwaves "is sickening to me." "If he's not man enough to let us know who he is," Matthews declared, "he needs to keep his mouth shut." He further told listeners, "I don't have to prove anything to him or anyone else about where I got my ordination," but he referred all who questioned it to his AME bishop. Matthews also reiterated once more that "despite what a lot of these racist people are saying," local blacks "are not involved in violence." Matthews concluded his call by telling the white "coward" who constantly "uses my name freely on the air" that "I love him too—just as much as he loves me." Despite the often heated tone of the show, the program host declared audience behavior "has been quite acceptable this evening." He expressed surprise that "I did not have even had to get near the edit button," which reveals that prior episodes had become even more heated when callers discussed local racial issues.[33] The February 25 installment of "Pensacola Speaks," therefore, is important because it demonstrated the colossal rift that existed between whites and blacks in Escambia County concerning the uneven balance of local power and displays the conflicting motivations each group had for their interest in the local struggle. The program also revealed that his arrest the previous evening had not tempered Matthews's resolve in confronting racism. The leader of the local movement, then, demonstrated no signs of softening his approach to racial injustices after the mass arrests. Such resolve made Matthews a courageous leader to some and a hated rabble rouser to others.

While residents addressed the local movement in public forums, the county judicial system joined the local sheriff's department to restrict black activism. On February 25, the circuit court issued an injunction that prohibited picketing on county property. Demonstrators had to remain on the perimeter of designated areas, maintain a minimum of ten feet between each person, and not block the entrances or exits to any building. Violators faced a contempt of court charge with no trial and immediate sentencing, while deputies in full riot gear guarded county facilities. Because the injunction served its intended purpose, Jim Edson discontinued his daily surveillance of black gatherings near county property on February 28. Despite the effort of white officials to establish a "police state" in Escambia County, Matthews organized the largest march to date through downtown Pensacola and scheduled the demonstration to take place on February 27. County law enforcement officials prepared for the gathering as soon as they learned of it from News Journal reporters.[34]

Sheriff Untreiner activated every deputy and reserve officer for duty during the demonstration, and instructed riot squad supervisor Jim Edson to prepare his twenty-man riot squad for the likelihood of violence. Untreiner equipped Edson's squad with small explosives that could kill anyone standing twenty feet from its detonation point and authorized their usage. Despite heightened uncertainties and the preparation for violence by black and white leaders alike, five hundred black and white demonstrators marched over a mile through downtown Pensacola during the demonstration. Gooden, Brooks, and Matthews delivered an hour-long address at Lee Square while approximately forty officers in civilian clothing mingled conspicuously in the crowd. Matthews urged the audience to "press for our constitutional rights against action we feel is unjust" and reminded them that "protests and demonstrations are our legal weapons to use against those seeking to oppress us and to attempt to deny us our freedom." Leaders repeated that "We want Deputy Doug Raines fired and in a chain gang," according to Brooks, for deliberately killing Blackwell. Gooden predicted that "violence is just around the corner" and warned that if the white power structure could not protect blacks, "we will destroy it and the system along with it." Governor Askew, Gooden promised the audience, "will not walk over the grave of Wendel Blackwell and into the White House." Police officers who monitored the gathering reported no violent incidents and left the downtown area two hours after the march began.[35] The large protest revealed that the February arrests did little in their immediate aftermath to discourage the black struggle for racial justice in Pensacola. Matthews, in fact, noticed an increase in both crowd size and enthusiasm in the mass meetings that followed the incarceration of their leaders.

Matthews, Brooks, and Gooden continued to hold nightly meetings at local churches to discuss black tribulations in the weeks that followed the February 24 arrests. They also led picket lines at selected businesses and led protestors around the sheriff's department in automobiles with their horns blaring. Several individuals acted as personal bodyguards for Matthews because he received numerous death threats during the controversy. They protected the Matthews home each night after someone threw a brick through a living room window. Armed black males also guarded church entrances during evening meetings and several possessed firearms inside the building. At the movement's peak, white downtown businessmen even offered Matthews a considerable cash sum to end the demonstrations, which he refused.[36] Sheriff Untreiner also intensified his efforts to end African American protests after February 24. He implored the state attorney general to file additional criminal charges against Matthews without success, and asked the Escambia County Commission for financial assistance to combat the persistent demonstrations. The commission gave the sheriff $30,000 to fund overtime bonuses for his depu-

B. J. Brooks (front left with bullhorn in his right hand) and R. N. Gooden (front, looking back), lead over five hundred protestors from Robert E. Lee Park to downtown Pensacola, 1975. The procession stretched over two blocks. H. K. Matthews (front right with bullhorn on his left arm), marches beside Elaine Blackwell. © Tampa Bay Times/ZUMAPRESS.com.

ties and purchase more advanced equipment for the riot control squad, which black leaders vehemently protested. County tax money, they argued, should benefit all citizens and not be allocated for use against a specific segment of the population.[37] African Americans soon took to the streets once more against the county sheriff's department, but their renewed anger had nothing to do with funding issues.

The tumult in Pensacola attracted attention from across the state and the *St. Petersburg Times*, like many other newspapers, sent a reporter to investigate the recent unrest. *Times* journalist Jane Daugherty interviewed riot control sergeant Edson as he prepared for the February 27 Pensacola march. He told her that he had prepared his deputies to play a game called "Selma." Edson described the rules as simply, "You grab a club and hit a nigger." He confessed, "Now I don't want you to think I'm a racist, I like black folks." In fact, he continued, "I'd like to have two of them in my back yard for the dogs to play with." He concluded that for his canines, "Niggers are better than Milkbones." Edson's remarks indicated that racial affairs in the county had reached potentially life threatening levels and involved issues much deeper and more divisive than a dispute surrounding the Blackwell shooting. The 1970s movement now clearly confronted the institutionalized racism that permeated white systems of control such as the county sheriff's department. The *Times* article that publicized Edson's incendiary words chronicled the area's history of racial unrest and concluded that "deputies know they can shoot blacks in Pensacola without fear of punishment." Yet Daugherty blamed many others for provoking racial unrest in Escambia County. She castigated local whites for ignoring black protests and not demanding that the sheriff's department at least suspend Raines for killing Blackwell. Daugherty also blasted the *Pensacola News Journal* for heightening city racial tensions by criticizing African American activities and ignoring white brutality. *Journal* reporters, the *Times* claimed, "openly report to the sheriff's department after covering protests" and allowed deputies to edit their stories. *News Journal* editor Bill Gordon admitted to Daugherty that his paper reported misleadingly low black crowd estimates and refused to cover most black meetings, demonstrations, and news conferences because he did not want to "inflame the situation" between area whites and blacks. Finally, Daugherty claimed the city's elected officials ignored the plight of area African Americans and only appointed "Uncle Toms" as black representatives on key advisory committees. The *Times* article ominously concluded that Panhandle blacks "are committed to seeing justice served here" at any cost, despite the stringent white resistance that desperately wanted to silence African American leaders.[38] Edson initially denied making any disparaging remarks against blacks, but later admitted that he made a comparison between Pensacola and Selma when Daugherty produced an audio recording of his comments.

On the evening after the *St. Petersburg Times* published its scathing report of the Pensacola crisis, the local SCLC and NAACP added Jim Edson to the list of people they demanded be terminated from the county sheriff's department and implored Governor Reubin Askew to intervene in the situation immediately.[39] Sheriff Untreiner defended his riot squad leader in the wake of the *Times* article and the charge that Edson "pronounced genocide on all black people in this county." A civilian, Untreiner surmised, likely made the negative remarks that Daugherty attributed to Edson, if anyone made them at all. Besides, Edson had committed no offense and "cannot be suspended or reprimanded without cause," despite the fact that the sheriff issued a 1971 directive that prohibited deputies from using racial slurs. Untreiner further declared

Edson "one of my best officers" and declared without irony that "I take pride in the way he handles himself during a crisis." Edson's past, Untreiner concluded, demonstrated "he is worthy of praise." Local television reporter Milt Derina supported Untreiner's office during a WEAR editorial concerning the incident and called Edson's comments "ridiculously minor."[40] Governor Askew proved no more responsive to black pleas for help.

Demands for the termination of Edson reached Tallahassee soon after the *St. Petersburg Times* published his provocative comments. Newspaper editors, civil rights leaders, and concerned citizens implored Askew to, at the very least, suspend Edson from his position. A letter from a white Panhandle resident called Edson "the shame of Pensacola" and cited the Escambia County Sheriff's Department as proof that Florida remained "two centuries behind" the rest of the nation in its racial progress. Even the *Pensacola Journal*, a bastion of white supremacy in the Panhandle, tempered its support of the Escambia County Sheriff's Department. The paper admitted that it initially dismissed the *St. Petersburg Times* report because they believed it "incredible" that "a deputy in a highly sensitive position would have the blindness to say such a thing in the presence of strangers, particularly news reporters." Yet the paper verified the quote with witnesses and acknowledged that Edson's words "understandably incensed" black leaders. The essay also criticized Untreiner and defended blacks for the first time during the period's racial unrest because the sheriff took no action against Edson for his statements. "How can we expect blacks to maintain any confidence whatsoever in evenhanded justice," *Journal* editors maintained, "when the man assigned to control these tense situations stands accused, at least by two witnesses, of uttering blatantly racist slurs?" The paper declared that officers must at least "maintain a public image of impartiality" when it came to handling racial affairs and wondered, "Where is the integrity of the sheriff's department when this situation is allowed to stand uncorrected?"[41] The reference of "image" over practices indicated the editors' primary concern. The Human Relations Commission and the Pensacola Inter Faith Council each implored Governor Askew to resolve the tension in his hometown. The HRC proclaimed that "racial issues in our city are getting out of hand and is [sic] about to become a national issue," while Executive Director Alain Hebert believed indicated that sheriff's deputies had Untreiner's "permission" to treat African Americans as second class citizens. The Inter Faith Council informed Governor Askew

Sgt. Jim Edson, 1976. Pensacola Historical Society Collection,
UWF Historic Trust.

that "black leaders have said from the beginning that *they* (emphasis in
original) want to sit down with responsible people in local government
and law enforcement," but the sheriff's department refused. The governor, according to the council, should use his office to promote "healing
and reconciliation" and force Untreiner to meet with area civil rights
groups. Askew, though, refused to intervene. The governor's general
counsel, Arthur Canady, maintained the state constitution prohibited the
governor from taking any action against Edson.[42] Askew's explanation
that he could take no action against a sheriff's deputy in Escambia County
is consistent with his previous inaction concerning racial unrest in the
Panhandle and further frustrated those who requested his assistance during the crisis. In an act of utter defiance to outside perceptions, Untreiner named Edson the sheriff's department's 1975 "Officer of the Year"
and awarded him a 5 percent "merit raise" because "of the way he handles all school and racial troubles—with excellent results."[43] While local
attention remained fixed on Blackwell's death and the conflicts that followed, a local grand jury released its report on the chaos that inundated
Escambia High twenty-six months earlier.

The grand jury that Golden assembled in the aftermath of the first
EHS riot made its investigation conclusions public on February 28. The
group focused on the Escambia High tumult but examined racial tensions in all county public schools. Although the grand jury concluded

that "a portion of" violent episodes in local schools "does have racial overtones," the report did not mention Confederate symbols or white resistance to integration as causes of school unrest. The grand jury, in fact, declared that "the citizens of Escambia County can take justifiable pride in the general harmony between the races in our area and that, despite some allegations to the contrary, most of our citizens of both races have accepted and welcomed integration with good will." The absence of "strict, no-nonsense discipline," the report documented, represented the most serious problem the county school board faced. The grand jury suggested the board establish alternative schools to separate "continual trouble-makers from the other students." The report implored the county "to increase security precautions, add security personnel where necessary and place increased emphasis on student discipline" until the school board established the alternative accommodations.[44]

The report on area school violence mirrored the monumental divide that existed between whites and blacks in Northwest Florida. The grand jury echoed white beliefs that a minority of malcontents, not racial strife, caused most of the upheaval in county classrooms. Their findings implicitly denied that racial agitation played any role in the campus unrest and did not cite white use of Confederate symbols as possible reasons for the troubles at Escambia High. African American students and parents, in other words, had nothing to complain about. Increased discipline, not action concerning school images that one group considered racially insensitive, would right all wrongs in the county system. The grand jury disclosures provided additional material that marginalized black activists and placed their leaders even more on the defensive, as the report judged the concerns of people like Matthews and Brooks as exaggerations, if not outright fabrications. The report provided yet another piece of official evidence to fuel white claims that black activists exploited the unfortunate series of events in Escambia County for their own selfish reasons and, along with the racist comments of Jim Edson, embodied the challenges and limitations the black freedom struggle in Northwest Florida faced in the era beyond integration. Even in a community like Pensacola, which possessed a tradition of protest against racial injustices that characterized much of the twentieth century, whites preserved their racial privileges in meaningful forms that withstood the legislative and judicial challenges the 1960s movement produced. Institutions that preserved the area's racial hierarchy, such as the Pensacola City Council, Escambia County Commission, school board, the state attorney's office, and sheriff's department, remained firmly under white control. These groups were the most instrumental in extending and protecting white supremacy into the 1970s and represent a manifestation of what Michelle Alexander labeled "systems of control" on a more common, pervasive level than she utilized. These white-dominated systems accommodated the basic changes that the movement produced and tolerated African Americans to an unprecedented degree, but they did so in ways that did not challenge or alter the existing racial status quo. Simultaneously, a belief that the legislative and judicial reforms of the 1960s ended discrimination and provided blacks the racial equality they demanded formed the foundations of a populist white conservatism that jealously guarded their status as a racial majority against perceived attacks. As time passed, the belief that persistent civil rights activism acted as an unwarranted, unjustified infringement upon their rights only strengthened. The retention of power and a popular conservative resistance combined to ensure that a robust, long-lasting, and multifaceted racism survived the 1960s in Escambia County. The persistence of practical segregation, furthermore, often occurred without the race-specific language that accompanied prior expressions of white racial superiority, which made Edson's comments all the more revelatory. Still, the sergeant's reprehensible remarks and the subsequent local response they elicited demonstrated both the endurance of white supremacy and the failure of traditional protest measures to alter the unequal power balance. The UKA capitalized upon the racial discord and growing white backlash against the Panhandle's long civil rights movement and formed one of the organization's largest and most active Florida chapters after Wendel Blackwell's death.

CHAPTER SIX

Opposition Familiar and Unanticipated

In the mid-1970s, the United Klans of America rose as a part of what historian David Chalmers termed the "fourth period revival" of the Ku Klux Klan and its related factions throughout the South.[1] Pensacola contained numerous elements that made the area "a potential hotbed for (UKA) recruiting." In the fall of 1974, then, UKA titan Charles E. Carroll met with fifteen people at Stokes Glass Company in Pensacola to officially form Klavern 109. The UKA established the klavern "to demonstrate and present demands for rights and objections of white citizens in the same manner as black citizens in Pensacola" and, more importantly, to "render assistance" and support to the "local law enforcement officers who have been the subject of many recent black protest demonstrations" since the Blackwell shooting. Within nine months, Klavern 109 became the state's largest and most organized UKA chapter, with approximately 350 members. A *New York Times* reporter called the klavern's establishment "the latest occurrence in a racial situation that has all the characteristics of the South in the turbulent days of the early 1960s" while Arthur Teitelbaum, leader of the Jewish Anti-Defamation League in Miami, stated the UKA "is probably no stronger anywhere in the deep South than in West Florida."[2] Perhaps most interesting, though, the klavern established a recorded telephone messaging system to recruit members and spread its alarmist propaganda.

Area resident and Klavern 109 member Bob McConnell started the "Voice of the Klan" to publicize the political, social, and economic views of white "rednecks" and "intellectuals" with "an element of humor" on a weekly basis. The messages were anything but comical and had specific purposes. First, the recordings denigrated and threatened local blacks. In particular, the messages identified H. K. Matthews and the Escambia County SCLC as the klavern's primary targets. Various Klan messages, for instance, called Matthews a "black felon" and identified his organization as one that "supports and encourages niggers guilty of wrongdoing." The "Voice" did more than just target and ridicule Pensacola's black leaders. It also broadened its hateful messages to address all "white-hating, tax-consuming, nigger parasites" in Northwest Florida. One message berated all "street niggers" who "terrified white ladies,"

Ku Klux Klan members surround a young African American prior to their May 24, 1975, march in downtown Pensacola. AP Photo/Mark Foley.

while another identified one "arrogant nigger deputy" as "a real smart ass" who "wants to make it with a white girl. Go ahead, nigger," the message warned, "Hell's not half full." Second, the recordings kept callers informed of local events from the perspective of Klavern 109. One diatribe stated that Escambia High School administrators refused to allow blacks onto bus number 36C because they previously smoked "so much pot that the white female bus driver became sick." The Klan claimed that black riders also "expose themselves indecently to the public, and throw missiles at cars and pedestrians." Out of retaliation for having their riding privileges revoked, "the driver was attacked with literally hundreds of eggs thrown by students and adults" African Americans later in the week. "The news media suppressed" the incident, the message claimed, "because niggers were involved. If white students had've planned this, it would have made headlines." The "Voice" also offered social and political commentaries on a regular basis. One message called commercials containing black actors "a Jewish device" to expose "literate and erudite" blacks to white viewers. The same recording mocked the appearance of African American actors in a sleep disorder commercial, saying "Have you ever heard of a nigger with insomnia? They can and will fall asleep like a hound dog under a tree." The UKA consistently attacked President Jimmy Carter as "that Jew-controlled monster from

Plains, Georgia" and informed listeners that "culture is non-existent in a nigger environment."[3]

The *Pensacola News Journal* found that "The Voice of the Klan" received an average of thirty-five hundred calls each week, including those from state and federal offices in Tallahassee, Miami, and Washington, D.C. Yet the recordings represented more than the incoherent ramblings of a sole racist who had an obvious penchant for hyperbole. The "Voice of the Klan" recordings magnify some important aspects of the extremist white response to Northwest Florida's long civil rights movement. First, the messages reveal that white supremacists still used the defense of white womanhood as a justification for their beliefs and actions, just as they did in numerous other locations throughout the South a decade earlier. It is telling that the "Voice" repeatedly referred to the driver of EHS bus 36C as "a white female" and attacked the hiring of black deputies because of their unrestrained desire for "white women." Historians have documented the importance of gender-based arguments to the preservation of white supremacy from Reconstruction through the 1960s civil rights movements but have not determined when, or even if, the defense of white femininity remained central to the Klan's post-1960s rhetoric. Surviving "Voice" recordings suggest that it did. Second, the anti-Semitic and antigovernment diatribes indicate that the fourth period revival of the Klan maintained a traditional hatred of blacks, but also reflected the group's realization of and frustration with their loss of perceived social control and growing cultural marginalization. Third, the "Voice of the Klan" exhibited the deep permeation of white resistance in Florida's Panhandle. Klavern 109 claimed that it had "trusted informants" within the Escambia County Sheriff's Department, PPD, and local media outlets. In addition, the group boasted that eighteen of its members worked at Pensacola and Escambia High as teachers and administrators. Klan representatives, the recordings claimed, "keep us well informed" of campus affairs. Black leaders repeatedly levied similar accusations. The presence of Klan sympathizers partially explained the semi-organized actions of white students who initiated several episodes of racial unrest at EHS. Whether their claims held some truth or not, the "Voice" remained a regular feature in Pensacola until whites successfully crushed African American activism in the latter 1970s. Finally, and perhaps most importantly, the "Voice of the Klan" and establishment of Klavern 109 represented both past oppression and continued resistance to meaningful social change in Escambia County. After Matthews announced that SCLC president Ralph Abernathy would return to Pensacola and lead another march through its downtown area, the UKA planned a demonstration of its own.[4]

UKA titan Charles Carroll returned to the Panhandle on March 14 and met with members of Klavern 109 and approximately twenty others who wanted to join the racist fraternity. Afterward, Carroll announced that on May 24, the day after Abernathy's return to the city, the klavern would lead a march through downtown Pensacola and hold an evening event at a nearby racetrack. Carroll made the UKA's objectives very clear during his press conference. "One race or the other," the titan maintained, "has to be assigned to be superior and that ought to be the white man." In an article that documented the emerging area Klan presence, the *News Journal* rhetorically asked, "What is happening to our community when . . . outsiders decide we have 'a good potential' for the revival of the KKK?" The editor wondered "Are we, as a community, simply going to let this situation drift out of control?" and implored local whites to "reject the Klan, no matter how bitter some of the actions of black protest leaders have made" them.[5] The caveat added to the plea that whites reject the organization's recruitment efforts shows that the *News Journal* blamed black activists for arousing the racial unease which allowed a group like the UKA to flourish in Pensacola. White perceptions of their actions notwithstanding, the Klan's preparations put the SCLC in a difficult position. The group could cancel its May march, which would undoubtedly please Klansmen and encourage the UKA to plan counterdemonstrations each time black activists held a public event, or the SCLC could follow through with its rally and legitimize, for many local whites, the UKA's subsequent activities. The SCLC decided to follow through with Abernathy's visit and downtown assembly.

As the Escambia County SCLC prepared for its showdown with the UKA and awaited the trials of those arrested at the county jail, it maintained picket lines near the facility and continued to hold mass meetings on an almost nightly basis. The mood of the meetings, though, changed after the jailhouse arrests. The optimism, moments of levity, and joyous outbursts that characterized prior assemblies disappeared. Anxiousness, desperation, and themes that bordered on despair characterized the spring messages. Consequently, their rhetoric became increasingly aggressive. Matthews encapsulated the change when he proclaimed at one mass meeting, "We're going to have to teach every cracker in this city a lesson. Every last one of them. There ain't no sense in playing tiddly-

Ku Klux Klan members light their torches from that of their local Klan
leader Charles Carroll (right) during a Pensacola membership rally, 1975.
AP Photo/John Lent.

winks with crackers and playing hanky panky with niggers." Brooks,
Matthews, and Leverette all admitted publicly that they carried firearms
in their vehicles for protection against white vigilantes and vengeful deputies. Brooks encouraged his followers to do the same and reminded
them, "It's not against the law to have a gun." To bolster his congregation's courage, Matthews told the story of one "cracker" who asked what
the preacher would do if he found a cross burning on his property. "If I
caught you burning a cross in my yard," Matthews replied defiantly, "I
would leave you there for evidence. And that didn't just go for that white
boy. That went for any black boy" who threatened him. Matthews's flir-
tation with militancy nearly became a steady courtship. He called his perceived aggressiveness "not an action, but a reaction" because the local
power structure left area African Americans with few alternatives.[6] The
controversial preacher bolstered the increasingly militant image of the
Escambia County movement when he invited a member of a nearby
organization to speak at a local mass meeting.

Marzine Emmett represented an organization from Mobile, Alabama,
called Neighborhoods Organizing Workers (NOW). NOW adopted a
similar stance to civil rights as Brooks, Gooden, and Matthews in that
the group demanded immediate social, political, and economic equality,
but NOW's methods differed greatly from those that the NAACP and

SCLC utilized. NOW advocated the use of force when confronted with violence and discouraged its members from resorting to nonviolent resistance when whites brutalized them. Emmett made those themes clear during his Pensacola appearance. He began his address by telling the congregation his name and admitting, "I think about raising hell with the honky every time I see him." Less than five minutes into his speech, he held up a lighter and stated, "These things were made for more than lighting cigarettes," which suggested that audience members use incendiary devices against their most ardent oppressors. He further declared that the "one thing a honky respects is violence" and advised area activists to arm themselves. Emmett even cited slave insurrectionist Nat Turner, whom he cited as a "bad nigger," as the ultimate example all black activists should follow. The NOW member claimed that he did not preach violence for its own sake and but did endorse "necessary violence." "I am just as peaceful as you let me be," he claimed, but "I am just as violent as that honky wants me to be." Emmett saved his most direct threats for blacks who undermined area activities. He estimated "that there is somebody out there that the white man downtown sent" to the meeting as an informant and promised, "Somebody here's going to get hurt." The message concluded after Emmett pledged, "If I ever found out that was a black man that was going to those white people and telling them what was going on, I'd take care of them." The NOW representative received a very reserved round of applause from the congregation when his address ended, which differed tremendously from the rousing cheers they showered upon Matthews and Gooden at the same point in their sermons.[7]

Still, Emmett's address affirmed that the tone, mood, and atmosphere of the Pensacola mass meetings became more combative as 1975 progressed and demonstrated that blacks possessed no innate predisposition toward nonviolence when protesting the continued suppression of their perceived rights. The use of violence against their oppressors, even if impractical, remained an option available to blacks and highlights the significance of continued nonviolence during the years beyond integration in Northwest Florida. Matthews was militant in language but nonviolent in practice; an intriguing combination that continued the work of scholars such as Timothy Tyson, Emilye Crosby, and Akinyele Umoja to extend understanding of movement leadership beyond the seemingly contradictory and reductive "black power" and nonviolent dichotomies.[8] The black freedom struggle in Pensacola demonstrated that armed self-protection, inflammatory rhetoric, confident self-assertion, and non-violence coexisted and often reinforced each other during post-1960s freedom struggles at the local level. Panhandle blacks expressed discontent in ways that whites interpreted as threatening and dangerous, but they adhered to the nonviolence their leaders advocated. Divisions among African Americans in Escambia County exacerbated the anger and frustration that movement leaders increasingly expressed as their protests continued without relief.

Matthews, Brooks, Gooden, and Leverette expected whites to oppose their activities, but they did not anticipate resistance that they believe came from within the black community. Each minister held particular contempt for upper-class black professionals, particularly educators and those the city and county employed, whom the ministers blamed for undermining the local movement by their lack of public support. The men labeled such blacks "class niggers," "Uncle Toms," and "high-stepping, half-breed niggers" at their mass meetings. During one session, R. N. Gooden addressed "the seething unrest in Pensacola" that existed between its black citizens and predicted "that the ultimate outcome of this struggle will be violence in the streets" between them. Gooden envisioned "burnings, lootings, firebombings, shootings" and other unrest engulfing the city and stated, "I pray to God that if it happens, it doesn't happen to the masses but to the classes." If movement activities resulted in any deaths, he continued, "I hope it happens to one of our class niggers" who are formally educated yet "ain't got sense enough to realize what's been going on about our struggle." Gooden proclaimed on another occasion that cowardly blacks proved just as dangerous to the county movement as white racists. He summarized the concern one evening by asking the congregation, "Will you be an Uncle Tom or will you be a man?" and remarked after a particularly scathing Brooks sermon, "This kind of message should have converted some Uncle Toms."[9] Gooden and Brooks demonstrated a growing irritation with black elites, but their anger did not equal the rage Matthews expressed toward the same general sense of class-based abandonment.

It infuriated Matthews that the few blacks who reaped the benefits of past activism criticized activities that aimed to extend the same rights to all African Americans. The NAACP and SCLC, he maintained, opened opportunities for black economic, political, and social advancement years earlier in Northwest Florida. Yet when the organizations spoke against the institutionalized racism that permeated the county's sheriff's department and school system, blacks who could assist the movement either became silent or privately condemned the campaigns. Group unity served as one of Matthew's primary themes at the post-arrest mass meetings, as he often reminded congregations that "until all black folks are free, no black folks are free." Many black elites, though, undermined the solidarity Matthews desired in various ways. Some canceled their SCLC and NAACP memberships or shopped at downtown stores that black activists boycotted, which damaged the movement economically. Others criticized the movement's leaders and accused them of manufacturing racial tensions and using the subsequent conflicts for their own selfish interests. "The black intelligentsia," Matthews proclaimed, "looked down their noses at us, the uneducated" because "we made them uncomfortable and threatened what they had," even though they possessed their economic and social status "because of folks like us who put their necks on the line." Matthews acknowledged during one mass meeting, "There are some of you down there who are downgrading us up here. We may not be what you want," he admitted, "but we're all you have got right now." Escambia County blacks had only two things to depend upon—"each other and God."[10] Interestingly enough, movement leaders never singled out individuals or specific examples of subterfuge that black professionals committed against their campaigns. It is quite possible that their perceived enemies simply feared white retribution, particularly job loss, if they publicly supported the greater freedom struggle or that they simply disagreed with the tactics ministers employed to protest racial grievances. Nonparticipation did not always constitute opposition, but the stakes were such that those in leadership positions perceived it to be the case. Their struggle for racial equality necessitated African American unity, so movement leaders held great disdain for members of their own race whom they believed disparaged area campaigns. The 1970s Pensacola movement, then, revealed the class-based tensions that existed within the African American minority as well as the hostility that divided whites and blacks in Northwest Florida. Indeed, the response of the African American professional class to racial inequity after the public demonstrations ended assumed a very different form from those the black masses utilized at the movement's apex.

Even in the throes of complete frustration, though, the leaders of the Pensacola movement never completely abandoned nonviolent strategies or their appeals to the radical remnant of the African American church.

The mass meetings retained their revival-like atmosphere; ministers still led the congregations in spirituals and hymns, and individuals continued praying for both the activists and their adversaries. The foundation of the Escambia County struggle, therefore, remained the black church even as the rhetoric of its ministers became more bellicose. Gooden reminded parishioners that "without God, none of us will survive" a confrontation with the local white power structure, while Matthews declared, "The gains we have made have been because God has been in the movement." The long civil rights movement in Pensacola, then, demonstrates that the line between nonviolence and militancy in racial conflicts is not as clear as popularly perceived. The idea of using weapons to "fight back" when assaulted during the 1970s was "tempting," Matthews claimed, but "there is a time when common sense must come into play. Whites wanted any reason to crush the movement and violence would have given them the license to do just that." In addition, the decision to remain nonviolent was a practical one. "You can't fight a tank with a pea shooter," Matthews reasoned. A violent showdown between African Americans and white officials in Pensacola "was a war we could not have won. The other side had everything going for them" but "we had nothing but momentary rage. We would have never had a chance to survive."[11] The coexistence of nonviolent direct action and willingness to defend home, community, and leaders with force characterized the Pensacola movement during the 1970s, as it did in numerous other southern cities.

Yet while nonviolent philosophies and tactics worked against de facto forms of discrimination in the 1960s, they did not alter the power imbalance that characterized race relations during the 1970s. B. J. Brooks experienced the pervasiveness of institutionalized white supremacy when the Florida Department of Transportation suspended him without pay on March 21 for "conduct unbecoming a Department of Transportation employee." The department's county supervisors conducted no investigation into the charges, but cited a Florida law that banned anyone accused of a felony from state employment to justify the decision. The FDOT promised Brooks automatic reinstatement upon an acquittal and immediate termination if convicted. The national NAACP called the suspension "an act of discrimination and a complete mockery of our system of justice," while Brooks questioned why the department waited a month after his arrest to suspend him. He argued that he had never been convicted of a crime nor received due process and pled, "This is practically my whole livelihood they're playing around with." He appealed the decision to the Escambia County Career Service Commission less than two weeks after he received it.[12] The Brooks suspension, in short, came at a critical time in the Escambia County civil rights struggle and perpetuated the mistrust that existed between black leaders and state authorities. Whether or not the state intended to send Brooks a message with the suspension, he interpreted it as such and publicly vowed to decrease his activities in the Pensacola movement. As a result, the black community lost a valuable leader during an important juncture in their struggle. The FDOT decision also validated the fear of white retribution that likely deterred black professionals from becoming more involved in the local freedom struggle. If one of the community's most public proponents of racial equality could potentially lose his job with a state agency, the same could happen to African Americans in much more anonymous and less financially secure capacities. Gooden and Matthews, despite the significant setback, promised the SCLC and NAACP would continue their struggle for racial justice in the area. Yet what the two ministers did not realize is that the NAACP national and state office planned to fully withdraw all support from the Pensacola movement.

The NAACP's defense of Brooks at a time when the organization planned to abandon Pensacola appears contradictory, but such was not the case. Indeed, Brooks's suspension and delicate financial situation strengthened the position of the national and state offices because it gave them unprecedented power over county NAACP actions. Simply put, Brooks had to obey NAACP dictates as long as the national office funded his legal employment struggles. This uneven power relationship had a tremendous impact on racial affairs in Florida's Panhandle, as the national NAACP office placed its interests above the needs of those who participated in the local struggle.

The rift between the state and local NAACP that developed after Gooden and Brooks led their pilgrimage to the governor's mansion on January 31 grew after the February 24 arrests. The primary reason Florida NAACP president Charles Cherry wanted to distance his organization from the Pensacola movement was the presence of Matthews. Cherry wrote a letter to Gloster Current on March 6 and explained his interpretation of the Escambia County situation to the national office. Cherry admitted that Pensacola blacks needed help from their group because "it is a very conservative town, to say the least, and has a long history of unsolved crimes committed by whites against blacks." Yet Cherry believed the NAACP could provide only limited assistance in the area. "The black leadership has been diluted," he wrote, "because the Regional Coordinator of the SCLC, Rev. H. K. Matthews resides in Pensacola." Cherry described Matthews as "the most vocal, outspoken, and perhaps the most articulate Black Civil Rights leader and minister in" the area and an impediment to NAACP goals. His methods seemed too radical for Cherry, who claimed Matthews "refused to work with Brooks" and the NAACP office. The state president also reported that Matthews's "credibility has been questioned and attacked by the community on several occasions" and "ministers and other leaders . . . have been non-supportive of the Pensacola movement." Cherry concluded his erroneous observations on the Pensacola struggle by stating, "Most of the ingredients exist in Pensacola for a good branch. Organization, however, is lacking. Rhetoric and emotional appeal, as has been provided during the past 10 weeks, is not what is needed."[13] State and national NAACP leaders, therefore, refused to intervene fully in the Pensacola movement while Matthews remained the area's foremost black spokesman.

While the state and national NAACP conspired against them, the Escambia County SCLC maintained campaigns against the sheriff's department. A group of organization members awaited Governor Askew's arrival at the Pensacola airport upon his visit to a chamber of commerce event on April 2 to personally request his intervention in their struggle against Untreiner's regime. The governor's plane, however, landed at a private airstrip elsewhere in the county. During his speech later that evening at Scenic Hills Country Club, Askew ignored the area's simmering racial unrest. The numerous heavily armed, bulletproof vest–wearing sheriff's deputies reminded those present of the violent possibilities that permeated Escambia County. Local SCLC leaders reacted with anger and disappointment to Askew's insulation and his refusal to intervene in the city's racial affairs. Matthews called Askew's actions "a deliberate avoidance-of-blacks tactic," while Otha Leverette wrote a letter to the *Pensacola Journal* that called Askew's inaction "an outrageous act of cowardice."[14]

Despite his progressive stance on racial issues and popularity among black voters, Askew refused to upset the racial status quo in Escambia County. He considered the conflict a "local matter that local people should handle" without relying on outside intervention. The governor remembered the Pensacola episode as "a very explosive situation" that "I did not want to complicate" with "outside interference." Besides, he believed that Untreiner needed no assistance resolving local problems because he "was one of the better sheriffs in Florida" at the time. The governor also claimed that his inaction did not represent a desire to silence leading activist Matthews, whom he knew since the 1960s and considered a personal friend. He expressed reservations to his advisers concerning Matthews's felony charge because the extortion and death threat allegations "were out of character for H. K." Askew's later actions concerning Matthews's case validated the claim that he did not agree with the initial verdict. The reason or reasons that Askew failed to pursue racial peace more aggressively in Escambia County, therefore, remain speculative. Scholars, however, must take one crucial factor into consideration when examining the issue: Askew had decided in 1975 to pursue the Democratic Party nomination for the presidential election of 1980.[15] Becoming involved in the political minefield of race relations in Pensacola possessed the potential to sabotage Askew's national campaign before it began. Any decision he made in the affair promised to alienate one group of voters, which Askew could not afford to risk with his vast aspirations. Whatever his reasoning, though, Askew's refusal to act decisively during the racial crisis that engulfed his hometown tarnishes his progressive image.

The absence of Reverend Brooks and the Pensacola NAACP in protests following the minister's job suspension also weakened the Escambia County black freedom struggle. After the FDOT suspended Brooks, state NAACP president Charles Cherry convinced him to publicly repudiate the activities of Matthews, Gooden, and Leverette. Less than a month after losing his job, Brooks publicly distanced the NAACP from Matthews and the SCLC, declaring, "I can no longer support the ideas and philosophies of the present leadership of the protest." He explained that Matthews and Gooden "do not have the interest of our people at heart" and called their tactics "underhanded." Brooks summarized his decision by stating, "It is not the policy of the NAACP to encourage citizens to break the law, and it is not the policy of the organization to castigate citizens for non-involvement," ploys he claimed the others embraced. Brooks asserted that Matthews and Gooden "want to blow this thing up" in Pensacola despite NAACP pleas to the contrary. He denied that the Department of Transportation suspension influenced the leadership split, but the NAACP provided legal counsel for Brooks and pledged to overturn his suspension. It is doubtful that the organization would have expended time and resources on a person who remained closely allied with someone it considered anathema to their philosophies.

Regardless of his reasons, Brooks pledged that the Pensacola branch would shift its struggle against racial injustice from the city's streets to its courtrooms and "take no part in future protest marches and demonstrations in Pensacola."[16] Neither Matthews, Gooden, nor Leverette publicly responded to Brooks' declarations. The organization continued to subvert the Escambia County campaign when it took action against another key leader.

On May 2, the Florida NAACP dismissed R. N. Gooden as its field director. According to state president Charles Cherry, the NAACP terminated Gooden because it demanded their representatives "use more negotiation and less demonstrations" in communicating with white leaders in Pensacola. Gooden, though, defied the recommendation, organized mass protests, and "defected to the SCLC." Cherry cited the fact that the NAACP paid for none of Gooden's seventeen documented trips to Escambia County as proof that the minister received payment from the rival organization, thus abandoning his responsibilities to the NAACP. Cherry denounced Gooden for joining SCLC activities because the organization advocated direct action protests, while the NAACP utilized legal maneuvering and private negotiations to achieve racial harmony. Instead, the Escambia County NAACP "has had nightly marches and other direct action" protests and, according to Cherry, "we feel that is wrong."[17]

National NAACP official Gloster Current endorsed Cherry's decision and deemed Gooden's actions "extremely covert," although no one from the national office met with Gooden or presented him with evidence that he had broken NAACP regulations. Gooden also stated that he, not the SCLC, paid for his Pensacola trips and noted that he served the NAACP without pay while a minister in Tallahassee since he became state field director in 1972. Gooden maintained his dismissal occurred "for reasons other than those submitted by Mr. Cherry" but did not explain the comment. The public battle between Gooden and Cherry had an immediate impact upon the Northwest Florida movement, as Gooden returned to Tallahassee following the rift.[18] Interestingly, Brooks protested Gooden's dismissal as state field director. He explained in a letter to the NAACP board of directors, "Rev. Gooden is the most vocal voice for the NAACP in Florida" and his dismissal "ought not be tolerated by the national office." If the decision stood, Brooks argued, "the NAACP will be the loser in Florida and the SCLC would most certainly take advantage of this articulation and ability to corrale [sic] people." Brooks concluded his passionate note by accusing president Cherry of being "remiss in his duties by not rendering assistance to the Pensacola branch. We pay our assessment and feel that we are entitled to whatever assistance the Conference can give."[19]

The correspondence demonstrated that a division existed both within the NAACP and between it and the SCLC. The fact that Brooks so harshly criticized Cherry following his earlier recommendation to distance himself from Gooden and Matthews suggests that Brooks did not fully agree with the order. It is very likely that the state office used Brooks's employment situation against him in their mandate to separate their branch from the controversial Pensacola ministers. Brooks needed the NAACP to provide counsel for his FDOT appeal and his upcoming felony trial. He had a chance to express his frustrations with Cherry when he dismissed Gooden, and Brooks took advantage of the opportunity. He used the NAACP's struggle with SCLC to justify his anger and maintained that the rival organization would use Gooden's situation to their potential advantage. Basing his criticism on the best interests of the NAACP, Brooks remained loyal to the national office and protected himself from the abandonment Matthews and Gooden experienced. Still, the letter illustrates that tactical and philosophical divisions embittered relationships within groups as well as between leaders of competing organizations. The dissensions within the NAACP and its national office and SCLC peaked in the days leading to the felony trials of Brooks and Matthews. The two pled not guilty to the extortion charges on April 17.[20]

On April 30, county court judge Walter Lagergren tried twenty-three blacks arrested with Brooks and Matthews on misdemeanor counts. The jury found all guilty of trespassing and seventeen guilty of unlawful assembly at the sheriff's department on February 24. The judge delayed sentencing while NAACP defense attorney Ed Duffee appealed the verdicts.[21] Matthews appeared alone before the court approximately a week later to face his misdemeanor charges, and an all-white jury found him guilty of unlawful assembly and malicious trespassing. Judge Lagergren sentenced Matthews, who he deemed "a troublemaker" that "needs to be in jail," to sixty days in prison on each count. The judge denied bail because Matthews "would continue to make public announcements that will cause anxiety and unrest in the community," and gave the pastor twenty-four hours to turn himself in to local authorities. The circuit court reversed Lagergren's denial of bail, and Matthews missed the incarceration deadline by twelve minutes. Despite his near jailing, the

SCLC maintained plans to march with Abernathy through downtown Pensacola on May 23 and invited individuals from around the region to participate.[22] While SCLC prepared for the demonstrations, the Escambia County School Board announced a new policy regarding another divisive local issue—the images at Escambia High School.

The board revived the EHS Confederate iconography debate during its April 30 meeting. Approximately three months earlier, the Fifth Circuit Court of Appeals overturned Arnow's permanent injunction against the symbols and gave the county school board sole authority concerning their fate. Yet instead of keeping the Confederate images out of EHS as the courts suggested and black leaders desired, the board proposed another student mascot and nickname vote. Whites who attended the meeting expressed such passion concerning the topic that the board called city police to maintain order during their proceedings. Judge Arnow reluctantly endorsed the second vote but stipulated the board first explain their decision at a public forum. Most of those who attended the July 9 session criticized the proposed election, albeit for different reasons. Leverette, the only local SCLC or NAACP official who attended, argued that a majority vote meant certain victory for "Rebel" proponents because African Americans still constituted a minority of the EHS student body, while white speakers claimed the appeals court's decision meant the board should reinstate all of the Confederate imagery immediately. After several hours of contentious debate, the school board formalized its original plan—a student vote would reinstate both the school nickname and use of the Confederate battle flag if two-thirds of those who cast ballots approved the controversial images. Until the vote occurred on an unannounced date during the 1975–76 school year, "Raiders" remained the EHS mascot. The compromise satisfied few in attendance, but each side believed the provision guaranteed them victory.[23] While the drama surrounding the symbols at EHS mounted, a much more public confrontation between the races occurred when African American activists and white supremacists gathered in Pensacola on consecutive days.

SCLC president Ralph Abernathy returned to the city as planned on May 23 and led 250 protestors to the Escambia County courthouse, where participants chanted "Stop racism in Florida." Abernathy and SCLC national communications director Tyrone Brooks addressed several topics during the hour-long rally. First, they discussed the circuit court's February 25 injunction against protesting on county property. No other county in the nation existed, Abernathy claimed, "where a judge has the tenacity to issue an injunction" that prohibited citizens from "exercising their first amendment right" to congregate "in peaceful, orderly protest." As Brooks declared, "ain't no foolish cracker judge going to tell us when we can march, where we're going to march to, what time we are going to march, how many we're going to have in the march, and how we want to march. That," he, concluded, "ain't SCLC." Second, Abernathy focused on the pending trials of Brooks and Matthews, two "nonviolent people" whom deputies arrested for "exercising their constitutional and God-given rights." The charges, Abernathy joked, indicated that white officials "aren't even intelligent enough to know what 'incarcerate' means. They get it mixed up with 'assassinate.'" Besides, "we don't have to assassinate Governor Askew" over the racial injustices that permeated Northwest Florida when "we can tell Jesus about it." Tyrone Brooks was particularly concerned with the continued local support of Matthews, whom he described as "for real" and someone who "ain't going to sell them out for a dime." SCLC, Brooks declared, supported Matthews, Gooden, and Leverette "one thousand percent" and would "tolerate no movement where people cannot respect their leaders." Brooks told the assembled to "get out of the movement" if they could not support county SCLC officials. Third, both Tyrone Brooks and Ralph Abernathy acknowledged the division that existed between the NAACP and SCLC. Brooks said that problems between the groups could be settled "behind closed doors" and warned that SCLC would tolerate "no more backstabbing" for organizational advancement. Abernathy was much more conciliatory than his communications director and confessed that he remained a lifetime NAACP member even as SCLC president. The two organizations, he declared, were not enemies. "Let's get together and iron out our differences," he told local NAACP officials, because "we don't have anything against you." The split "between this handful of black people who love freedom" but belonged to different organizations in Pensacola, Abernathy forcefully proclaimed to rousing applause, "ain't nothing but a bunch of crap!" The NAACP and SCLC had to unite in Escambia County or "you are all going to wake up and discover that" the UKA and George Wallace, both of whom would be downtown the next day, will "destroy us all." Finally, the SCLC rally revealed that the organization's leaders maintained a fascination with the Atlanta Five case that bordered on obsession. The national SCLC, Abernathy announced, had exhumed one of the men's bodies and "gained new evidence" that county officials made a "deliberate effort" to "hide

Young demonstrators join hands during a downtown march, 1975.
© Tampa Bay Times/ZUMAPRESS.com.

and cover up the truth about this horrible crime." Abernathy refused to reveal the new findings that proved white leaders conspired to protect the Atlanta Five murderers, but still demanded a federal investigation of the incident. The revelation and subsequent demand drew little reaction from the crowd, which had responded with boisterous enthusiasm to his previous declarations.[24]

The speech that Abernathy later delivered at a mass meeting differed greatly from the one he gave in downtown Pensacola. He repeated some themes, but focused more on the problems that besieged the local movement. Abernathy, then, was much more pessimistic and subdued at the second gathering. He acknowledged that "white people are not right in Pensacola" but worried that "there are some black people who are selling us out." Organizational squabbling over "who is going to get credit for this and who is going to get credit for that" threatened to undermine the continuing local movement, so Abernathy asked to personally address local NAACP president B. J. Brooks from the pulpit. When told that Brooks was not present, Abernathy said "he should be" because "the Black President of America" and one of *Ebony* magazine's "100 Most Outstanding and Influential Black People is in town." The irony of asking a rival organization to place their interests behind them for the local cause while simultaneously proclaiming his own importance did not resonate with Abernathy, who observed that conflicts between the NAACP and SCLC had allowed whites to "get away with murder." Yet Abernathy intensified the organizational rivalry by telling the audience that R. N. Gooden, whom the NAACP dismissed "simply because they heard that he had been employed by SCLC," now had "a place in SCLC." Abernathy welcomed Gooden into the fold "to do your work under the banner of SCLC." Although the minister had promised Pensacola blacks hours earlier that the national organization "ain't going, dammit, we ain't goin' nowhere," he left the city after the mass meeting and never again returned to Escambia County during the continuing crisis.[25] The next day, as promised, the United Klans of America held two events of their own in Pensacola.

The May 24 events marked the klavern's first public gatherings in Escambia County since the Blackwell shooting. The hour-long UKA march began at 10 A.M., proceeded from Lee Square to the Pensacola Municipal Auditorium, and ended near the Confederate Memorial in a downtown park. UKA imperial wizard Robert Shelton and Florida grand dragon John Paul Rogers led approximately 135 robed Klansmen through

Ku Klux Klan members march through downtown Pensacola on May 24, 1975.
AP Photo/Mark Foley.

downtown streets waving Confederate flags. Several blacks lined the
route and silently observed the spectacle, although Klan leaders warned
them to stay away from the rally. Many more whites watched the procession and several cheered as Klansmen passed. One white female told
a *News Journal* reporter that while she did not understand the exact purpose of the newly formed Klan, "I liked the old image a lot. I wish," she
stated, that "what they did" in the past "they would do now." The march's
finale coincided with the noon speech of former Alabama governor and
presidential candidate George C. Wallace for Law Enforcement Appreciation Day. Klansmen joined thirty-four hundred residents to hear Wallace speak at the county courthouse when their parade ended. Although
Wallace did not address the area's racial turmoil or acknowledge the Klan
presence, his speech praised law enforcement officials for restoring order to the community during the previous months. Shelton linked the
Klan rally to Wallace's appearance by telling reporters that the UKA gathered "as a show-of-strength for law enforcement in Escambia County."
Later that evening, the klavern sponsored a rally at the Pensacola Five
Flags Speedway where UKA officials addressed between four and five
thousand spectators.[26]

At the three and a half hour event, Klan leaders urged those in attendance to join Klavern 109 and, as Shelton declared, "put a stop to this

crap Abernathy is starting up in Pensacola." Shelton also focused on the Escambia High symbols controversy and said, "Your board of education has lost control of your children" and are "bringing whites down to the level of blacks." UKA titan Charles Carroll echoed Shelton's claims, called county board members "robots controlled by federal bureaucracy," and claimed Matthews "is one of my best recruiters." Florida grand dragon John Paul Rogers implored the audience to "protect the rights of whites like black protesters protect their rights," and wondered why "people think nothing of Rev. Ralph Abernathy marching publicly in Pensacola, but they object to our marching." The day's events ended with a ceremonial cross burning at the speedway. In the days following their assembly, the *Pensacola News Journal* published a letter from Klavern 109 officials that thanked all who attended the rally. The note specifically lauded Sheriff Untreiner and his deputies "for the outstanding manner in which they aided and assisted our organization during the entire day."[27] The May 24 events, though, served somewhat conflicting purposes. Both the national UKA and Klavern 109 hoped the event would attract additional members, while the Tuscaloosa office hoped the rally would "call attention to the group and bring it out in the open after years of being underground." In contrast to the UKA's regionally ambitious aspirations, the leaders of Klavern 109 had goals that local events dictated. Klavern officials also wanted their group to serve "as a countermeasure to the continued black protest marches" and provide a catalyst for the return of "law and order" to the Panhandle.[28] The differences between the local and regional UKA worked against the attainment of both sets of objectives, but the rapid rise of Klavern 109 contributed most to its swift collapse.

The group's public ascendancy attracted interest from the Federal Bureau of Investigation. The director of the FBI's Jacksonville office shared news of the klavern's endeavors with the Department of Justice's Civil Rights Division, the U.S. Secret Service, and the U.S. Attorney in the Northern District of Florida. The bureau also contacted federal agents in Atlanta, Birmingham, Mobile, and Tampa to collect and share information on the UKA and its Escambia County leaders. Most importantly, the FBI Intelligence Division used two members of Klavern 109 as informants, which brought the number of total informants the FBI used in Escambia County to six, including Sheriff Untreiner. It is unclear whether the FBI infiltrated the klavern with outside agents or if the bureau used existing UKA members for their purposes, but the relatively short time frame between Klavern 109's formation and the beginning of FBI surveillance of the group suggests the latter. Existing records are also unclear as to how the FBI obtained the services of its informants or what motivated the men to assist federal agents. Regardless, FBI sources provided information that resulted in a year-long investigation of UKA activities in Escambia County. The agency eventually compiled a membership list which noted each Klansman's preferred weapon, attributed approximately thirty cross burnings to Klavern 109, and documented threats group members made against local SCLC officials. Despite having evidence that Klan members engaged in many unlawful activities, the FBI's Jacksonville office refused to open a formal civil rights investigation regarding Klavern 109 because no "substantive information" existed that its members violated federal laws.[29]

As the felony trials of Brooks and Matthews approached, then, the long struggle for racial equality in Escambia County encountered obstacles from organizations both familiar and unanticipated. Sheriff Untreiner remained steadfast in his refusal to discipline Raines or Edson for their actions, and the UKA organized several events to rejuvenate the Florida Klan. SCLC and NAACP actions, though, proved the most surprising and tragic. Intensified resistance from two bastions of white supremacy in Northwest Florida—the sheriff's department and Klavern 109—did not surprise movement leaders, but they did not foresee their own organizations as impediments to local objectives. The roles national civil rights organizations played in area affairs, therefore, raise two issues that complicate understanding of the county freedom struggle. It demonstrates that discord within the NAACP distanced the local, state, and national offices from each other and suggests that tensions existed between the NAACP and SCLC. Each conflict eventually undermined and divided local leaders at the expense of group members. The self-interests of the NAACP and SCLC national offices, along with their mutual distrust and jealousy of each other, proved as damaging to the Pensacola movement as the white resistance activists encountered. An examination of the situations concerning Brooks and Matthews leads to a critical analysis of the goals and influence traditional organizations such as the NAACP and SCLC possessed beyond the 1960s. The two groups could do little, then, when the unrestrained white backlash to the long civil rights movement in Northwest Florida cost both of its primary leaders their livelihood and one his freedom.

CHAPTER SEVEN

The State of Florida v. B. J. Brooks
and H. K. Matthews

The extortion trial of H. K. Matthews and B. J. Brooks began in Escambia County circuit court on June 9 before Judge Kirke M. Beall. Brooks spoke to reporters before proceedings began, which marked his first public comments since his split with Matthews. The local NAACP leader called the "trumped up" felony charges "ridiculous," and deemed the trial a "political case" because local white officials wanted to intimidate, discredit, and silence black leaders. The NAACP supported Brooks's contentions and pledged to sponsor his case all the way to the U.S. Supreme Court if necessary. The organization made no similar promises concerning Matthews. Still, the two men agreed that the felony charges levied against them represented "nothing more than a thinly-veiled case of political persecution" because they never committed the alleged crimes.[1] The aggressive nature of the state's prosecution fueled the beliefs of Brooks and Matthews.

State attorney Curtis Golden and his assistant, Barry Beroset, served as counsel for the prosecution. Beroset asked most of the questions during witness questioning, but Golden attended both trial days. Golden's involvement proved ominous for the two civil rights leaders. Each man, particularly Matthews, had crossed paths with Golden numerous times during local protests and accused the attorney of obstructing justice for Panhandle blacks. Golden, whom Governor Reubin Askew had suspended for misconduct and abuse of power pertaining to an unrelated case less than a month after the Blackwell shooting, helped arrange the February 24 arrests of Matthews and Brooks on felony charges. The defendants both used Ed Duffee, a Tallahassee-based NAACP attorney who also represented *Augustus* plaintiffs in their fight against Confederate symbols at EHS, as their lawyer. The NAACP appointed Duffee to represent Brooks, but Matthews had to pay for his own representation. Duffee was an unwise choice as defense counselor. He did not familiarize himself with the county's recent racial past and, according to observers, did not prepare for the trial adequately. Duffee, for instance, interviewed no one prior to the trial day and never reviewed the prosecution's evidence.[2] No existing documents suggest that the NAACP offered Duffee legal assistance or that he requested help from the national office. Duffee's lack of preparedness, coupled with the state's determination to finally silence Brooks and Matthews, first became clear during jury selection.

Beroset and Duffee questioned thirty-seven potential jurors, all but six of whom were white. One of the first questions Duffee asked the group was, "Are there any of you all not aware of what's been going on here in Pensacola insofar as Rev. Brooks and Rev. Matthews are concerned?" Only two raised their hands, both of them young white women who had attended college outside of Florida during the previous seven months. The response surprised Duffee, so he reworded the question and received the same answer. A juror named Oscar Moss even voiced his opinions about Brooks and Matthews when Beroset asked if anyone had preconceived ideas concerning the guilt or innocence of either. Moss replied that he did and based his opinion "on the fact that there's been a lot of agitation (in Pensacola), and it just seems as though these two people are usually involved in it." But he did not stop there. He proclaimed that he had a negative experience during one of the downtown demonstrations that Matthews organized. Moss alleged that he was in the area during a protest when approximately fifty African Americans surrounded his vehicle and threatened his life. He also admitted that he personally knew both Jim Edson and Curtis Golden. Later in the jury selection process, Moss asked to be excused from the pool because of his involvement in other city projects. His prejudicial statements and attempts to evade service evidently did not matter, for Oscar Moss was selected to serve on the all-white jury. Five men and one woman constituted the body, and the two females who had never heard of Brooks or Matthews were not selected. Duffee only lodged one protest concerning the jury's composition, stating that he had "no individual challenges, per se" but objected that each juror had heard of the arrests and discussed the circumstances among themselves.[3] Duffee's incompetence became more evident when he filed a change of venue motion after jury selection ended.

In the request, Duffee argued that Brooks and Matthews could not have an impartial trial in Escambia County because of the "undue publicity to activities and circumstances surrounding the charges filed against" them. Duffee presented numerous newspaper clippings and signed affidavits to Judge Beall that supported his point, and made the claim, only half-jokingly, that the jury knew more about the charges against Brooks and Matthews than the defendants did. Yet Duffee submitted the necessary venue change documentation to the court on the morning of the trial, ten days after its due date. Duffee's carelessness gave Judge Beall a legal reason to deny the request and opening arguments in the case commenced in Pensacola on the afternoon of June 9.[4]

Prosecution attorney Barry Beroset spoke first and outlined the state's charges against Brooks and Matthews. Beroset acknowledged that the Blackwell shooting was the primary reason for local black discontent, but he reminded jurors that a grand jury ruled Doug Raines used "justifiable homicide" to defend his life and cleared him of any fault. Yet from January 24 through mid-February, Matthews and Brooks organized demonstrations on the county courthouse and prison grounds that grew increasingly menacing. The men, Beroset charged, "verbally and maliciously" threatened numerous Escambia County deputies and tried using the crowd to intimidate Sheriff Royal Untreiner, against his will, into firing Raines. Black anger peaked on February 19, Beroset continued, the night their leaders first allegedly threatened to "assassinate" Sheriff Untreiner, Deputy Raines, and Governor Askew. The protestors brandished weapons, threatened deputies, moved police barricades, and "totally abused and intimidated the officers" as the nightly protests progressed. The prosecution's opening argument concluded in an interesting manner. Matthews, Beroset maintained, acted as the demonstrators' primary leader because he "used the group as a tool" to force Untreiner to unwillingly suspend an "exonerated" man. Beroset's claim implied that the state viewed both men as guilty for committing felony extortion against a county official but held Matthews more responsible due to his role as the most outspoken leader of the local black community. Each person who testified for the prosecution reiterated Beroset's claim.[5]

Jim Edson testified first, and his appearance set the tone for the entire trial. Edson repeatedly portrayed Matthews as the individual who instigated and controlled an increasingly violent mob. The riot control director stated that at each gathering, "Matthews had his bullhorn and seemed to be the evident leader or the spokesman for the group, and Mr. Brooks was in his accompaniment," and later reiterated that "Matthews carried the megaphone, the portable bullhorn, and he used it exclusively." The sergeant recalled that Matthews ordered others to block all traffic coming in and out of the jail and refused to let deputies pass through the crowd unmolested. The situation grew even more serious on February 19, Edson declared, because it marked the first time blacks allegedly used the "assassination" chant. Matthews, according to Edson, climbed the stairs of the county jail's front porch that evening and sang through the bullhorn, "Two, four, six, eight, who shall we assassinate? Doug Raines, Sheriff Untreiner, Askew, and the whole bunch of you pigs." The protestors pointed at the deputies, repeated the chant three more times, and concluded the last of by saying, "and especially you, Jim Edson." Reports he previously made concerning the evening's activities, though, indicate that Edson embellished much of his testimony concerning the threats. The sergeant told the jury that when he heard the threatening chant it made him "quite nervous" because "I hadn't done anything to provoke this group. I couldn't figure out why my name would be included in the assassination chant." Edson also stated that on that same night he saw a number of black men who slapped two-foot-long clubs in their palms while standing three inches from officers' noses, which intimidated the present deputies. Female dispatchers even refused to come in to work that night because of the menacing crowd. Yet despite the near riotous scene, Edson ordered no arrests because he did not "want to try to provoke the situation."[6] The crowd was so dangerous that Edson allowed them to gather again the next evening so he could record their threats on audio tape.

Edson made two recordings of the February 20 protest which proved, he maintained, that Matthews used an increasingly violent mob to do his bidding. The first conflict of the night pertained to four barriers that the sheriff's department erected to block all entrances and exits to the county jail. Matthews told the frenzied crowd, according to Edson, "We're going to remove those barricades, and if anyone tries to interfere with us, we will remove them, too; we will meet force with force." Matthews ignored police orders and instructed his followers to move all the obstacles, although Deputy Bill Sandiford later testified that no black ever tried to move the barricades. Edson also recalled that African Americans vandalized department vehicles, spat on deputies, and threatened the lives of law enforcement officials. One man, for instance, told Edson, "We are going down there in the rich white neighborhood to the sheriff's house," while another claimed that six blacks watched the sergeant's home at night from their parked vehicles. Edson told the jury that during the protests, angry blacks telephoned death threats to his home, cut his phone lines, and threw flammable materials at his house. Armed friends, he claimed, guarded his home for almost two months while the deputy worked. The prosecution offered no evidence that any of those things happened or that they had anything to do with Matthews or Brooks, but Duffee offered no objections during the sergeant's testimony. Edson portrayed the February 24 arrests, then, as a necessary last resort to preserve communal order and protect county deputies.[7]

Five other members of the Escambia County Sheriff's Department testified for the prosecution. Each officer, much as Edson did during this questioning, portrayed the black protestors as dangerous revolutionaries. The deputies, though, also gave contradictory testimonies. Curtis Mitchell admitted that deputies carried no firearms during the demonstrations because "there was no need to," despite the fact all officers testified that they feared for their lives at one time or another during the nightly campaign. Mitchell also said that he thought the black cheer threatened to "castrate" those named until Edson told him differently. Bill Sandifer, furthermore, stated that demonstrators did not use the word "assassinate" in their chants on February 19 and said that the gatherings did not evolve into a "more hostile, frightening-type situation" until the night before deputies made their arrests, despite Edson's claim that both occurred days earlier. One consistent element of each deputy's testimony, though, was that Matthews acted as the group's primary leader at every demonstration. Officers described him as the "most vocal" leader, "the spokesman and leader of the group," and the conductor of each assassination chant. One deputy said Matthews shook his fist inches within an officer's nose and snorted "oink, oink, oink" in an attempt to provoke a riot, while another claimed that the minister repeatedly called the officers "sons-of-a-bitches." Cardwell testified that Matthews also told him, "Boy, we'll eliminate you, too, if you don't straighten up" after the reverend led his "assassination cheer." Cardwell added that Matthews ordered blacks to "go to our homes" and "destroy" their property.[8]

The most climactic moment of the prosecution's case came when Deputy Dan Collins took the stand. Collins made two audio recordings that the state claimed proved Matthews led demonstrators in several "assassination" chants. Collins made his first recording, which lasted twenty-eight minutes, from the back seat of a police cruiser while he held a microphone extension out of an opened window. Collins made the second tape, which lasted twelve minutes, from the front steps of the jail. Both recordings contained several versions of the controversial "two, four, six, eight" verse. Collins initially identified Matthews as the clear leader of the chants and testified that he used the word "assassinate" each time, but admitted that he could not recognize from the recordings who directed the other six songs and chants. Collins also claimed at different points during his testimony that "a group of young men" in the crowd "started a lot of these chants," stating, "I don't know that anyone led them," and that "no one person led the chants" because most "were spontaneous." He even attested that, "I don't recall Rev. Matthews using a bullhorn" on the night he made the tapes, which contradicted his previous comments.[9] Still, the prosecution introduced the sheriff's department's audio tapes as evidence and asked to play them for the jury. Duffee's reaction to the recordings advanced speculation concerning his capabilities.

The defense attorney objected to the tapes' introduction as evidence and proclaimed that he knew nothing of their existence. Beroset, however, presented proof that he sent paperwork that cited the tapes as evidence to Duffee during the discovery process. Duffee had let the May 6 deadline to file a motion to suppress the materials pass. The existence of the recordings and the change of trial venue appeal, therefore, represented two crucial elements in the case that worked against Brooks and Matthews because of their attorney's negligence. Judge Beall allowed prosecutors to play each recording, but they revealed nothing that indicted Matthews or Brooks. In fact, a *Pensacola News Journal* reporter wrote that the tapes "revealed festive activity at the jail with joking, singing, and praying" by those present. He heard the contested "two, four, six, eight" chant but thought it concluded, "Who shall we castigate" instead of "assassinate." The journalist further deemed the recordings "barely audible" and doubted that any person in the courtroom heard the demonstrators say anything in unison. A *St. Petersburg Times* correspondent heard the tapes and asked his readers rhetorically, "Have you ever listened, with white ears, to a thin, splotched, monaural tape of a crowd of shouting blacks, all locked in the rhythmic slide of syllables, repeated in the endless cadence of a chant?" Matthews thought, "Thank God. That exonerates me right there" after the recordings ended because he heard the word "incarcerate" at its end and did not hear his voice on either tape. Another man, Rev. Jimmie Lee Savage, led the disputed hymn each night and his voice, not Matthews's or Brooks's, appeared on the audio recordings.[10] Not only, then, did the disputed words not clearly appear on the tapes, but neither defendant led the pivotal chant.

The state's two most important witnesses, Sheriff Untreiner and Deputy Raines, closed prosecution testimonies and both men stressed their mutual fear of Matthews and his followers. Untreiner stated that blacks threatened to burn down his house, rape his wife, and shoot him while he patrolled the city. The sheriff claimed he installed "bullet-proof glass on the windows of my office" and "put in a security device at my own home," which deputies guarded nightly, to protect himself and his family from vigilantes. Furthermore, he removed his reserved parking sign at department headquarters so his enemies could not detect his automobile, and he used several vehicles each day to frustrate potential assassins. Untreiner feared the crowds so much that he placed informants in the mass meetings at Greater Mount Lilly Baptist Church to record their proceedings and learned that the ministers delivered "very inflammatory" speeches that "were very hostile toward the sheriff," Raines, and Governor Askew. Untreiner had no other alternative, he claimed, but to contact state attorney Curtis Golden and arrange the mass arrests on February 24. Yet Untreiner did not charge Matthews and Brooks with a felony immediately upon their incarceration, despite the fact that they allegedly threatened to kill three elected officials. The sheriff failed to explain the reason for the delay during his testimony. When Raines took the stand, he reconstructed a similar campaign of terror that the black masses conducted against him. The prosecution used Raines to elicit more compassion from an already sympathetic jury, as the beleaguered deputy detailed numerous threats that blacks made on his life and discussed his transferal to a departmental desk job that Sheriff Untreiner ordered for "security reasons." Raines also recalled that someone cut his phone lines and vandalized his home at the height of protests against him. He lived in such fear, Raines testified, that he changed his phone number several times and moved his family frequently during the ordeal. The Blackwell shooting never surfaced during his questioning.[11]

Three major flaws surfaced in the prosecution's case during witness testimonies. First, Brooks was not at the prison demonstration on the night that Deputy Collins made his tapes. Brooks missed the February 20 gathering due to illness, and several written accounts confirmed his absence. Because the tapes provided the basis of the extortion charge, Brooks endured an arrest and trial for a crime he physically could not have committed. Second, Edson lied about blacks using his name in their chants. Demonstrators did not add Edson's name to their demands until he made his infamous "Selma" comments in the weeks that followed the arrests. Blacks simply had no reason to include Edson's name in their chants on February 20, as he later alleged. The false allegation casts suspicion on the rest of his testimony concerning black activists and their leaders. Finally, the prosecution never reconciled their consistent claims of black militancy and ferocity with the paucity of evidence they possessed concerning the allegations. Witnesses stated that blacks possessed weapons at the gatherings and even used them to intimidate officers, but the prosecution produced no confiscated weapons as exhibits. Deputies repeated claims of blacks breaking the law on almost a nightly basis, but the only arrests came over a month after the demonstrations began. Instead of providing evidence, prosecution witnesses used anecdotal stories of black harassment as fact. Defense attorney Ed Duffee exploited none of these weaknesses in the prosecution's case and called only two witnesses on his clients' behalf. His case opened with an intriguing witness, to say the least: Sgt. Edson.

Edson's use as a defense witness backfired against Brooks and Matthews. Duffee asked no original questions and provided the sergeant with a chance to reinforce his earlier claims. The only original element Edson contributed in his second testimony was that Gooden appeared at the jailhouse gatherings "one time." No other witness mentioned Gooden's presence at any of the assemblies, which reveals that the main target of county officials throughout the ordeal remained Matthews.[12] When Edson's second testimony against Brooks and Matthews concluded, Duffee called Rev. Jimmie Lee Savage, the pastor of New Providence Baptist Church in Pensacola, to the stand. Savage corrected one of the state's most egregious errors and admitted that he initiated and led the "two, four, six, eight" chorus, which prosecutors blamed on Matthews. "My main role at the jail," Savage testified, "was to help in controlling the audience, getting their attention if necessary," and starting the "one particular chant that I would always preface and lead." The sole question he asked during the chant, Savage testified, was "Who shall we incarcerate?" He denied using any other words in his tune and proclaimed, "The first time I heard the word 'assassinate' in connection with this demonstration was the day after the massive arrests of February the 24." No one else, Savage insisted, ever led the chant. In addition, he insisted that no audience member possessed weapons at any demonstration and that Matthews never ordered any barricades removed. The prosecution realized that Savage had weakened their case dramatically and asked Judge Beall to drop the extortion counts against Matthews and Brooks to "attempted extortion" before closing arguments began. While the prosecution's evidence did not support extortion charges, a conviction on the grounds of "attempted extortion" appeared more likely. For that reason, Duffee refused to accept the lesser charge.[13]

Before the jury retired for deliberations, Beall gave them instructions that increased the likelihood of a guilty verdict against Brooks and Matthews. The judge explained that the state did not have to prove that the two men committed any crime on February 20, the night Deputy Collins made his recordings, or February 24, the night of the arrests. Instead, "if the evidence established beyond a reasonable doubt that the crime was committed sometime within two years immediately prior to the filing of the information (April 28, 1975)," the jury could find each defendant guilty of extortion.[14] Not only, then, were the activists held responsible for the local black protests that had taken place since Blackwell's murder with no evidence that they committed any crimes, but the judge held them accountable for all such activities that had occurred in the area since the spring of 1973. Not coincidentally, the judge backdated his instructions to cover the period of unrest that transpired over the Confederate symbols at EHS, in which Matthews was actively involved. Judge Beall, the sheriff's department, and the white power structure in Pensacola, therefore, saw the felony trial as their best chance to silence the local civil rights movement and did everything possible to ensure that the jury reached a decision they desired. The verdict surprised few.

After sixty-five minutes of deliberation on the afternoon of June 10, the jury returned guilty verdicts against Brooks and Matthews. "At the trial," the *Lakeland Ledger* summarized, "it was whites against blacks. The jury believed the whites." The two activists faced a maximum penalty of fifteen years in state prison for the second-degree felony conviction. Beall delayed sentencing until July 24 because he wanted to research their backgrounds. In the meantime, Duffee appealed the verdict and the court released each man on $20,000 bond. Matthews and Brooks responded to the verdict in ways that reflected their contrasting personalities and leadership styles. Matthews called the ruling "justice, Escambia County style" and "the penalty you pay for being black in this community." He predicted his "conviction will be overturned and I will probably never serve any jail sentence" because "somewhere in the state there are people who would sit on an honest jury and listen to evidence proving" his innocence. He also fired Duffee and hired a local attorney, Paul Shimek, to represent him during the appeals process. Brooks, though, repudiated Matthews's bold post-trial statements and said "I'm not going to be criticizing jurors or the court." Yet despite his acquiescence, the Florida Department of Transportation terminated Brooks from his position two days after the conviction.[15]

As Brooks and Matthews anxiously awaited sentencing for the felony convictions, their unlawful assembly and malicious trespassing trials approached. The county circuit court tried Brooks for his February 24 misdemeanor arrests on July 9. He and Rev. Otha Leverette were scheduled to face the jury together, but Judge Lagergren granted Leverette's appeal for a separate trial at the last minute. On the day of Brooks's misdemeanor trial, attorney Ed Duffee failed to appear at the county courthouse. Brooks later discovered that Duffee had confused his trial date. Still, Brooks waived his right to postpone the trial and threw himself upon the mercy of the judge and all-white jury. Three deputies even testified on his behalf and said that Brooks never used foul language, threatened anyone, or tried to incite violence during the demonstrations. Brooks's conciliatory tactics did not work, though, and the jury found him guilty of both charges. On May 1, the court found seventeen other blacks guilty of the same charges. They were given short probations or fined between $200 and $400 each. Brooks and Matthews, however, faced 120 days in jail and a $1,000 fine for the same transgressions. The NAACP pledged to fight the Brooks convictions but made no comment regarding Matthews.[16]

The felony convictions of Brooks and Matthews paralyzed the civil rights struggle in Northwest Florida and continued a period of white retribution against the two, particularly Matthews, for the leadership roles they occupied during the movement. The verdicts served as a warning to future activists, intimidated protestors, created a leadership void in the black community, and mired local race relations in suspicion and mistrust. Most importantly, the convictions demonstrate the power of the local white systems of control in the mid-1970s to silence social protest that it considered unpopular, unwarranted, or inconvenient. This became abundantly clear in the days following the convictions when H. K. Matthews contacted Ralph Abernathy, admitted he needed assistance in sustaining the local struggle, and asked the national office to help reinvigorate the Northwest Florida movement. Abernathy promised to arrive in Pensacola within days and Matthews announced, "Pensacola is going to have the biggest demonstration it had ever seen" on July 12. Yet less than twenty-four hours after Matthews made his announcement, Judge Beall revoked the minister's bond and ordered him jailed. Beall told Matthews at his July 10 hearing that he revoked bond because the minister continued to plan local marches and demonstrations. "I would have to be a damned fool," Beall announced, to "allow Matthews freedom while he continued the same activities he was convicted of." Apparently in Beall's opinion, the jury convicted Matthews for organizing civil rights demonstrations and not because he used force to extort anything from the white power structure. The judge, therefore, refused to grant Matthews bond, declared him "a threat to the community," and ordered him imprisoned until sentencing. Matthews's attorney appealed the decision to the Florida Supreme Court, the county SCLC canceled all scheduled events, and Abernathy never again visited Pensacola.[17] The felony convictions, therefore, displayed the failure of the local black freedom struggle to alter the white-dominated power structure in Escambia County, which could still crush dissent with relative impunity well into the 1970s.

In spite of the tense atmosphere which existed, Matthews did not expect to enter state prison. He knew that some inmates had been at the county facility for months awaiting their transport to the Raiford state prison and believed that the state Supreme Court would rule in his favor before he had to serve time in the infamous facility. Much to his surprise, though, deputies woke him at two o'clock on the morning after Beall revoked bond and transferred him to the North Florida Reception Center (NFRC) in Lake Butler for processing into Raiford. He registered at the facility as state inmate number 047832. Guards initially placed Matthews in minimum security holdings, but prison authorities transferred him to a maximum security cell because he had threatened to assassinate the governor and was, therefore, a dangerous inmate capable of organizing prisoners and encouraging violent behavior.[18] While Matthews awaited extradition to Raiford state prison, Beall announced the felony sentences for both Matthews and Brooks on July 17.

Judge Beall sentenced Matthews to five years in state prison "at hard labor," but gave Brooks five years of probation with the stipulation that he "not conduct or participate in any public demonstration in the state" during the term. The judge defended his decision by stating that he found "nothing adverse" in Brooks's past and those interviewed had "very favorable" things to say about his character, while the people he interviewed concerning Matthews "had nothing good to say about him." Beall refused to make his investigation discoveries public and warned attorneys against criticizing the judgments to the press. Attorneys for each man appealed the sentences after their announcement.[19] Matthews ignored Beall's admonition and called his punishment "no surprise" because "the judge has a personal vendetta against me." Yet he did receive support from one unlikely source. In a July 18 editorial, the *Pensacola Journal* questioned the discrepancy between the two judgments. In a headline that asked "Why was Matthews'[*sic*] treated differently from Brooks?," one writer called the minister's five-year prison term "an exceptionally harsh penalty for someone who is, in reality, guilty of not much more than an excess of rhetoric." It suggested the verdict provided a way to silence Matthews, who to many local whites "has long been a thorn bush obstructing the long and gingerly-trod road to racial harmony." It further urged Judge Beall to release his investigation findings so the community could evaluate the reasoning behind the sentences and determine "whether justice has prevailed, or whether one more black man who has become a nuisance has been trod upon and kicked aside" by the white power structure. Beall ignored each plea and denied Matthews's bail request because the minister possessed "an utter and total disregard for law and the legal process and, more particularly, law enforcement officers." Four days later, the First District Court of Appeal in Tallahassee granted Matthews a $20,000 bond until it heard the appeal of his extortion conviction. Matthews posted bail three days later.[20]

Newly appointed Florida SCLC field director R. N. Gooden and Otha Leverette organized a meeting at St. John Divine Baptist Church to celebrate Matthews's release and announce future activities. In his first public appearance since leaving prison, Matthews promised over five hundred individuals in the cramped church "to fight until Hell freezes over for the rights of my people." During his emotionally charged speech, Matthews read his sentence and release forms to the crowd, held up his wrist which still had a green prison band attached, and proclaimed proudly, "I got it fighting for my folks." Thunderous applause interrupted the speech numerous times.[21] The jubilation, excitement, and cheering crowds, however, proved a temporary panacea. A day after Matthews delivered his speech, Leverette resigned as SCLC's Escambia County chairman. He claimed that no one pressured his resignation but admitted that his legal costs already exceeded $10,000. Leverette's withdrawal from the SCLC left Matthews alone in his increasingly quixotic struggle to bring the national organization to the area. Matthews repeatedly reiterated his promise to continue the fight for racial equality in Pensacola, but local black activism waned dramatically after his release from prison. In addition, what police called "an organized group" set afire crosses on twelve county school campuses, including Escambia High, on August 5. Neither the sheriff's department nor the Pensacola Police ever named the responsible group and no records of any subsequent investigations survive.[22] Demonstrations thereafter subsided, protests were abandoned, and civil rights groups struggled to retain members. Matthews's growing frustration and despair increased after he experienced an unexpected betrayal.

F. L. Henderson, in his first action as newly elected president of the county SCLC, severed the group's relationship with Matthews and stated that he "is not authorized to speak, collect, or solicit funds for this organization." Henderson portrayed Matthews as a radical leader that had infiltrated and corrupted a peaceful group. SCLC, the new president observed, "was designed to be a peaceful, nonviolent organization" and "we do not advocate violence," so the group had "to eliminate it where it might exist." SCLC national headquarters supported Henderson's proclamations and sent a memorandum to "All News Media Personnel throughout Pensacola, Escambia County and the North Florida Area" which stated that only he, Henderson, possessed the authority to represent or speak for the local SCLC. "If you receive news and information that doesn't have" Henderson's signature, the correspondence proclaimed, "please ignore it completely" as "all activity involving the SCLC will and must be coordinated and conducted through our Escambia County Chapter."[23] With the SCLC action, both civil rights organizations that Matthews had represented and for which he received jail sentences while serving abandoned him.

The fact that national civil rights groups placed their own agendas before the interests of area leaders in Pensacola proved one of the local movement's largest tragedies. For the national organizations, particularly the SCLC, the events offered an opportunity to reclaim lost prestige. Local and national media representatives who covered the conflicts and SCLC activism, for instance, would have given Abernathy and his group the national publicity they craved. In addition, the Escambia County situation possessed elements familiar to the SCLC and NAACP. The protests had visible targets in Raines and Untreiner, encountered police brutality and judicial racism, and implemented nonviolent tactics SCLC and NAACP activists utilized during the previous decade. Most importantly, the area movement could have benefited from the intervention of a national civil rights organization. It would have brought exposure, participants, and a degree of interorganizational cohesion to the local movement, all of which it needed at one time or another during its duration. Instead, something much different happened.

The NAACP and SCLC revived tensions that had characterized their relationship since 1957. The NAACP's national and state offices expressed resentment, jealousy, and frustration concerning their rival organization in Escambia County and its charismatic leader. Consequently, the NAACP withdrew support from the Pensacola black freedom struggle and even used the fragile economic circumstances of Brooks, the president of its local branch, against him for the organization's self-interest. Soon thereafter, SCLC followed suit by denouncing Matthews and withdrawing all support from the movement in Northwest Florida at its most crucial point. The local civil rights struggle thus collapsed while its foremost spokesman served a questionable prison term. Matthews, therefore, faced legal reprisals with little support and subsequently severed ties with the black freedom struggle in Northwest Florida.

Matthews left the Escambia County movement to find employment elsewhere in November 1975. Potential local employers used his felony conviction as a convenient justification to deny his job applications. His economic situation had become so dire that Matthews lived in a downtown men's shelter after his release and often asked strangers for donations so he could eat. AME Zion Church officials offered him three temporary pastorates in Conecuh County, Alabama, and he accepted the positions out of financial necessity. Matthews, therefore, concluded that "I can't lead Escambia County from Alabama" and believed any attempt to do so constituted "a disservice to me and to this community." Before his departure, Matthews held a press conference to "set some things straight" considering the tribulations he endured in Pensacola, "the most racist and backwards city in this whole country."[24] The farewell demonstrated that the depth of his immense rage had many sources.

Matthews expressed immediate frustration with area whites who targeted him as the reason for racial unrest in the Panhandle. His leadership role, Matthews acknowledged, "gained the wrath of the entire racist element in the white community who feel that any sassy or uppity black should be done away with," but he denied creating any unrest in Pensacola during the previous years. Instead, white racism and deeply rooted racial injustices caused the problems. He merely organized and directed black dissatisfaction with the existing racial hierarchy. "I'm a little sick and tired of warped minds blaming me for everything that happens in this city," Matthews declared. "It's reached the point that if Santa Claus doesn't come, if the Easter Bunny gets delayed, if white bigots tear up Escambia High School while white deputies stand around and watch, then blame H. K. Matthews." "If I can cause that much trouble," the reverend proclaimed, "give me credit for it. Name two or three streets after H. K. Matthews" in Pensacola and "build a statue in my honor." Matthews concluded his address by saying, "If this one little black boy can upset a city that much, then he must be a helluva fellow." His decision to leave Pensacola, then, depended upon economic circumstances as well as Matthews's public resolution to not "allow myself to be kicked and walked on by bigots" any longer.[25]

Although Matthews articulated tremendous disdain for racist whites at his final press conference, he voiced greater contempt for local black professionals who he believed "are running off at the mouth" and "turn their noses up at me" due to his past behavior and activities. His statements reveal the extreme amount of personal angst Matthews endured as a result of his perceived betrayal by those for whom he most ardently fought. He admitted that African Americans had produced "many bitter experiences" for him during the struggle, and that black businessmen even refused to hire him in minimum wage positions after he returned from prison. His message to the Pensacola black community grew more passionate as it progressed. Matthews expressed regret that "some of these black folk who have benefitted most from my efforts . . . seem to forget who I am or chose not to think about how they got where they are." Black elites, he charged, "are more interested in being pacified and pleasing the white establishment than they are in achieving racial justice and equality" and "mistreated the one person who has risked more than any single individual in this town to fight for black folks." Despite the fact that "I am solely responsible for them being where they are," Matthews proclaimed with characteristic immodesty, "I never, regardless of my personal circumstances, stooped to the point that I have sold my people down the river."[26]

Yet before he concluded his speech, Matthews returned to the faith and the moral certainty that sustained him through the trials and tribulations he endured as the face of black resistance during the Escambia County struggle. He also pledged, "Nothing short of death will stop me from fighting for the rights of black people who want me to fight for them" because "God has ordained me to do so." He reminded those he addressed that "the God I serve is a good God," and "I've got a God on my side that can do everything but fail." He ended the press conference with a prayer for those who "are giving me hell" and "have kicked me while I am down." When the prayer, which emphasized the need to address one's own faults before condemning others, concluded, Matthews declared, "That's for all the good colored folks in this community who have torn me down." Even after he left Pensacola, area whites threatened his life so often the Federal Bureau of Investigation monitored his activities while Matthews lived in Alabama.[27]

Although he tried to build a new life for himself in another state, Matthews continued to fight his felony conviction. Attorney Paul Shimek, who had the minister's misdemeanor sentence reduced to time served, filed a motion for a second extortion trial for the former SCLC president and B. J. Brooks on January 20, 1976. Shimek based his request on newly discovered evidence that he said exonerated the two men. Over a month earlier, Shimek had given the police recordings of the alleged assassination chant, the prosecution's most important evidence, to an expert for analysis. Vince Ponciano, the owner of a Pensacola electronics store, conducted a series of detailed examinations on the tape contents and concluded that the protestors chanted "incarcerate" several times, but "definitely, absolutely not the word 'assassinate.'" Ponciano blamed misinterpretation of the words on an inferior tape player that the court used. Judge Beall denied the motion, which Shimek appealed to the First Circuit Court of Appeal.[28] While the legal ordeals of the two activists and former friends progressed into a new year, racial turmoil again engulfed Escambia High School. On this occasion, the violence between white and black students demonstrated how weakened the local movement and the leaders who spoke for area blacks had become since the 1975 arrests and trials of Brooks and Matthews.

CHAPTER EIGHT

Clouds of Interracial Revolution

On February 3, 1976, several hundred white students staged a sit-in demonstration in Escambia High's lobby to protest the absence of a school symbols vote. They returned to class only after Principal Chris Banakas promised an election within two weeks. The settlement did not satisfy the most vociferous Rebels who wanted to vote sooner, so they remained home from school the next day in protest. Much to their dismay, Banakas held the mascot election on February 4 and announced that none of the 338 absent students, most of whom were white, would be able to cast late ballots. Before school dismissed on that election day, Banakas announced that the "Rebels" nickname garnered 1,649 votes to 661 for "Raiders," but fell 116 votes or approximately 4 percent short of constituting a two-thirds majority. "Raiders," then, remained Escambia High's nickname and mascot. Tensions permeated the campus as white and black students left the school, but no violent incidents occurred. The situation changed dramatically before classes began the following day.[1]

At approximately 7:30 A.M. that Thursday, a group of white EHS students raised a Confederate banner on the school's flagpole in defiance of the election results. Those who gathered in front of the school carried miniature rebel flags and harassed black students while they awaited the morning bell. Others circled the school's perimeter roads in vehicles and waved Confederate flags from their windows, particularly near the area where school buses unloaded. Many students who assembled on the school's front lawn possessed knives, chains, bottles, bricks, and a number of other weapons. Some distributed a leaflet that asked, "How would you feel if you got 71 percent of the vote—and then lost the election???" Students who addressed the crowd near the front entrance called the election unfair because of its secrecy, the administration's refusal to accept absentee ballots, and the fact that a student majority wanted the Confederate imagery reinstated. "If the school board doesn't give us our name back," one speaker threatened, "we'll handle it our own way." Although they had quietly watched over the morning events without responding, the few present deputies made the whites remove their raised flag. The students resisted the order and several black males approached

Escambia High students wave Rebel flags during the February 5, 1976, riot. The resulting melee involved approximately 1,500 students, lasted more than four hours, and took thirty-five riot squad officers to subdue. © Tampa Bay Times /ZUMAPRESS.com.

the flagpole. A fistfight broke out between the two groups which quickly developed into a riot that engulfed the EHS campus.[2]

Enraged whites threw empty soda bottles, rocks, bricks, wooden boards, and other projectiles at any African American they saw. Some white students darted across school grounds and sought sanctuary from the violence in a nearby Catholic church, but most remained on campus. Whites consequently controlled the school grounds, while agitated blacks gathered inside of the EHS lobby. The rock throwing and vandalism came in waves, as whites dared blacks to exit the building while blacks taunted whites from behind school walls. "As fast as the bricks went" into the lobby, one deputy reported, "the black students threw them back." Most students had gathered in their homerooms and awaited the morning bell when the fighting started, so they moved away from windows and hid under desks as rocks thrown from the grounds outside shattered glass that littered the floor. Teachers called the frightened teenagers running through the hallways into their classrooms and locked the doors, while other students sought refuge inside of the library,

cafeteria, gymnasium, and band room when the riot started. Those bar-
ricaded behind locked doors listened as a cacophony of screams, chants,
breaking glass, crying, and curses ebbed and flowed from the outside
over the next three-plus hours. Groups of up to twenty blacks, some of
whom were not EHS students, roamed school corridors and terrorized
those gathered behind closed doors. They attacked isolated whites, destroyed the trophy cases, overturned tables, and hurled desks through
windows. The mobs also ripped water fountains from their bases, which
flooded the hallways, and pounded the heavy appliances against classrooms doors and student lockers. Those trapped inside were "extremely
intimidated" and "felt like hostages in our classroom," due in part because
there was no communication between school administrators in the main
office and the classrooms. At least one group of fifteen blacks broke
through a classroom door, overturned desks, and hit students with the
two-by-four planks they wielded. A few students—white and black—
tried to escape through their classroom windows and cut themselves on
jagged glass as they spilled to the outside lawn, while others broke the
legs off of tables or chairs to protect themselves. Students were not the
only ones inside the school who panicked. Band teacher Gerald Boone,
for instance, armed himself with a color guard sword to defend those
locked inside his room. "Minor stabbings, beatings, and rock throwing,"
WCOA reporter Don Priest observed, "were the order of the day at Escambia High."[3]

The deputies stationed on campus initially tried to stop the fighting
but did little else to curtail the violence and harassment black students
endured after the brick and bottle throwing began. Many white officers
sympathized with student complaints and only deployed tear gas canis-
ters into the white crowd after the mob pelted them with rubble. Officers arrested whites who resisted or assaulted deputies, but students
often distracted the deputies while others opened cruiser doors and allowed those inside to escape. The sheriff's department riot squad arrived
at the school almost an hour after the tumult began, but its members focused on escorting the growing number of parents inside the school
who had arrived to pick up their children. Separate groups of white and
black students, then, continued to smash windows, burst exterior water
pipes, start fires, vandalize automobiles, and assault others long after the
riot squad arrived at EHS. To make matters worse, school officials refused to use their buses to shuttle black students off the grounds for fear
the mob would damage county vehicles. The decision forced African

Students at Escambia High School disperse after deputies use tear gas to quell the February 5, 1976, riot. © Tampa Bay Times/ZUMAPRESS.com.

Americans to remain on campus while tensions raged, which stoked white anger and prolonged the crisis. Blacks who received no police escort had to make their way through crowds of incensed whites who taunted, pushed, spat on, and hit them as they tried to reach their friends and relatives inside the school. A black parent who witnessed such violent episodes asked a present reporter incredulously, "Why are [white students] being allowed to remain out front?" The most serious violence occurred, then, when the races came in contact with each other outside of the school. Most of the thirty people who required hospitalization after the riot received their injuries near the school's front entrance or parking areas, including three students hit by gunfire.[4]

Like many others, a twenty-two-year-old African American named Raymond Lindsey arrived at Escambia High after the riot began to pick up several kin who attended the school. Lindsey braved the hostile crowds, found three of his relatives in their classrooms, and escorted them to a waiting automobile. He returned inside to search for additional family members but did not locate them. A "mob of screaming whites" harangued Lindsey as he again exited the school lobby, but this time he exchanged insults with enraged whites and shouted, among other things, "All of y'all honkies are gonna die [sic]." An EHS senior who heard the threat later told officers, "The white kids were mad" so "we started throwing rocks at him." Deputy Tony Lewis saw "a hail of stones" strike Lindsey before he crouched behind a parked automobile, pulled a

Deputies take Raymond Lindsey into custody after he fired shots during the February 5, 1976, riot at Escambia High School when rioting broke out. © Tampa Bay Times/ZUMAPRESS.com.

.22 pistol from his pocket, stood, and fired two shots "directly at the crowd." Lindsey then threw the gun into a nearby thicket of bushes and ran to his Ford van, where his awaiting family watched in terror as events unfolded. Deputies apprehended Lindsay as he tried to leave the crime scene. The arresting officer noted that "a mob of approximately 150 students carrying rocks and clubs" followed as he walked the handcuffed suspect to a cruiser. Incensed whites pounded on the vehicle's doors, hood, and windows as it left campus. In the meantime, others crowded near the occupied van, showered it with rubble, and threatened those inside. Lindsey's relatives cried in fear as their grandmother prayed aloud from the front seat. Bricks broke the van's windows, but deputies intervened and escorted the blacks to safety before they received serious injuries. Frenzied whites overturned and vandalized the empty vehicle "until it was nearly demolished." When a tow truck arrived to remove the van from campus hours later, the driver found an attached poster that advertised a local Ku Klux Klan meeting on March 6.[5]

Lindsey told deputies that he fired his pistol "to scare (the mob) away" and he "wasn't going to try to kill nobody," but his shots wounded three white EHS students including Keith Hughes, the sixteen-year-old starting quarterback for the school football team. Bullet fragments hit Hughes in the thigh and caused superficial wounds, but his hospitalization and status as a campus celebrity provided him with a platform to address the unrest. Hughes told reporters that the riot occurred because "the blacks kept making fun of us and we had to do something." He said whites wanted to retain Confederate images at the school for traditional purposes, not racial reasons, yet proclaimed after the riot, "I don't care what they name it. Either way there's going to be fighting" between white and black students "for a long time" at Escambia High. Dale Shuel and Timothy Gardner were also hit in the leg and suffered minor gunshot injuries, but Franklin Whitmire suffered much more serious wounds. Whitmire was not near the area where Lindsey fired his pistol and initially thought a rock struck his head. Yet doctors discovered bullet fragments lodged between his skull and scalp during a second hospital visit. Deputies charged Lindsey with three counts of aggravated assault for the injuries to Hughes, Shuel, and Gardner, but they never charged anyone for shooting Whitmire.[6]

Deputies arrested two more people, both African Americans, on firearms-related charges during the campus unrest about three hours after it began. Twenty-three-year-old Foster Snyder brought a Ruger .22 to campus that he tucked into the front of his pants. The arresting officer noticed the protruding gun butt, searched Smith, and discovered the pistol. The gun, according to the deputy's report, "was in a fully cocked position ready to fire." Snyder was charged with "carrying a concealed firearm." Thirty-seven-year-old Vinnie J. Smith drove from EHS with her son when whites started throwing rocks at the car in front of her, which made both vehicles come to a complete stop. Smith held a .38 revolver out of her window and fired a shot in the air, which cleared the immediate vicinity. Deputies apprehended her for "discharging a firearm in public." Officers arrested three adults—Lindsey, Snyder, and Smith—and twenty juveniles during the February 5 riot. The sheriff's department later dropped all charges against seventeen of the white youth.[7]

As noon approached, the white crowd milled around the EHS grounds, ignored deputy orders to leave campus, and periodically threw rocks and bottles toward the building where approximately two hundred people remained inside. The journalist Don Priest got into the school and captured the fear and frustration many African Americans experienced from the lobby. One infuriated male told Priest, "Those whites want to get in here and get us blacks for no damn reason at all. I don't see why they're fighting us." Another stated a desire to leave campus but heard whites promise "to shoot the bus" that transported them away. An anxious voice asked Priest, "What kind of country is this y'all are running?" while another summarized the mood of most trapped inside by stating, "We just want to go home." White students outside of the school also shouted their sentiments at the reporter. One told him that concerning the blacks Priest interviewed, "We are mad and we're going to kill em." As the unruly crowd slowly dissipated, Sergeant Jim Edson defended his riot squad's relative inaction to Priest and *News Journal* reporters and said, "Sure, we could come out here with our night sticks and bust heads, but we don't want to do that." Edson admitted that the riot lasted so long because of his squad's delayed arrival but reasoned that "most of the violence stopped" eventually. The arrival of state representative Smokey Peaden finally ended the tumult at Escambia High, but only because he directed the remaining protestors to turn their anger toward another target.[8]

Peaden arrived at the school shortly before noon to assess the situation. He spoke to white protestors through a deputy's bullhorn and repeatedly told students to return home. Yet he also questioned the fairness of the previous day's election and criticized Escambia High administrators and county school board officials for allowing the vote, which reinforced student passions. Peaden told the crowd that he and W. D. Childers demanded an immediate audience with the Escambia County School Board, where they would represent "the interest of the majority" concerning the symbols issue. While Peaden addressed the crowd, school administrators changed their minds regarding the use of school buses. Faculty and staff members directed the buses to side entrances where they transported black students safely away. The group that gathered in front of the school dispersed when Peaden led approximately one hundred students to the school board office to air their grievances. Board members refused to meet with anyone but promised a final decision concerning the issue within a week. The announcement pacified whites and ended the Escambia High riot, which caused over $5,000 in property damages at the school.[9]

Confusion and frustration gripped Pensacola in the aftermath of the latest EHS disturbance. Principal Chris Banakas canceled classes for the following day and made no public comment concerning the symbols controversy. The county riot squad guarded the empty school to prevent additional vandalism, and arrested two white EHS students who climbed a fence onto campus later that evening. Officers at the sheriff's department proofread media reports of the campus unrest and, according to the *Pensacola Journal*, "clamped rigid censorship on details of the entire

rioting" by ordering media representatives "to not reveal any information whatsoever" concerning the discord's origins. Despite such efforts,
news of the unrest reached a national audience. On the February 5 edition of the "CBS Evening News," anchorman Walter Cronkite reported
that the "controversial student election" concerning a school nickname
"that has racial overtones . . . led to rioting by about 1,000 black and white
students, almost half the enrollment. Before it was over," Cronkite stated,
"three white students had been shot," county deputies "used tear gas to
break up the fighting," and "the heavily damaged school was closed until
Monday." *Jet* magazine also highlighted the incident in an issue that followed the riot, and declared that, "Pensacola is beginning to look like a
raccoon. With one eye blackened by the murder of five Black fishermen
two years ago, the Northwestern Florida town received another shiner
when white racist-led students rioted over the nickname of a high school's
athletic team." The "faculty and students" at EHS even received an open
letter from a Wisconsin man that condemned their actions and compared
those who supported Confederate imagery to "a bunch of crazed gradu-
ates from a Hitler youth [*sic*] jamboree."[10] The Escambia-Pensacola HRC,
the Florida Commission of Human Relations, and numerous Escambia
County residents contacted the governor's office and demanded that Governor Reubin Askew intervene in the crisis. Askew dispatched one of
his executive assistants, Harvey Cotton, to investigate the situation and
report directly to him. The governor also placed Dr. Donald Spence, an
African American Pensacola city councilman, on the county school board
to fill a vacancy and represent the interests of local blacks on the committee, but the governor did nothing else to immediately mollify local
tensions.[11] Another local politician, though, championed those who
supported the school's Confederate images.

Senator W. D. Childers arrived in Pensacola following the EHS disorder and attempted for two days to organize a public meeting concerning the situation, but no public or private establishment donated their
facilities for the assembly. Peaden also continued efforts to influence the
school board actions and declared, "This is not a race issue, but is about
what is fair and what is not." Each official promised they intended to use
their political clout and numerous local connections to force another vote
on the symbols issue. The chamber of commerce's Task Force on Minority Involvement urged Childers and Peaden to advocate moderation
and interracial cooperation among their constituents, while the Pensacola Christian Ministers' Association publicly asked all local churches

to set aside time during Sunday services to pray for a solution to the EHS turmoil. Even local newspapers released articles that pled for peace at the school. The usually belligerent *Pensacola Journal* appealed to "the whole community" in Northwest Florida to "remain calm and cooperative" concerning the Escambia High situation, for "We must not allow ourselves to strip civilization away and return to mob rule." The *Escambia County Beacon* published a similar letter addressed to all EHS students that listed a number of reasons why the symbols-related violence had to cease.[12] The failure of Childers to find a meeting area to mobilize whites in immediate defense of the divisive symbols, the intervention of local civic groups in the situation, and the response of two area newspapers to the latest violence demonstrated that for some whites, communal stability superseded the preservation of Lost Cause imagery at Escambia High School. The argument would become more prominent as the weeks passed and the unresolved issue continued to incite racial tensions in the area.

One of the most notable differences between the EHS unrest and previous racial incidents in the area was the relative inaction of organized African Americans. Local black leaders, who were divided, silenced, and weakened during the previous year, provided no unified, organized response to the outpouring of vitriol at Escambia High. The NAACP, for instance, issued no reaction to the campus unrest. New Northwest Florida SCLC president F. L. Henderson only implored white parents to set a positive example for their children and asked the county school board to devise a solution to the mascot controversy that would "appease the whole community," regardless of race. H. K. Matthews issued a statement that blamed the violence on "a vocal group who did not get their way," but the reverend's Alabama residency and legal tribulations rendered his protests inaudible. Peaden recognized the diminished role Matthews played in the local black community and ridiculed the minister's comments by stating sarcastically, "I thought he was still serving his (prison) sentence." Peaden added, "I don't refer to H. K. Matthews as 'Reverend' because I have too much respect for religion."[13] Local civil rights organizations, then, remained fragmented and powerless during the most contentious period of racial upheaval at Escambia High.

On February 9, classes at Escambia High resumed under the surveillance of seventy county riot squad officers. Only 1,023 of the 2,523 enrolled at EHS, including 100 of the school's 600 African American students, were in attendance. Thirty more deputies patrolled campus hallways while students attended classes. They locked all doors to the school and made students enter through metal detectors that officers installed at the front entrance. Across the street from EHS, a worker at Simmon's store dispersed white supremacy literature to students, reporters, and customers. Despite the presence of armed deputies, white students greeted buses that delivered the few blacks to campus with jeers and threats. Officers arrested one white for displaying an eighteen-inch long chain as blacks exited the vehicles. Deputies broke up numerous fights and checked purses, backpacks, and lockers at random as the day progressed. Riot Control sergeant Jim Edson supervised the reopening and told reporters that due to the high black absentee rate, "not one thing went wrong today, not even one cross word." Principal Banakas suspended thirteen blacks and fourteen whites for their roles in the February 5 disturbance, which indicates that he held each race equally responsible for initiating and prolonging the riot.[14] The coordinated actions of those who attempted to raise the Confederate flag that morning, brought numerous weapons to school, and distributed fliers that detailed their grievances concerning the symbols vote indicate that the most belligerent white students caused the riot. Despite the attempts to project an image of stability at EHS, Sheriff Royal Untreiner privately indicated that racial unrest threatened to again upset the tenuous calm.

Untreiner called Governor Askew's office the day after EHS reopened and requested help maintaining racial peace in Pensacola. Local pawnshops, he reported, had sold out of hand guns, knives, machetes, and other potential weapons in preparation for what he thought was an impending race war. Askew immediately dispatched 132 state law enforcement officials to the embattled campus, including forty members of the Florida Highway Patrol riot control squad. It is unclear whether Untreiner believed his assessment of the situation, which contradicted all public pronouncements his office made regarding the matter, or if he exaggerated claims to deter further violence. Whatever his reasoning, the feared countywide race riot never transpired. Untreiner told Askew that the state show of force "kept us from having violence at the school" and was "a life saver for this county." EHS Principal Chris Banakas, though, almost undermined the fragile peace when he announced that a twenty-student biracial committee would resolve the images controversy. Banakas urged students and parents that disagreed with his decision to attend a 2 P.M. school board meeting the next day.[15]

On February 11, over three hundred white students walked out of EHS classrooms and joined their adult supporters at school board headquarters. One hundred and thirty state troopers and approximately seventy county riot officers prevented the outbreak of violence at board offices before, during, and after the meeting. State legislators W. D. Childers, Tom Tobiassen, and Smokey Peaden met with students at the downtown facility and pledged to represent them during the proceedings. Childers acted as student spokesman and delivered a passionate speech to the school board. He called the "highly improper election" an "unprecedented affront to the whole American process of election procedures" because school officials issued the vote without warning and refused to accept absentee ballots. Childers concluded his address by insisting the board restore the school's Confederate imagery for "the safety of students at Escambia High." Dr. Donald Spence, the only African American county school board member, described Childers's statement as "political hogwash," but it was the only dialogue the school board allowed from the audience. No one else, the board chairman explained, had requested a place on the meeting agenda. After it exhibited what a WEAR editorial called "a sample of side stepping and fancy footwork that would score well in the Olympics," the Escambia County School Board took no action regarding the symbols and advised EHS students to resolve the matter on their own. The editorial called the determination that "students are more capable of solving this crisis than the school board" an "unbelievable decision."[16] The board's intransigence prolonged the crisis at Escambia High School.

On the morning after the meeting, state troopers stopped a group of thirty-five white students who again tried to raise a Confederate flag on the pole in front of Escambia High. The absentee rate exceeded 21 percent on February 12, as the SCLC asked black parents "to keep their children home rather than wage warfare against the troublemakers" at the school. The whites that attended classes wore black armbands which, according to one teen, "symbolizes the death of democracy at Escambia High School." *Pensacola Journal* editor Paul Jasper wrote an editorial two days later that addressed the issue. His article was a work of revisionist history that demonstrated that racial concerns remained at the center of the issue. Jasper's essay, for instance, claimed that Confederates never rebelled against the Union, Lincoln recognized "Dixie" as a magnificent song, and slavery played no role in the Civil War's outbreak. Jasper published his interpretations because he maintained, "If the community is going to quarrel, it may as well know what it is quarreling about." The paper also published a statement from Representative Smokey Peaden. "A free and impartial election with sufficient notice given" to the student body would, Peaden promised, "return an atmosphere of learning and pride to Escambia High School" and "bring a garden of Eden to" Northwest Florida. The majority vote, he concluded, "is right in the sight of God." The *Pensacola Beacon* addressed the topic with even more venom and claimed, "The reasoning of blacks that the Confederate flag or 'Dixie' constitute a personal affront to a student born in the 1960s holds about as much water as a teenage descendent of a Confederate veteran of Appomattox being emotionally upset by the display of pictures of Lee and Grant." The column asked African Americans, "How silly can you get?" and concluded that white resistance "stemmed not so much from undying devotion to a couple of symbols as to an irritation at having their own innate sense of the American fairness of majority rule trampled by a loud and vociferous minority." Indeed, as the upheaval regarding the EHS images progressed, whites increasingly used the claim of "majority rights" to defend their positions. As one resident expressed in a letter to state senator Tom Tobiassen, "When you remove a school name, flag and song when the majority wants it—then that is an injustice." Whites in Northwest Florida, then, considered themselves victims, "treated second class to blacks," and demanded someone "correct the injustices perpetrated against us."[17] White officials echoed their constituents' beliefs and shifted responsibility for the EHS riot to local blacks at a time when their leaders and organizations remained weak, divided, and on the defensive. Their situation further deteriorated when UKA Klavern 109 intensified its terroristic activities against perceived enemies.

UKA members made a number of bombing, burning, and death threats against numerous public officials in the aftermath of the 1976 EHS riot. Matthews, EHS principal Chris Banakas, Pensacola city councilmen, school board members, Human Relations Commission leaders, and a number of their relatives all received menacing telephone calls during the period. The fact that many of the individuals had unlisted or recently changed phone numbers made the threats even more unsettling. Dudley Clendinen, a *St. Petersburg Times* journalist, described the threats as "shows of strength" from the area Klan and concluded, "There is an ugly meanness here, and an abiding toleration of it" from white authorities. The number of crosses burned on county school grounds proved so numerous during February and March of 1976 that Utica Mutual Insurance

Alain Hebert comforts fellow commission member Teresa Hunt after arsonists destroyed her home, 1976. The KKK claimed responsibility for the attack. Pensacola Historical Society Collection, UWF Historic Trust.

Company canceled the Escambia County school system's fire coverage. Black school board member Donald Spence and two of his white colleagues—board chairman Richard Leeper and HRC representative Teresa Hunt—discovered burning crosses in their yards on separate occasions. Arsonists later destroyed the Hunt home on February 26. In addition, terrorists fired gunshots into the Spence residence and repeatedly telephoned bomb threats to school board offices. Leeper wrote a letter to the *News Journal* that stated, "It should be very obvious to you now, as it has been to the board all along, that the problems of Escambia High are deeply rooted racial problems and not the superficial problem of a questionable election over a school nickname." Klan members burned another cross in his yard the next evening. The volatile situation, Clendinen reported, demonstrated that "it is a time to be scared" for the Klan's enemies in Pensacola. HRC director Alain Hebert responded to Klan activity by appealing directly to Governor Askew for assistance.[18]

In a telegram he wired to the governor on February 26, Hebert claimed the racial situation in Northwest Florida "is worsening" because it "has shifted from the school to the community as a whole." Hebert reported that "numerous individuals have or are receiving threats to their property, family, and selves," and "I am amongst them." Indeed, the "Voice of the Klan" targeted "that nigger-lover Hebert" for white retribution, and a UKA member called a local radio station and said his group planned to kill the HRC executive director. The Department of Justice moved Hebert's family out of Pensacola, and the city police chief advised him to carry a firearm for self-protection. Hebert told Askew, then, that the Klan "is attempting to promote a direct interracial conflict" in Northwest Florida. "The black community has exhibited remarkable restraint," Hebert continued, but warned that their pacifism "can easily change." The telegram concluded by imploring Askew for assistance, "as I see the clouds of interracial revolution gathering, and I deeply fear for the safety of our community." Askew never responded to Hebert's plea, and the frustrated and discouraged HRC director resigned from his position soon thereafter.[19] The county school board exacerbated unease when it proposed an immediate reinstatement of EHS's controversial mascot.

At a March 10 meeting characterized by "bitter exchanges" between the county school board and several EHS students, their parents, and African Americans, board members Peter Gindl, A. P. Bell, and Carl West wanted to change the existing "Raiders" mascot to "Rebels," while fellow board members Richard Leeper and Donald Spence protested the move. Only intervention from board attorney William Davenport prevented the measure from passing. Davenport claimed the board could not legally change a school nickname and assured them Judge Arnow would hold any member who voted for such decisions in contempt of his previous ruling. In exchange for his advice, the school board voted three to two to fire Davenport. He had never lost a case as board attorney. A week later, the board finally reached a decision concerning the symbols that they hoped satisfied all involved. At their March 17 session, board member Carl West proposed changing the EHS nickname to "Patriots" in commemoration of America's bicentennial. As it had pointed out numerous times over the past three years, the school board had no authority to change school nicknames or mascots. West, nevertheless, reasoned that anyone who objected to the new mascot "isn't a true American." A. P. Bell and Peter Gindl, "Rebels" in both sentiment and practice, voted against the name, but the measure passed. The board formally announced Escambia High's new nickname and ended their meeting. On the morning after the announcement, nearly one thousand

Two proud Rebels react to the school board action changing the Escambia High School nickname and mascot to "Patriots," 1976. Pensacola Historical Society Collection, UWF Historic Trust.

white EHS students staged another demonstration in front of the school before classes began to protest their fourth mascot in less than twelve months. They remained out of classes for three days and presented the board with a twenty-three hundred signature petition that demanded it change the school nickname.[20] Student objections, though, did not pose the greatest challenge to the area's delicate stability, for Childers introduced a bill in the state legislature concerning the symbols on April 21 that expanded the issue well beyond Escambia High.

The controversial act proposed a countywide general election concerning Confederate imagery at EHS. It also made the county school superintendent an elected office rather than a board-appointed position and added two at-large members, which would further dilute black voting power and the ability to influence school board decisions.[21] The board did not need to do as Childers wanted, though, because his plan threatened community interests in Northwest Florida. The idea of communal stability operated in Pensacola similar to the ways the concept of civility brought the façade of racial harmony to Greensboro, North

Carolina. In his influential study of the city's civil rights movement, the historian William Chafe argued that civility, which he defined as "courtesy, concern about an associate's family, children and health, a personal grace that smooths contact with strangers and obscures conflict with foes," was "a way of dealing with people and problems that made good manners more important than substantial action." The "progressive mystique" that civility reinforced "provides a veneer for more oppression" by white leaders who protected their civic "power under the guise of sharing it."[22] As the tumult concerning EHS images deepened and became a political issue that threatened to consume the entire county, some civic leaders realized that the fight over the school's Confederate icons provided an ever-present source of racial tension in the area. The possibility of reinstating "Rebels," the battle flag, and "Dixie" as EHS symbols, therefore, had to end. Yet convincing the icons' most belligerent defenders to accept defeat without inciting even more violence was challenging. The idea of communal harmony, like the concept of civility in Greensboro, made a peaceful resolution possible without altering the social and political status quo in Escambia County. White civic leaders maintained that numerous reasons besides racial ones—from better grades to civilized rule to school board sovereignty—necessitated an end to the icons crisis. The power over such decisions, therefore, remained firmly in white hands and African Americans could do little to influence them. The editorials that a local television station broadcast demonstrated how the local white power structure rationalized changing the Confederate symbols at EHS without acknowledging black reasons for doing do.

In the days that followed the 1976 EHS unrest, white WEAR manager Milt Derina delivered a number of editorials concerning the issue during evening news broadcasts. The theme that Derina most emphasized was the negative impact that racial upheaval had upon Pensacola's image to potential investors. In one editorial, Derina proclaimed that outside media coverage of "the racial strife that has beset this community continuously since 1973" suggested "that this county is, very simply, a very badly governed area, plagued with inadequate law enforcement, and the inability to solve its most pressing problems." Consequently, Derina stated in another editorial "the reputation, the peace and quiet, and very definitely the economic progress of an entire community has been nailed to the cross of hatred" because potential investors view area civic leaders as "inept bigots who were simply unable to manage our own affairs."

WEAR, the local ABC affiliate and only major station based in Northwest Florida, even produced a four-part series that examined "the image that news events of the last few years have created of Pensacola" and conceded that its negative reputation damaged "the overall welfare of the entire community." Racial unrest, Derina argued, "is the principle [sic] factor in our inability to attract new industry to Pensacola."[23]

In one commentary, Derina told of "representatives from a California electric firm" who visited Pensacola as a potential site for a research facility that would have created hundreds of local jobs. On their way to a chamber of commerce meeting, the group "encountered one of the many demonstrations associated with the Blackwell case, long after the grand jury had acted." The businessmen located their proposed facility elsewhere. Derina linked the two events and asked his audience rhetorically, "How could you have explained what was going on on the one hand, and what kind of a report would you have made to your company about Pensacola as a prospective site? The questions answer themselves, don't they? The vital question is why would a tourist, an industry, a career serviceman, or a southern vacationer want to spend his time and money in a community which was experiencing the kind of troubles we have had?" Derina declared that because of the communal instability that racial unrest caused, "Pensacola and Escambia County are at a crossroads—the pressure for us to manage our affairs in such way that we impart peace, quiet, and order to this community mounts every day. We need badly to change our image" because "tourists will not come, industry will get leery and the military watchful when civil strife exists." The editorials blamed the unrest not on racist images, "a totally ridiculous argument which should have been solved years ago" and one that only "extremist organizations" continued to use, but on the school board's failure to exhibit strong, decisive leadership.[24]

Derina echoed arguments that multiple civic leaders previously made when he blamed county school board members for perpetuating "this tragic nonsense" regarding the EHS symbols and not the objectionable nature of the images themselves. He declared that it was time that board members, "capable, responsible, men of good will who keep very clearly in mind that the overall welfare of the entire community is a stake," demonstrated "effective leadership" and took "bold decisive action" to end the controversy at EHS "one way or another." The board, he opined, "needs to go about the business of providing education and to forget about its role in providing racial battlefields." "The longer this controversy simmers," Derina maintained, "the more bloodshed there will be."[25] The WEAR narratives, then, demonstrated the powerlessness of African Americans to influence decisions they regarded as important with the white power structure on their terms. Instead of addressing the reasons Confederate imagery offended local blacks or probing the reasons whites defended them so vigorously, the public commentaries placed responsibility for the tumult on the Escambia County School Board and made its members accountable for the restoration of communal harmony in Northwest Florida. Ironically, white civic leadership advocated publicly for the calming of racial tensions in the best interests of the community only after black protests, organizations, and leaders were effectively silenced.

The *Pensacola News Journal* supported Derina's arguments and led local opposition to Childers's countywide mascot election bill. An April 22 editorial in the *Pensacola Journal* called the proposed vote "sheer insanity" and compared its potential effects on county race relations to "pouring oil on a fire." Paper editors envisioned "nothing more likely to inflame a community than to have it conducting a full-scale election on whether the name 'Rebels,' considered an ethnic slur by blacks, should once again be reconstituted as a school nickname." "If the mere raising of a Rebel flag on the school grounds can set off a volley of cursing and threats," the article continued, "think of what could happen if someone organizes a full-scale 'Return the Rebels' election campaign in this county." Editors also warned that "the Southern Christian Leadership Conference, not to mention the NAACP" would reemerge in Pensacola in the event of a countywide mascot vote. The *Journal* recommended that area citizens honor the latest school board ruling not in the interests of racial justice, but because resistance usurped the board's authority and threatened Pensacola's communal interests.[26] Anxiety concerning a county referendum on the iconography, though, ended soon after it surfaced.

As a Pensacola station broadcast the session live on local television, the Florida House Local Legislative Subcommittee voted 6–0 to reject Childers's election bill on May 7. Childers honored the decision and asked students to "concentrate on education so peace and tranquility will prevail at the school," but he made one last attempt to leave his mark on the county system. If he could not persuade or bully the school board into reinstating the "Rebels," Childers reasoned, he would change the school board's composition. The senator, then, resubmitted a revised version of his bill to the house subcommittee. The new legislation retained all of its original stipulations but dropped the countywide symbols election plan. Childers told fellow legislators that he proposed the measure "in direct retaliation for" the school board's failure to reinstate Confederate imagery at EHS. The subcommittee passed the revised resolution and Childers receded from Escambia County's racial politics. Governor Askew signed the Escambia County School Board Reapportionment Act into law on June 8, 1976. The bill increased the number of school board members from five to seven, which Escambia County voters had to approve or reject in a July 2 referendum election.[27] While the symbols issue affected local affairs issues considered by the state legislature, two former civil rights leaders continued to fight their felony convictions.

The First Circuit Court of Appeals rejected the appeal for a new hearing by H. K. Matthews and B. J. Brooks on April 26. Judges accepted expert analysis that the men threatened no public officials on the taped recording but reasoned "that whether the words spoken or chanted were 'assassinate,' 'castrate,' or 'incarcerate,' they are still coercive threats" that the protestors' menacing tone conveyed. Regardless of word choice, the court stated, Matthews and Brooks used the crowd as a weapon to threaten present officers with injury. The same court denied Matthews's extortion appeal three months later. The unanimous ruling proclaimed that Matthews led a violent, armed crowd, which proved that the minister "consciously embraced fear of bodily harm as an instrument of enforcing otherwise lawful demands" and "was sufficient to convict him of extortion." Yet justices exonerated Brooks from any responsibility in the matter and overturned his felony conviction, despite the fact that they previously refused to grant him a new trial. The court declared that Brooks played no role in most demonstrations, did not lead the assassination threats with Matthews, and kept jail traffic flowing without obstruction when he appeared at the assemblies. Although the court extended leniency to Brooks, it upheld his unlawful assembly and trespassing charges on August 10, 1976. Brooks accepted the verdict publicly without malice and stated, "I now see clearly the numerous errors I committed" during the previous year. The NAACP spent approximately $14,000 to appeal the misdemeanor conviction for Brooks, but contributed nothing to Matthews's defense. The organization used the reversal of Brooks's felony conviction in materials it distributed concerning state NAACP endeavors.[28] Brooks, then, escaped legal persecution relatively unscathed for his civil rights activities. The courts found him guilty of two misdemeanor charges, but the NAACP paid his fines and legal expenses. All Brooks had to do in exchange for almost total exoneration was repudiate his past transgressions and not participate in future civil rights activities. Whether the same compromise existed for Matthews is unknown, for he refused to do either. Regardless, the experiences of each man provided a stark contrast for future activists to consider.

While the convictions of Brooks and Matthews progressed through the appeals process toward their ultimate conclusion, area voters added two at-large positions to the school board in a July 2 referendum election. The measure, according to the historian James McGovern, "was designed to weaken black political influence in this community." The year's elections substantiated McGovern's conclusions and indicate the voting majority used the opportunity to punish board members who took unpopular stands during and after the EHS unrest.[29] Elmer Jenkins, an African American science professor at Pensacola Junior College, ran for one of the school board's new at-large positions. Jenkins seemed an ideal candidate on many levels. He earned a bachelor's degree from Florida A&M, a master's from the University of Illinois, and had begun doctoral coursework at Florida State. He had worked in education for over thirty years, belonged to neither the NAACP nor SCLC, and had no connection to past civil rights activities in the area. Yet Jenkins's opponents, most of whom had only a high school diploma, "made the EHS issue their main topic" and "attacked the school board for the stand they took on EHS symbols." White candidate Jim Bailey, for instance, openly supported the UKA in their attempts to organize a rally at Escambia High. The "Voice of the Klan" hotline and the county teacher's union endorsed Bailey, who defeated Elmer Jenkins by 6,250 ballots. Bailey won an at-large position on the board a month later in the general election. Jenkins attributed his defeat "solely due to the countywide method of electing officers" and pledged to not run for public office again as long as the existing system remained. "Any time the voting is at-large," Jenkins maintained, "it is racially polarized."[30] The polarization was even more evident in the contest for the District Four county school board seat.

Dr. Donald Spence, a self-employed African American dentist, first campaigned for a Pensacola City Council seat in 1963. He lost in the run-off election to a white candidate and suffered defeat again when he ran for the same position in 1975. Later the same year, the city council appointed him to fill a position vacancy and Spence became the second black to serve on the body. He resigned from the city council in 1976 to run for the county's District Four school board seat, a seat that Governor Askew had temporarily appointed him to that February. One of Spence's opponents in the race, Carol Ann Marshall, solicited support from the UKA. Marshall spoke at multiple Klan rallies, and known members, including Imperial Wizard Robert Shelton, attended her campaign functions in a show of solidarity. The UKA's "Voice of the Klan" messaging service, whose slogan before the local election was "get the nigger off the school board," endorsed Marshall and stated that even as a female with no political experience she was "the lesser of two evils" in the race. Marshall campaigned on the platforms that "a minority should not take away the rights of a majority" and "government should not be established on the basis of race," both indirect references to the symbols dispute at EHS. Marshall defeated Spence by only 129 votes in the primary but won by 9,930 votes in the runoff election. "I was defeated," Spence maintained, solely "because I was black." Marshall won the District Four school board seat with a landslide victory over her opponent in the November 2 general election. Soon after taking office, Marshall transferred her three children from predominantly black county schools to those with an overwhelming white majority.[31]

The area's recent racial unrest surfaced in two other local campaigns, albeit in different ways. UKA member James Cohron ran for an at-large school board vacancy to challenge what he deemed "the black dominance" of local politics. Cohron openly defended his Klavern 109 membership and campaigned on the sole promise of reinstating Confederate imagery at Escambia High. Yet Cohron received the second-lowest vote total of the six people who participated in the September primary. Dr. Frank Biasco, whom the "Voice of the Klan" labeled "debased" because he associated with "criminal" blacks, eventually won the school board seat. In addition to the county school board elections, Sheriff Untreiner referenced the area's turbulence during his 1976 reelection campaign and claimed, "My calming influence restored racial harmony" in the panhandle after the EHS upheaval. Untreiner also pointed out that interracial tensions "practically disappeared" since Matthews and Gooden left Escambia County "and transferred their racial agitation to other places." Some African Americans supported Untreiner's claims. HRC chairman Eugene Brown, for instance, publicly endorsed Untreiner despite the fact that its previous director, Alain Hebert, criticized him for not doing more to mollify area racial tensions. Untreiner, Brown now claimed, "has tried to help the black community in every way possible, but he didn't get the cooperation of some black leaders." Fellow black HRC member R. J. Calloway echoed Brown's sentiments and observed, "All of this marching has been done away with" by the sheriff. Many county voters undoubtedly agreed, and Untreiner won his primaries, ran unopposed in the general election, and remained Escambia County's sheriff. The outcomes of the 1976 local elections proved to African Americans that "a black candidate running for elected office stands about as much chance as a snowball in Hell" of winning the contest.[32] Only legal action, the two blacks believed, would equalize political access and reorganize the local power structure in a way that benefited their race. Four months later, the men filed monumental lawsuits to end the discriminatory election process at the city and county levels.

Although UKA's Klavern 109 played a public role in two school board campaigns in 1976, the organization's involvement represented a futile effort to remain locally relevant. The FBI's monitoring and infiltration offer one reason for UKA problems. The two klavern members who served as FBI informants provided the bureau with abundant information concerning Klan activities. Evidence exists which indicates klavern members suspected that law enforcement officials—possibly even federal agents—monitored their activities. In 1976 one klavern leader had resorted to giving lie detector tests to all current and potential members, indicating that he suspected some of his fellow Klansmen of dishonesty, duplicity or, at worst, subterfuge. In addition to FBI infiltration, "internal dissension, ineffective leadership, and rotation of leaders" also weakened Klavern 109. Seventeen klavern officers, including the exalted cyclops, resigned their positions and membership between October 12 and December 15, 1975, due in large part to the paranoia and suspicion that permeated the organization. The leadership turnover continued in 1976 and on May 16, the klavern's newest exalted cyclops denounced violence and expressed his "strong belief that the Klan should concentrate on political type activities and recruit a higher type of individual." Klavern 109, he declared, would project "a law and order image" because "better results can be achieved through a good image and the printed word." Whether the FBI influenced the klavern's attempted image transformation or if the local leadership had been infiltrated is unknown. With a philosophical reorientation and the relatively small group reduced to meeting in a shed behind a member's mobile home, the FBI closed their investigation of UKA Klavern 109 in July 1976. The FBI retained its two UKA informants after its inquiry into Klavern 109 officially ended, and the group made no public appearances after 1976.[33]

The development and decline of the UKA in Northwest Florida gives some understanding of how the federal government viewed Escambia County's racial situation. Its surveillance of Klavern 109 reveals that the FBI, as it demonstrated numerous times throughout the South during the previous decade, had little interest in protecting local blacks. Despite the fact that the agency possessed substantial evidence that klavern officers armed themselves, patrolled black neighborhoods to harass and intimidate residents, threatened SCLC officials, and burned crosses on public and private property, the FBI refused to arrest any Klavern 109 members because their actions did not violate federal laws. The bureau did not turn any of its evidence over to the Escambia County Sheriff's Department or the PPD, and only intervened in local affairs when Klansmen committed arson on federal land in nearby Okaloosa County. Knowledge of how the FBI handled Klavern 109 undermined any faith local African Americans had that law enforcement would intervene proactively in the racial problems that pervaded Northwest Florida during the 1970s, and demonstrates the continuity of black political powerlessness in the years after desegregation occurred. On numerous occasions, black leaders and organizations looked to the federal government as a potential ally and, often, as their greatest hope in the local struggles for racial justice. Yet the FBI had no interest in protecting the civil rights of African Americans on the local level and even characterized SCLC protests as evidence of "black extremist activities" in Northwest Florida.[34] The bureau passed knowledge of SCLC rallies and events to Sheriff Untreiner and Pensacola police chief James Davis, but never informed county law enforcement of any Klan-sponsored events.

Perhaps most interestingly, the establishment of Klavern 109 gives a unique look into the "fourth period revival" of the Klan. The UKA proved reactionary and reflected the frustrations of marginalized white southerners with their loss of social and economic standing in a very different region from the one in which they were born. UKA members vented their frustration with black activists in the Panhandle, but they also expressed anger toward those who seemingly sympathized with or advocated equal treatment of African Americans. The rhetoric that emanated from UKA events in Northwest Florida reflected a worldview under siege from forces beyond klavern control. One Klansman, for instance, decried the "black dominance" of local, state, and national politics, and claimed that Jimmy Carter gave African Americans social privileges because "he bought their votes" with promises made during the 1976 presidential election. Florida grand dragon John Paul Rogers attributed the growth of Klavern 109 to the fact that "blacks have achieved a form of reverse discrimination. They get jobs over whites simply because they are black." He asked rhetorically, "How do you explain to a man that he can't have a job because he's white and then talk about equal rights?" The widespread UKA insistence that "if you're born white you already have two strikes against you" demonstrates the social alienation and loss of cultural control its members felt. To Klan members and those who sympathized with them, black equality equaled a loss of white rights. The majority had moved, in a relatively short period of time, from oppressor to perceived victim.[35]

Ironically, the presence of the UKA in Escambia County shows that the white supremacist organization had something in common with the national office of its rival, the SCLC. Both groups used the Pensacola situation for their own purposes with little regard for the local people they claimed to represent. For the SCLC, the greater objective was national rejuvenation of the moribund organization. Similarly, the UKA hoped the Pensacola situation would attract new members, inspire the formation of new klaverns, and increase the organization's inconsequential presence throughout the South. Both the SCLC and UKA proved equally inept at capitalizing upon the tumultuous racial situation because each viewed the local situation as the means to a greater end, not as their primary objective. The lack of concern for the specific issues that divided the races in Northwest Florida intensified racial animosities in the area, which African Americans and white leaders had to navigate on their own.

CHAPTER NINE

The Consequences of Powerlessness

The black freedom struggle in Northwest Florida exhibited both change and continuity between the 1976 Escambia County School Board elections through the 1980s. Most substantive activity shifted from downtown Pensacola and the Escambia High campus to area courtrooms, but the local movement still highlighted the power imbalance that characterized race relations in the years beyond integration. As the decade progressed, former movement leaders experienced continued consequences for the roles they previously played. On September 9, 1976, the First District Court of Appeals rejected a trial rehearing appeal for H. K. Matthews. His attorney took the ruling to the Florida Supreme Court, but Escambia County Circuit Court judge Kirke Beall again denied Matthews bail and ordered the minister to turn himself in to the sheriff's department by September 22. Matthews subsequently submitted to county authorities and read in the newspaper during his return trip to the NFRC in Lake Butler that his wife had filed for divorce. An appeals court granted him bond on October 22, and he returned to Alabama while awaiting a Florida Supreme Court hearing.[1] Like Matthews, Rev. B. J. Brooks also endured reprisals for the leadership he exercised during the local movement. Unlike his former friend, though, Brooks recouped some of his financial losses.

The Escambia County Career Service Commission reviewed Brooks's wrongful termination grievance against the FDOT and ruled on January 1, 1976, that the agency had to rehire Brooks, reimburse approximately $25,000 in lost pay and legal expenses, restore all benefits, and revise its departmental suspension and termination procedures. The First District Court of Appeals upheld the ruling, and Brooks returned to his job on August 8, 1976. He remained a state employee until retirement nearly a decade later. The NAACP played an important early role in the legal plight of their branch president, but his ordeal severed the relationship between the national office and local branch. The Pensacola chapter exhausted its funds in litigation and was unable "to send money to the National Office as we have in the past." The organization, consequently, ceased paying Brooks's legal costs, which led to a bitter battle between his attorney and the national office.[2] By 1978, Pensacola NAACP membership dropped to a decade-low ninety-four people. Twenty-four of Florida's fifty-eight NAACP branches had more members than the Pensacola chapter, which contributed $575 to the state office between 1972 and 1977. The amount represented .02 percent of the total receipts state branches contributed during the period.[3] The branch's financial travails replicated those the national organization simultaneously encountered.

In August 1976, a Mississippi court ruled against the association in a boycotting case against a group of white Port Gibson merchants and ordered the NAACP to pay $1.25 million in damages. According to movement historians Timothy Minchin and John Salmond, NAACP "leaders became wary of endorsing direct action and, instead, fought to overturn the decision" in its immediate aftermath. The U.S. Supreme Court upheld the organization's successful appeal over six years later, but the NAACP remained $1.2 million in debt. In addition to its financial troubles, the national office experienced a leadership change while the Pensacola chapter floundered. In 1977, seventy-six-year-old Roy Wilkins stepped down as NAACP Executive Director after serving the association for fifty years. Dr. Benjamin L. Hooks filled the tremendous leadership void and, according to Minchin and Salmond, "addressed financial shortfalls by accepting more funding from corporations, a move that dented the NAACP's social activism."[4] The miniscule membership and financial offerings that the Pensacola NAACP provided its state and national offices, particularly during a period of heightened local activity and internal crisis at the highest levels, made the branch largely inconsequential given the association's greater issues. It is unlikely that the group could have provided meaningful assistance to the Northwest Florida freedom struggle if it wanted. The local and national discord also partially explains the secondary role the Pensacola NAACP played in relation to the SCLC in mobilizing the local black community in public campaigns again police brutality and Confederate imagery.

The SCLC, much like the NAACP, also faced numerous problems and diminished in local significance as the 1970s concluded. The county branch remained mired in the substantial debt that it incurred years earlier and requested used copiers, typewriters, and other necessary materials from Atlanta headquarters to continue operations. The national office never responded to the request and remained uninvolved when Escambia County deputies arrested F. L. Henderson on two felony counts of rape on July 1. One black female charged the father of six of forcing her at gunpoint to have sex at the SCLC office, while another claimed

Henderson raped her in his car. Henderson said he knew neither woman and called his arrest a "frame-up to stop the black movement in Pensacola," a ploy the sheriff's department utilized to silence past Panhandle activists. Henry Arnold, the Escambia County SCLC communications director, assured the national office that the charges were unsubstantiated and noted "the past character of Mr. F. L. Henderson speaks for itself." Henderson quit his position less than a year later amidst the rape allegations and accusations of financial impropriety from organization members. His arrest and subsequent resignation represented the final blow to the county SCLC which effectively collapsed as the national office, similar to the NAACP, experienced tremendous internal disarray just when the Escambia County movement most needed its help.[5]

In the summer of 1976, a group of four SCLC officials asked Ralph Abernathy to resign the organization's presidency because of "our lack of substantial achievements, our failing revenues, [and] our diminished reputation" during the previous three years. Abernathy vacated the position months later when he ran for the congressional seat that Andrew Young's appointment to the United Nations opened. Although Abernathy lost the election, it allowed him to "withdraw gracefully from the presidency of the SCLC."[6] Joseph Lowery, the new SCLC leader, turned the organization's attention increasingly to the "political prisoners" who languished in U.S. prisons because of their civil rights activities. The national office, perpetually in search of an issue that could resurrect its fading influence and fill its empty coffers, named Matthews the nation's "Number One Political Prisoner" at its 1978 national convention and pledged to support his case financially through an appeal to the Supreme Court if needed. The organization never fulfilled the numerous promises it made concerning Matthews, but did use his cause in their annual fundraising drive later that year. In a letter that it sent all members, the SCLC referenced Matthews as an example that "the criminal justice system is still being used against us" and cited his conviction "for singing a popular marching chant" to solicit contributions to the organization. Yet Matthews received no financial aid from the campaign and only knew about it because an SCLC member gave him a copy of the correspondence.[7] The SCLC and NAACP, then, floundered aimlessly in their shared search for purpose, members, and relevance as the decade neared conclusion. Local blacks, meanwhile, never filled the leadership void that characterized the Escambia County freedom struggle after 1976, which reveals the most conspicuous flaw of the traditional approach to local organizing.

The reliance upon charismatic ministers and their organizational affiliations provided a model of community coordination that was successful in securing tangible racial change during the 1960s in Pensacola and many other southern locales. African Americans in the Panhandle, particularly teenagers and young adults, responded enthusiastically to and provided the core components of numerous marches, demonstrations, boycotts, and other direct action campaigns. Yet the felony convictions of Brooks and Matthews and the subsequent withdrawal of the NAACP and SCLC from local affairs debilitated a movement that depended upon a strong hierarchy. The Matthews sentence, in particular, demonstrated the white power structure's ability to cripple the local freedom struggle both temporarily by targeting specific key individuals and in the long term by providing an example to others who dared fill the leadership void. African Americans viewed the ordeal of Matthews, "the one they made the example of and put in jail," as what "shut the black community down." John Davis, a black Pensacolian and city community relations coordinator, observed in 1981 that the leadership vacuum meant local African Americans had to muster "more unity and cooperation" to improve their collective economic, social, and political conditions. The fact that the masses remained directionless and viewed remaining leaders as only "letdowns and sellouts" revealed a fatal flaw in the local organizing tradition.[8] A movement constructed upon the foundation of top-down leadership and direction collapsed with the removal of those select few. With meager options from which to choose, a small group of African Americans turned once again to the judicial system to improve economic, political, and social conditions for Escambia County blacks. The lawsuits and series of events they initiated reinforced the power imbalance that existed between the races in Northwest Florida as a new decade began.

The 1976 county school board referendum results prompted ten African Americans to contest the at-large selection process for board membership, but they expanded their complaint to include two additional institutions that utilized the same system. On March 18, 1977, Henry T. McMillan, Robert Crane, Charles L. Scott, William F. Maxwell and Clifford Stokes filed suit against the Escambia County Commission and school board, while Elmer Jenkins, Woodrow Cushon, Henry Burrell, Samuel Horton, and Bradley Seabrook did so against the Pensacola City Council. Federal Judge Winston Arnow consolidated the two cases on May 18 as *McMillan v. Escambia County, et al.* Plaintiffs charged that "the at-large election systems for all three local governmental bodies were racially conceived" and used "as instruments of purposeful discrimination against black voters," who represented one-third of the city population and one-fifth of the county residents. *McMillan* was the second southern suit that challenged at-large voting as discriminatory, as a district court ordered the Mobile (Alabama) City Commission, county commission, and school board to reorganize in 1976. *Bolden v. City of Mobile, et al.* represented the first time a federal court reorganized a city government during the twentieth century.[9]

McMillan outlined two ways in which the county electoral process impacted African Americans. First, the certainty of defeat discouraged blacks from seeking public office. Since 1955, African Americans ran for the Escambia County Commission four times, the school board five times, and the city council nineteen times. Only two men, both of whom had been previously appointed to their positions by white city councilmen, won their campaigns. Second, the at-large system made civic leaders "less responsive to the needs of the black citizens than they are to the needs of white citizens." White officials in Escambia County, Henry McMillan claimed, ignored black needs because "he knows he can get elected without your vote." As a result, "black neighborhoods endure a disproportionate share of unpaved and poorly-paved streets, inadequate recreational facilities and other inadequate municipal services." Attorneys demonstrated that 70 percent of blacks who lived within Pensacola's city limits lived in five census tracts that contained an African American population that exceeded 90 percent. In Escambia County, 43 percent of black residents lived within five tracts that possessed at least an 80 percent African American majority. The residential patterns, plaintiffs maintained, made the at-large election of a black candidate impossible and violated the 1965 Voting Rights Act. In place of the "fundamentally unfair" process, *McMillan* proposed the establishment of five single-member district elections for the city council, county commission, and county school board "so the voting strength of black citizens is not debased, diluted, minimized, or cancelled out" due to residential segregation. The redistricting gave black voters a majority in one of the five residential districts, which corresponded to their county population rate.[10] Editors at the *Pensacola News Journal*, as they typically did when charges of racial discrimination surfaced, vigorously defended the status quo.

News Journal editors characterized any outside meddling in county affairs as "a dangerous precedent" whose "real danger" to local autonomy "rests in the growing proclivity of the courts to preempt legislative authority." The *McMillan* suit, then, represented more than a voting rights suit. It would "lead to subversion of the other two branches of government and a destruction of the checks and balances which are the bedrock upon which this republic stands." Besides, the goal of *McMillan* plaintiffs to obtain "a court order which practically guarantees the election of a black—or anyone on the basis of race, sex, or party affiliation— simply institutionalizes discrimination instead of ending it." Columnists rejected the "judicial fiat" against the local electoral process that *McMillan* desired and endorsed the existing at-large system. The solution to any perceived electoral inequities, editors argued, "is not dismantlement of a government structure" but the election of "candidates, black or white, who will represent everyone" regardless of race. "The people of Escambia County," the *News Journal* concluded, "simply cannot be convinced that a change in governmental forms is either necessary or desirable."[11]

McMillan v. Escambia County sustained the struggle for racial equality in Northwest Florida, but it presented many discontinuities in the local freedom struggle. Rev. W. C. Dobbins, the Pensacola Council of Ministers, the NAACP, Matthews, and the SCLC each utilized public direct action campaigns, economic boycotts, voter registration drives, or a combination of nonviolent tactics to improve social conditions for local blacks. The protests responded to a specific event or incident and had a clearly defined short term goal, such as greater minority employment or the removal of deputies who allegedly brutalized African American suspects. The *McMillan* plaintiffs, though, utilized a different strategy altogether. The men filed suit with no advance warning, public mobilization, or assistance from any civil rights organization. The litigants expected a prolonged legal struggle, anticipated little to no cooperation from local or state elected officials, and appealed first to the courts for relief. Each of the plaintiffs, for instance, distanced themselves from and criticized area civil rights groups. None of the ten had ever joined SCLC. Only two men, Henry McMillan and Charles Scott, claimed NAACP membership, but each testified in depositions and at trial that they did not participate in organizational activities during the 1970s. *McMillan* litigants also expressed interest in local political participation. Elmer Jenkins ran for county positions in 1968, 1974, and 1976, and others wanted to campaign for public office under a more equitable electoral system. Unlike prior African American leaders who wanted to use the political process primarily to oust officials that ignored their grievances, the *McMillan* complainants wanted to alter the balance of local political power from within the system as members of the city and county governing bodies. The *McMillan* plaintiffs also possessed a religious diversity that differentiated them from prior black leaders. Unlike Matthews, Brooks, Leverette, and Gooden, none of those who brought suit against the local electoral systems were ministers. Crane and Jenkins were AME church members, Stokes attended Zion Hope Primitive Baptist Church, Seabrook and McMillan were Catholic, and the remaining five plaintiffs did not associate themselves with any denomination. Religious motivations, particularly the evangelical beliefs that inspired Matthews and his associates, played little to no role in the lawsuits brought against the at-large electoral system. Most importantly, though, each of the *McMillan* plaintiffs belonged to the professional middle class. Jenkins, McMillan, and Cushon had taught in county schools for multiple years, while Scott, Stokes, Seabrook, Horton, and Maxwell held federal positions at the Pensacola Naval Air Station. Retired entrepreneur Robert Crane and U.S. Postal Service employee Henry Burrell were the remaining litigants. The *McMillan* case, then, demonstrated that a group of men very different in personality, social standing, and methods from the ones who organized and led public direct action campaigns during the previous decade petitioned for political equity in Northwest Florida. They represented the "class niggers" that SCLC and NAACP leaders disparaged from their pulpits, but the *McMillan* ten sought a deliberate redistribution of local political power which, unlike the recent direct action protests, threatened a crucial mechanism that the white power structure used to maintain their political, economic, and racial supremacy.[12]

While attorneys for the plaintiffs and defendants in *McMillan v. Escambia County, et al.* prepared to try their case before Judge Winston Arnow, the controversy surrounding EHS's imagery finally ended. On August 11, 1977, his first day as the new principal at Escambia High School, Eugene Key declared it time to resolve the lingering nickname controversy "in a calm and deliberate manner" and announced that EHS students would elect a permanent mascot on September 7. Principal Key formed a committee of fifty EHS students, parents, and faculty members and charged them with selecting two mascots that students could choose between on election day. Key excluded all previous mascots from

Officials at Escambia High School test voting machines prior to yet another nickname vote, 1976. Pensacola Historical Society Collection, UWF Historic Trust.

consideration because he wanted to distance the school from its past troubles. A majority vote, the principal decided, would determine the winner. The committee selected "Gators" and "Sharks" as the mascot finalists. Seventy-four percent of the student body at Escambia High participated in the election, and "Gators" received 1,749 votes to 306 for "Sharks." The school board approved the results at its next meeting with a five to one vote and promised to accept the outcome as final. The mascot and nickname survived its first year without significant unrest, and the Escambia High class of 1978 fondly deemed themselves "the class of Gators, Rebels, Raiders, Patriots, and Escambians," each of which represented the school at some point during the four-year period. "Gators" remains the nickname and mascot at Escambia High School.[13]

The judicial process occupied a central role in the Escambia County freedom struggle as the decade concluded. On May 15, 1978, arguments in the *McMillan* suit against the at-large election process for the Escambia County Board of Commissioners, school board, and Pensacola City Council began. Although a group of men very different from those who had organized and led the black community initiated the litigation, and witnesses made few specific references to the racial unrest that had previously consumed the area, the power imbalance that B. J. Brooks, H. K.

Matthews, and their direct action campaigns highlighted surfaced repeatedly throughout the case proceedings. The fact that Otha Leverette and Brooks testified for the *McMillan* plaintiffs indicated that the ministers used the platform as an opportunity to obtain a greater degree of political and, eventually, economic and social empowerment than African Americans in Northwest Florida previously possessed. *McMillan* and the 1970 mass freedom struggle, then, demonstrated a simultaneous continuity of purpose and discontinuity of method. Judge Winston Arnow presided over the nine-day-long nonjury trial, during which prosecution witnesses maintained that the current system diluted African American voting strength, made elected officials less responsive to their minority constituents, and discouraged black political participation. Leverette described the issue most succinctly in a prepared statement that he read during his testimony. "I am an educated man," he proclaimed, "but if an illiterate ran against me the only thing he is got to be [*sic*] is white and he can beat me." Clifford Stokes connected black political disillusionment to the ambivalence that elected white officials demonstrated in response to the Blackwell shooting and Matthews's conviction. "Most black people," he explained, were "unaware," "afraid of," or suspicious of the "political system" in the city and county "because of past experience." Multiple witnesses also contended the at-large election system heightened racial tensions when an African American declared his candidacy for local office.[14]

F. L. Henderson ran for a city council position in 1971 and testified that angry residents vandalized his property and made "several" threatening phone calls to his residence during the campaign. The night before the election, someone placed a dead black cat on his front doorstep. Henderson lost the race in a landslide and said he would not run for public office again because, "There is no possible way I feel I could win under the present system." Elmer Jenkins, a college professor with a graduate degree, lost his 1974 school board campaign to an eighteen-year-old white high school student. Nathaniel Dedmond, the only practicing black attorney in Pensacola, ran for county office in 1972. He received few campaign contributions from African American voters because "they thought I have no chance of winning and it was a question of whether they should throw good money" away on a futile campaign. Dr. Charles Cotrell, a political scientist at St. Mary's University and expert witness for the plaintiffs, acknowledged that "many qualified black citizens" in Northwest Florida refused to run for office because "of the unlikelihood that a black person will be elected." In total, fourteen African American men testified that they would not campaign for political office in Pensacola or Escambia County due to the improbability of victory under the at-large system. As Donald Spence summarized straightforwardly, "If the Lord himself was black and ran for political office in Escambia County, he'd be defeated."[15]

One of the most important testimonies that Judge Arnow heard came from the Florida governor. Attorneys for the plaintiffs called Reubin Askew to the stand on May 22, the trial's sixth day. Askew recalled that he belonged to the state House of Representative's district legislative committee when it approved the act that gave Pensacola voters the chance to change its election of city councilmen from the district to at-large process in 1959, but he had since changed his position on the issue. The governor admitted that he now supported single-member voting districts as "the single most important step you can take to try to better insure representation to minorities" and claimed, "I don't know how we can say that government is truly representative of the people" under the existing system. Askew called the district process "right" and "fair," and concluded his testimony by blaming the current process for "indirectly disenfranchising a lot of people from fair representation."[16] Both his powerful indictment against at-large elections and the endorsement of district-based voting in the *McMillan* trial were Governor Askew's most important contribution to the progression of racial equality in his home county. The fact that he provided such insight while under oath and made no such public declarations regarding the case indicates that the governor still hoped to keep the racial tensions in Escambia County at a distance. Winston Arnow was not a jurist that was easily influenced with anything besides a literal reading of the law, but the decisive perspective that Reubin Askew offered strengthened the plaintiffs' case.

The *McMillan* witnesses for the plaintiffs, then, made a clear connection between the at-large election system and the marginalization of African Americans in Pensacola and Escambia County. Yet equally crucial were the indirect repercussions of black voting powerlessness that surfaced at trial. Four social consequences of African American political impotence, in fact, became recurring themes during the *McMillan* proceedings. Dilapidated and inferior infrastructure where many blacks resided was one such effect. Many witnesses linked their political powerlessness to the "neighborhood blight" that white elected officials, through either benign or willful indifference, never addressed. Plaintiffs compared the recreational facilities throughout the city and county and concluded that authorities generally neglected those in African American neighborhoods. Broken glass, litter, weeds, and uncut grass engulfed tennis courts and ball fields. Damaged and rusted playground equipment sat unrepaired. Unfilled swimming pools closed, and blown lights were not replaced. Similar facilities that lay in white residential areas, though, exhibited no such problems. The discrepancies stretched into other public services such as road and sidewalk maintenance, the number of street lights, sewage and water drainage, and the availability of fire hydrants in predominantly white and black residential areas. Attorneys submitted evidence that also documented higher rates of the "social pathologies" that differentiated black and white zones. For example, 26.2 percent of black residences in Escambia County lacked indoor plumbing compared to only 2.4 percent of white homes. The figures differed little inside the Pensacola city limits.[17] The absence of political representation, therefore, had a detrimental impact on the public services available to Escambia County blacks. Witnesses made similar observations concerning the situation in area schools.

Continued discrimination within the county school system represented a second residual effect of the racial inequities that at-large elections perpetuated. *McMillan* attorneys, for instance, demonstrated that the number of black principals, coaches, and school administrators in 1967 exceeded the number employed in Escambia County ten years later. Punishment and labeling discrepancies also concerned African American witnesses. In the 1975–76 term, African Americans constituted 25 percent of the county student population but were 56 percent of those suspended and 61.4 percent of those labeled "mentally handicapped." Conversely, blacks constituted only 6 per cent of students the county labeled as "gifted." The average white pupil was almost six times more likely than their black counterpart to enter advanced academic classes while 61 percent of students suspended more than once and five of every eight expelled students were African American. The *McMillan* plaintiffs, then, contended county educators funneled "black students that white teachers label 'problematic'" into special education programs and concluded white school officials "don't care nothing about blacks," "ignored" minority pupils, or "forced" African Americans "out of the school system" through an "unequal discipline of students." The conditions illustrated what Leon Hall, the director of the Southern Regional Council's School Desegregation Project and SCLC member, called "the student push-out," which occurred when white school administrators suspended or expelled minority students under questionable circumstances or whose "intolerable hostility" caused African Americans to quit school altogether. Hall termed this phenomenon "the implementors' revenge," and maintained that allowing the same people who initially opposed school desegregation to oversee its implementation represented the greatest obstacle to educational equality in southern classrooms. The solution to such institutionalized discrimination in Escambia County schools, Woodrow Cushon believed, was "single district voting" because it elected leaders "more responsive to the people within their district" and thus more likely to address the issues that their African American constituents encountered. The witnesses and discoveries presented in *McMillan*, then, related the at-large county election process to the persistence of racial inequities and "implementors' revenge" that characterized in local schools.[18]

The unequal treatment of African Americans by Pensacola police and Escambia County sheriff's deputies represented the third element that *McMillan* linked to the absence of black political power via its discriminatory election structure. Attorneys produced evidence that "law enforcement and political leaders" possessed "a laissez-faire attitude" on "the use of firearms by officers." City police and county deputies, consequently, exercised "dual firearms policies based on [the] racial, social, or economic irresponsible status" of suspects. One witness made the association between black political impotence and police brutality clear because of personal experience. B. J. Brooks, the former Pensacola NAACP president and movement co-leader, testified that African Americans met with elected officials "more about police brutality and the attitude of police officers when they are arresting blacks" than any other local issue, including the Escambia High nickname controversy, during the 1970s and "got no results, none whatsoever." In fact, Brooks stated, "I've been arrested for trying to speak out against police brutality." Other witnesses echoed Brooks's conclusions. Elmer Jenkins ran for a city council seat because "we were having too much police brutality in some of the black areas," while Samuel Horton testified that city "police just don't have the same attitudes for protecting a black citizen" as they did for whites. "A black city councilman," Horton proclaimed, would demand "a better attitude" than local law enforcement typically possessed when officers interacted with African Americans. The "widespread" fear of local law enforcement, attorneys argued, remained "a threat to the city's very existence."[19] The black inability to secure representation under the at-large electoral system, then, allowed allegations that local law enforcement brutalized and even murdered African American suspects to persist without recourse.

The final element that surfaced during the *McMillan* trial as a related consequence of black electoral helplessness was the economic disparity between the races in Northwest Florida. Attorneys highlighted black underemployment figures within the city and county, while witnesses linked the problem to an absence of black representation on the governing bodies of each entity. Pensacola and Escambia County, research demonstrated, were two of the largest employers in Northwest Florida. Blacks represented 24.3 percent of the county-employed workforce between 1973 and 1978, a percentage that approximated their population rate, but the majority occupied positions in the lowest job classification categories. The county classified 45 percent of African Americans as "service/maintenance" workers and 44 percent as "para-professionals." Conversely, blacks represented between only three and 10.5 percent of those who held professional, skilled, and better paying county jobs. Annual salaries also revealed a tremendous discrepancy. From 1973 through 1978, 21 percent of African Americans and 57.8 percent of whites earned more than $8,000 annually. In two of those years, 57.8 percent of black county employees earned less than $6,000. In 1975 and 1976, 27.8 percent of whites and 19.8 percent of African Americans received salaries that exceeded $10,000, while seventy whites and only six blacks earned more than $16,000 per year. The county's unemployment rate mirrored the wage disparity. In 1977, 9.9 percent of blacks and 3.5 percent of white residents, a differential one witness called "statistically significant," had no job.[20] The situation differed little for those within the city of Pensacola. Between 1974 and 1977, 24.9 percent of the city's workforce was African American and the majority, like those the county employed, occupied the lowest job and salary classification ranks. African Americans constituted 55.5 percent of "service/maintenance" positions, a higher percentage than they held within the county. Only the "skilled craftsmen" category, in which blacks occupied 27 percent of the positions, represented a significant improvement from county figures. Average salaries for black city workers also fell short of county levels. In 1974, 83 percent of black and 30.6 percent of white city employees made less than $8,000 annually. Over the next two years, 37 percent of white city workers and only 3.9 percent of African Americans earned more than $10,000. One hundred thirty-one whites and one black had an annual salary that exceeded $16,000 during the same period, and areas populated by a 95 percent or greater black majority documented an 18.6 percent unemployment rate.[21] "The people who control the economic power base of our community," Brooks testified, "seem to know what's best for black people" and, therefore, hired them only in subservient positions with wages that reached subsistence levels alone. Neighborhood blight, continued discrimination within county schools, police brutality, and black underemployment, then, surfaced during *McMillan* testimonies as the indirect social consequences of the political powerlessness that African Americans possessed due to the existing election process. Judge Winston Arnow's ruling, much like the ones he delivered in *Augustus*, had the potential to impact area race relations for years after its announcement.

On July 10, 1978, Arnow ruled the at-large election process for the county board of commissioners, school board, and Pensacola City Council unconstitutional because white officials used "the at-large system as a method of rendering black voters politically impotent to the desires of the white majority." The at-large procedure, therefore, "had a racially discriminatory intent" and diluted "black voting strength and participation in government." In his thirty-nine page opinion, Arnow traced the histories of the three governing entities and cited specific incidents where officials made decisions that consciously undermined the black vote and rendered minority representation on the ruling bodies almost impossible. Candidate filing fees, "an active Ku Klux Klan" in the area, and elected officials who were "unresponsive" to their minority constituents, Arnow claimed, also discouraged black political activity in Northwest Florida. The judge cited contemporary conditions and the region's contentious recent past to conclude that "the city, like the county, is, by and large, a race conscious society" which perpetuated "a dilution of black voting strength" at all levels of government in Northwest Florida.[22] His closing statements indicated that Judge Arnow empathized with both blacks and whites in his adopted home county:

Discrimination against blacks, stemming from long years of conscious and deliberate oppression and discrimination against blacks by whites, does not disappear quickly. It is a gradual and ongoing process, and the process is still going on here. The race discrimination that was so manifest in the earlier years in this state, and in this county and city, though diminished, has not yet disappeared. Because this county and this city have made so much progress in complying with the commands of the Constitution and the law in these recent years, this case is not an easy one to decide. . . . One day, hopefully, the time will come in our nation's ongoing progress when we as a people, or at least a sufficient number of us, have so eliminated race consciousness and discrimination from our hearts and minds that such is not reflected in governmental processes and procedures. Then there will be no need for suits such as these. Then there will be no justification for orders such as the ones entered here that interfere with the right of the people to establish for themselves the details of their government because, in doing so, they themselves will have complied with constitutional and legal requirements. As it has not in so many other places in our nation, that day has not yet come to Escambia County and to Pensacola.[23]

Arnow gave the board of commissioners, school board, and city council forty-five days to submit revised reapportionment and election plans. Although the judge wanted a new process in place before the September 1978 general elections, all three governing entities appealed the verdict.[24] The action delayed local elections indefinitely.

While some African Americans hoped the judicial process would bring meaningful political changes to Northwest Florida, the courts provided no relief for H. K. Matthews. Seventeen days after Arnow declared the city and county electoral processes unconstitutional, the Florida Supreme Court upheld Matthews's extortion conviction and five-year prison sentence with a four to two decision. Although he once intended to take his case to the U.S. Supreme Court if needed, the lengthy struggle took a physical, psychological, and emotional toll on Matthews. The exhausted minister asked Governor Askew for a pardon, despite its implication of guilt. Yet Askew urged Matthews to petition the state courts for a rehearing of his case, which the Florida Supreme Court denied on November 28, 1978.[25] Consequently, the governor asked the state clemency board to commute the minister's sentence to the sixty-three days he had already served. He refused to pardon Matthews, Askew explained, because he hoped the minister would appeal his conviction to the U.S. Supreme Court and establish a precedent against future cases that violated free speech rights. A pardon nullified any subsequent appeals. Askew called all of the decisions rendered against the minister "bad law" and compared Matthews to Dr. Martin Luther King Jr. for the harassment and persecution that he endured in Escambia County, while Florida secretary of state Jess McCrary, the only African American on Askew's cabinet, claimed the group "ought to hang our heads in disgrace" for the way their state handled the case. Despite a protest letter from Sheriff Royal Untreiner that called the clemency recommendation "a gross miscarriage of justice," Askew's cabinet voted 7–0 to commute Matthews's sentence. Despite his proclaimed admiration for and support of Matthews, Askew waited until a month before his tenure as governor ended before he publicly supported the maligned leader. The U.S. Supreme Court eventually dismissed Matthews's appeal and Florida governor Robert Graham pardoned him of the felony conviction in 1979.[26] The decision represented a pyrrhic victory, though, as a frustrated and indignant Matthews left a divided and equally embittered community with no intention of returning to Northwest Florida. While the legal process eventually exonerated Matthews of any alleged crime he committed during his public civil rights activities, the conflicts of the 1970s increased local attention on the activities and procedures of the Escambia County Sheriff's Department. A multitude of humiliating discoveries soon followed for those most involved with Matthews's incarceration.

Numerous scandals inundated Untreiner's department in the years after the local black freedom struggle subsided. The Blackwell shooting, for instance, represented the first of many brutality complaints citizens filed against Douglas Raines. He was accused of striking a drunken man with a revolver, allegedly beating a prisoner unconscious for not acknowledging an order, and breaking a man's arm while removing him from a Pensacola nightclub. Although departmental records did not record the race of Raines's alleged victims, Untreiner had to rotate him among many positions within the department because the deputy's reputation as "a nigger killer" inevitably impeded his job duties. The department suspended Raines in 1981 for showing pornographic movies to, taking nude photographs of, and having sex with a juvenile. On March 11, 1982, a disciplinary board found Raines guilty of the charges and finally dismissed him from the force "in bad standing."[27] It is unclear whether the Blackwell shooting or his racist reputation played a role in the board's decision. Escambia County riot squad sergeant Jim Edson, the crucial prosecution witness at Matthews's extortion trial, also experienced a humiliating conclusion to his career in law enforcement.

In October 1978, a young Boston-bred reporter for the *Pensacola News Journal* named Mark O'Brien discovered that Edson falsified documents

H. K. Matthews stands on courthouse steps with documents signed by Governor Reubin Askew commuting his felony sentence. Manuscript, Archive, and Rare Book Library, Emory University.

to receive a promotion to his current position. He had changed the name on his son's college transcript to his own to satisfy the assignment's educational requirement and submitted it to the county civil service board with his application. Edson received a thirty-day suspension and a demotion for his fraudulence but, more importantly, the forgery raised questions about the role Edson played in the Matthews conviction. Dudley Clendinen, a white *St. Petersburg Times* reporter, titled his article concerning the incident, "Deputy lied about his record; did he lie about Rev. Matthews?" The piece outlined the city's recent racial turmoil and placed Edson, "the sheriff's main man, his enforcer" and "a chief bigot," at the center of the case that resulted in Matthews's incarceration. One journalist wondered if Edson did "falsify records concerning his education and training, then is it not also reasonable to assume that his testimony in the Matthews' case might likewise be false?" while another asked more directly, "If you were seeking a good used car, who would you buy it from—Deputy Jim Edson or Rev. H. K. Matthews?" Others, though, maintained unwavering support for Edson. The president of the

Knights of the Ku Klux Klan, for instance, sent a letter to Sheriff Untreiner that asked him to reinstate the beleaguered officer for his work "in preventing heated racial confrontations in this community." The Klansman lauded Edson "for the courage he displayed during these trying times in our city" and reminded the sheriff that "all humans make errors." Untreiner needed little urging, though, to staunchly defend his close personal friend and suggested that Edson's enemies, such as Matthews, forged and planted the transcript to embarrass the sheriff's department. Yet a grand jury that formed to investigate the sergeant's credentials and subsequent promotion uncovered more damning evidence against him. Jurors discovered that Edson stole vehicles from the police impound lot, which deputies called the "boneyard," and sold them or gave them away as gifts. The state charged Edson with twenty counts of grand larceny and deputies arrested him twelve days after his initial thirty-day suspension ended. The disgraced Riot and Crowd Control officer, whom one editorial labeled "a liar and a fraud," resigned from the department before he faced trial for the thefts. A jury later found him guilty on eight felony grand larceny counts and one petty larceny count. The judge sentenced Edson to three years in state prison and twenty years of probation. African Americans suggested the sheriff's department rename its impound lot the "Milk Boneyard," referring to Edson's infamous quote that "Niggers are better than Milkbones" for his dogs.[28]

The controversies involving Raines and Edson sparked additional grand jury investigations of sheriff's department practices and produced larceny and perjury indictments against four of Untreiner's top officers. The state attorney even levied charges against the sheriff's secretary for lying to protect her boss from another grand jury investigation. Scandal so plagued the Untreiner administration after 1978 that WEAR and the *Pensacola News Journal* demanded his resignation. Untreiner did not run for reelection in 1980 and retired from the sheriff's department when his term ended on January 5, 1981. He died unexpectedly on January 26, 1989.[29] In addition to law enforcement personnel, state representative R. W. "Smokey" Peaden encountered an ignominious conclusion to his public service career. Peaden, the self-proclaimed "gospel music entertainer" and former state legislator, became one of the most vociferous opponents of black efforts to remove the Confederate imagery at Escambia High and even expressed a desire to shoot African Americans in his home city. Yet Peaden enjoyed tremendous support from his white constituents and campaigned for the Escambia County sheriff's position

"Call 'Em Off, Ya Heah?" December 12, 1978. J. Earle Bowden captured the beginning of numerous scandals that characterized the Escambia County Sheriff's Department during the late 1970s. J. Earle Bowden Cartoon Archive, University of West Florida Libraries.

in 1980. To finance his candidacy, the former Pensacola police officer organized a cocaine distribution operation in Florida and Texas. Deputies arrested six other people, including former Klansman and school board candidate James Cohron, in connection with the drug ring. Each individual pled guilty to the charges and implicated Peaden in masterminding the scheme, which severely compromised his election plans. In 1982, a federal court declared Peaden guilty of narcotics distribution and sentenced him to fourteen years in prison and $25,000 in fines. He died on March 7, 1999.[30]

The abuse of power by those in positions of authority was a consequence, not a cause, of the measures they took to preserve white supremacy in Northwest Florida during the 1970s. It is inviting, given each official's ultimate fate, to interpret their vehement opposition to the continued freedom struggle as one component of a greater personal and professional hubris which ultimately ended their public careers. But this is not the case. The greater white power structure allowed the sheriff's department and certain elected officials to extend their power into matters the racial majority considered unpopular. Civil authorities at the city and county levels gave their implicit and explicit support to those who could obstruct, frustrate, and ultimately crush the local movement. The Pensacola City Council, Escambia County Commission, school board, and state legislature remained silent when African Americans protested the unethical and often illegal actions of those under one of the group's supervision. The white-dominated control systems only responded when law enforcement and those elected officials extended their extralegal privileges outside of those pertaining to racial affairs and brought negative attention to or embarrassed civic leadership. The white power structure, then, encouraged and enabled public servants to abuse their authority in the defense of white supremacy. The empowerment carried into other areas and ultimately damaged careers and reputations irreparably, but it represented a fitting conclusion to a pattern of previously acceptable practices that the local control systems allowed in exchange for crippling—perhaps permanently—the black freedom struggle in Escambia County.

The multiple scandals that law enforcement leaders encountered validated African American complaints concerning sheriff's department integrity, and claims that an institutionalized racism still characterized the interaction between deputies and blacks continued into the 1980s. Yet the local white power structure impaired one of the only area civic agencies that tried to alleviate tensions between the two groups. The Pensacola City Council and Escambia County Board of Commissioners altered the purpose of the Human Relations Commission after Alain Hebert resigned as its executive director in 1978. "Instead of being out on the street," civic officials decided, the HRC should offer more individualized social services to local residents and act in "a more administrative kind of capacity" than it had during the Blackwell and Escambia High controversies. In essence, the commission changed from a proactive agency that served as an advocate for improved race relations in the city and county to a reactive group that investigated discriminatory practices only when residents filed formal complaints through HRC auspices. The organization organized a variety of new social programs for low income residents during the 1980s, such as job fairs, general education classes, sports leagues, neighborhood watch programs, and Christmas toy drives, but it could only collect and submit data when African Americans filed complaints against local officers.[31] Police brutality remained a concern for Escambia County blacks, but civic leaders rendered the HRC helpless in confronting the issue. One such issue highlighted the agency's primary purpose and subsequent impotence.

In October 1979, a week after an officer shot and killed an unarmed black for fleeing the scene of a burglary, the HRC asked the city council for a formal investigation of the PPD. The incident represented the fifth fatal shooting of an unarmed black male by city officers in a five-year period. Councilmen ignored the request, and the police chief exonerated each officer involved in the shootings. The committee also documented complaints concerning the Escambia County Sheriff's Department, learned that state agencies received more complaints concerning the Escambia County jail than any other in Florida during the 1970s, and investigated the shootings of four African Americans that occurred in the months that followed Wendel Blackwell's death. The HRC forwarded its findings to the city council and county commissioners, requested a formal grand jury inquest into the shootings, and asked civic leaders to "do something about the conduct of the sheriff's department." City councilmen and county commissioners took no additional actions, while the state attorney's office ruled each death a "justifiable homicide" and refused to empanel a grand jury.[32] The HRC's impotence provided another indication of the black powerlessness to influence decisions directly regarding their experiences with the white power structure in the years beyond integration. The local black freedom struggle continued into the new decade, but African Americans could do little that brought meaningful racial change to Northwest Florida. The continuation of the *McMillan* suits, for instance, indicated that the battle against racially discriminatory election procedures in the city and county remained unresolved.

In July 1979 the Pensacola City Council, Escambia County School Board, and county commission responded to Judge Arnow's order and submitted similar election plans to the court as ordered in his crucial *McMillan* ruling. The twenty-eight page charter proposed a mixed single-member district and at-large plan in which voters selected five representatives from their residential wards and two who could reside anywhere in their jurisdiction. Arnow initially rejected any scheme that contained general positions, but accepted the two seats provided county voters approved the charter in a November Special Referendum election. County voters rejected the revised election plan by 2,035 ballots on November 6, 1979. The fifteen northernmost county precincts, a rural, white-dominated area that prompted the *McMillan* plaintiffs to request single-member district representation, provided the charter's margin of defeat. The result left *News Journal* editors and their readers wondering, in regard to local elections, "Where does this leave us?" While a series of appeals and counterappeals left the election procedure unresolved, a federal report on the state of Northwest Florida race relations surfaced.[33]

On April 21, 1981, the Florida Advisory Committee (FAC) to the U.S. Commission on Civil Rights released a twenty-page study titled *The Administration of Justice in Pensacola and Escambia County*. Local residents informed the FAC of another incident in which an Escambia County deputy shot an unarmed black suspect in December 1979, and the committee launched an investigation for two reasons. First, the number and severity of area racial incidents that occurred between 1973 and 1980 alarmed civil rights committees at both the state and national levels, and each wanted to research, document, and understand why the tumult transpired. Second, the FAC's initial investigation indicated "some [black] community leaders still feel blacks are treated unfairly by the police and the courts," and that perception fueled local racial anxieties. The FAC concluded after a year-long investigation that "a lack of mutual understanding and respect" between "black residents, the Escambia County Sheriff's and the Pensacola Police Department's officers" explained many of the area's lingering tensions. In addition, the FAC found, "There is no formal means of communication between the community and either the Escambia County Sheriff's Department or the Pensacola Police Department." Although white "officials and community leaders" denied the existence of racial problems in the area, "the mere fact that some citizens and their leaders *perceive* that a problem exists is reason enough for concern [emphasis in original]." Simply put, "Cooperation and support from all segments of a community are necessary to effective police work, and those vital elements are not fully evident in Pensacola and Escambia County."[34]

The FAC identified the Blackwell shooting as the nadir of Panhandle race relations. The death and events which followed, the study proclaimed, "are fundamental to understanding the distrust some blacks have for local law enforcement and the judicial system." The subsequent convictions of Brooks and Matthews "'broke the back' of the civil rights movement in Pensacola" and perpetuated the belief "that law officers could treat blacks as they wished and anyone who objected was inviting persecution by the authorities." The FAC concluded that police brutality, particularly the shooting of unarmed black men by white officers, represented the most serious threat to communal stability in Northwest Florida.[35] The FAC report, then, made some vital suggestions to rectify the situation. First, the FAC urged the Pensacola City Council and Escambia County Commission to "reexamine their commitment to bettering human relations through the Escambia-Pensacola Human Relations Commission." The FAC labeled the "understaffed" HRC "a small and sparsely funded public agency." It employed one full-time director, a part-time employee, and two temporary workers with a $25,000 annual budget, and thus had only a "limited impact" upon local race relations. The state committee urged city and county administrators to allocate a small portion of the $3.7 million in federal revenue sharing funds it received in 1980 toward organizational rejuvenation. The FAC also implored the city and county to form separate biracial committees. Each committee, the FAC reasoned, would open communication between the police and area residents, assist law enforcement in reviewing proposed and existing departmental policies, and provide previously neglected residential areas with a forum to initiate grassroots neighborhood improvement campaigns. Most importantly, the FAC hoped the biracial committees would address minority underemployment within the Pensacola Police and the Escambia County Sheriff's Departments.[36]

The paucity of black law enforcement personnel in Northwest Florida explained much of the interracial tension that characterized the area for, as the state committee noted, "where poor police-minority relations exist, minorities have, without fail, been underrepresented on the police force." In 1978, 154 deputies served Escambia County, and only four were African American. The following year, the city employed 126 white and four black officers. "Given the overwhelming dominance of white males in both police agencies," the commission concluded, "it is little wonder why many blacks believe police-community relations are poor. Hostility toward any segment of government is easily bred when given segments of a community are policed and disciplined by a system in which they and their peers are effectively excluded." The FAC encouraged the PPD and Escambia County Sheriff's Department to hire more African Americans and promote them above their peak rank of sergeant. *News Journal* editors and elected officials at both the city and county positions, however, ignored the report.[37]

The legacy of the 1970s black freedom struggle in Northwest Florida, then, influenced area race relations into a new decade. The trials and travails that Matthews and Brooks endured crippled direct action protests against racial injustices, provided a cautionary tale for anyone who publicly threatened the Escambia County power structure, and revealed the primary shortcomings of the traditional approach to local organizing. Tensions within local civil rights groups, between their local and national chapters, and the continued rivalry organizations had with each other further undermined the Panhandle movement, as did a reorientation of the Human Relations Commission's primary purpose and functions. The controversy concerning the images and nickname at Escambia High finally ended, but the changes transpired with no white acknowledgment of why African Americans objected to the Confederate images. The *McMillan* suit continued the struggle for black empowerment in a different way than the mass mobilization efforts of the 1970s. Ten African Americans, all from the professional upper-middle class and each of whom repudiated public demonstrations and organizational posturing in sworn statements, responded to the controversial 1976 school board elections by seeking to dismantle the at-large election process for the county's three most influential governing bodies. *McMillan* drifted through the federal courts and endured a myriad of appeals and countermeasures as the 1980s began, which pertained to much more than electoral procedures for area political offices. The case also highlighted the economic disparities between whites and blacks, prejudicial practices that persisted in county schools, an unequal distribution of social services in residential areas that different races populated, and the contentious relationship between local law enforcement agencies and African Americans. *McMillan v. Escambia County*, therefore, was the legal instrument through which local blacks pursued political power to bring economic and social change to Northwest Florida as the 1980s progressed. The suit's settlement inspired hope for improved local race relations, but white control over county power systems remained absolute as the twenty-first century began.

CHAPTER TEN

Legacy of a Struggle

> To believe that some day in some nebulous future, whites
> and others will come to comprehend that the complex set
> of circumstances involving race and class that bring about
> inequalities in American society will disappear seems
> almost naive.
>
> —ORA WILLS, educator, writer, and eighty-year
> Pensacola resident

The many hearings, appeals, and public referendums that followed Judge
Winston Arnow's initial 1978 *McMillan v. Escambia County* verdict indefinitely delayed all county commission, school board, and Pensacola City
Council elections. The county school board spent $48,000 on the case
and estimated it needed an additional $200,000 to continue the appeals
process, a figure its members were unwilling to sacrifice. The board, then,
dropped its appeal of Arnow's ruling and became the first governing
body in Escambia County to implement district-based elections. The city
council and county commission, however, fought to preserve the at-large
system until the Supreme Court's 1982 *Rogers v. Lodge* decision, which
provided the district courts greater latitude to rule on electoral discrimination cases. In the wake of *Rogers*, the Fifth Circuit justices affirmed
Winston Arnow's ruling on the unconstitutionality of the traditional
election process, and he ordered his court to schedule county commission and Pensacola City Council elections by separate residential districts
before December 28, 1982. The council dropped its appeal of *McMillan*
and accepted a ten-seat reapportionment with seven single-member districts and three at-large positions. The county appealed to the Supreme
Court for an emergency stay of elections, but the court rejected the motion on December 2. Escambia County, which had held no commission
elections since 1978 and suffered from what one columnist called "a se-
vere case of political constipation," finally prepared for a vote under the
modified process.[1]

At a March 10, 1983, hearing, Judge Arnow accepted a reapportionment
plan from the Escambia County Board of Commissioners that divided
the county into the same five single-member districts that determined

school board representation zones. The scheme, Arnow maintained, "best complies with the one-person, one-vote rule and avoids diluting the potential voting strength of the blacks." He also set November 1 as the day of general elections for District One, District Three, and District Five, representatives of which would serve five-year terms. All commission seats, the judge determined, would shift to four-year service terms after staggered elections in 1986 and 1988. Defense attorneys filed a final appeal to stay commission elections, which the Supreme Court again rejected. In 1983, county voters elected commissioners for the first time in five years.[2] Under the revised plan, five African American candidates ran for the commission seat in District Three, which possessed a 56 percent black voting majority. White citizens, however, did not respond positively to the change. Only 17 percent of registered white voters in District Three participated in the 1983 election because, according to one person, "there wasn't anyone to vote for. They were all black." County election supervisor Joe Oldmixon even distributed "Judge Arnow's phone number" to the numerous people who complained about the new election process. Yet only 41 percent of the district's registered black voters cast ballots in the general election, which surprised African American candidates and seemingly confirmed black political apathy in the minds of whites who opposed electoral reform. Black candidates blamed the underwhelming and disappointing turnout on their constituency's traditional distrust of the overall local political process. "Why should I vote," one African American proclaimed, when elected politicians of any race "are not going to do anything anyway" to improve social and economic conditions?[3] Suspicion of the traditional political establishment remained a crucial legacy from the 1970s civil rights struggles for local blacks.

In spite of the low county voter participation rate of 29 percent, Willie Junior defeated his Republican opponent in the District Three race with a convincing 4,988 to 1,356 result and became the first African American elected to the Escambia County Commission. As 1983 ended, three African Americans served on the ten-member city council, two occupied seats on the five-person school board, and Junior was one of five county commissioners. "Let's give them all a chance," News Journal editors urged, "to show what they are willing to do." On December 19, 1984, the Fifth Circuit Court of Appeals determined that the at-large elections in Northwest Florida violated section two of the Voting Rights Act which, for all intents and purposes, ended proceedings in McMillan v. Escambia County. Voters still elected city councilmen, county commissioners, and school board members through single-member representation districts.[4] Although one significant lawsuit against racially discriminatory practices in Escambia County ended, the case that regulated county school integration remained open for almost fifteen more years.

In the fall of 1999, the NAACP and Escambia County School Board submitted a joint proposal to close the *Augustus* suit. The court approved the settlement and ordered the board to publish the agreement in local newspapers. Citizens who objected to the plan had sixty days to write and request a Fairness Hearing before U.S. District Court judge Lacey A. Collier. The court received only seven letters, and most supported case closure. Judge Collier acknowledged "that there are continuing racial disparities in certain areas of school system operation." Four county schools, he noted, still possessed a 90 percent or higher African American student majority and they constituted 60 percent of the student suspensions in Escambia County schools. Most importantly, blacks made up 35 percent of students but only 12 percent of the faculty and staff in district schools. Despite his reservations, Collier scheduled no further hearings on the case because of "the sparse response to the Notice published." The court announced that the Escambia County School System had achieved "full unitary status" and closed the *Augustus* suit on December 12, 1999.[5]

The *McMillan* and *Augustus* cases represented the most consequential legal challenges to the institutionalized white supremacy that permeated Escambia County race relations. The suits brought change to the education system and election procedures in Northwest Florida, but they also revealed the inability of local blacks to alter the power imbalance that divided the races throughout the twentieth century. The economic inequalities and educational discrepancies that African Americans continued to experience highlight the limitations and shortcomings that the black freedom struggle encountered during the years beyond integration in Escambia County. The local movement of the 1960s and 1970s, therefore, had little to no impact on the quality of life for those who needed it most. Differences in poverty rates, unemployment figures, mean household incomes, mean earnings, and per capita incomes reveal three important economic attributes for blacks and whites in Northwest Florida between 1970 and 2000 (see table A.1).[6]

First, the state averages for African Americans were typically higher than those at the local levels. The assessment that black Floridians were more likely than whites to live in poverty, for instance, dropped

173 percent during the thirty-year period. In Escambia County, the same figure decreased 38 percent, while the likelihood that blacks lived below poverty levels in Pensacola increased 58 percent from 1970 to 2000 (see table A.1). The amount that blacks earned for each per capita white dollar over the thirty-year period increased 14.9 cents in Florida and 10.8 cents in Escambia County, but decreased .8 cents during the same span in Pensacola (see table A.1 and figures A.1–A.3). Median household income figures revealed similar trends. African American households in Florida brought home 68.7 cents for every white dollar in 2000, a 12.5 cent increase since 1970 (see table A.1 and figure A.4). Black households in Escambia County brought home 59.7 cents for every dollar the average white household received, an increase of eight cents over thirty years, but African American households in Pensacola lost 5.7 cents on every dollar whites earned over the thirty-year period (see table A.1 and figures A.5–A.6). While the gap between white and black households narrowed, albeit slightly, a greater income disparity characterized black and white households in Pensacola in 2000 than it did in 1970.[7]

Second, the economic indicators reveal that only limited substantive economic gain occurred for Escambia County blacks between 1970 and 2000. In 1970, for instance, African Americans who lived in the county were 274 percent more likely than white residents to live below poverty standards. The percentage fell to 209 percent by 2000. The relative unemployment percentage of black to white workers dropped 70 percent during the period, but county African Americans were still 65 percent more likely than white workers to be unemployed in 2000. Finally, the mean earnings differential between black and white workers in Escambia County increased a paltry 2.4 cents—from 61.4 to 63.8 cents—between 1970 and 2000. The per capita income differential between whites and blacks diminished between 1970 and 2000, but still fell 4.1 cents below the average black earning growth rate at the state level (see table A.1 and figure A.2).[8] Little meaningful improvement, then, bridged the economic disparities between whites and blacks in Escambia County from 1970 through 2000.

Finally, statistics reveal that financial conditions for African Americans who resided in Pensacola were worse in 2000 than they were thirty years earlier. The percentage of African Americans living in poverty fell 65 percent in Escambia County and 387 percent statewide between 1970 and 2000, but it increased 58 percent for Pensacola blacks. In 2000, African Americans in Pensacola were 380 percent more likely than city whites to be mired below poverty levels and 89 percent more likely to be un-employed. The per capita income differential between whites and blacks decreased in Florida and Escambia County from 1970 to 2000 by 14.9 and 10.8 cents, respectively, but increased for African Americans in Pensacola by almost a cent during the era (see table A.1 and figures A.1–A.3). Pensacola blacks received 53.5 cents for every white per capita dollar in 2000, despite the fact that African American high school graduation percentages and the mean number of educational years for blacks increased each decade after the 1960s. Mean earnings and household incomes disparities between black and white workers in Pensacola also increased between 1970 and 2000 (see figures A.4 and A.6). One black civic leader claimed as early as 1980 that economic figures indicated, "Pensacola is basically where it was fifty years ago in relation to job opportunities for blacks and poor whites." The "economic racism" and absence of "upward mobility" opportunities for black residents that NAACP president Robert Walker said afflicted his city contributed to the decline of Pensacola's black population by an average of 9.5 percent for each decade between 1970 and 2000, while it increased 64 percent in Escambia County and 44.6 percent across Florida (see table A.1).[9]

In addition to the persistent economic inequities, African Americans faced significant obstacles in Escambia County schools throughout the 1980s and 1990s. Between 1982 and 1992, black students constituted 29.4 percent of those enrolled in the county schools (see figure A.7). Yet 63.8 percent of all students labeled "mentally handicapped" were African American, and only 3.9 percent of those admitted to "gifted" programs were black (see figures A.8 and A.9). In addition, African Americans represented 46.5 percent of county students suspended one or more days from school for disciplinary reasons between 1981 and 1984 (see figure A.10).[10] To complicate matters, the electoral reforms that *McMillan* introduced had little impact in county schools. Only five African American candidates ran for school board positions on eight separate occasions between 1980 and 2000 and two of the three winners, Henry McMillan and Elmer Jenkins, were plaintiffs in the suits that altered the local election processes.[11] African Americans in Escambia County, therefore, encountered numerous economic and educational challenges in the years following the settlement of the *McMillan* and *Augustus* suits, but unresolved issues from prior decades continued to plague local race relations for the century's remainder.

In 1999 Movement for Change (MFC), a grassroots group that emerged during the decade to fill the organizational void left by SCLC and NAACP, asked the Pensacola City Council to remove the Confederate battle flag from the city's official "Five Flags" logo and public displays. Fifty years earlier, Pensacola civic boosters declared theirs "The City of Five Flags" to promote local tourism and erected poles to fly the Spanish, French, British, Confederate, and American flags near the downtown waterfront. A "Fiesta of Five Flags" subsequently became an annual festival that both reflected immense civic pride and brought scores of tourists to the historic area. The Confederate flag did not occupy a prominent role in Fiesta events or the Five Flags celebrations because, according to the historian John Coski, "civic boosters chose to use the familiar and popular battle flag, without much thought to either historical accuracy or racial innuendo." Yet MFC representatives protested the image and informed councilmen that the flag, as it did at Escambia High School almost thirty years earlier, offended African Americans.[12] When MFC leaders asked the city council to remove the battle flag from official use, it challenged a long-standing cultural tradition and source of civic identity in Northwest Florida that whites believed possessed no racial connotations. The decision to remove the Confederate battle flag from official city use, then, demonstrated that images still had tremendous meaning for whites and blacks in Pensacola.

Pensacola city manager Tom Bonfield proposed a resolution to the city council in January 2000 that the body replace the Confederate battle flag with the Stars and Bars in all city displays. He defended the issue as "a matter of historical accuracy," not because the standard agitated some residents, could offend city visitors, or because similar controversies raged in Georgia and South Carolina. The Stars and Bars, Bonfield explained, was the Confederacy's first official flag and the only such banner to fly over Pensacola because the city remained under Confederate control only through the spring of 1862. The city's solution, much like the county school board's decisions pertaining to the Confederate images at Escambia High School, angered black and white activists alike. For African Americans, it represented another episode in which white officials removed Confederate imagery with no acknowledgment of its racially offensive meaning while flag supporters, much as they did during the EHS symbols crisis, accused their opponents of dishonoring Confederate veterans and "rewriting history." Over 300 people attended the

February 10 Pensacola City Council meeting, where the body approved the flag change with a seven-to-two vote. At its next session, the Escambia County Commission voted unanimously to retain the battle flag for Five Flags observances that occurred outside of city limits.[13] The fight over Confederate imagery, therefore, still polarized the races in Northwest Florida as the twentieth century ended. Yet the persistent debate over the symbols' meaning was only one continuity in area race relations. The black mistrust of local law enforcement, particularly the Escambia County Sheriff's Department, survived the end of Royal Untreiner's administration and continued into the 1990s.

The shooting of black suspects by white officers remained a central issue for African Americans long after the 1975 death of Wendel Blackwell. From 1992 to 2000, Pensacola police officers shot and killed six suspects, two of whom were black. County deputies, in comparison, killed eight people during the same period. Five of the victims were African American, and white deputies fired each of the deadly shots. On June 9, 2000, MFC announced that it would stage a demonstration on the Pensacola Bay bridge during the coming Independence Day weekend to protest local police brutality. MFC's "Countdown to Shutdown" campaign intended to block tourist access to local beaches during the summer's busiest weekend in hopes that it would initiate a Justice Department investigation of Pensacola Police and Escambia Sheriff's Department policies. The threat of civic and racial unrest brought a federal mediator to the Panhandle, and he organized negotiations between community leaders and residents at the sheriff's department. MFC leaders suspended their planned demonstration pending continued dialogue with local white officials. The plan reminded many of past black campaigns against similar practices with good reason. H. K. Matthews helped MFC president LeRoy Boyd organize the direct action protest.[14]

Unlike most of the individuals who were involved in the circumstances concerning the incarceration of H. K. Matthews, numerous organizations and civic groups recognized the sacrifices and contributions that the fiery minister made for racial equality in Northwest Florida as the century ended. The late 1980s and 1990s, in short, solidified Matthews's position as the "Martin Luther King of Pensacola," even though he never again established a residence in Florida. The *Pensacola New American*, for instance, maintained in 1988, "There is no way for us to mention Dr. King and the struggle without mentioning Rev. Matthews. . . . And we're sure Dr. King would think the same" because "Matthews was in the forefront of every major civil rights push in this area." As the years passed, the Escambia County SCLC, the Pensacola NAACP, several local heritage and fraternal organizations, the Northwest Florida Afro-American Hall of Fame, the Chicago City Council, numerous area churches, and the Escambia-Pensacola Human Relations Committee presented Matthews with numerous awards for his contributions to the local and national civil rights movement. B. J. Brooks compared his former colleague and estranged friend to "Nelson Mandela" because his conviction "was all political," and the Pensacola City Council declared July 12, 1987, "H. K. Matthews Day" in Escambia County. Over 1,000 people attended the ceremony at Zion Hope Primitive Baptist Church, at which Rev. R. N. Gooden delivered the keynote address and Mayor Vince Whibbs presented Matthews with a key to the city. The irony of the affair did not escape the still-perceptive minister, as he noted that "the town has given me its keys for organizing and leading the same activities that basically got me exiled a decade earlier."[15] The recognition and accolades that Matthews received, though, came because of the emphasis the approach to local organizing placed upon individual leaders and not because his initiatives brought substantial social and economic improvements for blacks in Northwest Florida. The powerlessness of area African Americans to alter the racial status quo, influence the local power structure to acknowledge the validity of black concerns, or initiate meaningful reform in those areas remain the most enduring legacy of the area freedom struggle.

The shortcomings of the local movement have only became more pronounced as the twenty-first century progresses. The legacy of the "implementors' revenge," for instance, endures in county schools. Black public school students remain less likely to enter advanced placement courses and more likely to drop out of school than whites. In 2008, Escambia County had the third-highest black dropout rate in the state—6.6 percent—which tripled the same statistic for white pupils. By 2012, African Americans comprised 35.1 percent of county students and 54 percent of those with "intellectual disabilities," but only 12.2 percent of those enrolled in gifted programs. Whites, put another way, were six and one half times more likely than blacks to enter advanced courses while blacks were over twice as likely as whites to be labeled intellectually handicapped. In addition, blacks represented 61.5 percent of all student suspensions during the 2012–13 school year, which meant that African Americans had a three times higher likelihood than whites of being suspended.[16] Economic discrepancies along racial lines also persist in Northwest Florida. In 2010, black per capita income was $14,058 lower than whites in Escambia County and $24,799 lower in Pensacola. Median black household income was $22,787 and $31,329 lower in each locale. The gap between each measurable data point was wider than in any prior census year, with the per capita income division almost doubling since 2000. In addition, African American households in Escambia County were 3.5 times more likely than white households to receive food stamps and 4.7 times more likely to do so in Pensacola in 2010.[17] Yet most importantly, the shooting of black citizens by white sheriff's deputies characterizes the racial divide that permeates the region into the twenty-first century's second decade. In July 2013, sixty-year-old Pensacola resident Roy Middleton was mistaken for a car thief in his own yard and shot fifteen times by two sheriff's deputies. The officers claimed Middleton, who was searching his vehicle for a cigarette, lunged toward them with what they believed was a metal object in his hand. Sheriff David Morgan placed the two men on paid administrative leave until a grand jury ruled that they committed no crime. Morgan, in a press conference that would have made Royal Untreiner swell with pride, claimed "non-compliance to the directions of law enforcement officers" represented "the tragedy" of Middleton's shooting. Besides, the sheriff noted with unintended irony, "this is a common occurrence" because "we live in a very violent society." Middleton survived the shooting, which differentiated his case from Wendel Blackwell's in the most crucial way.[18]

An examination of the black freedom struggle in Escambia County, Florida, then, expands existing academic and popular understanding of the broader struggle for racial justice across the South in many ways. It contributes to the growing body of scholarship that extends the movement's traditional timeline beyond a reductive "dominant narrative" and demonstrates in communities such as Pensacola that the black freedom struggle endured and evolved after the 1960s ended. The Panhandle movement also challenges the antiquated yet still pervasive "Florida exceptionalism" argument which situates the state outside the racial tumult that engulfed much of the region. The area movement, instead, places Florida with a greater regional context and illustrates how whites modified the methods and tactics they used to preserve white supremacy after the monumental legislative victories of the Second Reconstruction. The rise and fall of Klavern 109, commonplace invocation of "majority rights," and the display and defense of Confederate iconography in the public realm offer a number of ways that white southerners responded to persistent challenges to their racial superiority during the 1970s and beyond, which places Northwest Florida in a position from which scholars can assess the development of white popular conservatism, and movement change and continuity in locales where African Americans were a distinct minority of the overall population. Furthermore, the Panhandle freedom struggle illuminates the discord that existed both between and within organizations such as the NAACP and SCLC at the local, state, and national levels. Their struggles for members, financial security, and renewed relevance affected area movements in unforeseen ways during the 1970s and suggests that there is a need for a critical assessment of the role and practicality of institutional involvement in contemporary local racial affairs. Finally, the Escambia County movement demonstrates how both the top-down and grassroots approaches provided the foundation of a unique yet ultimately flawed local organizing approach.

An array of African American leaders, particularly ministers, used their influential positions within the black community to coordinate direct action campaigns and take legal actions against specific targets during the Pensacola movement that depended upon community support to succeed. The organizational model worked against segregated public facilities, discriminatory statutes and, to a lesser degree, employment inequities, but it failed to alter the power imbalance that still characterized local race relations beyond the 1960s. Marches, demonstrations, mass meetings, and economic boycotts had little effect against de facto forms of white supremacy and such tactics fueled a resurging majority backlash against black activism. In addition, the ability of white systems of control to successfully target and subsequently silence specific black leaders provided an example to the African American population and crippled the area struggle. As a result of the emphasis local blacks placed on charismatic individual leaders and guidance from civil rights groups, the Pensacola freedom struggle foundered with little direction or purpose into the twenty-first century. Blacks continue to mobilize, but they target traditional obstacles with little focus or direction. Tremendous educational and economic gaps, some of which are greater than they were fifty years earlier, characterize contemporary race relations, demonstrate the limits of traditional forms of community mobilization in altering the possession and application of meaningful civic power in Escambia County, and reflect the persistence of white supremacy even after Jim Crow formally ended.

Yet the most important feature of the Northwest Florida freedom struggle during the years beyond integration is the national relevance of Pensacola's experience. The lessons of the Escambia County movement transcend local, state, or even regional context. The story of racial power, privilege, change, and continuity is not this community's alone, for others throughout the United States encountered similar conflicts. The Panhandle movement highlights the shifting nature of the movement's orientation from laws to practices, culture, and the possession of power that a racial majority possesses in cities throughout the nation. It also places the origins of the "New Jim Crow" that Michelle Alexander described in the context of these 1970s struggles over the status of black students in school where they were a racial minority and the power that white-dominated law enforcement bodies and local courts wielded—often in discriminatory and unjust fashion—over African Americans. The pattern of an emerging school-to-prison pipeline takes shape in Escambia County during this vital period and additional research is needed to connect the mass incarceration of black males to the ways whites implemented school integration, as well as the limitations and challenges the national black freedom struggle encountered during the 1970s and beyond. The Pensacola experience does, however, extend conclusions that Alexander and other scholars of social change, inequality studies, and civil rights history have reached regarding new forms of discrimination beyond the criminal justice system and the war on drugs to more pervasive and benign systems of white supremacy. The display, use, and defense of divisive symbols still polarize the races. The gap between white and black incomes continues to expand. Inequities in public education for African American students persist. Most importantly, the failure of the justice system to hold law enforcement officers accountable for using excessive force against and even killing black citizens demonstrates that the national struggle for racial equality, as Northwest Florida experienced almost fifty years ago, is far from over. The deaths of black men at the hands of white police under questionable circumstances—whether it is Wendel Blackwell in Pensacola, Michael Brown in Ferguson, Eric Garner in New York City, Walter Scott in North Charleston, or Freddie Gray in Baltimore—reinforce the failure of the 1960s civil rights movement to alter the power imbalance that still characterizes race relations in the United States.

Demographic, Economic, and Educational Data Referenced in Chapter 10

TABLE A.1 Data for Escambia County, Pensacola, and Florida

Escambia County	1960*	1970**	1980	1990	2000
Total population	173,829	205,334	233,794	262,798	294,410
White population	137,425	163,014	181,204	201,235	213,008
Black population	36,404	40,362	45,853	52,618	63,010
White poverty rate (%)	N/A	12.2	24.9	10.8	10.3
Black poverty rate (%)	N/A	45.6	51.0	39.6	31.8
White median household incomes***	$5,670	$8,702	$16,004	$27,830	$38,881
Black median household incomes***	$2,896	$4,645	$8,680	$13,764	$22,846
White mean earnings	N/A	$8,427	$18,401	$32,301	$47,309
Black mean earnings	N/A	$5,170	$11,695	$20,303	$30,185
White unemployment, in %	4.0	4.1	6.0	5.7	3.7
Black unemployment, in %	9.4	10.2	13.8	12.9	6.1
White per capita income	N/A	$2,589	$6,960	$13,773	$18,641
Black per capita income	N/A	$1,299	$3,412	$6,599	$11,386

Pensacola—city	1960*	1970**	1980	1990	2000
Total population	56,752	59,507	57,619	58,165	56,255
White population	37,134	39,539	36,841	38,198	36,514
Black population	19,618	19,709	19,457	18,557	17,203
White poverty rate (%)	N/A	10.4	7.9	7.6	7.1
Black poverty rate (%)	N/A	43.9	41.0	41.2	34.1
White median household incomes***	$5,204	$9,872	$17,791	$31,617	$40,377
Black median household incomes***	$3,013	$4,523	$8,083	$12,552	$20,405
White mean earnings	N/A	$8,394	$21,576	$39,574	$53,088
Black mean earnings	N/A	$5,087	$11,566	$20,035	$28,409
White unemployment, in %	3.4	4.1	4.6	5.4	3.8
Black unemployment, in %	8.7	10.5	12.0	13.5	7.2
White per capita income	N/A	$2,623	$8,754	$18,732	$21,438
Black per capita income	N/A	$1,398	$3,493	$6,854	$11,256

(continued)

Florida	1960*	1970**	1980	1990	2000
Total population	4,951,560	6,789,443	9,746,324	12,937,926	15,982,378
White population	4,063,881	5,719,343	8,184,513	10,749,285	12,465,029
Black population	887,679	1,041,651	1,342,688	1,759,534	2,335,505
White poverty rate (%)	N/A	6.3	11.8	9.4	9.5
Black poverty rate (%)	N/A	41.6	41.1	31.5	25.9
White median household incomes***	$5,174	$7,690	$15,446	$28,981	$40,819
Black median household incomes***	$2,789	$4,320	$9,423	$18,055	$28,033
White mean earnings	N/A	$9,692	$19,511	$37,886	$54,761
Black mean earnings	N/A	$5,618	$13,017	$25,318	$38,030
White unemployment, in %	4.8	3.6	3.2	4.9	3.2
Black unemployment, in %	7.2	5.6	8.6	11.3	6.2
White per capita income	N/A	$3,390	$7,895	$16,483	$21,557
Black per capita income	N/A	$1,473	$3,832	$7,648	$12,585

* In 1960 the category 'non-white' was used.

** In 1970 the category 'Negro' was used.

*** The category 'family income' became 'household income' in 1970.

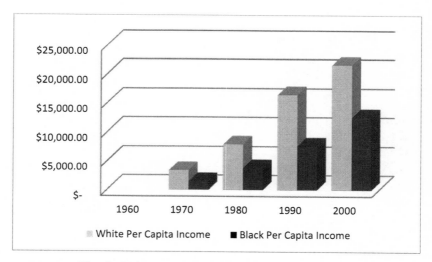

FIGURE A.1 Florida. White vs. Black Per Capita Income

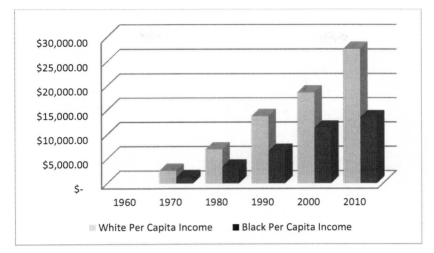

FIGURE A.2 Escambia County. White vs. Black Per Capita Income

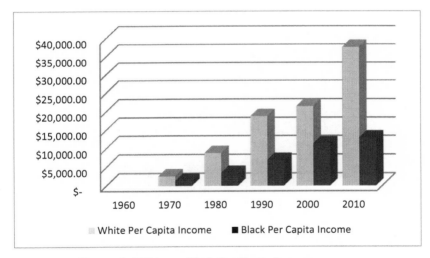

FIGURE A.3 Pensacola. White vs. Black Per Capita Income

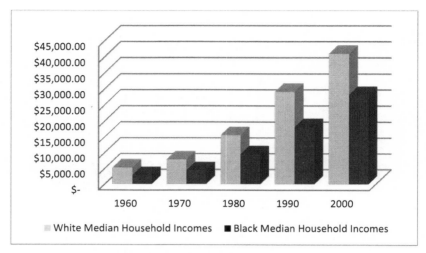

FIGURE A.4 Florida. White vs. Black Household Income

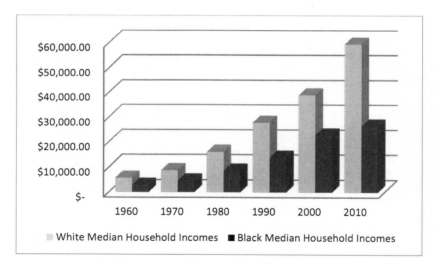

FIGURE A.5 Escambia County. White vs. Black Household Income

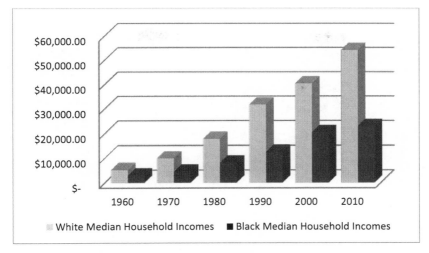

FIGURE A.6 Pensacola. White vs. Black Household Income

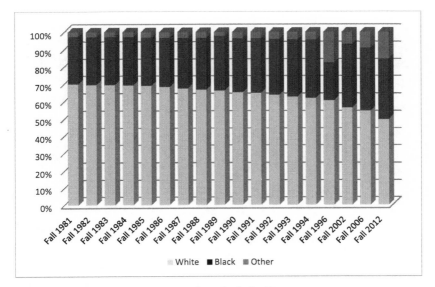

FIGURE A.7 Escambia County. Student Body by Race

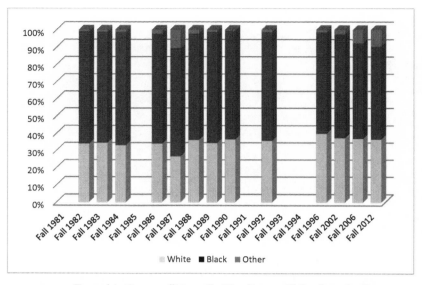

FIGURE A.8 Escambia County. "Mentally Handicapped" Students by Race

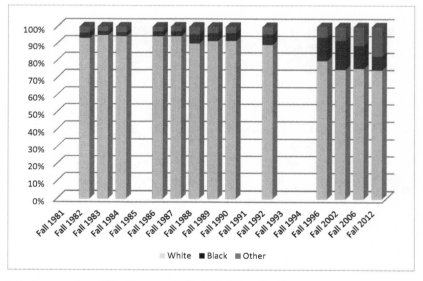

FIGURE A.9 Escambia County. "Gifted" Students by Race

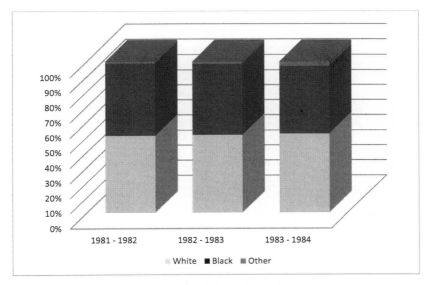

FIGURE A.10 Escambia County. Suspended Students by Race

Notes

Abbreviations Used in the Notes

Augustus v. ECBOE   Case file of *Charles A. Augustus, et al. v. Escambia County Board of Education et al.*, PCA 1064, U.S. District Court, Northern District of Florida, Pensacola Division, Escambia County Clerk of Court Records Office, Pensacola, Fla.

Blackwell v. Untreiner   Case file of *Elaine R. Blackwell v. Royal Untreiner, Douglas Raines, and U.S. Fidelity and Guaranty Company*, civil case number 76–651, Escambia County Clerk of Court Archives and Records, Pensacola, Fla.

Brooks v. FDOT   Case file of *Billie Joe Brooks v. Department of Transportation, State of Florida*, civil case number 77–2163, Escambia County Clerk of Court Archives and Records, Pensacola, Fla.

COINTELPRO   The Counter-Intelligence Program of the FBI, microfilm collection, "White Hate Groups," reels eighteen through twenty, Wilmington, Del., 1978.

ECCCP   Escambia County Community Council papers, Pensacola Historical Society, Pensacola, Fla.

ECSBMB   Escambia County School Board Minute Books and Clippings File, Escambia County School Superintendent's Office, Pensacola, Fla.

ECSDR   Escambia County Sheriff's Department Records, Escambia County Sheriff's Office Administrative Building, Pensacola, Fla.

EPHRCP   Escambia-Pensacola Human Relations Commission papers, Escambia-Pensacola Human Relations Commission, Pensacola, Fla.

Escambian   Escambia High School Yearbook, EHS library, Pensacola, Fla.

Fla. v. Brooks and Matthews

Case file of *Florida v. Brooks, Billie Joe Sr. and Matthews, Hawthorne Konrade*, case number 50,350, Florida Supreme Court Case Files, 1825–2011, State Archives of Florida, Tallahassee, Fla. The original case was numbered 75–390 while pending in the Florida First District Court of Appeal.

Fla. v. HKM	Case file of *Florida v. Matthews, Hawthorne Konrade*, case number 73–911B, Escambia County Clerk of Court Archives and Records, Pensacola, Fla.
Fla. v. HKM, FSA	Case file of *Florida v. Matthews, Hawthorne Konrad*, case number 50–350, Florida Supreme Court Case Files, 1825–2011, State Archives of Florida, Tallahassee, Fla. The file combines the Florida First District Court of Appeal cases numbered z-133, z-166, z-275, BB-401.
HKMAR	H. K. Matthews Audio Recordings, private collection, Brewton, Ala.
HKMP	H. K. Matthews Papers, private collection, Brewton, Ala.
HKP	Howard King Papers, Pensacola Historical Society, Pensacola, Fla.
JMCP	John Moreno Coe Papers, 1919–1973, Manuscript, Archives, and Rare Book Library, Emory University, Atlanta, Ga.
LFP	LeBaron Family Papers, University Archives and West Florida History Center, John C. Pace Memorial Library, University of West Florida, Pensacola, Fla.
McMillan	Case file of *Henry McMillan, et al. v. Escambia County, et al.*, U.S. District Court for the Northern District of Florida, RG 21, National Archives at Atlanta.
McMillan UWF	*McMillan v. Escambia County* case file, University Archives and West Florida History Center, John C. Pace Memorial Library, University of West Florida, Pensacola, Fla.
MHWP	Mary Harrison Washington Papers, private collection, Mapleton, Ga.
MTGP	Marion T. Gaines Papers, University Archives and West Florida History Center, John C. Pace Memorial Library, University of West Florida, Pensacola, Fla.
NAACPP	National Association for the Advancement of Colored People Papers, Library of Congress Manuscript Division, Washington, D.C.
NWABR	*Newsweek* Atlanta Bureau records, 1953–1979, Manuscript, Archives, and Rare Book Library, Emory University, Atlanta, Ga.
PPDF	Pensacola Police Department files, Pensacola, Fla.
RO'DAP	Governor Reubin O'Donovan Askew Papers, RG 103, State Archives of Florida, Tallahassee, Fla.
SCLCR	Southern Christian Leadership Conference records, 1864–2012, Manuscript, Archives, and Rare Book Library, Emory University, Atlanta, Ga.
Smith v. St. Tammany	Case file of *Thomas J. Smith v. St. Tammany Parish School Board, et al.* Records of U.S. Fifth Circuit Court of Appeals, RG 276, John Burgess facility, National Archives at Fort Worth, Tex.

SOE Files	Escambia County Supervisor of Elections files, Escambia County Supervisor of Elections Office, Pensacola, Fla.
TTP	Tom Tobiassen Papers, University Archives and West Florida History Center, John C. Pace Memorial Library, University of West Florida, Pensacola, Fla.

Newspapers and Magazines

AA	Atmore (Alabama) Advance
AC	Atlanta Constitution
ADW	Atlanta Daily World
BAA	Baltimore African-American
Broad.	Broadview
BS	Brewton (Alabama) Standard
CA	Cleveland Advocate
CCP	Cleveland Call and Post
CD	Chicago Defender
DBMJ	Daytona Beach Morning Journal
ECPB	Escambia County—Pensacola Beacon
FT	Florida Tropic
FTU	Florida Times-Union
LL	Lakeland Ledger
MA	Montgomery Advertiser
MDN	Miami Daily News
MH	Miami Herald
MPR	Mobile Press Register
NOTP	New Orleans Times-Picayune
NW	Newsweek
NYT	New York Times
PC	Pittsburgh Courier
PCP	Pensacola Call and Post
PJ	Pensacola Journal
PN	Pensacola News
PNA	Pensacola New American
PNJ	Pensacola News Journal
PT	Philadelphia Tribune
PV	Pensacola Voice
RRLR	Race Relations Law Reporter
SHT	Sarasota Herald Tribune
SPI	St. Petersburg Independent
SPT	St. Petersburg Times
SSN	Southern School News
SUM	The Summation: A News Publication of the Escambia-Santa Rosa Florida Bar Association

SZ   *Star of Zion*
TCL   *Tri-City (Alabama) Ledger*

Introduction

1. *PJ*, January 23, 1975.

2. *PJ*, June 10, 1975; *PN*, July 17, 1975.

3. Hall, "Long Civil Rights Movement," 1233.

4. Ibid., 1233–34; Eagles, "Toward New Histories," 838, 848.

5. Steven Lawson's essay, "Freedom Then, Freedom Now" first challenged the concept of a "long movement" and inspired a number of scholars who answered his call for a new model of civil rights study that kept the classic phase of the movement (1954–1968) central to their works. "The Long Origins for the Short Civil Rights Movement," skillfully articulated the objections some scholars have with the "long civil rights" framework and opened a volume of essays that offered "new perspectives" on the greater movement. According to Lawson, the "long" concept "blurs the lines of the historic changes within the black freedom struggle that gave the period from 1954 to 1968 its distinct context and character." Lawson defends a "short civil rights movement," a period "defined by the robust interconnections among the federal government, community activists, national and local organizations, and charismatic and group-centered leaders" that evolved into and inspired the continuing struggle for a broader "struggle for freedom rights." Lawson, "Long Origins of the Short Civil Rights Movement," 14, 26. See also the remaining essays in McGuire and Dittmer, eds., *Freedom Rights*.

6. Crosby, *A Little Taste of Freedom*, xiv; Moye, *Let the People Decide*, 204; Green, *Battling the Plantation Mentality*, 312; See also Crosby, *Civil Rights History from the Ground Up*; Fleming, *In the Shadow of Selma*; Jeffries, *Bloody Lowndes*; Hamlin, *Crossroads at Clarksdale*; and Brown-Nagin, *Courage to Dissent*.

7. Alexander, *The New Jim Crow*, 3, 12, 13, 72. For more on the criticisms of *The New Jim Crow*, see Forman Jr., "Racial Critiques of Mass Incarceration," 101–46; Osel, "Black Out"; Osel, "Toward Détournement"; Thomas, "Why Some Like the New Jim Crow So Much." For more on the historical importance of the issue, see Heather Thompson, "Why Mass Incarceration Matters."

8. Payne, *I've Got the Light of Freedom*, 217.

9. Crespino, *In Search of Another Country*, 11, 18; Kruse, *White Flight*; Lassiter, *The Silent Majority*.

10. Key Jr., *Southern Politics in State and Nation*, 83. See also Phillips, "The Central Theme of Southern History," 30–43; Price, *The Negro and Southern Politics*; Matthews and Prothro, *Negroes and the New Southern Politics*; and Dauer, "Florida: The Different State."

11. For more on works that challenge the myth of Florida exceptionalism, see Mohl and Mormino, "The Big Change in the Sunshine State"; Green, *Before His Time*; Rabby, *The Pain and the Promise*; Newton, *The Invisible Empire*; Ortiz, *Emancipation Betrayed*; Winsboro, "Image, Illusion, and Reality," 1–21; Marvin Dunn, "The Illusion of Moderation," 22–46; Ortiz, "Old South, New South, or Down

South?," 220–44; Gilbert King, *Devil in the Grove*; Wilkerson, *The Warmth of Other Suns*; and Cassenello, *To Render Invisible*.

12. These are the three dichotomies that Numan Bartley claims characterized the response of southern business leaders to civil rights activities in their cities, but it also applies well to the greater reaction of other white civic leaders in those areas. Bartley, *The Rise of Massive Resistance*, 313–15.

13. This organizing approach should not be confused with the "organizing tradition" that Charles Payne addressed in *I've Got the Light of Freedom*. He build his work, one of the most significant in movement scholarship, around SNCC activist Bob Moses's insight that the movement is divided into "organizing" and "mobilizing" traditions. The former, which Payne argues developed in the Mississippi Delta during the early 1960s, possessed a broader definition of freedom than community mobilization efforts and placed "a greater emphasis on the long-term development of leadership in ordinary men and women." Payne, *I've Got the Light of Freedom*, 3. The Northwest Florida movement, in contrast, actually combined the two traditions and relied upon charismatic leaders, particularly ministers, to organize and lead large-scale local campaigns that had long-term goals. The approach to organizing African Americans in Escambia County, then, is much different than the traditions that Payne analyzed in his seminal study.

14. U.S. Commission on Civil Rights and Katie Harris, *The Administration of Justice*, 4.

15. Laurie B. Green argues similarly in her work that Memphis blacks defined freedom broadly to include constitutional, human, and social rights. The city's sanitation strike evolved out of the expanded conceptualization; Greene, *Battling the Plantation Mentality*, 2007. Hasan Kwame Jeffries used the term "freedom rights" to describe the changing nature of African American objectives during the long civil rights movement. "Freedom rights," Jeffries maintains, "is a new paradigm for understanding the civil rights movement" that "included those enumerated in the U.S. Constitution and in various state constitutions, such as freedom of speech, religion, and assembly, and the right to due process, keep and bear arms, and vote. They also included rights that everyone is born to without restriction such as the right to own property, move without restriction, and receive an education." It is a useful term, but I chose not to use it here because black organizers in Lowndes County conceived of freedom rights "primarily as a political struggle" beyond the 1960s; Jeffries, *Bloody Lowndes*, 8, 56. In Escambia County, those rights extended into the cultural realm.

16. Martin Luther King Jr., *Where Do We Go From Here*, 8.

17. Ibid., 4; Ayers and Naylor, eds., *You Can't Eat Magnolias*, ix–x, 24; Bowden, interview.

Chapter One

1. Arnade, "Raids, Sieges, and International Wars," 106; Coker, "Pensacola, 1686–1763," 117–19, 114; William Edward Dunn, *Spanish and French Rivalry in the Gulf Region*, 61, 158, 172–73; Lloyd, "Development of the Plan of Pensacola," 253–55.

See Landers, *Black Society in Spanish Florida*; Rivers, *Slavery in Florida*; Saunt, "'The English Has Now a Mind Make Slaves of Them All'"; and Canter Brown, "Race Relations in Territorial Florida."

2. Ortiz, *Emancipation Betrayed*, 17, 103.

3. McGovern, *The Emergence of a City in the Modern South*, 7–8; McGovern, "The Rise of Pensacola," 36–37; and Shofner, "The Cultural Legacy of the Gulf Coast," 55.

4. Winsboro and Bartley, "Race, Education, and Regionalism," 721–22; Newton, *The Invisible Empire*, xv; Ortiz, *Emancipation Betrayed*, xvii, xx, 12. For more on Pensacola's black community during the era, see Hunter, *A History of Pensacola's Black Community*; Edward Davis, *A Half Century of Struggle for Freedom in Florida*, 66; Bragaw, "Status of Negroes in a Southern Port City in the Progressive Era," 288–90; and Meier and Rudwick, "Negro Boycotts of Segregated Streetcars in Florida," 525–33.

5. McGovern, "The Rise of Pensacola," 41, 66; Meier and Rudwick, "Negro Boycotts of Segregated Streetcars in Florida," 532; Bragaw, "Status of Negroes in a Southern Port City," 300, 303; McGovern, "Pensacola, Florida: A Military City in the New South," 31; Bragaw, "Loss of Identity on Pensacola's Past," 415.

6. James McGovern deposition, March 2, 1978, in *McMillan*; McGovern, *The Emergence of a City in the Modern South*, 67–70. For contemporary accounts of the Shaw lynching, see *PJ*, July 30 and 31, 1908, and August 1 and 2, 1908.

7. Pearce, *The U.S. Navy in Pensacola*, 132–43, 148, 158. For more on the Great Migration in Florida, see Ortiz, *Emancipation Betrayed*, 128–41.

8. Bragaw, "Status of Negroes in a Southern Port City in the Progressive Era," 298–300; McGovern, *The Emergence of a City in the Modern South*, 81, 107; Arnesen, "What's on the Black Worker's Mind?," 12–13; Gilbert, "Racial Attitudes Expressed in the *Pensacola News Journal*," 31–57. One area that requires more examination is the relationship between labor organizations and the struggle for racial equality during the twentieth century. For some works which address this concern, see Draper, *Conflict of Interests*; Honey, *Southern Labor and Black Civil Rights*; Korstad and Lichtenstein, "Opportunities Lost and Found," 786–811; "NAACP Branch files, Pensacola, Florida, 1919, 1921–28," group 1, box G42, NAACPP; *CD*, February 22, 1919; *CA*, March 20, 1919.

9. Key West formed the first NAACP branch in Florida. *PNJ*, February 28, 1986. For more on the Pensacola NAACP's campaign against the white primary, see "NAACP Branch files, Pensacola, Florida, 1919, 1921–28, 1935–37," group 1, box G42, "NAACP Legal Files, Cases Supported, H. D. Goode," group 1, box D58, both in NAACPP.

10. McGovern, "The Rise of Pensacola," 42; McGovern, *The Emergence of a City in the Modern South*, 91–93, 128, 138, 140, 150.

11. Parks, *Pensacola: Spaniards to Space Age*, 99; Kane, *The Golden Coast*, 21; McGovern, "The Rise of Pensacola," 38, 43; McGovern, *The Emergence of a City in the Modern South*, 155–57. Pensacola's population in 1940 was 37,449 and 43,479 in 1950. Escambia County's population in 1940 was 74,594 and 112,707 in 1950. "Plaintiffs'

Post-Trial Proposed Findings of Fact," June 5, 1978 in *McMillan*. For more on how the war transformed southern society, see Daniel, *Lost Revolutions*.

12. Mormino, "World War II," 328; Reese, "Giant of the Pine Forest," 34, 38, 43, 54, 95; Ellsworth and Ellsworth, *Pensacola: The Deep Water City*, 120, 132.

13. "Plaintiffs' Post-Trial Proposed Findings of Fact," June 5, 1978, and "Order," July 10, 1978, both in *McMillan*.

14. Klarman, "How *Brown* Changed Race Relations," 81–117; McGovern deposition, March 2, 1978, in *McMillan*; Kluger, *Simple Justice*, 724.

15. *PNJ*, September 13, 1959; "Order," July 10, 1978, and Charlie Taite deposition, May 16, 1978, both in *McMillan*.

16. Taite deposition, May 16, 1978, and "Appendix C: 'Summary of Black Candidacies in City Elections,'" July 10, 1978, both in *McMillan*.

17. Hyde, *Sunbelt Revolution*, 3–4.

18. Padgett, "The Tallahassee Bus Boycott," 190. For more on the Tallahassee movement and Rev. C. K. Steele, see Padgett, "C. K. Steele: A Biography," and Rabby, *The Pain and the Promise*.

19. Julian Banfell deposition, May 17, 1978, Reubin Askew deposition, May 22, 1978, James McGovern deposition, March 2, 1978, "Plaintiffs' Post-Trial Proposed Findings of Fact," June 5, 1978, "Order," July 10, 1978, and "Plaintiff's Post-Trial Brief," n.d., all in *McMillan*.

20. Banfell deposition, May 17, 1978, Askew deposition, May 22, 1978, and "Plaintiff's Post-Trial Brief," n.d., both in *McMillan*; *PJ*, April 30, 1959, and October 6 and 9, 1959.

21. See Green, *Before His Time*, and Gilbert King, *Devil in the Grove*. Siegel, "Why Equal Protection no Longer Protects," 1113.

22. For more on the Pensacola newspaper and its civic importance, see Perry Jr., *Never Say Impossible*. Bowden interview; Gilbert, "Racial Attitudes Expressed in *The Pensacola News Journal*," 57; Appleyard interview; McGovern deposition, March 2, 1978, and J. Earle Bowden testimony, May 19, 1978, both in *McMillan*.

23. *PNJ*, April 1, October 14, 1956, and August 23, 1959; Undated letters to the *PNJ* editor, in *McMillan* UWF.

24. ECSBMB, October 1958–August 1960, 135–36, 293; William J. Woodham deposition, July 5, 1960, "Depositions, Brief, Etc." file, in *Augustus v. ECBOE*; *PJ*, May 14, May 15, August 21, and October 29, 1959; *PN*, May 15, 1959; *CCP*, May 30, 1959; *SSN*, October, 1959; *PNJ*, January 27, 2012.

25. Journal of the Senate: Extra-Ordinary Session, State of Florida, 1956, "An Act Relating to the Management of the Public Schools at the Local Level," 10 and 50, State of Florida, State Library; "Rules and Regulations for Implementation of the Pupil Assignment Law," n.d., "Depositions, Brief, Etc." file, both in *Augustus v. ECBOE*; *SPT*, May 9, May 25, 1955; *SSN*, June 1955; Winsboro and Bartley, "Race, Education, and Regionalism," 736.

26. "Criteria for Applications of Reassignment in Escambia County Schools" and "State Board of Education Minutes," October 13, 1959, and Woodham deposition, July 5, 1960, "Depositions, Brief, Etc." file and W. J. Woodham to Lillie

May Robinson, November 25, 1959, "Plaintiff's Exhibits" file, all in *Augustus v. EC-BOE*; ECSBMB, October 1958–August 1960, 293.

27. *PJ*, February 2, 1960; "N.A.A.C.P. Begins a Suit in Florida," *NYT*, February 2, 1960, 20; *SPT*, February 2, 1960. The Dade and Palm Beach County School Boards faced school integration suits when *Augustus* was filed. *SSN*, March 1960, 14.

28. "N.A.A.C.P. Begins a Suit in Florida," *NYT*, February 2, 1960, 20; ECSBMB, October 1958–August 1960, 351–52; *MA*, February 11, 1960; *PN*, February 26, 1960; *ADW*, March 11, 1960; *PT*, March 12, 1960; *SSN*, March 1960, 14.

29. *PJ*, June 23, 1960; *SSN*, June 1960, 5; *RRLR*, Fall 1960, 645–49; "Motion to Dismiss Case," February 19, 1960, "Depositions, Briefs, Etc." file in *Augustus v. ECBOE*; "Motion to Strike," April 20, 1960, "Depositions, Briefs, Etc." file in *Augustus v. ECBOE*.

30. "Oppositions to Defendants' Motion to Strike," May 25, 1960, and "Plaintiff's Brief: Preliminary Statement," January 16, 1961," Depositions, Briefs, Etc." file, and "Trial Transcript," January 16, 1961, 17–20, 26, 29–31, 41, 70, 79–83, 89–90, 93, 96–97, all in *Augustus v. ECBOE*; ECSBMB, August 1960–March 1962, 146; *SSN*, February 1961, 7.

31. "Resolution of Board of Public Instruction," March 17, June 14, 1961, and "Order of Court," and "Notice of Appeal," September 8, 1961, "Depositions, Briefs, Etc." file, all in *Augustus v. ECBOE*; *SSN*, April and November 1961; *PJ*, March 18, April 12, 1961; ECSBMB, August 1960–March 1962, 188–89.

32. ECSBMB, March 1962–September 1963, 54–56; *PJ*, May 24, 1962; "Pensacola Will Integrate 13 Negroes in School Plan," *NYT*, May 25, 1962, 21; *NOTP*, May 31, 1962; *PC*, June 9, 1962; *SSN*, July 1962, 14.

33. "Court of Appeals Opinion," September 5, 1962, "Depositions, Briefs, Etc." file, in *Augustus v. ECBOE*; ECSBMB, March 1962–September 1963, 131; *SPT*, July 25, 1972; *Time*, February 2, 1970: 8–9; *FTU*, August 26, 1962.

34. *PJ*, May 24, July 12, August 5, 1962; *PN*, July 11, 1962; *PNJ*, August 26, 1962.

35. *PN*, August 27, 1962; "9 Schools in Pensacola Area Admit Negroes for First Time," *NYT*, August 28, 1962, 19; *SPT*, August 28, 1962; *NOTP*, August 28, 1962; *PJ*, August 28, 1962; *MDN*, August 29, 1962.

36. *ADW*, August 28, September 6, 1962; *PNJ*, May 20, 1979, and July 27, 1987, and January 27, 2012; Harrison interview.

37. "Order," November 29, 1962, "Depositions, Briefs, Etc." file, both in *Augustus v. ECBOE*; *SSN*, October 1962, 16; *SSN*, January 10, and October 9, 1963; *SPT*, August 31, 1963.

38. *SSN*, September 1964, 7; *RRLR*, Spring 1966, 148–49; "Motion for Further Relief," November 11, 1964, "Order," February 5, March 4, 1965, "Request for Admission of Facts," March 8, 1965, "Motion for Reconsideration," March 10, 1965, "Response to Request for Admission," March 19, 1965, "Denied Motion," April 20, 1965, "Plaintiff's Statement Concerning the Racially Discriminatory Operation of Defendant's Desegregation Plan," April 27, 1965, "Order Denying Motion," October 6, 1965, "Depositions, Briefs, Etc." file, all in *Augustus v. ECBOE*; Harrison interview.

39."Journal of the Tennessee Annual Conference of the United Methodist Church," *Sixteenth Session of the 170th Annual Conference,* June 13–16, 1983, 256; "Journal of the Central Alabama Annual Conference of the Methodist Church," *Eighty-Eighth Annual Session,* May 16–19, 1963, 10 and 30; "Journal of the Central Alabama Annual Conference of the Methodist Church," *Eighty-Ninth Session,* May 28–31, 1964, 10 and 29; Carter Sr. interview; Matthews, interview, October 27, 2000; Young interview; Von Unruh, Chair of United Methodist Church Tennessee Conference, email to author, August 13, 2002; Smith and Wynn, *Freedom Facts and Firsts,* 293–94; W. C. Dobbins, "A Brief History of the Pensacola Council of Ministers," July 23, 1963, in HKP.

40. "NAACP Youth File, Charter Applications, Florida, 1957–1965," Pensacola file, group 3, box E17, NAACPP; Harvey interview, May 15, 2010; Jonas, "'All God's Chillun Got Wings,'" 58–59.

41. Washington interview; Wills interview; Jonas, "'All God's Chillun Got Wings,'" 59–60. For more on the Greensboro sit-ins, see Chafe, *Civilities and Civil Rights,* 79–101.

42. "NAACP Youth File, Florida, Pensacola–West Palm Beach, 1956–65," group 3, box E3, NAACPP; *PNJ,* April 3, 1960; *PN,* April 5, 1960; *PJ,* April 6, 1960; *SPT,* April 7, 1960; Harvey interview, May 15, 2006; Harrison interview, March 13, 2006.

43. Harrison interview; Harvey interview, May 15, 2010; Dobbins, "A Brief History of the Pensacola Council of Ministers," July 23, 1963, in HKP.

44. "NAACP Branch Department Files, Florida, Pensacola Branch, 1945–1970," group 4, box C83, NAACPP. For more on the Pensacola Merchants' Association and the meetings it had with the PCM, see "Escambia County Community Council, Special Committee Report," March 6, 1962, in HKP.

45. Matthews interview, November 23, 2001; Harvey interview, March 15, 2006; Washington interview.

46. Harrison, interview; Harvey, interview, March 15, 2006; Washington, interview; Huff interview with Angela Dobbins, May 7, 2015; Jonas, "'All God's Chillun Got Wings,'" 78.

47. Matthews, interview, October 16, 2001; Harrison, interview; Harvey, interview, May 15, 2010; Washington, interview; Chafe, *Civilities and Civil Rights,* 101.

48. *SPT,* June 14, June 16, June 17, 1961; *PN,* June 16, July 2–3, July 10–12, 1961; *PJ,* July 7, July 10, July 12–14, 1961; Carter, interview; Harrison, interview; Harvey, interview, May 15, 2010; "Docket and Record of Police Court: City of Pensacola," June 15–18, 1961, in PPDF; Pensacola NAACP Youth Council "Newsletter," July 8, 1961, in MHWP.

49. Harrison, interview; Harvey, interview, May 15, 2010; Pensacola NAACP Youth Council "Newsletter," July 8, 1961, in MHWP; Dobbins, "A Brief History of the Pensacola Council of Ministers," July 23, 1963, in HKP; *PC,* January 13, 1962.

50. *PN,* July 12, 1961; Special Committee meeting minutes, October 12, 16, 26, and November 29, 1961, in ECCCP.

51. Special Committee meeting minutes, December 11, 15, 1961, and January 4, 23, February 7, 15, 19, 26, 1962, in ECCCP.

52. Special Committee meeting minutes, January 25, February 22, 26, March 5, 12, 1962, in ECCCP; Pensacola Biracial Committee meeting minutes, July 16, 1963, in HKP.

53. Harrison, interview; Matthews, interview, October 16, 2001; Jonas, " 'All God's Chillun Got Wings,' " 129.

54. *BAA*, December 30, 1961, and October 13, 1962; *PT*, March 6, 1962; *MA*, February 23, 1962; "NAACP Branch Files, 1956–65, Florida Annual Reports," group 3, box E3, NAACPP; Dobbins, "A Brief History of the Pensacola Council of Ministers," July 23, 1963, in HKP.

Chapter Two

1. Dobbins to King, July 9, 1963, in HKP; "Information Sheet: Human Relations Commission," February 2, 1973, in EPHRCP; *PN*, August 14, 1963, and July 16, 1973; Howard King interview.

2. *PN*, June 28, July 2, July 9, 1963; Pensacola Biracial Committee meeting minutes (referred to hereafter as "BRC minutes"), July 2, 1963, in HKP. Wallace King, Ira Bascle, Rev. H. C. Calloway, and Raymond Soto joined the committee on July 9, 1963. BRC minutes, July 16, 1963, in HKP.

3. Eskew, *But for Birmingham*, 338.

4. *PJ*, September 25, 1963; BRC minutes, July 2, October 1, 1963, in HKP; King interview.

5. *PNJ*, June 16, July 14, 1963; *PJ*, June 20, August 23, September 25, September 29, October 2, 1963; *PN*, August 6, 1963; BRC minutes, September 24, 1963, in HKP.

6. "Pensacola," group 3, box C24, NAACPP. For more on the relationship between the Pensacola Police Department and the local black community, see Hennessy, "The Racial Integration of Urban Police Departments in the South."

7. "Report of Bi-Racial Committee to City Council of Pensacola," August 8, 1963, and "Recommended Program of Voluntary Action for Improvement of Race Relations in Pensacola," n.d., in HKP; BRC minutes, August 27, September 24, October 15, 1963, and January 28, February 4, 1964, in HKP; *PJ*, September 27 and October 2, 1963; King interview.

8. *PJ*, April 30, May 1, and June 30, 1964.

9. Loevy, *The Civil Rights Act of 1964*, 357–61.

10. *Journal of the Tennessee Annual Conference of the United Methodist Church*, Sixteenth Session of the 170th Annual Conference, 256; "The Methodist Church," United Methodist Church Archives and Information Center, Huntingdon College Library; *Journal of the Central Alabama Annual Conference of the Methodist Church*, May 16–19, 1963, 10; *Journal of the Central Alabama Conference of the Methodist Church*, May 28–31, 1964, 10, 29; Harvey interview, March 15, 2006; Matthews interview, November 23, 2001; Roy Finley to C. P. Mason, November 17, 1964, in HKP. Dobbins remained in Alabama until 1968, when he became pastor at Clark Memorial Church in Nashville, Tennessee. He remained there and served the UMC in a number of capacities until his death on January 24, 1983. Von Unruh,

Chair of United Methodist Church Tennessee Conference, email to author, August 13, 2002; Frances Lyons-Bristol, reference archivist at UMC General Commission on Archives and History, email to author, July 15, 2015.

11. Matthews and Butler, *Victory after the Fall*, 35–40, 57–58.

12. Matthews interview, September 15, 2001; Special Committee "Monthly Report: October 10, 1963–November 12, 1963," in ECCCP.

13. Harvey interview, March 15, 2006; Matthews interview, November 23, 2001.

14. Matthews and Butler, *Victory after the Fall*, 85–92. Numerous organizations have repeatedly recognized Matthews's participation in the Selma March. The SCLC even invited him to participate in the March 7, 1995, "30th Anniversary of the Voting Rights Campaign and the Selma to Montgomery March." See Fred Taylor to H. K. Matthews, February 13, 1995, in HKMP.

15. *PN*, March 29, 1965.

16. Matthews interview, November 23, 2001; Wiley, "An Agent for Change," 95.

17. Matthews interviews, November 23, 2001, and June 18, 2007.

18. Ibid. For more on prophetic Christianity and the role it occupied during the civil rights movement, see Chappell, *A Stone of Hope*.

19. *PJ*, April 8, 1968; Matthews interview, November 23, 2001; Wiley, "An Agent for Change," 95–96; "NAACP Youth File, Florida, Pensacola–West Palm Beach, 1956–65," group 3, box E3, NAACPP; Advisory Board to James Brown, March 6, 1969; Dr. P. F. Baranco to Marion T. Gaines, October 9, 1968, both in EPHRCP; NAACP Youth Advisors to Pensacola Mayor and City Council, November 8, 1968, in "Information Sheet: Human Relations Commission," February 2, 1973, in EPHRCP; Matthews interview, July 19, 2015.

20. The four FAMU students were in Pensacola because they were enrolled in the Public Health Nursing class at the Escambia County Health Department. *PJ*, April 8, 1968; Matthews, interview, November 23, 2001; *PCP*, June 21, 1969; "Information Sheet: Human Relations Commission," February 2, 1973, in EPHRCP; Letter to Human Relations Committee, April 13, 1969, in EPHRCP; Meeting minutes, April 15, 1969, in EPHRCP; Rev. Robert Sidentopf to Miss Cheryl Dearring, April 17, 1969, in EPHRCP.

21. *PCP*, June 7, 1969; *PNJ*, March 16, 1969; *Broad.*, August 1971, 1–5; Appleyard interview; Mott interview; Bowden interview; Hebert interview.

22. *PN*, August 14, 1963; "Information Sheet: Human Relations Commission," February 2, 1973, in EPHRCP. For more on the Biracial Committee, see HKP.

23. HRC minutes, October 4, 1966, and February 11, February 13, April 9, May 14, August 12, September 10, November 17, 1968, and July 2, 1969, in MTGP; *PJ*, December 16, 1971.

24. HRC minutes, February 16, 1966, in MTGP; Citizens United for Racial Equality to Commission, July 8, 1968, in EPHRCP; Meeting minutes, September 10, 1968, and May 20, February 18, April 15, August 20, December 17, 1969, and October 15, 1971, in EPHRCP; Murray E. Wilcox to Rev. Robert Siedentopf, February 28, 1969, in EPHRCP; "NAACP Youth Council, College Chapter, and Adult Branch" flier, in EPHRCP; *PJ*, October 5, October 6, 1969, and January 22, May 5, 1970; *PCP*, June 14, 1969.

25. "Human Relations Commission, 1966–71" file, in MTGP; Bowden interview.

26. Brooks replaced Matthews as president of the Pensacola branch in the first weeks of 1969. See part 6, box C83, NAACPP. According to Matthews, he resigned as president of the adult branch to have more time for duties as senior advisor of the Youth Council. Matthews and Butler, *Victory after the Fall*, 105–07. Minchin, "Making Best Use of the New Laws," 673; Matthews interview, November 23, 2001; Part 6, group 4, NAACPP.

27. The national SCLC office in Atlanta gave the Escambia County chapter its "Certificate of Affiliation" on February 23, 1971. T. Y. Rogers Jr. letter to H. K. Matthews, February 23, 1971, SCLCR; Matthews interview, November 23, 2001; Matthews interview, February 13, 2002; Matthews and Butler, *Victory after the Fall*, 101.

28. "Application for Affiliation," n.d., SCLCR; Matthews interview, February 13, 2002, and July 19, 2015.

29. *PNJ*, March 16, 1969; *Broad*, August 1971; *PN*, April 20, 1971.

30. W. J. Cash, *The Mind of the South*, 303; Myrdal, *An American Dilemma*, 535–36; O'Brien, *The Color of the Law*, 143; Moore, *Black Rage in New Orleans*, 2; Jeffries, *Bloody Lowndes*, 34–35; Greene, "Challenging the Civil Rights Narrative," 66. For more on police violence in the post-1965 movement, see Greene, *Battling the Plantation Mentality*, 91–82, 106–11; Minchin, *From Rights to Economics*, 1, 5; Tyson, *Blood Done Signed My Name*; Umoja, *We Will Shoot Back*; De Jong, *Invisible Enemy*, 84–85.

31. Matthews interview, November 23, 2001; Watson interview; Hoard interview.

32. Hennessy, "The Racial Integration of Urban Police Departments in the South," 78; Matthews interview, Nov. 23, 2001; Watson interview; Hoard interview. In 1971, a black prisoner named Robert Lee Adams filed a law suit against the Escambia County Sheriff's Department that called the maintenance and use of the bullets "cruel and unusual punishment." The department settled the suit for $1,000 and dismantled the cells by year's end. *Robert Lee Adams vs. Sheriff, Escambia County* in JMCP.

33. In 1966, for instance, the Human Relations Commission documented instances of "near riots" between the races at PHS football games, a dance held that a local National Guard armory sponsored, and a busy intersection where black and white pedestrians frequently passed. The presence of Escambia County sheriff's deputies exacerbated racial tensions in each episode. HRC minutes, February 16, 1966, in MTGP; *PJ*, November 6, 1966. Meeting minutes, May 20, 1969, and Pensacola NAACP Youth Council to Pensacola Police Chief D. P. Caldwell, July 10, 1970, both in EPHRCP.

34. Matthews interview, November 23, 2001; "Investigation Findings" of the Glover/Huff drownings, undated report, in EPHRCP.

35. *PJ*, August 1, August 3, August 4, 1970; "Investigation Findings" of the Glover/Huff drownings, undated report, in EPHRCP.

36. *PNJ*, January 27, 1989; Behr interview; Royal Untreiner Personnel File, in ECSDR; Appleyard, *The Peacekeepers*, 109–10.

37. "Report: Escambia County School Board," June 23, 1967, *Augustus v. ECBOE*; Leroy D. Clark, NAACP Assistant Counsel, to J. Edwin Holsberry, Esq., July 8, 1966, *Augustus v. ECBOE*; Theodore R. Bowers to J. Edwin Holsberry, Esq., July 19, 1966, *Augustus v. ECBOE*; "Decree: Judge Harold Carswell," April 14, 1967, *Augustus v. ECBOE*.

38. U.S. Commission on Civil Rights, *The Diminishing Barrier*; "Report: Escambia County School Board," June 23, 1967, *Augustus v. ECBOE*; "Motion for further relief, NAACP," November 26, 1968, *Augustus v. ECBOE*.

39. *Charles C. Green et al. v. County School Board of New Kent County, VA et al.* 381 U.S. 438–42 (1968); Patterson, *Brown v. Board of Education*, 146; *RRLR*, Summer 1967, 796–97; *PNJ*, October 13, 1969; "Motion for further relief, NAACP LDF," November 26, 1968, *Augustus v. ECBOE*.

40. The Senate rejected Carswell's appointment, due primarily to his poor civil rights record and reputation as an "obstructionist." For more on Carswell's nomination and rejection, see *Time*, February 2, 1970, 8–9; *Newsweek*, February 9, 1970, 22–24; *Newsweek*, March 16, 1970, 29–30; *Time*, March 30, 1970, 18–19; *Time*, April 20, 1970, 11; *The New Yorker*, December 5, 1970, 160–61; *The New Yorker*, December 12, 1970, 53–131.

41. Federal Judicial Center, "Biographical Directory of Federal Judges"; Stafford, "Winston E. Arnow: The Man and the Building," "Winston E. Arnow Federal Building Designation Act," *Congressional Record*; *PNJ*, November 29, November 30, 1994.

42. "Order," January 23, and April 4, 1969, *Augustus v. ECBOE*.

43. U.S. Commission on Civil Rights, *The Diminishing Barrier*; "Order," April 21, 1969, *Augustus v. ECBOE*; *PNJ*, January 18, 1973.

44. The PHS halftime show featured a song that represented each of the five flags that flew over Pensacola during its history, and the band played "Dixie" to commemorate the Confederate period. The band performed the same routine at its first home football game a week later, but the director allowed the few blacks who remained in the group to abstain from playing the song. They placed their instruments by their side the next week in protest of the Confederate anthem. It was the last time the PHS band performed the song. Watson interview, Matthews interview, February 13, 2002.

45. Bowden interview; *PNJ* editorial, n.d., HKMP.

Chapter Three

1. U.S. Commission on Civil Rights, *The Diminishing Barrier*, 11.

2. Mott interview; "Racial Violence in Public Schools," n.d., in TTP.

3. U.S. Commission on Civil Rights, *The Diminishing Barrier*, 13, 14; "Racial Violence in Public Schools," n.d., in TTP; Wiley, "An Agent for Change," 80, 90; Watson interview; "A Summarized Report Concerning the Establishment and Maintainance [sic] of Human Relations Committees in Schools for the City of Pensacola and Escambia County, Florida," n.d., in EPHRCP.

4. U.S. Commission on Civil Rights, *The Diminishing Barrier*, 13; Meeting minutes, October 15, 1971, in EPHRCP.

5. During the 1970–71 school year, 13,443 blacks and 404 other undesignated racial minorities attended Escambia County public schools; only 202 blacks attended Escambia High School. "Report by Defendants," October 20, 1970, in *Augustus v. ECBOE*; "Pre-Trial Stipulation," June 26, 1973, in *Augustus v. ECBOE*; Mott interview; *PJ*, February 23, 1963; 1964 *Escambian*, 19, 45; 1965 *Escambian*, 14; 1967 *Escambian*, 20, 170; 1968 *Escambian*, 20, 185; 1969 *Escambian*, 39; 1970 *Escambian*, 120, 126–27; 1971 *Escambian*, 4–5, 16; 1972 *Escambian*, 3, 10, 14–15, 87, 95, 136, 192, 206, 276–77, 282; 1973 *Escambian*, 62, 119, 122, 144, 200; "Exhibits" file, in *Augustus v. ECBOE*. The terms "Confederate flag" and "battle flag" refers to the familiar blue St. Andrews cross on a red field, with thirteen white stars arranged within the blue diagonal bars. The "Stars and Bars" designation is sometimes erroneously used to reference the more popular "battle flag" design. The Stars and Bars, though, has one white and two red horizontal stripes with a circle of white stars on a blue field in the upper left corner. The Stars and Bars served as the First National Confederate flag. For more see Coski, *The Confederate Battle Flag*.

6. "Exhibits" file, in *Augustus v. ECBOE*; Anixbia Strong testimony, "Non-Jury Trial," July 11, 1973, in *Augustus v. ECBOE*; 1972 *Escambian*, 10, 192. For more on the *Escambian*'s curious portrayal of blacks and the glorification of its school's Confederate imagery, see 1970 *Escambian*, 120, 126–27; 1971 *Escambian*, 4–5, 16; 1972 *Escambian*, 3, 10, 14–15, 87, 95, 136, 192, 206, 276–77, 282; 1973 *Escambian*, 62, 119, 122, 144, 200.

7. Testimonies of Nicky Scapin, Zenobia White, Richard Leeper, and Belinda Jackson, "Non-Jury Trial," July 11, 1973, in *Augustus v. ECBOE*; "Hearing Before Winston E. Arnow," January 24, 1973, in *Augustus v. ECBOE*.

8. Coski, *The Confederate Battle Flag*, viii, 95–105, 124, 135, 207, 211; Southern Regional Council, *The South and Her Children*, 12–13.

9. Testimonies of Linda Packer, Jackson, B. J. Brooks, Nicky Scapin, Sidney Nelson, David Howell, Zenobia White, and Strong, "Hearing," January 24, 1973, in *Augustus v. ECBOE*; *PN*, November 16, November 17, 1972; *PJ*, November 28, 1972; Matthews interview, October 27, 2000; "NAACP Legal Department Case Files, *Augustus v. School Board*, 1972–75," group 5, box 387, NAACPP; Rufus C. Huffman to Franz Marshall, January 17, 1973.

10. *PJ*, December 13, December 14, 1972, and July 12, 1973; *SPI*, December 14, 1972.

11. *PJ*, December 14, 1972; ECSBMB, 1972–73, 149.

12. *PJ*, December 14, December 15, 1972; "Hearing," January 24, 1973, Brooks testimony, in *Augustus v. ECBOE*.

13. Appleyard, *The History of Education in Escambia County*, 70; *PJ*, December 16, December 19, December 20, 1972; *PN*, December 20, 1972; "Racial Violence in Public Schools," n.d., in TTP; Bowden interview.

14. Bowden interview; *MH*, January 21, 1973; *PJ*, December 15, December 19, 1972.

15. William Reed memoranda to Askew, January 5, 1973, S126 in RO'DAP; ECSBMB, 1972–73, 150–74; *PJ*, December 21, December 23, 1972; *MH*, January 21, 1973.

16. Smokey Peaden to Askew, January 31, 1973, S125 in RO'DAP; ECSBMB, 1972–73, 174–76; *PJ*, December 21, December 22, 1972; *PN*, December 21, 1972; *MH*, January 21, 1973.

17. ECSBMB, 1972–73, 174–76; *PJ*, December 21, December 22, 1972; *MH*, January 21, 1973.

18. *PJ*, December 29, 1972, and January 1, 1973.

19. Ibid.; *PNJ*, December 24, December 31, 1972; *PJ*, January 1, 1973.

20. President Lyndon B. Johnson formed the "National Advisory Commission on Civil Disorders" in 1967 to investigate the causes of race riots that devastated urban areas each year since 1964 and provide recommendations based on its findings. The group released the "Kerner Report," named for Illinois governor and committee chair Otto Kerner, on February 29, 1968. Kerner Commission, *Report of the National Advisory Commission on Civil Disorders*; Hebert interview.

21. Thomas, "Civil War," 605; Wilson, *Baptized in Blood*, 5, 13, 15, 118, 161. Rollin G. Osterweis and Paul Gaston preceded Wilson in the use of the term "myth" to describe the Lost Cause, while Gaines Foster followed Wilson and used "tradition" to explain the ideology. See Osterweis, *The Myth of the Lost Cause*, Gaston, *The New South Creed*, and Foster, *Ghosts of the Confederacy*. I prefer the term "civil religion" because it emphasizes the importance of religion in the construction and preservation of the Lost Cause, but also believe that it can be used interchangeably with "myth" and "tradition" without losing its fundamental character. Although many scholars have done a fine job of examining the development of the Lost Cause from the Civil War's end through the civil rights movement, few have analyzed the impact the ideology had on southern whites in the post–civil rights South. The Escambia County case study indicates that the Lost Cause experienced a revival in the area due to the immense social changes that transpired, particularly to the racial status quo, in a relatively short period of time.

22. Crespino, *In Search of Another Country*, 18; Mott interview; Wilson, *Baptized in Blood*, 118.

23. *PJ*, January 5, 1973.

24. Mott interview; Bowden interview; Appleyard interview.

25. *PJ*, January 2, 1973; *PN*, January 2, 1973; *MH*, January 3, January 21, 1973; Rufus C. Huffman to Franz Marshall, January 17, 1973, "NAACP Legal Department Case Files, *Augustus v. School Board*, 1972–75," group 5, box 387, NAACPP; Mott interview; "Hearing," January 24, 1973, Brooks testimony, in *Augustus v. ECBOE*.

26. ECSBMB, 1972–73, 182; "A Summarized Report Concerning the Establishment and Maintainance [sic] of Human Relations Committees in Schools for the City of Pensacola and Escambia County, Florida," n.d., in EPHRCP; *MH*, January 3, 1973; *PJ*, January 3, 1973; *PN*, January 3, 1973.

27. *PJ*, January 3, 1973; *PN*, January 3, 1973.

28. Billy Pelham memorandum to Sec. Revell, January 3, 1973, and Doug Stowell memorandum to Askew, January 5, 1973, S126 in RO'DAP.

29. Gordon E. Harvey, *A Question of Justice*, 67.

30. Kaalina, *Claude Kirk and the Politics of Confrontation*, 172; Dyckman, *Floridian of His Century*, 264; Colburn and Scher, *Florida's Gubernatorial Politics in the Twentieth Century*, 281, 288; Harvey, *A Question of Justice*, 90; Dyckman, *Reubin O'D. Askew and the Golden Age of Florida Politics*, 129, 140–42, 191; Oral History Interview with Reubin Askew, July 8, 1974, Interview A-0045, Southern Oral History Program Collection, Southern Historical Collection, the Wilson Library, University of North Carolina at Chapel Hill. Interestingly, Dyckman's study of Askew's years as governor makes no mention of the racial tumult that engulfed Pensacola.

31. Anderson memorandum to Askew, January 5, 1973, and William Reed memorandum to Askew, January 5, 1973, S126 in RO'DAP; Askew memorandum to Peaden, February 16, 1973, and letter to Mrs. S. D. Groves, February 16, 1973, S125 in RO'DAP; Askew to Bonnie Bobe, November 7, 1973, S70 in RO'DAP.

32. *PN*, January 3, 1973; *PJ*, January 4, 1973.

33. *PN*, January 5, 1973; ECSBMB, 1972–73, 185–87; *PJ*, January 6, 1973.

34. *PJ*, January 7, 1973.

35. "Hearing," January 24, 1973, testimonies of Packer and Brooks testimony, in *Augustus v. ECBOE*; *PN*, January 8, January 9, 1973; *ADW*, January 9, 1973.

Chapter Four

1. *PJ* January 10, January 11, 1973.

2. Ibid.; Mrs. Jessie Matthews to Winston Arnow, January 23, 1973, S126 in RO'DAP.

3. ECSBMB, 1972–73, 190–201; Blankenship to Father Leonard Duncan, February 13, 1973, S126 in RO'DAP; *PN*, January 11, 1973; *PJ*, January 11, January 12, January 13, 1973; WCOA news, "1973: The Year's News in Review," in HKMAR, vol. 6.

4. When classes began in January, 120 students attended Escambia High School. Only 7 percent of the total enrollment, or 238 students—were black. Lipscomb testimony, January 24, 1973, in *Augustus v. ECBOE*; ECSBMB, 1972–73, 202–03; Testimonies of Leeper and Lipscomb, July 11, 1973, and "Hearing," January 24, 1973, in *Augustus v. ECBOE*; *PJ*, January 16, January 17, 1973; *PNJ*, January 14, 1973; *PN*, January 16, January 17, 1973; WCOA news, "1973: The Year's News in Review," in HKMAR, vol. 6.

5. *PJ*, January 16, January 17, January 20, 1973; *PN*, January 24, 1973; *PNJ*, January 21, 1973; Rufus C. Huffman to Franz Marshall, January 17, 1973, "NAACP Legal Department Case Files, *Augustus v. School Board*, 1972–75," group 5, box 387, NAACPP; Gooden to Nathaniel Jones, July 23, 1973, "NAACP Branch Department Files, Field Staff, R. N. Gooden Correspondence, 1973–75," group 6, box C29, NAACPP.

6. "Motion to Intervene as Plaintiff," January 19, 1973, and "Memorandum in Support of Motion to Intervene," January 22, 1973, both in *Augustus v. ECBOE*.

7. *Smith v. St. Tammany* case file.

8. Anderson to Askew, July 20, 1977, S126 in RO'DAP; *PJ*, January 18, January 19, 1973; *MH*, January 21, 1973; *SHT*, February 6, 1973; "Racial Violence in Public Schools" report, n.d., TTP.

9. *PNJ*, January 21, January 31, February 11, 1973.

10. *PJ*, January 13, January 21, January 28, 1973; *PNJ*, February 4, February 11, 1973; *PN*, February 5, 1973.

11. "Hearing," January 24, 1973, "Memorandum of Law in Opposition of Motion to Intervene," January 22, 1973, and "Answer of Defendants," February 14, 1973, in *Augustus v. ECBOE.*

12. "County Files—Escambia," Florida Senate Bill SB 452, section 230.221, S126 in RO'DAP; *PJ*, January 24, 1973; *PN*, January 24, 1973.

13. "Hearing," January 24, 1973, in *Augustus v. ECBOE.*

14. Ibid.

15. "Hearing," January 24, 1973, "Order," January 24, 1973, "Order," January 26, 1973, all in *Augustus v. ECBOE*; *PJ*, January 25, January 26, January 30, 1973; *PN*, January 25, January 26, 1973; ECSBMC, 1972–73, 204.

16. *PN*, January 26, January 29, February 1, 1973; *DBMJ*, February 1, 1973; *MH*, February 2, 1973; Rufus C. Huffman to Franz Marshall, January 17, 1973, "NAACP Legal Department Case Files, *Augustus v. School Board*, 1972–75," group 5, box 387, NAACPP; Peaden to Askew, January 31, 1973, S125 in RO'DAP; Blankenship to Peaden, February 13, 1973, Sessums to Blankenship, February 20, 1973, and Transcript of report by John Hayes, February 29, 1973, all in S126 in RO'DAP.

17. *MH*, February 2, 1973; *SPI*, February 5, 1973; *SHT*, February 6, 1973; Mott interview.

18. *PJ*, February 15, 1973; ECSBMB, 1972–73, 238, 246; "White Irritations," 1973, in TTP.

19. Brooks to Jones, February 23, 1973, "NAACP Legal Department Case Files, *Augustus v. School Board*, 1972–75," group 5, box 387, NAACPP.

20. Belinda Jackson, the plaintiff in the *Augustus* symbols motion, was among those arrested. *PJ*, March 22, 1973; "Grand Jury Indictment," 1973 Winter Term, in *Fla. v. HKM*; Matthews interview, October 27, 2000.

21. *PNJ*, May 20, 1973; Henry McMillan deposition, July 20, 1977, in *McMillan.*

22. "Jury verdict," June 14, 1973, in *Fla. v. HKM*; Matthews interview, February 13, 2002.

23. "Non-Jury Trial," July 11, 1973, Barfield opening statement, testimonies of White, Strong, Howell, Scapin, Leeper, Nelson, and Young, in *Augustus v. ECBOE*; *PN*, July 11, 1973; *PJ*, July 12, 1973.

24. "Final Judgment," July 24, 1973, in *Augustus v. ECBOE.*

25. *PN*, July 24, August 16, 1973; *PJ*, July 25, October 20, 1973, and April 10, 1975; "Potential for Violence," May 3, and July 3, 1973, COINTELPRO; WCOA news, "1973: The Year's News in Review," in HKMAR, vol. 6.

26. *PJ*, May 15, 1974; *PV*, May 4–10, 1974; *PN*, May 14, May 16, 1974; "Report," May 9, 1974, in EPHRCP.

27. Meeting minutes, March 21, 1972, "Information Sheet: Human Relations Commission," February 2, 1973, both in EPHRCP; U.S. Commission on Civil Rights and Harris, *The Administration of Justice in Pensacola and Escambia County*, 3; William H. Marshall, B. J. Brooks, Otha Leverette, Stephen Henderson, Lloyd

Wilkins, Nathaniel Smith to Barney Burke, October 20, 1973, in EPHRCP; *PN*, May 17, September 27, 1974; Hebert interview.

28. *PV*, May 4–10, 1974; Appleyard interview; Bowden interview; Hebert interview; Hoard interview; Matthews and Butler, *Victory after the Fall*, 162.

29. "Report," May 9, 1974, Alain C. Hebert to HRC, June 5, 1974, meeting minutes, July 5, 1974, in EPHRCP; U.S. Commission on Civil Rights and Harris, *The Administration of Justice in Pensacola and Escambia County*, 3; *PJ*, May 15, 1974; Eugene Brown to D. W. Timberlake, May 30, 1974, Alain C. Hebert to Hollice Williams, June 20, 1975, "Reccommendations [*sic*] of the Human Relations Commission Concerning Police Firearms Policies, 1974–1975," in *McMillan* UWF.

30. *PNJ*, December 1, 1974, January 19, 1975; *PJ*, December 2, December 3, December 5, December 6, December 7, 1974; "Pensacola, Florida, Drowning Murder Report," January 4, 1975, in *NWABR*.

31. *PJ*, December 13, 1974; *PNJ*, January 19, 1975; *Martin Luther King Speaks*, Program 7502, "Ralph David Abernathy Speech on Five Black Men Who Went Missing in Pensacola, Florida," January 11, 1975, in SCLCR.; *Jet*, March 4, 1976, 8–10.

32. For more on Abernathy's reservations concerning his ability to lead SCLC, see Abernathy, *And the Walls Came Tumbling Down*, 476–78, 494–99; Young, *An Easy Burden*, 490, 502; Peake, *Keeping the Dream Alive*, 285–97; Fairclough, *To Redeem the Soul of America*, 396–97.

33. Martin Luther King Jr., *Where Do We Go From Here?*, 12; Young, *An Easy Burden*, 502–3; Peake, *Keeping the Dream Alive*, 254, 261; Reynolds, *Jessie Jackson*, 359–61.

34. "Memorandum to all Board Members and Chapter Presidents," July 30, 1974, Abernathy letter to ministers, August 7, 1974, both in SCLCR; "Abernathy Group Ends Convention," *NYT*, August 17, 1974, 24; Peake, *Keeping the Dream Alive*, 301. Abernathy did not mention the failed Philadelphia convention in his memoirs.

35. C. K. Steele to Abernathy, March 6, 1972, SCLCR.

36. *Jet*, March 4, 1976, 8–10; "Pensacola, Florida, Drowning Murder Report," January 4, 1975, in *NWABR*; Doris Mason investigation notes, December 9, 1974, in SCLCR; *PN*, December 12, 1974.

37. "Drowning in Pensacola of Five Atlanta Fishermen," October 13, 1975, Abernathy to Gov. Jimmy Carter, January 4, 1975, "Pensacola Drownings: 1976" folder, all in S93 in RO'DAP; "Pensacola, Florida, Drowning Murder Report," January 4, 1975, in *NWABR*.

38. *PJ*, December 13, December 14, 1974; *AC*, December 14, 1974; "Abernathy to Gov. Jimmy Carter, January 4, 1975," "Pensacola Drownings: 1976" folder, both in S93 in RO'DAP; *Martin Luther King Speaks*, Program 7502, "Ralph David Abernathy Speech on Five Black Men Who Went Missing in Pensacola, Florida," January 11, 1975, in SCLCR.

39. *PNJ*, December 15, 1975; *PJ*, December 17, 1974; *Jet*, March 4, 1976, 8–10.

40. SCLC letter to Governor Reubin Askew, December 23, 1974, Abernathy to Governor Jimmy Carter, January 4, 1975, Jimmy Carter to Reubin Askew, January 7, 1975, Untreiner to Askew, January 7, 1975, Cooper memorandum to

Askew, October 13, 1975, Askew to Young, October 21, 1975, State Attorney Curtis Golden, "Supplemental Investigative Report," November 11, 1975, "Pensacola Drownings: 1976" folder, all in S93 in RO'DAP; "SCLC News Release," January 7, 1975, in NWABR; Andrew Young telegram to Rubin [*sic*] Askew, January 14, 1975; *Martin Luther King Speaks*, Program 7502, "Ralph David Abernathy Speech on Five Black Men Who Went Missing in Pensacola, Florida," January 11, 1975, both in SCLCR.

41. *PJ*, December 14, 1974.

42. King, "Gov. Carter Given Data on 5 Deaths," *NYT*, January 6, 1975, 15; *PJ*, January 9, 1975; Untreiner to Askew, January 7, 1975, "Pensacola Drownings: 1976" folder, S93 in RO'DAP.

43. Hebert interview.

44. *PJ*, December 13, December 14, December 16, 1974; *AC*, December 14, 1974; Matthews and Butler, *Victory after the Fall*, 160.

45. Matthews and Butler, *Victory after the Fall*, 160.

Chapter Five

1. Sergeant Don Powell, "Deputy Field Report," December 20, 1974, "Witness Statement" of Douglas Raines, Darrel Mumford, Roger Tyner, Leonard Rogers, Dillon Vickery, and Raymond Boisvert, December 20, 1974, in ECSDR; *PNJ*, January 12, 1975; "Grand Jury Report," January 22, 1975, Douglas Raines Personnel File, in ECSDR.

2. Powell, "Deputy Field Report," "Witness Statement," of Raines, Mumford, Tyner, Rogers, Vickery, Boisvert, December 20, 1974, in ECSDR; Depositions of Douglas Raines, May 18, 1976, Leonard Rogers, June 21, 1976, and J. Dillon Vickery, January 18, 1977, in *Blackwell v. Untreiner*.

3. Powell, "Deputy Field Report," and "Supplementary Officer Report," December 20, 1974, ECSDR records; Untreiner deposition, June 21, 1976, in *Blackwell v. Untreiner*; *PNJ*, December 22, 1974; Raines Personnel File, "Employee Evaluation," December 12, 1979, in ECSDR.

4. *PNJ*, December 22, 1974; *PJ*, December 27, December 28, 1974, January 7, 1975; HKMAR, vol. 1; "Transcript of Trial Rehearing," March 1, 1976, in *Fla. v. Brooks and Matthews*.

5. *PJ*, January 8, 1975; *PNJ*, January 19, 1975.

6. From July through December 1974, for instance, the HRC received approximately sixty formal complaints of discriminatory employment practices and the organization began a program to establish student HRCs in each county high school. See meeting minutes, October 30, December 19, 1974, in EPHRCP; "A Summarized Report Concerning the Establishment and Maintainance [*sic*] of Human Relations Committees in Schools for the City of Pensacola and Escambia County, Florida," n.d., in EPHRCP.

7. "Report on Wendel Blackwell Shooting," n.d., Hebert to Curtis Golden, January 15, 1975, EPHRCP; Hebert interview.

8. Dyson, *I May Not Get There With You*, 124.

9. Ibid., 126–28.

10. *PJ*, January 7, 1975; "Transcript of Trial Rehearing," March 1, 1976, 20, in *Fla. v. Brooks and Matthews*.

11. Mass meetings, n.d., in HKMAR, vols. 2 and 9.

12. Mass meetings, n.d., in HKMAR, vols. 2, 4, and 9.

13. Mass meetings, n.d., in HKMAR, vols. 2 and 9.

14. Mass meetings, n.d., in HKMAR, vol. 2; *PJ*, January 8, January 9, January 11, January 16, 1975.

15. Raines Personnel File, "Grand Jury Report," January 22, 1975, in ECSDR; *PNJ*, January 19, 1975; Jim Edson, "Deputy Field Report," January 24, January 31, 1975, in ECSDR; *PJ*, January 22, January 23, January 25, January 26, 1975; Mass meetings, n.d., in HKMAR, vol. 2.

16. U.S. District Court, Fifth Circuit Court of Appeals ruling, January 24, 1975, in *Augustus v. ECBOE*.

17. *PJ*, February 1, April 10, April 24, 1975; Matthews interview, October 27, 2000.

18. *PJ*, February 15, 1975; Matthews interview, October 27, 2000.

19. Gooden to "All Florida NAACP Branch Presidents," May 29, 1975, group 6, box C29, and Gloster B. Current to Gooden, n.d., "NAACP Branch Department Files, Field Staff, R. N. Gooden Correspondence, 1973–75," both in NAACPP.

20. Edson, "Deputy Field Report," February 6, February 7, February 11, February 14, February 18, 1975, ECSDR.

21. Edson, "Deputy Field Report," February 6, February 8, February 11, February 14, February 19, February 20, 1975, ECSDR.

22. *PN*, February 13, 1975.

23. *PJ*, February 22, 1975; Edson, "Deputy Field Report," February 21, 1975, in ECSDR.

24. Edson, "Deputy Field Report," February 21, February 23, 1975, and Richard Nix, "Deputy Field Report," February 23, 1975, all in ECSDR.

25. *PJ*, February 25, 1975; *SPT*, March 2, 1975; "Trial Transcript," June 10, 1975, 13, and "Transcript of Trial Rehearing," March 1, 1976, 20–22, in *Fla. v. Brooks and Matthews*; Matthews interview, October 27, 2000.

26. "1st District Court of Appeals opinion," July 26, 1976, in *Fla. v. Brooks and Matthews*; Edson, "Deputy Field Report," February 24, 1975, in ECSDR; Officer W. K. Sandifer, "Affidavit of Complaint," February 24, 1975, in *State v. Sylvester Gaines, et al.*, case file, case number 75-2715-Z-MM, Escambia County Clerk of Court Archives and Records Department; *PN*, February 25, June 10, 1975; *SPT*, March 2, 1975.

27. Edson, "Deputy Field Report," February 24, 1975; "Arrest report," February 24, 1975, in *State v. Robert T. Malden* case file, case number 75-2715-AA, Escambia County Clerk of Court Archives and Records Department; "Arrest report," February 24, 1975, in *State v. Etta Hall Davis* case file, case number 75-2715-DD, Escambia County Clerk of Court Archives and Records Department; "Arrest report," February 24, 1975, in *State v. James Leon Davis* case file, case number 75-2715-BB, Escambia County Clerk of Court Archives and Records Department; "Arrest

report," February 24, 1975, in *State v. Bertha Rene Bradley Jackson* case file, case number 75-2715-CC, Escambia County Clerk of Court Archives and Records Department; "Trial Transcript," June 10, 1975, 2–3, 10–17, 22, and "Extortion Complaints" and "Bond motion," June 27, 1975, in *Fla. v. Brooks and Matthews*; *PJ*, February 25, February 26, September 10, 1975; *PN*, February 25, 1975; *PNJ*, March 2, 1975; *SPT*, November 13, 1978.

28. Ibid. Each of the forty-seven individuals arrested on February 24 entered innocent pleas with the county court. *PN*, March 10, 1975.

29. Matthews interview, October 27, 2000; *SUM*, March 1975; *PN*, February 25, February 26, 1975; *PJ*, February 26, 1975; *PNJ*, March 2, 1975.

30. "Pensacola Speaks," February 25, 1975, in HKMAR, vol. 8.

31. Ibid.

32. Ibid.

33. Ibid.

34. *PN*, February 25, February 26, 1975; *PJ*, February 26, 1975; *PNJ*, March 2, 1975; Matthews interview, October 27, 2000; Edson, "Deputy Field Report," February 28, 1975, in ECSDR; *SUM*, March 1975.

35. Edson, "Deputy Field Report," February 25, February 26, February 27, 1975, in ECSDR; *SPT*, February 28, March 2, 1975; *PJ*, February 26, February 27, 1975; *PN*, February 26, February 27, February 28, 1975.

36. According to Matthews, a white business owner offered him $18,000 to "cool off your activities" and "back out" of any remaining African American protests. Matthews rejected the offer. Matthews interview, February 12, 2002.

37. *PNJ*, March 2, 1975; *PJ*, March 3, March 4, March 7, 1975; *PN*, March 5, March 10, 1975; Edson, "Deputy Field Report," February 28, 1975, in ECSDR.

38. *SPT*, March 2, 1975.

39. *SPT*, March 2, 1975; "Mass meetings," in HKMAR, vol. 2.

40. *PN*, March 17, 1975; *PN*, March 18, 1975; *PJ*, March 18, 1975; *PJ*, March 21, 1975; Untreiner letter to Dr. Robert N. Dorsey, December 20, 1972, Jim Edson Personnel File, in ECSDR; WBSR news, in HKMAR, vol. 3.

41. *PJ*, March 18, 1975. One of the reasons the *News Journal* responded as it did to Edson's comments is because one of its journalists, Randall Hinton, witnessed Edson's conversation with the *St. Petersburg Times* reporter and claimed he fabricated the story. Hinton later told state attorneys that the *Times* quoted Edson accurately. The Florida Attorney General charged Hinton with perjury and he lost his position at the newspaper. WBSR news, in HKMAR, vol. 3.

42. *PNJ*, March 2, March 9, 1975; *PN*, March 5, March 10, March 15, 1975; *PJ*, March 3, 1975; Meeting minutes, March 21, 1975, and Pensacola Inter Faith Council to Askew, March 25, 1975, both in EPHRCP; Lou Oliver to Governor Askew, March 25, 1975, and Arthur Canady to Lou Oliver, April 8, 1975, "Legal Affairs Correspondence" file, both in S93 in RO'DAP; Hebert interview.

43. "Escambia County Civil Service Board Personnel Action Form," August 18, 1975, Edson personnel file, in ECSDR.

44. Grand Jury report of "Violence in the Public High Schools of Escambia County, Florida," February 28, 1975, in TTP.

Chapter Six

1. Chalmers, *Hooded Americanism*, 406. For a case study on the UKA during the 1960s and 1970s in another southern state, see Cunningham, *Klansville, U.S.A.*

2. Jacksonville Intelligence Division to Directors of Atlanta, Birmingham, Mobile, and Tampa Offices, May 16, 1975, Jacksonville Intelligence Division to Birmingham Director, January 26, 1976, Carl A. Ekblad, "The United Klans of America, Inc., Knights of the Ku Klux Klan," February 2, 1976, Jacksonville Intelligence Division to FBI Director, "Investigative Summary, Extremist Matter—United Klans of America," February 17, 1976, FBI Director to Secret Service Director, "Investigative Summary, Extremist Matter—Klan," February 17, February 23, April 7, April 27, 1976, FBI Director to Secret Service Director, "Investigative Summary, Robert C. Yarter," March 18, 1976, all in COINTELPRO; King, "Racial Incidents in Pensacola Prompt Attempts by Klan to Get New Members," *NYT*, March 18, 1975, 74; *PN*, February 26, 1975; *PNJ*, December 12, 1976.

3. "The Voice of the Klan," n.d., in HKMAR, vol. 1; *PJ*, December 12, 1976; Hoard interview.

4. *PNJ*, December 12, 1976; "The Voice of the Klan," n.d., in HKMAR, vol. 1; WBSR news program "The Monitor," n.d., in HKMAR, vol. 14.

5. *PN*, February 26, 1975; *PJ*, March 15, 1975; King, "Racial Incidents in Pensacola Prompt Attempts by Klan to Get New Members," *NYT*, March 18, 1975, 74.

6. Mass meetings, n.d., in HKMAR, vols. 9, 11, and 14.

7. For more on NOW, see Frederick Douglas Richardson, *The Genesis and Exodus of NOW*; Mass meetings, n.d., in HKMAR, vol. 12.

8. See Crosby, *A Little Taste of Freedom*, Tyson, *Radio Free Dixie*, and Umoja, *We Will Shoot Back*.

9. Mass meetings, n.d., in HKMAR, vol. 12.

10. Mass meetings, n.d., in HKMAR, vols. 2, 9, and 12; Matthews, interview, June 18, 2007.

11. Mass meetings, n.d., in HKMAR, vol. 2; Matthews, interview, Florida, June 18, 2007.

12. *PJ*, March 27, March 28, 1975; "WCOA News," n.d., in HKMAR, vol. 3; "Career Service Commission" hearing, January 12, 1976, in *Brooks v. FDOT*; Legal Department to Theodore Bukowski, April 10, 1975, "NAACP Legal Department Case Files, Florida, *Brooks v. FDOT*, April 1975," group 5, box 390, NAACPP.

13. Legal Department to Theodore Bukowski, April 10, 1975, "NAACP Legal Department Case Files, Florida, *Brooks v. FDOT*, April 1975," group 5, box 390, NAACPP; Cherry to Current, March 6, 1975, "NAACP Branch Department Files, Florida, Pensacola Branch, 1974–77," group 6, box C83, NAACPP.

14. *PJ*, April 3, April 5, 1975; WCOA news, n.d., in HKMAR, vol. 4.

15. Dyckman, *Reubin O'D. Askew and the Golden Age of Florida Politics*, 126, 129; Askew interview.

16. *PJ*, April 26, 1975.

17. Cherry to Gooden, n. d., "NAACP Branch Department Files, Field Staff, R. N. Gooden Correspondence, 1973–75," group 6, box C29, NAACPP; *PJ*, May 3, 1975.

18. *PJ*, May 2, 1975; Matthews interview, October 27, 2000; "WCOA News," n.d., in HKMAR, vol. 4; Current to Nathaniel Jones, June 12, 1976, "NAACP Legal Department Case Files, Florida, *Brooks v. FDOT*, April 1975," group 5, box 390, NAACPP; Gooden to "All Branch Presidents," May 29, 1975, "NAACP Branch Department Files, Field Staff, R. N. Gooden Correspondence, 1973–75," group 6, box C29, NAACPP.

19. Brooks to "NAACP Board of Directors," April 11, 1975, "NAACP Branch Department Files, Field Staff, R. N. Gooden Correspondence, 1973–75," group 6, box C29, NAACPP.

20. *PJ*, April 17, 1975.

21. *PJ*, March 5, April 30, May 1, 1975; Officer W. K. Sandifer, "Affidavit of Complaint," February 24, 1975, in *State v. Sylvester Gaines, et al.*, case file, number 75-2715-Z-MM, *Florida v. Leverette, Matthews, Brooks, et al.*, case file, number 75-2716-MM, *State v. Sylvester Gaines, et al.*, case file, numbers 75-2715-Y-MM and 75-2715-Z-MM, *State v. Robert T. Malden*, case file, number 75-2715-AA, *State v. Etta Hall Davis*, case file, number 75-2715-DD, *State v. James Leon Davis*, case file, number 75-2715-BB, and *State v. Berth Rene Bradley Jackson*, case file, number 75-2715-CC, all case files in Escambia County Clerk of Court Archives and Records Department, Pensacola, Fla.

22. *PJ*, May 7, May 8, 1975.

23. *PJ*, May 1, May 31, July 8, 1975; *PN*, July 10, 1975; ECSBMB, 1974–75, 366–70, *Work Sessions and Conferences (April 24, 1974–June 21, 1976)*, July 7, 1975, 2, and 1975–76, 1–5.

24. *PNJ*, May 24, 1975; "Abernathy, Ralph David, March in Pensacola, Florida, May 23, 1975," *Martin Luther King Speaks*, Program 7522, June 21, 1975, SCLCR; "Tyrone Brooks, speech at rally in Pensacola, Florida on deaths of five black men," *Martin Luther King Speaks*, Program 7524, June 14, 1975, SCLCR; *ADW*, June 6, 1975.

25. "Abernathy, Ralph David, March in Pensacola, Florida, May 23, 1975," *Martin Luther King Speaks*, Program 7522, June 21, 1975, SCLCR.

26. *PJ*, May 24, 1975; *PNJ*, May 25, 1975; FBI Intelligence Communication, May 16, 1975, in COINTELPRO.

27. *PJ*, May 24, 1975; *PNJ*, May 25, 1975; *PN*, May 26, 1975; Klavern president George E. Kachelhofer and secretary James R. Cohron both signed the group's published letter. *PNJ*, June 9, 1975.

28. FBI Intelligence Communication, May 16, 1975, FBI Intelligence Division, "Informative Notes," May 20, 1975, Tampa Intelligence Division to Jacksonville Director, May 22, 1975, Jacksonville Office to Director, "Investigative Summary, Extremist Matter—United Klans of America," February 23, 1976, all in COINTELPRO.

29. FBI Intelligence Communication, May 16, 1975, FBI Intelligence Division, "Informative Notes," May 20, 1975, Jacksonville Office to FBI Director, "Investigative Summary, Extremist Matter—United Klans of America," February 23, 1976,

Tampa Intelligence Division to Jacksonville Director, May 22, 1975, Jacksonville Intelligence Division to Director of Birmingham, Miami, Mobile, and Tampa Offices, September 11, 1975, Jacksonville Office to Director of Birmingham Office, January 26, April 15, 1976, Ekblad Report, February 2, 1976, "The United Klans of America, Inc., Knights of the Ku Klux Klan," Director to U.S. Secret Service Director, "Investigative Summary, Extremist Matter—Klan," February 4, February 17, February 19 1976, Director to U.S. Secret Service Director, "Investigative Summary, Robert C. Yarter," March 18, 1976, Director to U.S. Secret Service Director, "Investigative Summary, Extremist Matter—Klan," April 7, 1976, Director to U.S. Secret Service Director, "Investigative Summary, Extremist Matter—Klan," April 19, 1976, Jacksonville Office to Assistant Attorney General, "Cross Burnings, Escambia County, Florida, June 23, 1976," June 28, 1976, all in COINTELPRO. The only UKA klavern member that the FBI documents mention is Robert C. Yarter, the Century unit's exalted cyclops. The remainder of names, particularly those of FBI informants, are redacted due to privacy concerns. Director to U.S. Secret Service Director, "Investigative Summary, Robert C. Yarter," March 18, 1976. For more on the Milton rally, see *PNJ*, September 12, 1976.

Chapter Seven

1. *PN*, June 9, 1975.

2. *PN*, June 9, 1975; William Wells to Nathaniel Jones, Memorandum, February 2, 1977, "NAACP Legal Department Case Files, Florida, *Brooks v. Florida Department of Transportation*, 1977–78," group 5, box 390, NAACPP; Arthur Herman affidavit, October 30, 1974, "Curtis Golden" folder, S94 in RO'DAP.

3. "Trial Transcript," June 9, 1975, 4, 11, 30–33, 51, 82, in *Fla. v. Brooks and Matthews*.

4. *PN*, June 9, June 10, 1975; "Request for Change of Venue," May 25, 1975, C. K. Bass and Elouise D. Savage affidavits, June 9, 1975, "Motion For New Trial," June 18, 1975, and "Trial Transcript," June 9, 1975, 78, 80, 87, 89, all in *Fla. v. Brooks and Matthews*.

5. "Trial Transcript," June 9, 1975, 82, 32–33, 36–43, in *Fla. v. Brooks and Matthews*.

6. "Trial Transcript," June 9, 1975, 104, 130, 135, 149, 133, in *Fla. v. Brooks and Matthews*.

7. Ibid., 143, 152–53, 170.

8. "Trial Transcript," June 9, 1975, 149, 164–65, 167–68, 179, and June 10, 1964, 10, 13, 19, 21–24, and "Transcript of Trial Rehearing," March 1, 1976, 20–22, in *Fla. v. Brooks and Matthews*.

9. "Trial Transcript," June 10, 1975, 59, in *Fla. v. Brooks and Matthews*.

10. Ibid., 118–24; *PN*, June 10, 1975; *SPT*, November 13, 1978.

11. "Trial Transcript," June 10, 1975, 59, 62–71, 77–82, in *Fla. v. Brooks and Matthews*.

12. Ibid., 99–100.

13. Ibid., 118, 120–24, 128, 140.

14. Ibid., 164, 176.

15. Ibid., 2–3A, 17, 22; *PJ*, June 11, June 13, 1975; *PN*, June 11, 1975; *PNJ*, July 13, 1975; *LL*, November 25, 1978; "Career Service Commission" hearing, January 12, 1976, in *Brooks v. FDOT*.

16. *PJ*, July 9, 1975; *SPT*, November 13, 1978. In March 1977, the Florida Supreme Court investigated and subsequently disbarred Ed Duffee for defrauding a client. Nathaniel Jones to Hinton King, August 22, 1975, "NAACP Legal Department Case Files, Florida, *Brooks v. Florida Department of Transportation,* April 1975," group 5, box 390, NAACPP.

17. Case docket in *Fla. v. Brooks and Matthews*; *PN*, July 10, July 11, July 14, 1975; *PJ*, July 11, July 12, 1975; *PNJ*, July 13, 1975.

18. Matthews interview, February 13, 2002; "WEAR appearance," n.d., in HKMAR, vol. 7.

19. "Order," July 17 and July 18, 1975, 59, in *Fla. v. Brooks and Matthews*; *PJ*, July 15, July 16, 1975; *PN*, July 17, 1975.

20. *PJ*, July 18, July 25, July 29, 1975; "Order Denying Bail," July 12, 1975, in *Fla. v. Brooks and Matthews*; "Order Granting Bail on Appeal," July 29, 1975, in *Fla. v. HKM*, FSA.

21. *PJ*, July 29, August 1, August 2, 1975.

22. *PJ*, August 4, August 5, 1975; Meeting minutes, August 28, 1975, in EPHRCP; "Press Conference," n.d., in HKMAR, vol. 5.

23. *PJ*, December 10, 1975; Bernard Lee to Matthews, March 8, 1976, and "SCLC Memorandum," March 10, 1976, both in SCLCR.

24. Press Conference, n.d., in HKMAR, vol. 5.

25. Ibid.

26. Ibid.

27. Ibid.; FBI Mobile Office to HRC, March 26, 1976, in EPHRCP.

28. "Order," December 11, 1975, "Affidavit of Vincent Ponciano," December 12, 1975, "Motion for New Trial," January 20, 1976, "Order Denying Amended Motion for New Trial," March 1, 1976, all in *Fla. v. Brooks and Matthews*.

Chapter Eight

1. *PN*, February 4, 1976; Kelly interview; *SPT*, February 6, 1976.

2. *PJ*, February 5, February 6, 1976; Edson, "Deputy Field Report," February 5, 1976, in ECSDR; Anonymous flier, "High School Incidents: Escambia High School, 1976" folder, n.d., S119 in RO'DAP. The flier proclaimed that 2,523 students attended EHS and 125 faculty worked there, which resulted in 2,648 eligible voters under the school board policy. A total of 1,649 voted for "Rebels," which equaled 62.2 percent of the ballots cast. The flier's declaration that the name received 71 percent of the vote, then, is inflated.

3. *PJ*, February 5, February 6, 1976; *SPT*, February 6, April 12, 1976; Kelly interview; Flynn interview; Deputy field reports of L. W. Roper, Robert Taylor, Joe Walker, Tom Wesley, February 5, 1976, and Tom Wesley, "Offense Report,"

February 11, 1976, all in ECSDR; WCOA news report, February 5, 1976, in HK-MAR, vol. 4.

4. *PJ*, February 5, 1976; *PN*, February 5, 1976; King, "Racial Animosity Turns to Violence in Pensacola, Fla., on Issue of Calling High School Teams 'Rebels,'" *NYT*, March 7, 1976, 33; Deputy field reports of Thomas Lewis, F. E. Hill, Lonnie Price, T. Watson, J. B. Mayton, February 5, 1976, and Lewis, "Offense Report," February 13, 1976, in ECSDR.

5. Lewis, "Deputy Field Report," February 5, 1976, "Supplementary Offense Report," February 5, 1976, Richard Nix and Tom Wesley, "Offense Report," February 6, 1976, Recorded statements of five white minors regarding February 5 EHS shooting, February 6, 1976, and Recorded statements of Raymond Lindsey, February 5, 1976, and Danny Matthews, Malcolm Lindsey, February 6, 1976, all in ECSDR; Anonymous flier, "High School Incidents: Escambia High School, 1976," n.d., S119 in RO'DAP; *SPT*, February 6, 1976.

6. *SPT*, February 7, 1976; David Hightower, "Deputy Field Report," February 5, 1976, in ECSDR.

7. Watson, "Deputy Field Report," and Price, "Deputy Field Report," February 5, 1976, in ECSDR.

8. *PJ*, February 6, 1976; WCOA news report, February 5, 1976, in HKMAR, vol. 4.

9. WCOA news report, February 5, 1976, in HKMAR, vol. 4; *PJ*, February 6, 1976; *PNJ*, February 8, 1976.

10. D. M. Barnes, "Arrest Report," February 5, 1976; *Jet*, March 4, 1976; "CBS Evening News" broadcast, February 5, 1976, record number 244665, Vanderbilt University Television News Archive, Nashville, Tenn.; James Cameron, "A Letter to the Faculty and Students of the Escambia County High School in Pensacola, Florida," n.d., in author's possession; *PJ*, February 7, 1976.

11. The telegrams are located in "High School Incidents: Escambia High School, 1976" folder, n.d., S119 in RO'DAP. Ralph Northberg to Askew, February 12, 1976, and Norman Jackson to Harvey Cotton, n.d., "High School Incidents: Escambia High School, 1976" folder, S119 in RO'DAP; *Pensacola Beacon*, February 12, 1976; Hebert interview.

12. *PJ*, February 6, February 7, 1976; Telegrams to Grover Robinson, Tobiassen, Childers, and Peaden, February 7, 1976, in EPHRCP; WCOA news report, February 6, 1976, in HKMAR, vol. 3; *Escambia County Beacon*, April 29, 1976.

13. WCOA news reports, February 5 and 6, 1976, in HKMAR, vols. 3 and 4.

14. *PN*, February 9, February 10, 1976; Don Smith, "Deputy Field Report," February 9, 1976, in ECSDR; ECSBMB, 1975–76, 351–52.

15. Unsigned handwritten note, February 10, 1976, Untreiner to Askew, February 13, "High School Incidents: Escambia High School, 1976" folder, all in S119 in RO'DAP; *PJ*, February 11, 1976.

16. *PJ*, February 11, February 12, 1976; *ADW*, February 13, 1976; ECSBMB, 1975–76, 329–31; Jackson to Cotton, February 12, 1976 and Untreiner to Askew, February 13, 1976, "High School Incidents: Escambia High School, 1976" folder, all in S119 in RO'DAP; "Statement by W. D. Childers to the Escambia County School

Board," February 11, 1976, in EPHRCP; Peter Gindl testimony, May 24, 1981, in *McMillan*; "WEAR Editorial" transcript, February 12, 1976, SCLCR.

17. Unsigned handwritten note and typed memoranda, February 12, 1976, "High School Incidents: Escambia High School, 1976" folder, S119 in RO'DAP; *Jet*, March 4, 1976, 7; *PJ*, February 11, February 14, 1976; *ECPB*, February 12, 1976; *PN*, February 12, 1976; Patrick Key to Tobiassen, April 19, 1976, in TTP.

18. Smith, "Deputy Field Report," February 26, 1976, in ECSDR; FBI Mobile office to Pensacola-Escambia Human Relations Committee, March 25, 1976, in EPHRCP; *PJ*, February 13, February 19, February 20, February 23, February 24, February 26, February 27, 1976; *PNJ*, February 22, February 29, 1976; *PN*, April 2, 1976; Hebert interview; *SPT*, April 12, 1976.

19. Hebert to Askew, February 26, 1975, in EPHRCP; Hebert interview.

20. *PN*, March 11, March 19, 1976; *PJ*, March 18, 1976; ECSBMB, 1975–76, 329–31, 366–68, 432–35, and "Board Work Sessions and Conferences," book 1, April 24, 1974–June 21, 1976: 3.

21. *PJ*, April 21, April 22, 1976; Gindl testimony, May 24, 1981, in *McMillan*.

22. Chafe, *Civilities and Civil Rights*, 8, 249.

23. "WEAR Editorial" transcripts, February 10–11, February 23–24, 1976, SCLCR.

24. "WEAR Editorial" transcripts, February 23–26 and March 11, 1976, SCLCR.

25. "WEAR Editorial" transcripts, February 10, 12, 23, 26, 1976, SCLCR.

26. *PJ*, April 22, 1976.

27. *PJ*, May 7, May 8, 1976; Grover Robinson to W. L. Malony, May 4, 1976, "High School Incidents: Escambia High School," 1976 folder, S119 in RO'DAP; Gindl testimony, May 24, 1981, in *McMillan*; For state law, ch. 356, see *History of Legislation: 1976 Regular Session*, 95–98, Florida House of Representatives Office of the Clerk, State Library and *The Clerk's Manual, 1974–76*, "Senate Bill Actions Report," 278–79, Florida House of Representatives Office of the Clerk, State Library.

28. "Order Denying Amended Motion for New Trial," March 1, 1976, and 1st District Court of Appeals "Opinion," July 26, 1976, both in *Fla. v. Brooks and Matthews*; *PN*, July 26, August 10, 1976; *PJ*, August 12, 1976; William Wells to Nathaniel Jones, August 17, 1976, "NAACP Legal Department Case Files, Florida, *Brooks v. FDOT*, May–September 1976," group 5, box 391, NAACPP.

29. The results for each referendum item were 12,119 in favor to 5,596 against the salary limitations, 12,763 for and 4,638 against nonpartisan board elections and the placement of "limitations on the activities of candidates for board membership," and 10,683 to 7,180 for the addition of two at-large board seats. "Escambia County School Referendum," ballot and election results, July 2, 1976, SOE Files. For the 1970 school board referendum results, see "Plaintiff's Post-Trial Proposed Findings of Fact," June 5, 1979, and McGovern deposition, March 2, 1978, in *McMillan*.

30. Depositions of Jenkins, July 21, 1977, *McMillan*, July 20 and December 6, 1977, and "Plaintiff's Post-Trial Proposed Findings of Fact," June 5, 1979, all in *McMillan*. In the September 28 runoff election, Bailey received 26,786 total votes

to 20,536 for Jenkins. Escambia County School Board District Seven election results, September 7, September 28, and November 2, 1976, SOE Files.

31. Spence testimony, May 16, 1978, Carol Ann Marshall testimony, May 24, 1978, Marshall, "Statement to the Escambia County School Board," October 13, 1977, all in *McMillan*; Escambia County School Board District Four election results, September 7, 1976, SOE Files. In the September primary, Marshall obtained 29,106 votes and Spence received 19,176. Marshall defeated her opponent in the general election 52,228 to 15,262. District Four School Board election results, September 28 and November 2, 1976, SOE Files.

32. Escambia County School Board District Six election results, September 7, and November 2, 1976, SOE Files; Escambia County Sheriff's election results, September 7, September 28, 1976, SOE Files; McMillan deposition, July 20 and December 6, 1977, and Dr. Frank Biasco testimony, May 24, 1978, all in *McMillan*; Tobiassen to Untreiner, April 12, 1976, in TTP; *PJ*, July 28, August 5, September 30, 1976; *PNJ*, August 15, September 12, 1976.

33. Ekblad Report, "The United Klans of America, Inc., Knights of the Ku Klux Klan," February 2, 1976, Director to Secret Service Director, "Investigative Summary, Extremist Matter—Klan," February 17–19, March 18, April 7, April 19, April 27, and June 26, June 30, 1976, Director to Secret Service Director, "Investigative Summary, Robert C. Yarter," March 18, 1976, Jacksonville Office to Director, "Investigative Summary, Extremist Matter—United Klans of America," February 17, February 23, 1976, Director to Secret Service Director, "Investigative Summary," February 19, May 21, July 19, 1976, and Jacksonville Intelligence Division to Atlanta, Birmingham, Mobile, and Tampa Offices, May 16, 1975, all in COINTELPRO. UKA membership continued to fall throughout Florida for the remainder of the decade. In January 1976, the UKA claimed 700 members in the state. The number fell to 500 in 1980 and 150 in 1984. In 1987, a civil court gave a $7 million dollar verdict and the literal keys to the UKA's Tuscaloosa headquarters to Buehlla Mae Donald, the mother of a young black named Michael Donald that two UKA members lynched in Mobile, Alabama. The suit effectively ended the United Klans of America. Newton, *The Invisible Empire*, 191, 206–8. For more on the Donald lynching, see Kirkland, "Pink Sheets and Black Ballots," 1999.

34. UKA, "Investigative Summary," June 26, 1976, in COINTELPRO.

35. *PNJ*, September 12, December 12, 1976; Newton, *The Invisible Empire*, 191.

Chapter Nine

1. *PN*, September 20, October 22, 1976; Matthews and Butler, *Victory after the Fall*, 271.

2. *Brooks v. FDOT* case file; "NAACP Legal Department Case Files, Florida, *Brooks v. FDOT*, March–April 1976," in Escambia County Clerk of Courts Records Office.

3. "Report to the 69th Annual National Convention," January 21, 1978, "Black Organizations" file, S126 in RO'DAP.

4. Minchin and Salmond, *After the Dream*, 202–3; Berg, *The Ticket to Freedom*, 239. For more on the Port Gibson suit, see Crosby, *A Little Taste of Freedom*, 111–13, 237–40.

5. Henderson to Abernathy, n.d., H. L. Arnold, "Events and Activities Report of Escambia County SCLC," July 12, 1976, Arnold, "Memo to All Media Personnel," n.d., and Lawrence Tolbert to Rev. Fred D. Taylor, April 12, 1977, all in SCLCR; *PN*, July 1, 1976; *ADW*, July 2, 1976; *PV*, July 3–9, 1976.

6. Abernathy, *And the Walls Came Tumbling Down*, 579–85.

7. DeRoche, *Andrew Young*, 102–3; *PJ*, August 18, 1978. For more on the division between the SCLC national office and its Escambia County chapter, see Shimek to Lowery, April 13, 1977, August 7, 1978, Matthews to Hosea Williams, August 5, 1978, Chauncey Eskridge to Julius Chambers, August 25, 1978, Levonne Chambers to Eric Snapper, September 7, 1978 all in SCLCR; Lowery to "SCLC Supporters," October/November 1978, HKMP.

8. Wiley, "An Agent for Change," 94–95; *PJ*, July 3, 1981.

9. The Board of County Commissioners was composed of five members who served staggered four-year terms. Candidates had to run for specific slots according to the district where they resided, but their election came from an at-large vote of the entire community. Each party held a primary where a majority vote was required for its nomination. No majority vote was required in the general election. The Escambia County School Board was composed of seven members who also served staggered four-year terms. Only five of the seven, though, had to reside in residential districts. The Pensacola City Council had ten members who ran for five numbered slots that corresponded to five city wards, and they had to live in the corresponding district. The election had no primary stage, and a majority vote in an at-large election determined service. "Complaint," March 18, 1977, in *McMillan*; *PN*, March 21, 1977; *Bolden v. City of Mobile*, 423 F. Supp. 384 (S.D. Ala. 1976).

10. "Complaint," March 18, 1977, McMillan deposition, July 20, 1977, and Appeals Court ruling, February 19, 1981, in *McMillan*; *PN*, March 21, 1977.

11. *PN*, March 23, 1977; *PJ*, July 11, July 12, August 17, 1978, and November 8, 1979.

12. Depositions of McMillan, July 20, 1977, Woodrow Cushon, July 21, 1977, Elmer Jenkins, July 21, 1977, Bradley M. Seabrook, July 25, 1977, Robert P. Crane, July 25, 1977, Clifford Stokes, July 25, 1977, William F. Maxwell, July 25, 1977, Samuel Horton, July 27, 1977, Henry N. Burrell, July 27, 1977, and Charles L. Scott, July 27, 1977, all in *McMillan*; Mass meetings, n.d., in HKMAR, vol. 12.

13. Sole objector James Bailey dissented because Key banned prior school nicknames from consideration. ECSBMB, 1977–78, 99; *PJ*, August 11, August 12, August 15, September 2, September 8, 1977; Ullrich interview.

14. Depositions of McMillan, July 20, 1977, Seabrook, July 25, 1977, and Stokes, July 25, 1977, and B. J. Brooks testimony, May 17, 1978, all in *McMillan*.

15. Testimonies of Donald Spence, May 16, 1978, F. L. Henderson, Elmer Jenkins, Nathaniel Dedmond, Cecil T. Hunter, May 17, 1978, and "Plaintiffs' Post-Trial Proposed Findings of Fact," June 5, 1978, all in *McMillan*; "Donald D. Spence to the Florida Constitution Revision Commission," August 18, 1977, in *McMillan* UWF.

16. Askew testimony, May 22, 1978, in *McMillan*.

17. "Plaintiffs' Post-Trial Proposed Findings of Fact," June 5, 1978, in *McMillan*. Attorneys discovered, for instance, that roads in sixty-one African American neighborhoods remained unpaved in December 1975. *McMillan* UWF; Depositions of Cushon and Jenkins, July 21, 1977, William F. Maxwell and Seabrook, July 25, 1977, Horton, July 27, 1977, and Brooks testimony, May 17, 1978, all in *McMillan*.

18. "Plaintiffs' Post-Trial Proposed Findings of Fact," June 5, 1978, "Order," July 10, 1978, and depositions of Cushon and Jenkins, July 21, 1977, Stokes and Seabrook, July 25, 1977, and Scott, July 27, 1977, all in *McMillan*. I combine students that state Education Department reports labeled "educable" and "trainable" mentally handicapped for my total calculations. "Statistical Report 76-10," May 1976, Florida Department of Education, Tallahassee, Fla. Leon Hall, "The Implementors' Revenge," 122–23.

19. Eugene Brown to D. W. Timberlake, May 30, 1974, and Hebert to Hollice Williams, June 20, 1975, in *McMillan* UWF; Depositions of Jenkins, July 21, 1977, and Horton, July 27, 1977, Testimony of Brooks, Hunter, May 17, 1978, and Brown, May 19, 1978, all in *McMillan*.

20. African Americans represented 3 percent of "clerical workers," 7 percent of "skilled craftsmen," and 10.5 percent of "protective services, police/fire" in the county. The files do not contain the same wage and employment figures for each year. "EEO-4 Analysis, job classification for Escambia County, 1973–1977," in *McMillan* UWF.

21. Blacks represented 4 percent of "clerical workers" and "police/fire" positions, 2.6 percent of "technicians," and 11.6 percent of "para-professionals" the city employed. "City of Pensacola EEO-4 Summary, showing employees by job classification, department and percentage of blacks, 1974–1977," in *McMillan* UWF; Brooks testimony, May 17, 1978, and "Pleadings file, #965-1213: 'Plaintiffs' Post-Trial Proposed Findings of Fact,'" June 5, 1978, both in *McMillan*.

22. "Memorandum Decision," July 10, 1978, in *McMillan*.

23. Ibid.

24. Ibid.

25. *PJ*, July 28, July 29, 1978; Florida Supreme Court "Opinion," July 27, 1978, and November 28, 1978, in *Fla. v. Brooks and Matthews*.

26. *PJ*, December 14, December 15, December 26, 1978; Matthews interview, October 27, 2000.

27. *PN*, July 28, 1975; Raines Personnel File, "Notice of Disciplinary Action," August 10, 1981, and "Order," March 25, 1982, both in ECSDR.

28. "Notice of Disciplinary Action," Edson personnel file, October 16, 1978, Knights of KKK to Royal Untreiner, November 29, 1978, "Notice of Disciplinary Action," November 30, 1978, and "Letter of Resignation," September 30, 1980, all in ECSDR; unknown newspaper, December 12, 1978, in HKMP; *LL*, November 25, 1978; *SPT*, November 13, 1978; *FT*, December 12, 1979.

29. "Notice of Termination," January 5, 1981, Untreiner personnel file, in ECSDR; *PNJ*, January 27, 1989.

30. *LL*, August 20, 1982, *DBMJ*, October 30, 1982; *U.S. v. Reubin W. Peaden*, 727 F.2d 1493 (No. 82-6050, U.S. Court of Appeals, Eleventh Circuit, 26 March 1984); *PNJ*, March 10, 1999.

31. "Correspondences: 1977" folder, and "Annual Report," 1978, 1979, 1982, 1983, in EPHRCP; Hebert interview.

32. U.S. Commission on Civil Rights and Harris, *The Administration of Justice*, 5; Meeting minutes, February 3, 1976, Curtis Golden to HRC, March 28, 1978, and Florida Clearinghouse on Criminal Justice to Hebert, November 17, 1975, all in EPHRCP.

33. The final vote in the Special Referendum Election was 15,128 against, 13,093 for the charter. *PNJ*, November 4, November 11, 1979; *PJ*, November 6, November 7, November 8, 1979. For more on the series of appeals and rulings, see U.S. Court of Appeals, Fifth Circuit, February 19, 1981, and United States Supreme Court, March 27, 1984, in *McMillan*.

34. *PNJ*, December 2, 1979; U.S. Commission on Civil Rights and Harris, *The Administration of Justice*, i, l, 16.

35. U.S. Commission on Civil Rights and Harris, *The Administration of Justice*, 4–6.

36. Ibid., ii, 16–18.

37. Ibid., 12, 15–17.

Chapter Ten

1. Although the Escambia County School Board abandoned its *McMillan* appeal, Carol Ann Marshall, the board member who defeated Donald Spence in 1976 elections with Klan support, continued as an individual appellant. Appleyard, *The History of Education in Escambia County*, 86, 91; "Order," December 28, 1982, in *McMillan*; *PJ*, December 22, 1982; *PNJ*, December 26, 1982; *PN*, December 27, 1982.

2. "Memorandum Decision," March 11, 1983, and "Case Docket," n.d., both in *McMillan*; *PJ*, March 11, 1983.

3. *PNJ*, March 13, September 25, November 6, 1983; *PJ*, November 2, November 3, 1983.

4. *PJ*, November 3, 1983; *PNJ*, November 6, 1983; "Memorandum Decision," March 27, 1984, and December 19, 1984, in *McMillan*. The Eleventh Circuit appellate court dismissed the defense's final appeal concerning *McMillan* on April 15, 1985. The issue, though, surrounded the settlement of legal fees and not the legality of city or county elections. "Case Docket," n.d., in *McMillan*. Willie Junior later became involved in a bribery scandal with W. D. Childers, who became a county commissioner in 2002. Junior accepted money from Childers in exchange for votes, agreed to testify against Childers, and was guaranteed a prison sentence of eighteen months maximum for pleading no contest to the eleven charges against him. Junior committed suicide the day before his sentencing. *PNJ*, March 30, 2003.

5. "Memo in Support of Joint Settlement," September 7, 1999, and "Finding of Fact and Conclusions," December 12, 1999, in *Augustus v. ECBOE*. The "Notice

of Settlement and Fairness Hearing" appeared in *PNJ*, October 3, 1999, and *PV*, October 30, 1999.

6. I have analyzed the economic divisions in these categories over time to determine if African Americans have narrowed the gaps and thus improved their economic standing in relation to whites, whether the gaps have remained similar and indicate little improvement, or if the gaps have increased. Poverty rates reveal whether the number of poor black families compared to poor white families has increased or decreased, while unemployment rates indicate if the number of unemployed black workers per unemployed white workers has changed. Median household earnings for whites and blacks are important, because the variable reflects the relative economic well-being of households by race. Similarly, a per capita income comparison discloses the ratio of available dollars to individual residents. These statistics provide the most straightforward measures of the economic gap between blacks and whites that has existed over thirty years. By analyzing these figures, researchers can determine if there has been progress or decline in the relative economic standing of white and black citizens in Florida overall, and specifically in Pensacola and Escambia County.

7. The percentage of black Floridians that were more likely than whites to live in poverty was 560 percent in 1970 and 387 percent in 2000; in Escambia County it was 247 and 209 percent, respectively, while in Pensacola, blacks were 322 and 320 percent more likely than whites to live in poverty in 1970 and 2000. U.S. Bureau of the Census, *Nineteenth Census, 1970*, vol. 11, "Florida," 214, 235, 308, 322, 327, 332, 506, 524, 530; Bureau of the Census, *Twenty-Second Census, 2000*, vol. PHC-2-11, "Florida," 94, 125, 183, 213.

8. U.S. Bureau of the Census, *Nineteenth Census, 1970*, vol. 11, "Florida," 488, 506, 524, 530; U.S. Bureau of the Census, *Twenty-Second Census, 2000*, vol. PHC-2-11, "Florida," 94, 125, 213.

9. See "Tables 1–3" for all statistics related to the black and white population, employment, and economic figures that I cite. U.S. Bureau of the Census, *Nineteenth Census, 1970*, vol. 11, "Florida," 212, 214, 235, 308, 312, 322, 327, 332, 476, 488, 506, 518, 524, 530; U.S. Bureau of the Census, *Twenty-Second Census, 2000*, vol. PHC-2-11, "Florida," 94, 125, 183, 213; *PPJ*, July 3, 1981; *PNJ*, February 9, 1986; *PNJ*, February 10, 1986; *PNJ*, March 1, 1986.

10. "Profiles of Florida School Districts, 2002–03," 34, "Dropout Demographics," November 2008, "Students in Florida Public Schools," 1980–81, 1981–82, "Students in Florida School Districts," 1982–83, 1983–84, 1984–85, "Membership in Florida Public Schools," Fall 1985, Fall 1986, Fall 1987, Fall 1988, Fall 1989, Fall 1990, Fall 1991, Fall 1992, Fall 1993, Fall 1994, 2003–04, 2012–13, "Membership in Programs for Exceptional Students," Fall 1986, Fall 1987, Fall 1989, Fall 1990, Fall 1992, Fall 1998, all in Florida Department of Education Reports, Education Information and Accountability Services, Tallahassee, Fla.

11. McMillan and Vernon McDaniel won their campaigns 1980, while Jenkins won the District Three races in 1986, 1990, 1994, and 1998. African Americans who ran for school board positions and lost were Joe Fountain (1980), McDaniel (1980

and 1984), and Alvin Wingate (1994). "Escambia County School Board Election Results," in SOE files.

12. Coski, *The Confederate Battle Flag*, 280–81.

13. The others used in the "Five Flags" displays represent the United States, Spain, Great Britain, and the French monarchy. *PNJ*, February 2, February 11, 2000. For more on the Pensacola City Council meeting and subsequent vote, see the body's February 10, 2000, "Minutes," http://www.cityofpensacola.com /departments/city-clerk/city-records/fortis-document-search (October 23, 2013).

14. For more on one of the most controversial police shootings since the Blackwell incident in Escambia County, see "NAACP Legal Department General Office Files, Florida, Police, 1974–1981," group 5, box 2754, NAACPP; AP State and Local Wire, November 22, 1999; *PNJ*, June 11, June 29, July 1, and July 17, 2000, and April 24, 2001; Boyd interview.

15. *PV*, July 12–22, 1987; *PNJ*, July 12, July 13, 1987. B. J. Brooks died on February 15, 1998. *PNJ*, February 16, 1998. For more on the numerous awards and accolades that Matthews received, see *PNA*, January 21–24, 1988; *PNJ*, July 13, 1987, April 22, 1997, June 11, December 6, 1998; *BS*, April 23, 1997, August 29, 2001; *PNJ* 1998; *AA*, February 13, 2000; *SZ*, August 3, 2000; *TCL*, July 19, 2001; *MPR*, August 25, 2001. The honors and accolades for Matthews extended into his new state during the twenty-first century. Governor Don Siegelman declared August 29, 1999, "H. K. Matthews Day" in Alabama and appointed him to the advisory board to the state tourism bureau in July 2001. On February 26, 2006, city officials dedicated Rev. H. K. Matthews Park at the corner of 12th Avenue and East Anderson Street in Pensacola. "An Appreciation for the Presiding Elder of the Brewton District: The Rev. H. K. Matthews," August 26, 2001, HKMP; *PNJ*, February 26, 2006.

16. "Dropout Demographics," November 2008, "Membership in Florida Public Schools, 2012–13," table 1, "Membership in Programs for Exceptional Students, 2012–13," tables 9 and 17, Florida Department of Education, Data Publications and Report Archive, http://www.fldoe.org/accountability/data-sys/edu-info -accountability-services/pk-12-public-school-data-pubs-reports/archive.stml (June 22, 2015). In 2012, as indicated in the archived records, 20,214 county public school students were white, and they represented 1,652 of those in gifted programs and 153 of those declared intellectually handicapped. In comparison, 14,297 students were black, and they represented 181 and 227, respectively, of the gifted or handicapped. A total of 8,088 students were suspended (4,978 blacks, 2,263 whites) in 2012–13. "Discipline Data Reports," 2012–13, FDOE. Email to author from Kenneth Dukes, FDOE Education Information and Program Specialist, January 7, 2015.

17. In 2010 white per capita income was $37,606 in Pensacola and $27,588 in Escambia County. White median household income was $54,144 in Pensacola and $49,279 in Escambia County. Black per capita income was $12,807 in Pensacola and $13,530 in Escambia County. Black household income was $26,492 in Escambia County and $22,815 in Pensacola. Food stamps were received by 5,968 of 84,911 white Escambia County households and 1,042 of 16,993 households in Pensacola, compared to 5,516 of 22,341 African American households in the county and 1,639

of 5,663 households within city limits. All figures are located at "American Fact Finder" www.factfinder.census.gov (November 25, 2013).

18. *PNJ*, October 16, 2013; *Slate*, August 15, 2013, http://www.slate.com/articles /news_and_politics/jurisprudence/2013/08/escambia_county_sheriff_david _morgan_his_bizarre_defense_of_the_shooting.html (June 22, 2015).

Bibliography

Archives and Collections

Atlanta, Georgia
  Emory University
    Coe, John Moreno Papers, 1919–1973
    Newsweek Atlanta Bureau records, 1953–1979
  The National Archives at Atlanta
    U.S. District Court Records
      McMillan et al. v. Escambia County, et al.
Brewton, Alabama
  H. K. Matthews Papers
Fort Worth, Tex.
  The National Archives at Fort Worth
    Records of the U.S. Fifth Circuit Court of Appeals
      Thomas J. Smith v. St. Tammany Parish School Board, et al.
Mapleton, Georgia
  Mary Harrison Washington Papers
Montgomery, Alabama
  Huntingdon College Library
    United Methodist Church Archive and Information Center
      Alabama–West Florida UMC Conference Records
Nashville, Tennessee
  Vanderbilt University
    Vanderbilt University Television News Archive
Pensacola, Florida
  Escambia County Civil Service Board
    Personnel Files
  Escambia County Clerk of Courts Records Office
  Escambia County Sheriff's Department Records Office
  Escambia County Supervisor of Elections Office
  Escambia High School Library
    Escambian Yearbook Collection
  Escambia-Pensacola Human Relations Commission
    Escambia-Pensacola Human Relations Commission Papers
  Pensacola Police Department
    Pensacola Police Department Files
  University of West Florida
    John C. Pace Memorial Library

University Archives and West Florida History Center
  LeBaron Family Papers
  Marion T. Gaines Papers
  McMillan v. Escambia County Case File
  Tom Tobiassen Papers
Tallahassee, Fla.
  Florida Department of Education
    Data Publications and Report Archive
    Education Information & Accountability Services
  State Archives of Florida
    Florida Supreme Court Case Files, 1825–2011
    Governor Reubin O'Donovan Askew Papers
  State Library of Florida
    Florida House of Representatives Office of the Clerk
      The Clerk's Manual, 1974–76
      History of Legislation: 1976 Regular Session
      Journal of the Senate: Extra-Ordinary Session, State of Florida, 1956
Washington, D.C.
  Federal Bureau of Investigation Records Management Division
  Library of Congress Manuscript Division
    National Association for the Advancement of Colored People Papers
  Robert S. Rankin Memorial Library
  U.S. Commission on Civil Rights
  United States Bureau of the Census
    U.S. Government Printing Office
      Census of Population: 1960. Vol. I, *Characteristics of the Population.* Part 11:
        Florida, 1963
      Census of Population: 1970. Vol. I, *Characteristics of the Population.* Part 11:
        Florida—Sections 1 and 2, 1973
      *Census of Population: 1980. Characteristics of the Population: Number of
        Inhabitants* and *General Social and Economic Characteristics*: Florida—
        Sections 1 and 2, 1983
      Census of Population: 1990. General Population Characteristics and *Social and
        Economic Characteristics*: Florida, 1993

Personal Interviews

Appleyard, John. Telephone interview with J. Michael Butler. May 3, 2010.
Askew, Reubin. Telephone interview with J. Michael Butler. August 14, 2002.
Behr, Jack. Interview with J. Michael Butler. Pensacola, Florida. April 30,
  2010.
Bennett, Ellison. Telephone interview with J. Michael Butler. January 6, 2015.
Bowden, J. Earle. Telephone interview with J. Michael Butler. May 3, 2010.
Boyd, LeRoy. Interview with J. Michael Butler. Pensacola, Florida. October 10,
  2000.

Carter, Charles, Sr. Interview with J. Michael Butler. Pensacola, Florida. July 10, 2002.

Flynn, Kevin. Interview with J. Michael Butler. Pensacola, Florida. April 30, 2010.

Harrison, Horace. Telephone interview with J. Michael Butler. March 13, 2006.

Harvey, Raymon. Telephone interview with J. Michael Butler. March 15, 2006.

———. Interview with J. Michael Butler. Pensacola, Florida. May 15, 2010.

Hebert, Alain. Telephone interview with J. Michael Butler. October 22, 2013.

Hoard, Barbara. Interview with J. Michael Butler, Pensacola, Florida. May 15, 2010.

Huff, Angela Dobbins. Telephone interview with J. Michael Butler. May 7, 2015.

Kelly, Lance. Interview with J. Michael Butler. Pensacola, Florida. April 20, 2012.

King, Howard. Telephone interview with J. Michael Butler. July 16, 2015.

Matthews, H. K. Interview with J. Michael Butler. Brewton, Alabama. October 27, 2000, October 16, November 23, 2001.

———. Interview with J. Michael Butler, Douglas, Georgia. September 15, September 16, 2001, February 13, 2002.

———. Telephone interview with J. Michael Butler. June 18, 2007, and July 19, 2015.

Mott, Roger. Interview with J. Michael Butler. Pensacola, Florida. May 1, 2010.

Ullrich, Bob. Telephone interview with J. Michael Butler. January 16, 2015.

Washington, Mary Harrison. Telephone interview with J. Michael Butler. March 16, 2006.

Watson, Susan. Telephone interview with J. Michael Butler. July 8, 2011.

Wills, Ora. Telephone interview with J. Michael Butler. December 31, 2014.

Young, James. Interview with J. Michael Butler. Pensacola, Florida. May 1, 2010.

Books and Articles

"9 Schools in Pensacola Area Admit Negroes for First Time." *NYT*, August 28, 1962, 19.

Abercrombie, Lelia. "Early Churches of Pensacola." *Florida Historical Quarterly* 37 (1959): 446–62.

Abernathy, Ralph David. *And the Walls Came Tumbling Down*. New York: HarperPerennial, 1990.

"Abernathy Group Ends Convention," *NYT*, August 17, 1974, 24.

Alexander, Michelle. *The New Jim Crow: Mass Incarceration in the Age of Colorblindness*. New York: The New Press, 2012.

Alilunas, Leo. "The Rise of the 'White Primary' Movement as a Means of Barring the Negro from the Polls." *The Journal of Negro History* 25, no. 2 (April 1940): 161–72.

Alvis, Joel L. *Religion and Race: Southern Presbyterians, 1946–1983*. Tuscaloosa: University of Alabama Press, 1994.

Appleyard, John. *Four Centuries . . . A Saga of Pensacola Port in Action*. Pensacola, Fla.: John Appleyard Agency, 1976.

———. *The History of Education in Escambia County, 1870–2005*. Pensacola, Fla.: John Appleyard Agency, 2005.

———. *The Peacekeepers: The Story of Escambia County, Florida's 43 Sheriffs*. Pensacola, Fla.: John Appleyard Agency, 2007.

Arnade, Charles W. "Raids, Sieges, and International Wars." In *The New History of Florida*, edited by Michael Gannon, 100–16. Gainesville: University Press of Florida, 1996.

———. "Tristan De Luna and Ochuse (Pensacola Bay), 1559." *Florida Historical Quarterly* 37 (1959): 201–23.

Arnesen, Eric. "What's on the Black Worker's Mind?: African American Workers and the Union Tradition." *Gulf Coast Historical Review* 10 (1994): 5–18.

Ayers, H. Brandt, and Thomas H. Naylor, eds. *You Can't Eat Magnolias*. With an introduction by Willie Morris. New York: McGraw-Hill, 1972.

Bartley, Numan V. *The Rise of Massive Resistance: Race and Politics in the South during the 1950s*. Baton Rouge: Louisiana State University Press, 1969.

Bearss, Edwin C. "Civil War Operations in and around Pensacola." *Florida Historical Quarterly* 36 (1957): 125–65.

Berg, Manfred. *"The Ticket to Freedom"*: *The NAACP and the Struggle for Black Political Integration*. Gainesville: University Press of Florida, 2005.

Berman, William C. *The Politics of Civil Rights in the Truman Administration*. Columbus: Ohio State University Press, 1970.

Blight, David W. *Race and Reunion: The Civil War in American Memory*. Cambridge, Mass.: Harvard University Press, 2001.

Bowden, Jesse Earl. *Pensacola: Florida's First Place City*. Norfolk, Va.: Donning Company, 1989.

Bragaw, Donald H. "Loss of Identity on Pensacola's Past: A Creole Footnote." *Florida Historical Quarterly* 50 (1972): 414–18.

———. "Status of Negroes in a Southern Port City in the Progressive Era." *Florida Historical Quarterly* 51 (1973): 281–302.

Branch, Taylor. *At Canaan's Edge: America in the King Years, 1965–1968*. New York: Simon & Schuster, 2006.

———. *Parting the Waters: America in the King Years, 1954–1963*. New York: Simon & Schuster, 1998.

———. *Pillar of Fire: America in the King Years, 1963–1965*. New York: Simon & Schuster, 1998.

Brown, Canter, Jr. "The Civil War, 1861–1865." In *The New History of Florida*, edited by Michael Gannon, 231–48. Gainesville: University Press of Florida, 1996.

———. "Race Relations in Territorial Florida, 1821–1845." *Florida Historical Quarterly* 73 (1995): 287–307.

Brown, Sara Hart. "Pensacola Progressive: John Moreno Coe and the Campaign of 1948." *Florida Historical Quarterly* 68 (1989): 1–26.

Brown-Nagin, Tomiko. *Courage to Dissent: Atlanta and the Long History of the Civil Rights Movement*. Oxford: Oxford University Press, 2012.

Burran, James A. "Urban Racial Violence in the South during World War II." In *From the Old South to the New*, edited by Walter J. Fraser Jr. and Winfred B. Moore Jr., 167–78. Philadelphia, Penn.: Temple University Press, 1980.

Cameron, James. "A Letter to the Faculty and Students of the Escambia County High School in Pensacola, Florida." No date. In author's possession.

Carageorge, Ted. "The Greeks of Pensacola." In *Ethnic Minorities in Gulf Coast Society*, edited by Jerrell H. Shofner and Linda V. Ellsworth, 56–68. Pensacola, Fla.: Gulf Coast History and Humanities Conference, 1979.

Cash, William Thomas. *The Story of Florida*. New York: American Historical Society, 1938.

Cash, W. J. *The Mind of the South*. New York: Knopf, 1941.

Cassenello, Robert. *To Render Invisible: Jim Crow and Public Life in New South Jacksonville*. Gainesville: University Press of Florida, 2013.

Chafe, William H. *Civilities and Civil Rights: Greensboro, North Carolina and the Black Struggle for Freedom*. New York: Oxford University Press, 1981.

Chalmers, David M. *Hooded Americanism: The History of the Ku Klux Klan*. New York: New Viewpoints, 1981.

Chappell, David L. *A Stone of Hope: Prophetic Religion and the Death of Jim Crow*. Chapel Hill: University of North Carolina Press, 2007.

Clubbs, Occie. "Pensacola in Retrospect: 1870–1890." *Florida Historical Quarterly* 37 (1959): 377–96.

Cobb, James C. *Away Down South: A History of Southern Identity*. Oxford: Oxford University Press, 2005.

Cohodas, Nadine. *The Band Played Dixie: Race and the Liberal Conscience at Ole Miss*. New York: The Free Press, 1997.

Coker, William S. "Pensacola, 1686–1763." In *The New History of Florida*, edited by Michael Gannon, 117–33. Gainesville: University Press of Florida, 1996.

Colburn, David R. *Racial Change and Community Crisis: St. Augustine, Florida, 1877–1980*. New York: Columbia University Press, 1985.

Colburn, David R., and Elizabeth Jacoway, eds. *Southern Businessmen and Desegregation*. Baton Rouge: Louisiana State University Press, 1982.

Colburn, David R., and Richard K. Scher. *Florida's Gubernatorial Politics in the Twentieth Century*. Tallahassee: University Presses of Florida, 1980.

Collins, Donald E. *When the Church Bell Rang Racist: The Methodist Church and the Civil Rights Movement in Alabama*. Macon, Ga.: Mercer University Press, 1999.

Coski, John M. *The Confederate Battle Flag: America's Most Embattled Emblem*. Cambridge, Mass.: Harvard University Press, 2005.

———. "The Confederate Battle Flag in American History and Culture." *Southern Cultures* 2 (1996): 195–231.

Crespino, Joseph. *In Search of Another Country: Mississippi and the Conservative Counterrevolution*. Princeton, N.J.: Princeton University Press, 2007.

Crosby, Emilye, ed. *Civil Rights History from the Ground Up: Local Struggles, a National Movement*. Athens: University of Georgia Press, 2011.

Crosby, Emilye. *A Little Taste of Freedom: The Black Freedom Struggle in Claiborne County, Mississippi.* Chapel Hill: University of North Carolina Press, 2005.

Cunningham, David. *Klansville, U.S.A.: The Rise and Fall of the Civil Rights Era Ku Klux Klan.* Oxford: Oxford University Press, 2014.

Dalfiume, Richard M. *Desegregation of the U.S. Armed Forces: Fighting on Two Fronts, 1939–1953.* Columbia: University of Missouri Press, 1969.

———. "The 'Forgotten Years' of the Negro Revolution." *Journal of American History* 55 (1968): 90–106.

Daniel, Pete. *Lost Revolutions: The South in the 1950s.* Chapel Hill: University of North Carolina Press, 2000.

Dauer, Manning J. "Florida: The Different State." In *Changing Politics of the South*, edited by William C. Havard, 92–164. Baton Rouge: Louisiana State University Press, 1972.

Davis, Edward D. *A Half Century of Struggle for Freedom in Florida.* Orlando, Fla.: Drake's Publishing, 1981.

Davis, John Walker. "An Air of Defiance: Georgia's State Flag Change of 1956." *Georgia Historical Quarterly* 82 (1998): 305–30.

Dawkins, Mary. "Religion in Pensacola: The Birth of Protestantism, 1822–1845." *Pensacola History Illustrated* 3 (1989): 22–32.

De Jong, Greta. *Invisible Enemy: The African American Freedom Struggle after 1965.* Hoboken, N.J.: Wiley-Blackwell, 2010.

DeRoche, Andrew J. *Andrew Young: Civil Rights Ambassador.* Wilmington, Del.: Scholarly Resources, Inc., 2003.

Dibble, Ernest F. "Slave Rentals to the Military: Pensacola and the Gulf Coast." *Civil War History* 23 (1977): 101–13.

Dierenfield, Bruce J. *The Civil Rights Movement.* Harlow, England: Pearson Longman, 2004.

Dillon, Patricia. "Civil Rights and School Desegregation in Sanford." *Florida Historical Quarterly* 76 (1998): 310–25.

Dittmer, John. *Local People: The Struggle for Civil Rights in Mississippi.* Urbana: University of Illinois Press, 1995.

Doherty, Herbert J. "Ante-bellum Pensacola: 1821–1860." *Florida Historical Quarterly* 37 (1959): 337–56.

Draper, Alan. *Conflict of Interests: Organized Labor and the Civil Rights Movement in the South, 1954–1968.* Ithaca, N.Y.: ILR Press, 1994.

Dunn, Marvin. "The Illusion of Moderation: A Recounting and Reassessing of Florida's Racial Past." In *Old South, New South, or Down South? Florida and the Modern Civil Rights Movement*, edited by Irvin D. S. Winsboro, 22–46. Morgantown: West Virginia University Press, 2009.

Dunn, William Edward. *Spanish and French Rivalry in the Gulf Region of the United States, 1678–1702: The Beginnings of Texas and Pensacola.* Freeport, N.Y.: Books for Libraries Press, 1971.

Dyckman, Martin A. *Floridian of His Century: The Courage of Governor Leroy Collins.* Gainesville: University Press of Florida, 2006.

———. *Reubin O'D. Askew and the Golden Age of Florida Politics*. Gainesville: University Press of Florida, 2011.

Dysart, Jane E. "Another Road to Disappearance: Assimilation of Creek Indians in Pensacola, Florida, during the Nineteenth Century." *Florida Historical Quarterly* 61 (1982): 37–48.

Dyson, Michael E. *I May Not Get There with You: The True Martin Luther King, Jr.* New York: Free Press, 2000.

Eagles, Charles. *Jonathan Daniels and Race Relations: The Evolution of a Southern Liberal*. Chapel Hill: University of North Carolina Press, 1982.

———. "Toward New Histories of the Civil Rights Era," *Journal of Southern History* 66, no. 4 (November 2000): 813–48.

Eisterhold, John A. "Lumber and Trade in PC and West Florida, 1800–1860." *Florida Historical Quarterly* 51 (1973): 267–80.

Ellsworth, Linda, and Lucius F. Ellsworth. *The Cultural Legacy of the Gulf Coast, 1870–1940*. Pensacola, Fla.: Gulf Coast History and Humanities Conference, 1976.

———. *Pensacola: The Deep Water City*. Tulsa, Okla.: Continental Heritage Press, 1982.

Ellsworth, Lucius F. "Raiford and Abercrombie: Pensacola's Premier Antebellum Manufacturer." *Florida Historical Quarterly* 52 (1974): 247–60.

Eskew, Glenn T. *But for Birmingham: The Local and National Movements in the Civil Rights Struggle*. Chapel Hill: University of North Carolina Press, 1997.

Fairclough, Adam. "The Southern Christian Leadership Conference and the Second Reconstruction, 1957–1973." *South Atlantic Quarterly* 80 (1981): 177–94.

———. *To Redeem the Soul of America: The Southern Christian Leadership Conference and Martin Luther King, Jr.* Athens: University of Georgia Press, 1987.

Federal Judicial Center. "Biographical Directory of Federal Judges." http://www.fjc.gov/servlet/nGetInfo?jid=63&cid=999&ctype=na&instate=na. June 22, 2015.

Ferris, William, and Charles R. Wilson, eds. *The Encyclopedia of Southern Culture*. Chapel Hill: University of North Carolina Press, 1989.

Findlay, James F., Jr. *Church People in the Struggle: The National Council of Churches and the Black Freedom Movement, 1950–1970*. New York: Oxford University Press, 1998.

Fleming, Cynthia Griggs. *In the Shadow of Selma: The Continuing Struggle for Civil Rights in the Rural South*. London: Rowman and Littlefield, 2004.

Florida Legislature. *The Clerk's Manual, 1974–76*, "Senate Bill Actions Report," 278–79. Tallahassee, Florida: State House of Representatives Office of the Clerk, State Library.

———. *History of Legislation: 1976 Regular Session*, 95–98. Tallahassee, Florida: State House of Representatives Office of the Clerk, State Library.

———. *Journal of the Senate: Extra-Ordinary Session, State of Florida, 1956*, "An Act Relating to the Management of the Public Schools at the Local Level," 10 and 50. Tallahassee, Florida: State of Florida, State Library.

Flynt, Wayne. "Pensacola Labor Problems and Political Radicalism." *Florida Historical Quarterly* 43 (1965): 315–32.

Foner, Eric. *Reconstruction: America's Unfinished Revolution, 1863–1877*. New York: Harper & Row, 1988.

Forman, James, Jr. "Racial Critiques of Mass Incarceration: Beyond the New Jim Crow." *New York University Law Review* 87 (2012): 101–46.

Foster, Gaines M. *Ghosts of the Confederacy: Defeat, the Lost Cause, and the Emergence of the New South, 1865–1913*. Oxford: Oxford University Press, 1988.

Franklin, John Hope. *Reconstruction after the Civil War*. Chicago: University of Chicago Press, 1961.

Fraser, Walter J., and Winfred B. Moore Jr., eds. *From the Old South to the New*. Philadelphia, Penn.: Temple University Press, 1980.

Friedland, Michael B. *Lift Up Your Voice Like a Trumpet: White Clergy and the Civil Rights and Antiwar Movements, 1954–1973*. Chapel Hill: University of North Carolina Press, 1998.

Gannon, Michael, ed. *The New History of Florida*. Gainesville: University Press of Florida, 1996.

Garrow, David. *Bearing the Cross: Martin Luther King, Jr. and the Southern Christian Leadership Conference*. New York: William Morrow, 1986.

———. *Protest at Selma: Martin Luther King, Jr. and the Voting Rights Act of 1965*. New Haven, Conn.: Yale University Press, 1978.

Gaston, Paul. *The New South Creed: A Study in Southern Mythmaking*. New York: Knopf, 1970.

Gilbert, Laura. "Racial Attitudes Expressed in The Pensacola News Journal, 1919–1925." M.A. thesis, University of West Florida, 1973.

Giles, Michael. "Racial Stability and Urban School Desegregation." *Urban Affairs Quarterly* 12 (1976): 499–510.

Goldfield, David R. *Still Fighting the Civil War: The American South and Southern History*. Baton Rouge: Louisiana State University Press, 2002.

Gould, Virginia. "In Defense of Their Creole Culture: The Free Creoles of Color of New Orleans, Mobile, and Pensacola." *Gulf Coast Historical Review* 9 (1993): 26–46.

Graham, Hugh Davis. *Crisis in Print: Desegregation and the Press in Tennessee*. Nashville, Tenn.: Vanderbilt University Press, 1967.

Green, Ben. *Before His Time: The Untold Story of Harry T. Moore, America's First Civil Rights Martyr*. New York: Free Press, 1999.

Green, Laurie B. *Battling the Plantation Mentality: Memphis and the Black Freedom Struggle*. Chapel Hill: University of North Carolina Press, 2007.

———. "Challenging the Civil Rights Narrative: Women, Gender, and the 'Politics of Protection.'" In *Civil Rights History from the Ground Up: Local Struggles, a National Movement*, edited by Emilye Crosby, 52–80. Athens: University of Georgia Press, 2011.

Griffen, William B. "Spanish Pensacola." *Florida Historical Quarterly* 37 (1959): 242–62.

Hall, Jacquelyn Dowd. "The Long Civil Rights Movement and the Political Use of the Past," *Journal of American History* 91, no. 4 (March 2005): 1233–63.

Hall, Leon. "The Implementors' Revenge." *Southern Exposure* 7 (Summer 1979): 122–24.

Hamilton, William. "The Warren Fish Company of Pensacola." *Pensacola History Illustrated* 4 (1993): 3–9.

Hamlin, Francoise Nicole. *Crossroads at Clarksdale: The Black Freedom Struggle in the Mississippi Delta after World War II*. Chapel Hill: University of North Carolina Press, 2012.

Harvey, Gordon E. *A Question of Justice: New South Governors and Education, 1968–1976*. Tuscaloosa: University of Alabama Press, 2002.

Harvey, Paul. *Freedom's Coming: Religious Culture and the Shaping of the South from the Civil War through the Civil Rights Era*. Chapel Hill: University of North Carolina Press, 2005.

Havard, William C., ed. *Changing Politics of the South*. Baton Rouge: Louisiana State University Press, 1972.

Hennessy, Brian C. "The Racial Integration of Urban Police Departments in the South: Case Studies of Three North Florida Cities." M.A. thesis, Florida State University, 1974.

Higginbotham, Evelyn Brooks. *Righteous Discontent: The Women's Movement in the Black Baptist Church, 1880–1920*. Cambridge, Mass.: Harvard University Press, 1993.

Hildreth, Charles H. "Railroads out of Pensacola, 1833–83." *Florida Historical Quarterly* 37 (1959): 397–417.

Hill, Lance. *Deacons for Defense: Armed Resistance and the Civil Rights Movement*. Chapel Hill: University of North Carolina Press, 2006.

Holt, Len. "Freedom Schools." *Southern Exposure* 9, no. 1 (1981): 42–45.

Honey, Michael K. *Southern Labor and Black Civil Rights: Organizing Memphis Workers*. Urbana: University of Illinois Press, 1993.

Horwitz, Tony. *Confederates in the Attic: Dispatches from the Unfinished Civil War*. New York: Pantheon Books, 1998.

Hunter, Charlene A. *A History of Pensacola's Black Community*. Pensacola, Fla.: Escarosa Humanities Center, 1971.

Hyde, Samuel C., Jr., ed. *Sunbelt Revolution: The Historical Progression of the Civil Rights Struggle in the Gulf South, 1866–2000*. Gainesville: University Press of Florida, 2003.

Jeffries, Hasan Kwame. *Bloody Lowndes: Civil Rights and Black Power in Alabama's Black Belt*. New York: New York University Press, 2009.

Johnson, Cecil. "Pensacola in the British Period: Summary and Significance." *Florida Historical Quarterly* 37 (1959): 263–80.

Jonas, Sarah Zahra. "'All God's Chillun Got Wings': How the NAACP Youth Council Desegregated the Lunch Counters of Pensacola, Florida, 1960 to 1962." Ed.D. diss., University of West Florida, 2014.

"Journal of the Central Alabama Annual Conference of the Methodist Church." In *Eighty-Eighth Annual Session, May 16–19, 1963*, 10 & 30. Alabama–West

Florida UMC Conference Records, Huntingdon College Library, United Methodist Church Archive and Information Center, Montgomery, Alabama.

———. In *Eighty-Ninth Session, May 28–31, 1964,* 10 & 29. Alabama–West Florida UMC Conference Records, Huntingdon College Library, United Methodist Church Archive and Information Center, Montgomery, Alabama.

"Journal of the Tennessee Annual Conference of the United Methodist Church." In *Sixteenth Session of the 170th Annual Conference, June 13–16, 1983,* 256. Nashville, Tenn.: West End United Methodist Church.

Kaalina, Edmund F. *Claude Kirk and the Politics of Confrontation.* Gainesville: University Press of Florida, 1993.

Kane, Harnett T. *The Golden Coast.* New York: Doubleday, 1959.

Kennedy, Stetson. *Jim Crow Guide to the U.S.A.: The Laws, Customs, and Etiquette Governing the Conduct of Nonwhites and Other Minorities as Second-Class Citizens.* London: Lawrence & Wishart, 1959.

———. *The Klan Unmasked.* Boca Raton, Fla.: Florida Atlantic University Press, 1990.

———. *Southern Exposure.* Garden City, N.Y.: Doubleday, 1946.

Kerner Commission. *Report of the National Advisory Commission on Civil Disorders.* Washington, D.C.: U.S. Government Printing Office, 1968.

Kesselman, Michael N. "An Historical Analysis of Desegregation on Miami Beach Public Secondary Schools, 1968–1977." Ed.D. diss., University of Miami, Fla., 1979.

Key, V. O., Jr., *Southern Politics in State and Nation.* Knoxville: University of Tennessee Press, 1949.

King, Gilbert. *Devil in the Grove: Thurgood Marshall, the Groveland Boys, and the Dawn of a New America.* New York: Harper, 2012.

King, Martin Luther Jr. "A Testament of Hope," in *A Testament of Hope: The Essential Writing and Speeches of Martin Luther King, Jr.* New York: Harper Collins, 1986.

———. *Where Do We Go From Here: Chaos or Community?* New York: Harper & Row, 1967.

King, Wayne. "Gov. Carter Given Data on 5 Deaths." *New York Times.* January 6, 1975, 15.

———. "Racial Animosity Turns to Violence in Pensacola, Fla., on Issue of Calling High School Teams 'Rebels.'" *New York Times.* March 7, 1976, 33.

———. "Racial Incidents in Pensacola Prompt Attempts by Klan to Get New Members." *New York Times.* March 18, 1975, 74.

Kirkland, Scotty E. "Pink Sheets and Black Ballots: Political and Civil Rights in Mobile, Alabama, 1945–85." M.A. thesis, University of South Alabama, 1999.

Klarman, Michael J. *From Jim Crow to Civil Rights: The Supreme Court and the Struggle for Racial Equality.* New York: Oxford University Press, 2006.

———. "How Brown Changed Race Relations: The Backlash Thesis." *Journal of American History* 81 (1994): 81–117.

Kluger, Richard. *Simple Justice: The History of "Brown v. Board of Education" and Black America's Struggle for Equality.* New York: Vintage, 1975.

Kneebone, John T. *Southern Liberal Journalists and the Issue of Race, 1920–1944*. Chapel Hill: University of North Carolina Press, 1985.

Korstad, Robert, and Nelson Lichtenstein. "Opportunities Lost and Found: Labor, Radicals, and the Early Civil Rights Movement." *Journal of American History* 75 (1998): 786–811.

Kruse, Kevin M. *White Flight: Atlanta and the Making of Modern Conservatism*. Princeton, N.J.: Princeton University Press, 2006.

Landers, Jane. *Black Society in Spanish Florida*. Urbana-Champaign: University of Illinois Press, 2009.

Lassiter, Matthew D. *The Silent Majority: Suburban Politics in the Sunbelt South*. Princeton, N.J.: Princeton University Press, 2006.

Lawson, Steven F. "Freedom Then, Freedom Now: The Historiography of the Civil Rights Movement." *American Historical Review* 96:2 (1991): 456–71.

———."From Sit-in to Race Riot: Businessmen, Blacks, and the Pursuit of Moderation in Tampa, 1960–1967," in *Southern Businessmen and Desegregation*, edited by David R. Colburn and Elizabeth Jacoway, 257–81. Baton Rouge: Louisiana State University Press, 1982.

———."Long Origins of the Short Civil Rights Movement, 1954–1968," in *Freedom Rights*, edited by Danielle L. McGuire and John Dittmer, 9–37. Lexington: University Press of Kentucky, 2011.

Leidholdt, Alexander. *Standing before the Shouting Mob: Lenoir Chambers and Virginia's Massive Resistance to Public-School Integration*. Tuscaloosa: University of Alabama Press, 1998.

Lloyd, Robert B. "Development of the Plan of Pensacola During the Colonial Period, 1559–1821." *Florida Historical Quarterly* 64, no. 3 (1986): 253–72.

Loevy, Robert D., ed. *The Civil Rights Act of 1964: The Passage of the Law That Ended Racial Segregation*. With contributions by Hubert H. Humphrey, Joseph L. Rauh Jr., and John G. Stewart. Albany: State University of New York Press, 1997.

Lufkin, Charles L. "War Council in Pensacola, January 17, 1861." *Gulf Coast Historical Review* 9 (1993): 47–64.

Manis, Andrew. *A Fire You Can't Put Out: The Civil Rights Life of Birmingham's Reverend Fred Shuttlesworth*. Tuscaloosa: University of Alabama Press, 1999.

Manucy, Albert C. "The Founding of Pensacola: Reasons and Reality." *Florida Historical Quarterly* 37 (1959): 223–41.

Marks, Henry R., and William R. Lux. "Pensacola: City Under Five Flags." *Americas* 24 (1973): 31–33.

Marsh, Charles. *God's Long Summer: Stories of Faith and Civil Rights*. Princeton, N.J.: Princeton University Press, 1997.

Marshall, Thurgood. "The Rise and Collapse of the 'White Democratic Primary.'" *The Journal of Negro Education* 26, no. 3 (Summer 1957): 249–54.

Martinez, J. Michael, William D. Richardson, and Ron McNinch-Su, eds. *Confederate Symbols in the Contemporary South*. Gainesville: University Press of Florida, 2000.

Matthews, Donald, and James Prothro. *Negroes and the New Southern Politics.* New York: Harcourt, Brace and World, 1966.

Matthews, H. K., and J. Michael Butler. *Victory after the Fall: Memories of a Civil Rights Activist.* Montgomery, Ala.: NewSouth Books, 2007.

McAlister, L. N. "Pensacola During the Second Spanish Period." *Florida Historical Quarterly* 37 (1959): 281–327.

McCoy, Donald R., and Richard T. Reutten. *Quest and Response: Minority Rights and the Truman Administration.* Lawrence: University of Kansas Press, 1973.

McGovern, James R., ed. *Andrew Jackson and Pensacola.* Vol. II. Pensacola, Fla.: The Pensacola Series Commemorating the American Revolution Bicentennial, 1974.

———. *The Emergence of a City in the Modern South: Pensacola, 1900–1945.* DeLeon Springs, Fla.: E. O. Painter, 1976.

———. " 'Miz Lizzie' and Her Special School." *Gulf Coast Historical Review* 1 (1985): 23–32.

———. "Pensacola, Florida: A Military City in the New South." *Florida Historical Quarterly* 59 (1980): 22–41.

———. "The Rise of Pensacola." In *The Cultural Legacy of the Gulf Coast*, edited by Linda and Lucius F. Ellsworth. Pensacola, Fla.: Gulf Coast History and Humanities Conference, 1976.

McGuire, Danielle L., and John Dittmer, eds. *Freedom Rights: New Perspectives on the Civil Rights Movement.* Lexington: University Press of Kentucky, 2011.

McNeil, Charles. "The Fishermen." *Pensacola History Illustrated* 4 (1993): 25–31.

Meier, August, and Elliott Rudwick. "Negro Boycotts of Segregated Streetcars in Florida, 1901–1905." *South Atlantic Quarterly* 69 (1970): 525–33.

Metcalf, George R. *From Little Rock to Boston: The History of School Desegregation.* Westport, Conn.: Greenwood Press, 1983.

Minchin, Timothy J. *From Rights to Economics: The Ongoing Struggle for Black Equality in the U.S. South.* Gainesville: University Press of Florida, 2007.

———. "Making Best Use of the New Laws: The NAACP and the Fight for Civil Rights in the South, 1965–1975." *Journal of Southern History* 74, no. 3 (2008): 669–702.

Minchin, Timothy J., and John A. Salmond, *After the Dream: Black and White Southerners since 1965.* Lexington: University Press of Kentucky, 2011.

Mohl, Raymond A., and Gary R. Mormino. "The Big Change in the Sunshine State: A Social History of Modern Florida." In *The New History of Florida*, edited by Michael Gannon, 418–45. Gainesville: University Press of Florida, 1996.

Montgomery, William E. *Under Their Own Vine and Fig Tree: The African-American Church in the South.* Baton Rouge: Louisiana State University Press, 1993.

Moore, Leonard N. *Black Rage in New Orleans: Police Brutality and African American Activism from World War II to Hurricane Katrina.* Baton Rouge: Louisiana State University Press, 2010.

Mormino, Gary R. "G.I. Joe Meets Jim Crow: Racial Violence and Reform in World War II Florida." *Florida Historical Quarterly* 73, no. 1 (1994): 23–42.

———. "A History of Florida's White Primary." In *Sunbelt Revolution: The Historical Progression of the Civil Rights Struggle in the Gulf South, 1866–2000*, edited by Samuel C. Hyde Jr., 133–50. Gainesville: University Press of Florida, 2003.

———. "World War II." In *The New History of Florida*, edited by Michael Gannon, 344–72. Gainesville: University Press of Florida, 1996.

Moye, J. Todd. *Let the People Decide: Black Freedom and White Resistance Movements in Sunflower County, Mississippi, 1945–1986*. Chapel Hill: University of North Carolina Press, 2004.

Muir, Thomas. "1920s East Zaragoza Street, Pensacola, Florida." *Gulf Coast Historical Review* 12 (1996): 171–87.

Myrdal, Gunnar. *An American Dilemma: The Negro Problem and Modern Democracy, Vol. II.* New Brunswick, N.J.: Transaction Publishers, 1996.

"N.A.A.C.P. Begins a Suit in Florida." *New York Times.* February 2, 1960, 20.

Newton, Michael. *The Invisible Empire: The Ku Klux Klan in Florida.* Gainesville: University Press of Florida, 2001.

Oates, Stephen B. *Let the Trumpet Sound: The Life of Martin Luther King, Jr.* New York: Harper & Row, 1982.

O'Brien, Gail. *The Color of the Law: Race, Violence, and Justice in the Post-World War II South.* Chapel Hill: University of North Carolina Press, 1999.

Ortiz, Paul. *Emancipation Betrayed: The Hidden History of Black Organizing and White Violence in Florida from Reconstruction to the Bloody Election of 1920.* Berkeley: University of California Press, 2005.

———. "Old South, New South, or Down South? Florida and the Modern Civil Rights Movement: Towards a New Civil Rights History in Florida." In *Old South, New South, or Down South? Florida and the Modern Civil Rights Movement*, edited by Irvin D. S. Winsboro, 220–44. Morgantown: West Virginia University Press, 2009.

Osel, Joseph D. "Black Out: Michelle Alexander's Operational Whitewash." *International Journal of Radical Critique.* http://www.radicalcritique.org/2012/03/black-out-michelle-alexanders.html. July 23, 2014.

———. "Toward Détournement of *The New Jim Crow*, or The Strange Career of the New Jim Crow," *International Journal of Radical Critique.* http://www.radicalcritique.org/2012/12/toward-detournement-of-new-jim-crow-or.html. July 23, 2014.

Osterweis, Rollin G. *The Myth of the Lost Cause, 1865–1900.* Hamden, Conn.: Archon Books, 1973.

Padgett, Gregory B. "C. K. Steele: A Biography." Ph.D. diss., Florida State University, 1994.

———. "The Tallahassee Bus Boycott." In *Sunbelt Revolution: The Historical Progression of the Civil Rights Struggle in the Gulf South, 1866–2000*, edited by Samuel C. Hyde Jr., 190–209. Gainesville: University Press of Florida, 2003.

Parks, Virginia. *Pensacola: Spaniards to Space Age.* Pensacola, Fla.: Pensacola Historical Society, 1986.

Patterson, James T. *Brown v. Board of Education: A Civil Rights Milestone and Its Troubled Legacy.* New York: Oxford University Press, 2001.

Paulson, Darryl, and Milly St. Julien. "Desegregating Public Schools in Manatee and Pinellas Counties, 1954–71." *Tampa Bay History* 7 (1985): 30–41.

Payne, Charles M. *I've Got the Light of Freedom: The Organizing Tradition and the Mississippi Freedom Struggle*. Berkeley: University of California Press, 1995.

Peake, Thomas R. *Keeping the Dream Alive: A History of the Southern Christian Leadership Conference from King to the Nineteen-Eighties*. New York: Lang, 1987.

Pearce, George F. *The U.S. Navy in Pensacola: From Sailing Ships to Naval Aviation (1825–1930)*. Pensacola: University Press of Florida, 1980.

"Pensacola Will Integrate 13 Negroes in School Plan." *New York Times*. May 25, 1962, 21.

Perry, John H., Jr., *Never Say Impossible: The Life and Times of an American Entrepreneur*. Charlottesville, Va.: Thomasson-Grant, 1996.

Phillips, Ulrich B. "The Central Theme of Southern History." *American Historical Review* 34 (1928): 30–43.

Price, Hugh Douglas. *The Negro and Southern Politics: A Chapter of Florida History*. New York: New York University Press, 1957.

Proctor, Samuel. "Prelude to the New Florida, 1877–1919." In *The New History of Florida*, edited by Michael Gannon, 266–86. Gainesville: University Press of Florida, 1996.

Rabby, Glenda A. *The Pain and the Promise: The Struggle for Civil Rights in Tallahassee, Florida*. Athens: University of Georgia Press, 1999.

Rea, Robert. "British Pensacola." *Pensacola History Illustrated* 3 (1990): 3–10.

Reese, John S. "Giant of the Pine Forest: A History of the Chemstrand/Monsanto Pensacola Nylon Plant, 1953–92." Ph.D. diss., Florida State University, 1992.

Reingold, Beth, and Richard S. Wilke. "Confederate Symbols, Southern Identity, and Racial Attitudes: The Case of the Georgia State Flag." *Social Sciences Quarterly* 79 (1998): 568–80.

Reynolds, Barbara A. *Jesse Jackson: The Man, the Movement, the Myth*. Chicago: Nelson Hall, 1975.

Richardson, Frederick Douglas. *The Genesis and Exodus of NOW*. Boynton Beach, Fla.: Futura Printing, Inc., 1996.

Richardson, Joe M. *The Negro in the Reconstruction of Florida, 1865–1877*. Tallahassee: The Florida State University, 1965.

Rivers, Larry Eugene. *Slavery in Florida: Territorial Days to Emancipation*. Gainesville: University Press of Florida, 2000.

Rothschild, Mary Aickin. "The Volunteers and the Freedom Schools: Education for Social Change in Mississippi." *History of Education Quarterly* 22 (1988): 401–20.

Rowe, Gary Thomas, Jr. *My Undercover Years with the Ku Klux Klan*. New York: Bantam Books, 1976.

Saunders, Robert W. *Bridging the Gap: Continuing the Florida NAACP Legacy of Harry T. Moore, 1952–1966*. Tampa, Fla.: University of Tampa Press, 2000.

Saunt, Claudio. "'The English Has Now a Mind to Make Slaves of Them All': Creeks, Seminoles and the Problem of Slavery." *American Indian Quarterly* 22 (Winter-Spring 1998): 157–80.

Schnur, James A. "Desegregation of Public Schools in Pinellas County, Florida." *Tampa Bay History* 13 (1991): 26–43.

Shattuck, Gardiner H., Jr. *Episcopalians and Race: Civil War to Civil Rights.* Lexington: University Press of Kentucky, 2000.

Shofner, Jerrell H. "The Cultural Legacy of the Gulf Coast, 1870–1940." In *The Cultural Legacy of the Gulf Coast*, edited by Linda and Lucius F. Ellsworth. Pensacola, Fla.: Gulf Coast History and Humanities Conference, 1976.

———. "Militant Negro Laborers in Reconstruction Florida." *Journal of Southern History* 39 (1973): 397–408.

———. *Nor Is It Over Yet: Florida in the Era of Reconstruction, 1863–1877.* Gainesville: University Press of Florida, 1974.

———. "The Pensacola Workingman's Association: A Militant Negro Labor Union during Reconstruction." *Labor History* 13 (1972): 555–59.

Shofner, Jerrell H., and Linda V. Ellsworth, eds. *Ethnic Minorities in Gulf Coast Society.* Pensacola, Fla.: Gulf Coast History and Humanities Conference, 1979.

Siegel, Reva. "Why Equal Protection No Longer Protects: The Evolving Forms of Status-Enforcing Action." *Stanford Law Review* 49 (1997): 1111–48.

Sims, Patsy. *The Klan.* 2nd ed. Lexington: University Press of Kentucky, 1996.

Sitkoff, Harvard. *The Struggle for Black Equality, 1954–1980.* New York: Hill and Wang, 1981.

Smith, Charles V. *The Civil Rights Movement in Florida and the United States: Historical and Contemporary Perspectives.* Tallahassee, Fla.: Father and Son Publishing, 1989.

Smith, Jessie Carney and Linda T. Wynn, eds. *Freedom Facts and Firsts: 400 Years of the African American Civil Rights Experience.* Canton, Mich.: Visible Ink Press, 2009.

Southern Regional Council. *The South and Her Children: School Desegregation, 1970–1971.* Atlanta, Ga.: SRC, Inc., 1971.

Stafford, William. "Winston E. Arnow: The Man and the Building." Escambia–Santa Rosa Bar Association. http://www.esrba.com/userfiles/arnowjdg2011 .pdf. June 22, 2015.

Stampp, Kenneth M. *The Era of Reconstruction, 1865–1877.* New York: Knopf, 1965.

Thomas, Emory. "Civil War." In *The Encyclopedia of Southern Culture*, edited by Charles Reagan Wilson and William Ferris, 605. Chapel Hill, University of North Carolina Press, 1989.

Thomas, Greg. "Why Some Like the New Jim Crow So Much." *Vox Union.* http://www.voxunion.com/why-some-like-the-new-jim-crow-so-much/. July 23, 2014.

Thompson, Heather Ann. "Why Mass Incarceration Matters: Rethinking Crisis, Decline, and Transformation in Postwar American History." *Journal of American History* 97, no. 3 (2010): 703–34.

Thornton, Kevin. "The Confederate Flag and the Meaning of Southern History." *Southern Cultures* 2 (1996): 233–45.

Tomberlin, Joseph A. "Florida and the School Desegregation Issue, 1954–1959: A Summary View." *Journal of Negro Education* 43, no. 4 (1974): 457–67.

———. "Florida Whites and the *Brown* Decision of 1954." *Florida Historical Quarterly* 51 (1972): 22–36.

Towns, Stuart W. "Honoring the Confederacy in Northwest Florida: The Confederate Monument Ritual." *Florida Historical Quarterly* 57 (1978): 205–12.

Tuck, Stephen G. N. *Beyond Atlanta: The Struggle for Racial Equality in Georgia, 1940–1980.* Athens: University of Georgia Press, 2001.

Tyson, Timothy B. *Blood Done Signed My Name: A True Story.* New York: Crown, 2004.

———. *Radio Free Dixie: Robert F. Williams and the Roots of Black Power.* Chapel Hill: University of North Carolina Press, 1999.

Umoja, Akinyele Omowale. *We Will Shoot Back: Armed Resistance in the Mississippi Freedom Movement.* New York: NYU Press, 2013.

U.S. Bureau of the Census. *Nineteenth Census, 1970.* Vol. 11, "Florida." Washington, D.C.: Government Printing Office, 1973.

———. *Twenty-Second Census, 2000.* Vol. PHC-2-11, "Florida." Washington, D.C.: Government Printing Office, 2003.

U.S. Commission on Civil Rights. *The Diminishing Barrier: A Report on School Desegregation in Nine Communities.* Washington, D.C.: Office of the General Counsel, 1972.

U.S. Commission on Civil Rights, and Katie Harris. *The Administration of Justice in Pensacola and Escambia County: A Report Prepared by the Florida Advisory Committee to the U.S. Commission on Civil Rights.* Washington, D.C.: U.S. Commission on Civil Rights, 1981.

Wagy, Thomas R. "Governor Leroy Collins of Florida and the Little Rock Crisis of 1957." *Arkansas Historical Quarterly* 38, no. 2 (1979): 99–115.

———. "Governor Leroy Collins of Florida and the Selma Crisis of 1956." *Florida Historical Quarterly* 57 (1979): 403–20.

Walker, Jenny. "A Media-Made Movement? Black Violence and Nonviolence in the Historiography of the Civil Rights Movement." In *Media, Culture, and the Modern African American Freedom Struggle*, edited by Brian Ward, 41–66. Gainesville, University Press of Florida, 2001.

Ward, Brian. "Forgotten Wails and Master Narratives: Media, Culture, and Memories of the Modern African American Freedom Struggle." In *Media, Culture, and the Modern African American Freedom Struggle*, edited by Brian Ward, 41–66. Gainesville: University Press of Florida, 2001.

———. *Just My Soul Responding: Rhythm and Blues, Black Consciousness, and Race Relations.* Berkeley: University of California Press, 1998.

Washington, Booker T. *The Negro in Business.* Boston: Hertel, Jenkins, 1907.

Washington, James Melvin. *Frustrated Fellowship: The Black Baptist Quest for Social Power.* Macon, Ga.: Mercer University Press, 1986.

Weedle, Robert S. *Changing Tides: Twilight and Dawn in the Spanish Sea, 1763–1803*. College Station: Texas A&M University Press, 1995.

———. *The French Thorn: Rival Explorers in the Spanish Sea, 1682–1762*. College Station: Texas A&M University Press, 1991.

Wendt, Simon. *The Spirit and the Shotgun: Armed Resistance and the Struggle for Civil Rights*. Gainesville: University Press of Florida, 2007.

Wiley, Lusharon. "An Agent for Change: The Story of Reverend H. K. Matthews." Ed.D. diss., University of West Florida, 2007.

Wilhoit, Francis. *The Politics of Mass Resistance*. New York: G. Braziller, 1973.

Wilkerson, Isabelle. *The Warmth of Other Suns: The Epic Story of America's Great Migration*. New York: Vintage, 2011.

Wilkinson III, J. Harvie. *From Brown to Bakke: The Supreme Court and School Integration, 1954–1978*. New York: Oxford University Press, 1981.

Williamson, Joel. *The Crucible of Race: Black-White Relations in the American South since Emancipation*. New York: Oxford University Press, 1985.

Wills, Ora. *Images in Black: A Pictorial History of Black Pensacola. Part II*. Pensacola, Fla.: African American Heritage Society, 2007.

Wilmore, Gayraud. *Black Religion and Black Radicalism*. New York: Doubleday, 1972.

Wilson, Charles R. *Baptized in Blood: The Religion of the Lost Cause, 1865–1920*. Athens: University of Georgia Press, 1980.

Wilson, Charles R., and William Ferris, eds. *The Encyclopedia of Southern Culture*. Chapel Hill: University of North Carolina Press, 1989.

Winsboro, Irvin D. S. "Image, Illusion, and Reality: Florida and the Modern Civil Rights Movement in Historical Perspective." In *Old South, New South, or Down South? Florida and the Modern Civil Rights Movement*, edited by Irvin D. S. Winsboro, 1–21. Morgantown: West Virginia University Press, 2009.

Winsboro, Irvin D. S., and Abel A. Bartley, "Race, Education, and Regionalism: The Long and Troubling History of School Desegregation in the Sunshine State." *Florida Historical Quarterly* 92, no. 4 (Spring 2014): 714–45.

"Winston E. Arnow Federal Building Designation Act." *Congressional Record* 149: 119 (Wednesday, September 3, 2003). H7798-H7800. Washington, D.C.: Government Printing Office, 2003.

Woodward, C. Vann. *Origins of the New South, 1877–1913*. Baton Rouge: Louisiana State University Press, 1971.

Wynn, Neil A. *The Afro-American and the Second World War*. London: Paul Elek, 1976.

Young, Andrew. *An Easy Burden: The Civil Rights Movement and the Transformation of America*. New York: HarperCollins, 1996.

Younge, Julien C. "Pensacola in the War for Southern Independence." *Florida Historical Quarterly* 37 (1959): 357–71.

Index

led by, 51, 58; Dobbins and, 37, 44; Matthews and, 135, 234–35, 250; on white response, 1, 18

King, Wallace, 54

Kirk, Claude, 71, 97

Klarman, Michael, 23

Kluger, Richard, 23

Kruse, Kevin M., 9

Ku Klux Klan (KKK, UKA), 20, 86, 163, 216, 237; attacks and threats by, 43, 207–9; decline of in Pensacola, 218, 290 (n. 33); and Escambia High riot, 207–8; FBI and, 178–79, 217–18, 285 (n. 29); formation of Pensacola chapter, 15, 159; "fourth period revival" of, 159, 218–19; marches by, 39, 160, 162, 176–77; membership in Pensacola, 159, 218; *Pensacola News Journal* and, 21, 161, 162, 177, 178; and SCLC, 159, 162–63, 219; "Voice of the Klan" hotline of, 159–61, 215, 216; and white backlash, 9–10, 158, 159, 218–19

Kyle, Merenda, 104

Lagergren, Walter, 172

Lakeland Ledger, 188

Landers, Jane, 19

Lanius, G. H., 88

Lassiter, Matthew D., 9

Lawson, Steven F., 11, 266 (n. 5)

Lee, Robert E., 88

Leeper, Richard, 84, 87–88, 115, 116, 208, 209

Leverette, Otha, 148, 163, 191, 228; and Atlanta Five case, 125, 126, 129; and Blackwell shooting, 134–35, 136, 141, 144; Brooks disassociation from, 170, 171; and Confederate image controversy, 86, 101, 173; and SCLC Educational Committee, 67

Lewis, John, 61

Lewis, Tony, 199–200

Lindsey, Raymond, 199–200, 201

Lipscomb, R. C., 85, 108

"Long civil rights movement" concept, 4–5, 266 (n. 5)

Lost Cause ideology, 89–91, 92–93, 277 (n. 21)

Lowery, Joseph, 222

Luna, Tristan de, 19

Lynch, Bill, 132

Lynching, 10, 20–21, 68

Marshall, Carol Ann, 216, 290 (n. 31), 293 (n. 1)

Marshall, Thurgood, 30

Martin, Bob, 107

Mason, Charles P., 24, 50

Mass meetings: Abernathy speech at, 176; around Blackwell death, 15, 134–38, 145, 152; confrontational rhetoric at, 162–63, 164–65, 186; decline of, 193; around Matthews-Brooks trial, 191; during downtown sit-in campaign, 44; revival-like atmosphere at, 137, 138, 167; during Selma struggle, 58

Matthews, H. K. (Hawthorne Konrad): appeal of conviction by, 214–15, 220; arrested at Escambia High, 113–14; and Askew, 170, 234–35; and Atlanta Five case, 125, 126, 129, 130; biographical background, 57; and black elite, 114, 165–66, 194; black support for, 63, 150, 152, 174; and Blackwell shooting protests, 1–2, 15, 133, 134–39, 141, 143–47, 151–52; break with NAACP by, 65–66, 274 (n. 26); and Brooks, 66–67, 170, 251; as central leader of Pensacola freedom struggle, 14, 56, 58; confrontational rhetoric of, 57–58, 76, 95–96, 99, 162–63, 164, 167; and Confederate image controversy, 86, 92, 93, 101; conviction and sentencing of, 2, 172; departure from Escambia County of, 193–94; and Dobbins, 57–58, 135; extortion charge against, 147–48, 172; FBI monitoring of, 195;

and February 1975 demonstration, 145–47; firearms carried by, 163; honoring of, 250–51, 295 (n. 15); imprisonment of, 2, 7–8, 189–90, 191, 222; and King, 135, 234–35, 250; on mistrust of police, 68; as NAACP Youth Council adviser, 62, 274 (n. 26); national NAACP and, 62, 168–69, 274 (n. 26); pardoning of, 7–8, 234–35, 236; photos of, 99, 144, 153; on police racism, 118, 120; regular columns by, 63; religious calling of, 60–62, 135, 194–95; SCLC chapter founded by, 66, 274 (n. 27); SCLC severs relationship with, 192, 193; and Selma actions, 58–60, 273 (n. 14); sentencing of, 190–91; threats against, 152, 159, 207; use of tape recordings by, 135–36; and "wash-in" protest, 62–63; white hostility to, 63–64, 74, 115, 138, 149, 150–51, 204. *See also* Brooks/Matthews extortion trial

Maxwell, William F., 223, 226
McArthur, L. D., 31
McCrary, Jess, 235
McCullough, Red, 25
McDaniel, Vernon, 294 (n. 11)
McGovern, George, 97
McGovern, James, 26, 215
McMillan, Henry T., 114–15, 223, 224, 225–26, 248, 294 (n. 11)
McMillan v. Escambia County, et al., 223–26, 227–34, 245; appeals of decision in, 244, 293 (n. 4); assessment of, 243, 246; ruling in, 233–34; testimony in, 227–33
Mellon, Churchill, 43
Merritt, Lonnie, 121
Miami Herald, 105
Middleton, Roy, 252
Migrations, 20, 21
Minchin, Timothy, 65–66, 221
The Mind of the South (Cash), 67
Mitchell, Curtis, 184

Mitchell, Lucien, 118
Mobile, Ala., 163
Montgomery bus boycott, 24–25
Moore, Harry T., 26
Moore, Leonard, 68
Morgan, David, 252
Morris, Willie, 18
Moses, Bob, 267 (n. 13)
Moss, Oscar, 181
Motley, Constance Baker, 30, 31
Mott, Roger, 78, 92, 105, 111–12
Movement for Change (MFC), 249, 250
Moye, J. Todd, 4
Mumford, Darryl, 132, 134
Mydral, Gunnar, 67

National Association for the Advancement of Colored People (NAACP), 53, 55, 118, 154, 204; black elite and, 165–66; and Blackwell shooting, 132–33, 136, 139, 141–42; and Confederate image controversy, 86–87, 93, 104; decline of local chapter, 56, 220–21; and defense of Brooks, 148, 167, 168, 180, 214–15, 220; direct action campaigns used by, 12, 39–40, 44, 46, 47–48, 49, 98–99, 139, 225; formation of Pensacola chapter, 19, 21; and Matthews, 65–66, 250; membership of Pensacola chapter, 66, 220–21; national finances of, 220, 221; rift between national and local/state, 100, 141–42, 168–69, 171–72, 179, 192; and school desegregation fight, 14, 27, 30, 32, 35, 74–75; SCLC tensions and rivalry with, 9, 15, 95–96, 129–30, 170–71, 172, 174, 176, 179, 193; white attacks on, 27, 64–65, 74; withdrawal of support for Pensacola movement by, 168
National Association for the Advancement of Colored People (NAACP)